Franklin Tuthill

The History of California

Franklin Tuthill

The History of California

ISBN/EAN: 9783741186172

Manufactured in Europe, USA, Canada, Australia, Japa

Cover: Foto ©ninafisch / pixelio.de

Manufactured and distributed by brebook publishing software (www.brebook.com)

Franklin Tuthill

The History of California

THE

HISTORY OF CALIFORNIA.

BY

FRANKLIN TUTHILL.

SAN FRANCISCO:
H. H. BANCROFT & COMPANY.
1866.

Entered according to Act of Congress, in the year 1866.

By H. H. BANCROFT & CO.,

In the Clerk's Office of the District Court of the United States for the Northern District of California.

PREFACE.

The following book was written because there seemed to be a demand for a History of California which should sketch the main events of the country from its discovery to the present time. The pioneer, under whose observation the most exciting of these events have occurred, confesses the need of such a book. The thousands who have entered the State since it assumed its present peaceful aspect, complain of the lack of a succinct story of what had to be done here to make the land so pleasant a home.

The material for a history of California is abundant. The log-books of ancient mariners who visited the coast—the voluminous, if not well-kept archives of the Government, while the territory was under Spanish or Mexican rule—the official reports and Congressional documents about the transfer to the United States—the files of newspapers since the land was Americanized—the scores of books of intelligent travellers, who have put their impressions on record, and the oral evidence of natives, and early immigrants, who mingled in all the affairs most interesting to us—from these sources may be drawn ample details of life in California, from dates as far in the past as any but enthusiastic antiquarians care to retire to.

There are several histories of California to be found in the libraries, some of them works of permanent value. One of the oldest, the "Jesuit Venegas," and the authority for the times and places of which it treats, was printed a century ago, when the California of the moderns was an unknown land. The history by Forbes, the Englishman, and the valuable report of explorations by De Mofras, the Frenchman, each much quoted and appreciated in the highest quarters, were written while our California was deemed by Americans the very remotest land of the globe, farther away for all practical purposes than the East Indies, more inaccessible than the antipodes. After the discovery of gold in California, there was quite an irruption of books about the country, and among them a few histories, which rendered the outlines of its past career familiar, and ministered admirably to the needs of the early adventurers. But since their period, though the term, counted by years, is very short, all has happened that is most stirring in California story. Those events, so impossible of repetition, seem, even to the actors in them, to belong to a distant antiquity. The sixteen years that have elapsed since the American occupation, embrace such physical and social changes as oftener require a full century for their development.

No doubt a better history can be written when the country is older, and time has more thoroughly tested some social experiments that seem already successful. But, considering by how large a portion of the population of the State its thrilling story is but dimly remembered, like a tale told long ago in a far-distant spot, concerning lands now familiar, but which the hearer never dreamed would become his home, this work is cheerfully submitted to the public, in hope that it will be received in the same spirit of charity with which it was written.

August, 1865.

CONTENTS.

CHAPTER I.
THE APPROACHES TO, AND DISCOVERY OF, CALIFORNIA.

Hindrances to the Earlier Discovery of California.—Columbus's Theory left no Room for California on the Globe.—First Voyagers on the Pacific.—Expeditions sent up the Coast by Cortez.—His Pilot, Ximenes, discovers Lower California, A. D. 1534.—Cabrillo discovers Upper California, A. D. 1542.—His Coast Survey Profitless.—Meaning of the Word California.—Boundaries of the Country..................... Pages 1—14

CHAPTER II.
A NOTABLE ENGLISHMAN IN CALIFORNIA.

Inducements to the Exploration of the Coast.—The Straits of Anian.—Sir Francis Drake about Cape Horn, and on the Pacific.—He Attempts Returning to Europe by a Northern Route.—Visits California, A. D. 1579, and names it New Albion.—A Pedestrian Trip through the Country.—The Climate gets a Bad Name.—Drake probably entered San Francisco Bay.—Reasons for the Belief.—Characteristics of the Natives.—Did they find Gold? .... Pages 15—27

CHAPTER III.
VISCAINO'S EXPLORATIONS ALONG THE CALIFORNIA COAST.

Philip II. orders the Settlement of California.—Viscaino's Settlement at La Paz.—His careful Exploration of the Coast, A. D. 1602.—Describes San Diego and Monterey.—His Crew suffers from Scurvy.—Did he Visit San Francisco?—The Results of his Voyage Wasted... Pages 28—36

CHAPTER IV.
UNSUCCESSFUL ATTEMPTS TO COLONIZE THE COUNTRY.

Pirates on the Coast.—Futile Attempt of Admiral Otondo and Father Kino to Colonize California in 1683.—The Jesuits decline the Job.—Topographical Reasons why the Spanish Navigators missed the best Harbor on the Coast............... Pages 37—41

CHAPTER V.
EXPERIMENTS OF THE JESUITS IN CALIFORNIA.

Jesuit Occupation of the Peninsula.—Fathers Kino and Salva Tierra undertake the Spiritual Conquest of California.—Settlement at Loreto, A. D. 1697.—Their Method with the Indians.—A Rebellion Met by Coercion.—Jealousy of the Jesuits Hinders their Success.—Hard Times.—Father Ugarte at the Mission.—Kino, from Sonora, furnishes Supplies.—Effort to Connect the Settlements of the Peninsula and the Main-Land by a Chain of Missions.—Overland Excursions from Sonora to Lower California.—Salva Tierra's Unwelcome Promotion, Release, and Death.—Alberoni's Grand Scheme and its Collapse.—The Pioneer Home-Built Vessel.—Ugarte Explores the Gulf.—Geographical Surveys.—Ugarte Dies.—A Success.—The Missions Relieve the Philippine

Galleon.—A Rebellion.—Life at the Mission.—Whipping Popular with the Indians.—The Pious Fund.—The Jesuits Expelled.—The Franciscans assume the Lower California Missions.—Begert's Blast against California.—The Dominicans Relieve the Franciscans, who (A. D. 1769) go to Upper California.—Venega's History and Curious Map.. Pages 42—71

CHAPTER VI.

OCCUPATION OF UPPER CALIFORNIA BY THE FRANCISCANS.

Galvez's and Junipero's Expedition, in four Detachments, to Settle Upper California.—They Rendezvous at San Diego.—A Mission Established, A. D. 1769.—Governor Portalá visits Monterey Harbor, Overland, without recognizing it.—Discovers San Francisco by Land.—Indian Outbreak at San Diego.—Monterey Discovered.—Joyful Reception of the News in Mexico.—Death of Father Junipero, A. D. 1784.—Location of the Missions.—A Vessel enters San Francisco Bay, June, 1775.—Order of Establishment of the Missions... Pages 72—87

CHAPTER VII.

THE ABORIGINES.

The Aborigines of Upper California.—Digger Mythology, Traditions, and Customs.—Their Food; Religious and Social Life; Medical Practice; the Sweat-House.—Burial or Burning of the Dead.—Their Ideas of Death... Pages 88—97

CHAPTER VIII.

DETAILS OF THE MISSION SYSTEM.

The Spanish Policy towards the Indians.—Theory of the Mission System.—The Mission Buildings.—The Indian Rancheria.—Government of the Mission.—The Presidio.—Collision of Priests and Soldiers.—The Pueblo of different Kinds.—Political Government of California under Spain.—Effect of the Manifold Order System. Pages 98—110

CHAPTER IX.

A CALM HALF CENTURY.

The Indians take kindly to Mission Life.—An Era of Tranquillity.—Number of Domesticated Indians at different Periods.—Population of each Mission, A. D. 1802.—Thriving Times.—Yankees Buy their Hides.—Fear of Earthquakes.—Dread of Foreigners.—The Viceroy's Orders to beware of Captain Cook.—Vancouver Well Treated.—Jealousy of American Visitors.—John Brown at San Francisco.—The Russian Occupation, from 1812 to 1842, of a Strip on the Coast... Pages 111—120

CHAPTER X.

CALIFORNIA UNDER MEXICAN RULE.

California Accepts Imperial Mexico's Rule (1822).—List of Governors of California while under Spain.—Becomes a Territory of Republican Mexico.—Proposed Change of Name.—Jedediah S. Smith arrives Overland from the East. A. D. 1826.—The Fur Business.—The Pious Fund diverted from the Ecclesiastics to the Spanish and Mexican Governments.—The Mexican Colonization Act of 1824.—Wealth of the Missions in 1831... Pages 121—129

CHAPTER XI.

THE MISSIONS SECULARIZED.

Trouble Comes.—Governor Echeandia tries to enforce the Secularization, A. D. 1830.—Soliz's Insurrection.—Governor Victoria Arrests the Secularization.—The Echeandia

CONTENTS. xi

Insurrection.—Portilla's Treachery.—Victoria Keeps his Promise, and Retires to Mexico.—Pio Pico appointed Governor by the Legislature.—Anarchy and Confusion.—Figueroa arrives through many Perils.—Division of the Missions: the Spanish Franciscans take those South of San Luis Obispo; the Mexican Franciscans take those North of it.—Director Hijar's Colony arrives at Solano.—The Missionaries hasten to Destroy their Property.—Great Slaughter of Cattle.—The Colonists Revolt, and are Exiled.—The Territorial Legislature turns over the Missions to Governor Figueroa.—Death of Figueroa, A. D. 1835 .... Pages 130—140

CHAPTER XII.

REBELLION, SECESSION, RESTORATION, PANICS.

Custom-House Quarrel.—Revolution.—Alvarado and Isaac Graham capture the Capital, and Proclaim the Independence of California.—Alvarado crushes out a Rebellion; is appointed Governor by Mexico, and Recognizes Mexico again as the Central Power.—Graham and other Foreigners Arrested and Exiled, but return again with Honor.—Governor Micheltorena arrives.—A Panic.—Commodore Jones hoists the American Flag at Monterey.—Hauls it down again, and Apologizes.—Alvarado and Vallejo capture the Governor's Ammunition.—Micheltorena Invokes Sutter's Aid.—Sutter obtains a "General Title" to certain Lands.—The Foreigners stand aside, leaving Mexicans and Californians to Fight it out.—The Mexicans Surrender.—Apparition from over the Mountains.—Fremont's Appearance.—List of Mexican Governors of California.
Pages 141—151

CHAPTER XIII.

THE "NATIVE CALIFORNIANS."

What they understood by "Independence."—Character of the People.—Great Riders.—Their Homes, Habits, Food, Dress, and Gardens.—Boston Traders arrive after 1822.—How Justice was Administered.—Whalers in the Port.—Immigrants, and the Impression that all is soon to be Americanized... Pages 152—161

CHAPTER XIV.

FREMONT AND THE BEAR PARTY REVOLUTION.

Fremont's Exploring Party asks Permission to Rest in the San Joaquin Valley, A. D. 1846.—Castro's Fair Promises and Treacherous Performances.—Fremont stands a Siege.—Proceeds Northward.—Is Overtaken by Lieutenant Gillespie with Dispatches from Home.—His Camp broken into by Indians.—Four of his Party Killed.—Resolves to Revolutionize the Government.—Returns to the Sacramento Valley.—Merritt's Party Captures Sonoma.—William B. Ide's Proclamation.—The Bear Flag.—Lieutenant Ford's Expedition routs De la Torre's Force.—Fremont Organizing a Battalion.—Arrives at Sonoma.—Declaration of Independence, July 5th.—The Bear Party Absorbed into the Battalion.—Fremont gives Chase to Castro................................. Pages 162—175

CHAPTER XV.

THE AMERICAN CONQUEST OF CALIFORNIA.

Movements of the United States Navy in the Pacific.—Commodore Sloat's Instructions.—A Race and its Consequences.—Sloat raises the United States Flag at Monterey, July 7th, 1846.—British Plots to secure California rendered Futile.—The United States Flag raised at San Francisco.—It replaces the Bear Flag at Sonoma.—Fremont anticipates Sloat's Messenger, and seizes the Government Arms at San Juan.—Reports to Sloat.—The Commodore Puzzled, and out of Spirits.—Refuses to Accept into Service Fremont's Battalion.—Arrival of Commodore Stockton.—He takes Command of the Land Forces.—Sloat Sails for Home.—Occupation of the Ports.—Stockton lands at San Pedro; Marches his Force to Los Angeles, and organizes a Territorial Government for California.—The Flores's Insurrection at the South.. Pages 176—192

CHAPTER XVI.

CALIFORNIA'S THREE CONQUERORS AND FIRST THREE AMERICAN GOVERNORS.

Stockton's Measures to Quell the Insurrection.—Captain Mervine's Party Repulsed near San Pedro, by the Californians.—News of General Kearny at San Pasqual.—Stockton sends him timely Relief.—Kearny arrives at San Diego.—The Advance upon Los Angeles.—The Engagement on the Plains of San Gabriel.—Stockton re-enters Los Angeles, January 10th, 1847.—Fremont's Battalion moves Southward.—He Pardons Jesus Pico.—A Toilsome March.—Fremont makes and Proclaims the Treaty of Conenga.—Delicate Relations of Stockton, Kearny, and Fremont.—Fremont Reports to Stockton.—Fremont as Governor.—Seven Weeks of Tranquil Splendor.—Kearny and Shubrick join to depose him.—Proclamation Ignoring the Conenga Treaty.—Fremont's Famous Ride—Is refused an Interview with Kearny, except in Presence of Colonel Mason.—Fremont Disobeys Orders.—Stevenson's Regiment Arrives.—Fremont goes East under Arrest.—His Trial and Sentence—Refuses the President's Clemency, and Retires from the Service... Pages 193—213

CHAPTER XVII.

SAN FRANCISCO AMERICANIZED.

The Land Escapes Mormonism.—Yerba Buena's Change of Name.—Its Newspapers.—Benicia.—First Alcaldes of San Francisco.—First Mayor and the Ayuntamiento.—Public Meetings.—Overland Immigrants Snow-stayed East of the Sierra Nevadas.—Terrible Sufferings of the Donner Party.—Meeting of Indignation concerning Fremont.—Growth of San Francisco, and its Sudden Depopulation.................. Pages 214—225

CHAPTER XVIII.

THE GOLD DISCOVERY.

Gold Discovered at Coloma, January 19th, 1848.—Governor Mason's Visit to the Placers.—His Report to the War Department.—How the News was Received at the East.—Previous Hints of Gold in California.—Circumstances of the Discovery of 1848.
Pages 226—234

CHAPTER XIX.

GRAND RUSH TO CALIFORNIA.

Peace between the United States and Mexico.—Terms of the Treaty.—The California Fever a World-wide Epidemic.—They come in Companies with strange Ventures in Rotten Bottoms.—Isthmus and Overland Immigrants.—The Grumblers.—Theories of the Gold Production.—Simultaneous Settlement of the Mining Region.—Society.—Crime and its Punishment in the Mines.—Anomalous Method of Civil Government.
Pages 235—248

CHAPTER XX.

CONGRESS FAILS TO PROVIDE A GOVERNMENT.

Unavailing Efforts to give California a Government.—Polk's Request and the Wilmot Proviso.—Senators Corwin, Calhoun, Benton, and Dix on California.—Clayton's Bill Passes the Senate, and is Defeated in the House.—Congress does nothing for California, 1847-'48.—President Polk's Letter to Californians.—Colonel Benton's Letter to the Same.—The Congress of 1848-'49.—Douglas's State Bill Adversely Reported.—A Special Committee Reports Favorably.—Senatorial Discussions.—Dayton says they can get a Constitutional Convention only by using the Lasso.—Webster advises a Military Government.—Proposition to Cede back California to Mexico.—A Territorial Bill put on the Appropriation Bill.—Dix regrets the Gold Discovery.—Webster and Calhoun Debate Constitutional Questions—A Stormy Sunday Morning Session.—Foote Raves.—Jefferson Davis would Sacrifice California to the Appropriations.—The Senate Recedes, and California gets no Government—Revenue Laws Extended over California.
Pages 249—261

CONTENTS.

CHAPTER XXI.
THE CONSTITUTIONAL CONVENTION.

The People of California Establish a Government.—Governor Riley's Proclamation for a State Convention.—Election of Delegates.—Small Vote Cast.—Constitutional Convention meets at Monterey, September, 1849.—The Antecedents of Members.—Organization of the Convention.—Slavery Prohibited Forever.—Debate concerning Negro Immigration.—State Boundaries.—The Slavery Question.—Lotteries, Duelling, Schools, Banks.—Expenses of Convention.—Concluding Courtesies.—The People Adopt the Constitution.. Pages 262—283

CHAPTER XXII.
THE FIRST STATE LEGISLATURE.

Meeting of the First Legislature at San José.—Governor Riley surrenders his Authority as Governor to Governor Burnett.—Fremont and Gwin elected U. S. Senators.—The Legislature's Reputation and Work.—Rate of Interest.—Foreign Miners' License.—Utah's Curious Petition.—Brief History of the Cities Chartered.—San Francisco's Growth.—The Hounds.—Sacramento.—Counties Organized.—Meaning and Origin of their Names.. Pages 284—305

CHAPTER XXIII.
WAITING ON CONGRESS FOR ADMISSION TO THE UNION.

President Taylor's Message, advising the Admission of California.—Admits that he urged the People to Organize a State.—Clay's Compromises Proposed.—California's Admission discussed by Senators Foote, Mason, Davis, Clay, King, Calhoun, Webster, and Seward.—Bell's Compromise Resolutions.—Debate on the Compromises submitted by Clay's Select Committee.—The California Bill passes the Senate.—Ten Senators Protest.—It passes the House, and is approved by the President, September, 1850.—The other Compromise Measures.—Repose.—What Disturbs and Ends it... Pages 306—323

CHAPTER XXIV.
"THE FALL OF '49 AND SPRING OF '50."

News of the Admission into the Union celebrated.—The Tent Era.—Flush, Thriftless Times.—Cost of Living in the "Fall of '49 and Spring of '50."—The Scarcity of Females.—Character of the Population.—All try the Mines.—The Currency.—Wages.—Labor Honorable with all.—State of the Market.—A Wet Winter.—Style of Houses.—Fires in San Francisco.—Mining Rushes.—Squatter Riots.—Gambling, Lynch Law, Politics.—Conservative Influences at Work.—Sources of State Pride and Hope.
Pages 324—345

CHAPTER XXV.
AFTER THE ADMISSION.

Product of the Mines.—New Mining Methods.—Quartz-Crushing and Water-Ditches.—Agriculture, Manufactures, and Commerce.—The Markets alternately Bare and Glutted.—Population of the State.—The Indians and Indian Wars.—Correspondence between Governor Bigler and the U. S. Agents concerning the Indians.—War Debt.—Reservations.—The Chinese Welcomed at first, but soon Disliked.—Their "Houses," Habits, Worship, and Employments.—A Chinese Fight.—Excitement in the Legislature about Negro Testimony... Pages 346—373

CHAPTER XXVI.
GROWTH AND HINDRANCES OF THE TOWNS AND CITIES.

San Francisco's Progress.—Real Estate.—Land Claims.—The Limantour Fraud.—Exorbitant Taxes.—The Peter Smith Judgments and Sale of City Property.—Sacramento.—

Fires and Floods.—Marysville.—Stockton.—Nevada City.—Grass Valley.—Placerville.—Other Towns and Cities.—Frequent Removals of the Capital......... Pages 379—392

CHAPTER XXVII.

FILLIBUSTERISM.

William Walker.—His Sonora Expedition.—Its Inglorious End.—The Mexican and French Consuls at San Francisco tried for Violating the Neutrality Laws...... Pages 393—401

CHAPTER XXVIII.

A FINANCIAL STORM.

The Financial Storm of 1855.—Failure of Page, Bacon & Co.—The Adams & Co. Muddle.—Their Books lost and found.—Alfred A. Cohen, Isaiah C. Woods, and Trenor W. Park.—Sketch of the Career of "James King, of Wm."—The Banker turned Editor.—The Subjects of his Assault.—Palmer, Cook & Co.—State Finances in a Bad Way.—Water-Front Extension.—Franchise-Hunting.—The Courts................. Pages 402—412

CHAPTER XXIX.

POLITICS.

Early Democracy of the State.—Governor Burnett.—Governor McDougall.—Governor Bigler.—Tammany and Chivalry Wings of the Democratic Party.—Double-headed Convention of 1854.—Know Nothing Victory.—First Election for U. S. Senators.—Fremont and Gwin chosen.—Failure to elect Fremont's Successor in 1854.—Weller elected in 1852.—The Struggle of 1854.—Broderick beaten.—Gwin still kept out of the Vacant Seat in 1855.—Narrow Escape from Henry S. Foote's Election in 1856.—How San Francisco and Sacramento Vote.—The real Ruling Classes.—Lynchings.—Increasing Violence and Crime.. Pages 413—431

CHAPTER XXX.

THE VIGILANCE COMMITTEE OF 1856.

Assassination of "James King, of Wm.," by Supervisor Casey.—Formation of the Vigilance Committee.—Newspaper Treatment of the Assassination.—Great Public Excitement.—The Pulpit on the Vigilance Movement.—Casey taken from the Jail by the People.—King's Burial.—Generous Provision for his Family.—Casey and Cora Executed by the Vigilance Committee.—Burial of the Executed.—Billy Mulligan's Life, Dream, and Suicide.—Governor Johnson asks for Federal Arms in vain.—The Committee make some Important Arrests.—Non-arrival of the expected Reaction.—Elements of Opposition to the Popular Movement.—A Law and Order Meeting.
Pages 432—454

CHAPTER XXXI.

COLLISIONS WITH THE STATE AUTHORITIES.

Governor Johnson proclaims San Francisco in a State of Insurrection.—He orders out the Militia.—Fort Gunny-Bags erected.—Citizens petition the Governor to withdraw his Proclamation.—He throws the Responsibility on the "Insurgents."—General Sherman Resigns his Major-Generalship of Militia.—News of Congressman Herbert's Murdering a Waiter.—Constitution and Method of the Vigilance Committee.—Its Arms and Funds.—Meeting of Sympathizers.—Great Vigilance Mass Meeting.—The Patent Ballot-Box.—Governor Johnson appeals to President Pierce for Aid, but receives none.
Pages 455—472

CHAPTER XXXII.

THE VIGILANCE COMMITTEE ASSUMES MORE DOUBTFUL POWERS.

A Case of Piracy alleged.—State Arms seized by the Vigilants.—One of their Agents stabbed by Judge Terry.—A General Alarm.—Vigilants Capture the Armories.—Volney

E. Howard's Official Report of Affairs.—Judge Terry in the Vigilants' Jail.—Commissioners from Sacramento plead for him.—The Governor Repudiates the Commission.—Terry's Friends in the United States Senate.—Senators concerning the Vigilance Committee.—Ubiquitous Metiowan.—The Banished trying to return.—Execution of Hetherington and Brace by the Vigilants.—A. A. Green gets the Pueblo Papers by a Stratagem.—How the Vigilants got them from him.—Vigilance Respect for Federal Authorities.—Judge Terry discharged... Pages 473—498

CHAPTER XXXIII.

THE VIGILANCE COMMITTEE DISBANDS.

The Supreme Court resumes Work.—The Vigilance Committee preparing to surrender Power.—Danger of being crowded into Politics.—Grand Final Parade.—Address of the Executive to the General Committee.—Head-Quarters under Public Inspection.—State Arms retained.—The "Pirates" Acquitted.—The Rooms closed.—Results of the Vigilance Committee's Work.—List of the Executed and Banished.—Popularity of the Movement.—The Rev. Dr. Scott in Trouble.—Members annoyed by Suits.—The Proclamation of Insurrection withdrawn... Pages 499—517

CHAPTER XXXIV.

PRESERVING THE FRUITS OF THE REFORM.

Organization of the People's Party.—The Reformed City Government.—Better Times.—Comparison of Municipal Expenses before and after the Revolution.—Method of the People's Party... Pages 518—524

CHAPTER XXXV.

FINANCIAL BREAKERS.

The State's Interest not paid.—An Unconstitutional Debt.—Vision of Threatening Repudiation.—The Debt assumed by a Popular Vote.—Restoration of the Civil Fund to the State refused.—Indian War Claim admitted.—State and Local Debts, and what to show for them.. Pages 525—531

CHAPTER XXXVI.

LAND TITLES.

Uncertainty of Land Titles.—Congressional Legislation concerning them.—Board of Land Commissioners.—Suffering entailed by every Decision, Right or Wrong.—Attorney-General Black's Sensational Communication.—Instances quoted by him of Fraud on a grand Scale.—A Better Era Dawning.. Pages 532—542

CHAPTER XXXVII.

BITTER PARTY STRIFES.

Governor Johnson's Administration.—The State Prison Blunder.—Bates's Defalcation.—Broderick is King of Caucus, and is elected U. S. Senator.—Gwin and Latham aspire to the vacant Seat.—Why Broderick gives it to Gwin.—Latham's Version of his Defeat.—Gwin's Letter proving the Bargain and his Abasement.—Broderick breaks with the Administration.—The Fugitive Slave Law tried.—The Campaign of 1859.—Broderick declines a Challenge.—His first Stump Speech.—Broderick, Gwin, and Latham enjoying great Freedom of Speech.—Attitude of the Republicans.—Greeley's Advice.—Pixley's Pamphlet.—Latham wins.. Pages 543—560

CHAPTER XXXVIII.

BRODERICK'S DEATH.—NOTABLE DUELS.

Judge Terry challenges Broderick.—The Challenge Accepted.—The Duel.—Broderick mortally wounded.—His Death and Burial.—Colonel Baker's Eulogy.—Baker's Life and

Death.—Broderick's Will.—Terry's Resignation.—The Farce of his Trial.—Notable Duels.—Gilbert killed by Denver in 1852.—G. Pen Johnston kills Senator Ferguson in 1858.—Piercy killed by Showalter in 1861.—Senator Haun announces Broderick's Death to the U. S. Senate... Pages 561—571

CHAPTER XXXIX.

A POLITICAL REVOLUTION.

Latham elected Senator in Broderick's Place.—Governor Downey vetoes the Bulkhead, and achieves extraordinary Popularity.—The Water-Front Question happily settled.—The State votes for Lincoln.—Legislature of 1861.—Free Gifts of Railroad Franchises.—General McDougall elected U. S. Senator.—A Republican State Ticket elected.—The Legislatures of 1862, 1863, and 1864................................... Pages 572—581

CHAPTER XL.

RELATIONS TO THE FEDERAL GOVERNMENT.

Perilous Position when the Southern States began to secede.—A. Sydney Johnston, commanding the Pacific Department, relieved by General Sumner.—The great Union May Meeting, 1861.—The Press and the Pulpit for Union.—Rev. Dr. Scott prefers Peace.—Important Services of T. Starr King.—His Method, Death, and Burial.—Political Parties on the War.—Downey's Fatal Sentence.—Democratic State Convention.—Edmund Randolph's Crazy Speech.—Stanford elected Governor.—Gwin's Hypocrisy.—Latham rides two Horses, and is thrown.—McDougall disappoints the Union Men.—Conner's Course.—Party Organizations sacrificed for Union.—Low elected Governor.—The Supreme Court Judges.—California's Contributions to the Army.—Gifts to the Sanitary Fund.—The Specific Contract Act.—Adherence to a Metallic Currency.—Taxing the Mines.—Californians in the Army and Navy.—In Rebel Service.—A California Pirate.—Arrests of Disloyal Persons.—General Wright's prudent Course.
Pages 582—600

CHAPTER XLI.

RESOURCES OF THE STATE.

The Gold Yield.—Profit of the various Modes of Mining.—Late Rushes out of the State.—Loss of Population in certain Districts.—Useful Mineral Products of the State.—The Mining Stock Mania, 1863-'4.—An Irruption of Prospecters.—Valuable Mineral Discoveries.—Agriculture.—Manufactures.—Exports and Imports.—Arrivals and Departures.—Insolvencies.—The Currency................... .... Pages 601—615

CHAPTER XLII.

QUARRELS WITH NATURE.—COMPENSATIONS FOR APPARENT MISFORTUNES.

Earthquakes, Floods, and Drought.—The Flood of 1861-'2.—Is there any Danger of another such?—Rainless Years.—Compensation of Fires, Floods, Droughts, and Rushes.—Much of the apparent Loss a real Gain to the Mining Towns................ Pages 616—627

CHAPTER XLIII.

THE PEOPLE AND THE PROSPECT.

Salubrity of the Climate.—What Diseases are not Uncommon.—Society rapidly improving.—The Schools.—Disproportion of the Sexes.—Sabbath Observance.—The Dashaways.—The Wine Question.—Charities.—The Indian Remnant.—Failure of the Reservation System.—The Chinese Puzzle.—Communications with the Atlantic States.—Overland Mail.—The Pony.—Telegraph across the Continent.—Awkward Task of the Historian.—The State on the Threshold of its Greatness.—Already a Mother of Territories and States .... Pages 628—644

THE HISTORY OF CALIFORNIA.

CHAPTER 1.

THE APPROACHES TO AND DISCOVERY OF CALIFORNIA.

It was about half a century after Columbus found America that the first discovery was made of Upper California. It was thirty-seven years later that the first Englishman set eyes on its soil. Still later, by one hundred and eighty-nine years, the first permanent settlement in it was successfully attempted. There was not enough known of its resources to attract much attention, until the American conquest of California, which occurred seventy-eight years later still, or three hundred and fifty-five years after the discovery of the New World.

The statement of Herodotus, that winged serpents guarded the cinnamon-trees of India, though historically fabulous, was poetically true enough; for though no such fantastic creatures as the historian described ever stood guard by any tree of earthly growth, the dis-

CHAP. I.

cases that hover over the spice-gardens on the verge of tropical jungles were scarcely less dangerous objects to encounter than winged serpents would have been. The dragons that so long protected from plunder or enjoyment the depositories of our California gold, the boundless opulence of our Pacific resources, commercial, agricultural, and mineral, were the reports carried back to Spain and England by successive navigators of intense cold in these middle latitudes, and of storms perpetually raging along our coast; the concealment of our harbors under thick and frightful fogs, behind reefs of outlying rocks or sand-bars, over which the breakers seemed to make a continuous breach; on the east, a sturdier dragon still defied approach—desert wastes, and impassable mountains of great breadth, whose frosty peaks and ridges were unbroken, except at far-distant passes, that only the most careful search revealed. During the course of three centuries the unceasing demand for safe harbors along the coast, the fact that pirates nestled in its sparse bays to the terror of lawful traders, stories of pearls in the rivers and gold in the soil, the sharp rivalry of empires conflicting for wider possessions, the assurance that whoever enjoyed its ports would control the avenues of the rich commerce of the Indies—all these motives conspired in vain to tempt to its thorough exploration and settlement. It will never cease to be a wonder how, so long after it was mapped, such a land lay hidden and almost forgotten, while explorers rummaged all corners of the earth beside, and dragged the sea for fresh prizes in the domain of Geography.

It was some years after the great Genoese found his new world before geographers comprehended that there was room enough on the globe for the land of which we write. When Columbus argued to the professors of Salamanca his pet and prolific theory of the rotundity of the earth, the wisest of them did not dispute its truth; but he shared with them the error of allowing too little length for a degree of longitude. In consequence, he looked in the vicinity of Florida for Marco Polo's famous Island of Cipango—the Japan of our maps; and the best charts of his day advanced the eastern boundary of Cathay or China as far east as the Sandwich Islands. So, when he came across the islands that picket the Western Continent, he had no doubt that he was near the threshold of the Eastern. When he had coasted scores of leagues along the southern shore of Cuba, and the crazy condition of his ships and his disheartened men made it necessary for him to turn to the eastward again, he took the sworn statements of all on board his fleet, from the captain to the ship-boy, in

CHAP. I.

1502.

confirmation of his own opinion that they had visited the eastern extremity of Asia. On his fourth voyage to America, in 1502, he diligently searched from the Bay of Honduras to Porto Bello, for the strait that the Spanish geographers believed must communicate between the Gulf of Mexico and a sea lying to the westward. But no such coveted outlet could he find, and he died firm in the faith that in crossing the Atlantic he had navigated the only ocean that divided the western edge of Europe from the eastern fringe of Asia. But as succeeding explorers pried into and retreated from each large river's mouth along the northern shore, investigated the whole curve of the Mexican Gulf, sought along the Caribbean Sea and up the broad La Plata, but everywhere in vain, for an opening westward, the islands, that most had held the new lands to be, grew beyond controversy into a continent—but not the Eastern Continent, for the natives everywhere persisted in the story that to the westward (and many of them said, not far off) lay an ocean. It piqued the chart-makers and the hardy navigators alike that it could not be reached.

1513.

That honor was not long reserved for Balboa, a noble Spaniard, who had settled with a colony of gold-seekers at Darien. In the year 1513 his guides took him to the top of a mountain, whence they told him that both seas might be seen. Pushing up to its summit, he found it as they had said. When the vision of a limitless expanse of waters to the south met his gaze, he fell on his knees, and, with uplifted hands, thanked Heaven for the honor of being the first European that had beheld "the sea beyond America." Then descending to the shore, he waded waist deep into the water, and took possession of it, and all the lands it washed, for Spain.

But the first European to sail on the waters of Balboa's "South Sea beyond America" was Fernando Magellan. This zealous and courageous Portuguese navigator had sailed as far east as the Malay Islands, where his countrymen were slowly effecting a settlement. But becoming dissatisfied with the remuneration he was receiving for his services, he went over to Spain, and without much difficulty convinced the court, inflamed by reports of the mines in Mexico, where about that time Cortez was urging his imperial conquests, that the coveted Spice Islands might be reached by sailing westward. There was a famous compact then existing between those maritime rivals, that whatever new lands might be discovered beyond the meridian one hundred and eighty degrees west of the Azores, should belong to Spain; and all east of that line were to be the property of Portugal. Spain could not resist the temptation to gain a point by intrigue when projected on so grand a scale, and Magellan was speedily dispatched with five small vessels to come up by a westward route behind the Portuguese possessions in the Malay Archipelago; and so, while adhering to the letter of the compact, to obtain a claim to that garden of the East which, without a question, the compact was intended to secure to Portugal.

Arrived off the South American main, Magellan left no gulf or inlet unexplored that promised an opening westward. On the 21st of October, 1520, he entered the strait between the mainland and the Island of Tierra del Fuego, which he named "The Strait of Ten Thousand Virgins," but which, ever since, has been known as the Straits of Magellan. He was sixty days threading this channel, crooked and thick-set with islands. Behind every headland that he passed a new creek opened or a new river emptied. The tide rose and fell thirty feet. The water rushed backward and forward like a torrent. The overhanging cliffs were capped with snow, yet a flaming mountain—so they reported—was generally in sight on the south. At last from this horrid place his little fleet emerged into an open sea, so calm, so gentle, so unlike the turbulent Atlantic, that he named it the Pacific. Once upon its bosom, his course lay westward towards the Philippines. Northward of his track no one yet had sailed on all this ocean.

But Cortez (in 1521) had completed the conquest of Mexico, and from the capital to both oceans the Spanish dominion was acknowledged. It was with no little curiosity that he awaited the return of the explorers he had sent out to find the western border of his New Spain. The next year he had the pleasure of announcing to his emperor that his agents had in three places discovered the South Sea. The responsive command to explore both coasts for an opening between the oceans, he welcomed as a relief from the languor that began to annoy him. It was comparatively an easy task to scour the eastern coast from Panama to Florida. But on the west he had work worthy of his genius; for, first of all, there were his harbors to find, then his ships to build, and then a sea of unknown perils to navigate, which as yet no keel had ever vexed.

But, to a man like Cortez, difficulties are a spur, and repeated failures are sharp incentives. He fitted ship after ship, and sometimes fleets of them, determined to know not only what sort of face the land he had conquered presented to the west, but also to be sure that no strait were left undiscovered, north or south, by which Spain might reach the Spice Islands without doubling the Cape of Good Hope; and it was his special purpose to inspect definitely the stormy channel through the continent where Magellan had passed from ocean to ocean. In 1534, one of his men, a mutineer and murderer, discovered Lower California, and was murdered there. Cortez had given to Becerra the command of one of two ships that were sent out to learn the fate of a missing vessel of a previous expedition. Becerra's crew mutinied under the lead of the pilot, Ximenes, a native of Biscay, who continued the voyage, crossed the Gulf of California, and landed. While near the bay afterwards known as La Paz, Ximenes and twenty of his Spaniards were killed by the Indians. The vessel, however, returned, with a good report of the country, its people, and its pearls.

During the same year, Cortez, seeking for the Moluccas, which he thought to be no great distance off, conducted in person an exploring expedition to the north. He left Tehuantepec with four ships; three of these were soon stranded along the coast. The one in which he himself sailed reached the gulf and the peninsula. From that time the Gulf of California was known as the "Sea of Cortez;" though when, soon afterwards, it was more explored, it gained the name of the Red or Vermilion Sea: perhaps from some resemblance

of its outline to the Red Sea that separates
Egypt from Arabia; perhaps from the color of
its waters near its head, as seen after the Colorado had disgorged into it a torrent more than
usually turbid. Cortez hoped to plant a colony
on the peninsula; but the discontent that grew
out of the sufferings of the little company from
famine, from excesses when relief came, and
from repulses by the Indians, made him glad
to hear the appeals from Mexico for succor,
that gave him an excuse to retreat from his
undertaking and return.

In 1537 he dispatched three ships, under
Francisco de Ulloa, who entered the Gulf of
California, explored it to its extremity, then
doubling the Cape, went up the western coast
of the peninsula to about the twenty-ninth
degree of north latitude. Ulloa, after a year's
absence, brought back accounts of a bare volcanic land, peopled by poor men—of "no country, in short, worthy the second visit." And
now the conqueror's conceit of rich islands and
vast territories of unbounded wealth was quite
deserting him. For all his princely outlays he
was reaping no profits either of glory or of
gold.

But that very year Mexico enjoyed a fresh
sensation. Of three hundred Spaniards, who,
ten years before, landed in Florida to conquer
it, four survivors wandered across to Cu-

CHAP. I.
1537.

liacan, whence they were sent to the capital. There they told such stories of the pearls and other riches that abounded on the coast of the South Sea, that all Mexico was fired for explorations. Cortez and the Viceroy Mendoza, with equal zeal, sprang to new enterprises. But the projects of the two were irreconcilable, and the star of the viceroy was in the ascendant. Cortez remained chafing at home, harassed by the lawyers, while the viceroy perfected his arrangements to send off, for the conquest of "the countries and islands north of Mexico," an army of a thousand men by land, and another by sea. Orders were given for the two armaments to meet in latitude thirty-six. The land forces penetrated northward by way of Sinaloa and Sonora to where they found seven wretched towns, with a population in the largest one of but four hundred men. The houses, though constructed of earth and unhewn logs, were occasionally of several stories in height. These places they identified as "the seven large towns, inhabited by civilized nations, with mountains round about, rich in metals and gems," and "the large town of Quivira, with houses seven stories high, celebrated for its riches," which a zealous Franciscan had reported to exist, and on whose representations as much as on those of the Florida wanderers the expedition was founded. In three years the inland army returned, sick, thinned, and disheartened, reporting a country barely tolerable, and but narrowly removed from the character of a desert. Meanwhile the fleet had achieved the disgrace of its commander by a very speedy return without the slightest advantage gained. They went, according to account, to the appointed place on the thirty-sixth degree of north latitude, which would have been up the Colorado River, above the Mohave Indian country; they erected some crosses, buried some bottles containing letters, and then went back again. As we hear nothing further of this landing in so high a latitude, as it was not spoken of as a point beyond preceding explorations, and as the commander of the fleet was disgraced, it is probable that there was some mistake about it, though that Alarcon was the discoverer of the mouth of the Colorado, about the year 1540, is not disputed.

Cortez now embarked for Spain, never to return. Before he left, however, he saw himself deserted by one who had always followed his fortunes. Pedro de Alvarado, ambitious of rivalling Cortez as an explorer, having asked of the emperor and received a commission, contracted for the building of twelve ships, a galley, and some smaller vessels, and for their thorough outfit with men, horses, arms, and provisions. To make his enterprise more sure, he allied himself with Mendoza, the viceroy, but

CHAP. I.

1540.

suffering death at the hands of the Indians, whom he had cruelly oppressed, his ships were left to rot in their harbors, until Mendoza refitted a portion of them, two of which he sent, under Juan Rodriguez Cabrillo, a native of Portugal, to explore the western coast of California.

1542.

Cabrillo left Natividad June 27, 1542. He touched on the peninsula of Lower California, ran up the coast, and often landed to question the docile Indians. In the Santa Barbara region he saw large houses, and being told by the natives that in the interior there lived white men, he wrote those white men a letter, and gave it to the Indians to be forwarded. When about on the fortieth degree of latitude, he saw mountains covered with snow, and between them a large cape, which he called De Mendoza (Mendocino), in honor of the viceroy. On the 10th of March, 1543, when in forty-four degrees, the cold being very intense, his provisions exhausted, and his ships in bad condition, he turned southward again, and sailed back towards Natividad.

The value of this expedition lay simply in the information it brought back of the trend and direction of the coast. Cabrillo fetched home no account of snug harbors, or of places proper to plant colonies in; indeed, the important geographical facts of his discovery seem to have been soon forgotten. The date which marked an era—the starting date, indeed, in California history—was no era to the cotemporaries of Cabrillo. The viceroy sent out no succeeding expeditions. Being soon afterwards promoted to the viceroyalty of Peru, he had little further opportunity to extend his researches; and the solitary enterprise of his successor in that direction proved a perfect failure. The efforts that had been put forth with so little profit for twenty years, to learn the configuration of the western coast of America, were intermitted for more than half a century.

The meaning of the word *California*, and how it came to be applied to the land we live in, is not to this day a settled matter. Venegas, the Jesuit historian, thinks that some words of the Indians having a sound similar to it, were mistaken by the Spaniards as the designation for the country, though investigation showed that the Indians did not so call it. Others have supposed or guessed that the name was deliberately framed by the Spaniards from the Latin *calida fornax*—a hot furnace. But this is improbable, as the Spaniards were not in the habit of manufacturing names by any such classical process; nor were men who were used to the heat of Acapulco likely to speak of any portion of California as a furnace, in comparison with that oven of cities.

The name first appears in the account written by Bernal Diaz, of one of Cortez's expeditions, he applying it only to the gulf. From this it seems to have spread to include all of the region that Spain claimed northward of Mexico on the Pacific, or west of the Gulf of California.

If a geographer of the time of Cabrillo had attempted to bound the region known as California, he would have said that it extended from the Vermilion Sea of Cortez and the ocean on the south, northward past Cape Mendocino, to the Straits of Anian, which separate America from the confines of Tartary; that eastward it was bounded by Canada, and on the southeast by a wild desert tract that cut off access to it from New Spain, above the termination of the Vermilion Sea.

CHAPTER II.

A NOTABLE ENGLISHMAN IN CALIFORNIA.

HITHERTO there had been three great inducements for prosecuting explorations in the Northern Pacific: First, a desire to find a route from Europe to the Indies, the Straits of Magellan being the only water passage yet known, and a return through them from west to east being industriously represented as quite impracticable. Second, the hope of finding rich regions that would rival the Spice Islands in the products of their forests, and the mines of Mexico in precious metals. Third, the ardent zeal of the Catholic sovereigns, inspired alike by policy and piety, to convert the heathen and give unknown nations to the Church. But now a new motive was added. A rich trade between the Philippine Islands and Spain was springing up. Every year a great galleon from the Malaysian Archipelago crossed the Pacific to Acapulco, whence its freight was conveyed either to Panama or across the continent to Vera Cruz. To avoid the easterly trade-winds, this galleon made the coast of America as far

CHAP.
II.
1578.

north as Cabrillo's Cape Mendocino, where the northwest winds were generally blowing, and from which point there was still a long voyage of some eighteen hundred miles to Acapulco, with no known harbors on the way into which she might put on emergency for supplies or repairs.

Then there were the Straits of Anian, much talked of by mariners and believed in by geographers, which were supposed to separate Asia and America; and the fancy was that they led eastward to the Atlantic, somewhere about Newfoundland. Suppose the English, who were beginning to be a threatening power on the sea, should force that upper passage and some fine morning appear with a fleet off Acapulco or Panama! What was to hinder their taking any port they pleased, or snatching all the plunder of captured galleon or sacked cities that they had the heart to covet or the ships to carry away? Or if there exist profound peace between England and Spain, the latter had not a single settlement north of Culiacan, and the doctrine was not then admitted, any more than now, that the planting of a cross in a land conferred a title to it that the next squatter sovereign could not cloud the day he took possession. As the Spaniards debated, the shadow of what they most dreaded stalked in upon them.

England and Spain were at peace, but no love was lost between them. Queen Elizabeth had no hesitation in smiling upon the undertakings of Francis Drake, who, "on his own account, was playing the seaman and the pirate," "had got a pretty store of money together," was fast earning the name of "Sea-King," and already "was very terrible to all Spaniards." On his third voyage to the West Indies and the Spanish Main, he was led to "that goodlie and great high tree" on the Isthmus of Panama, from which both oceans are visible at the same time.

As he looked out on the vision that had so affected Balboa sixty years before, he was "vehemently transported with desire to navigate the South Sea; and falling down there upon his knees, he implored the Divine assistance that he might at some time or other sail thither and make a perfect discovery of the same, and hereunto he bound himself with a vow. From that time forward his mind was pricked on continually, night and day, to perform his vow."

Five years later he set sail again, with great secrecy, for America, his fleet consisting of five vessels; the largest of one hundred, the smallest of fifteen tons! His own "ship" was named the *Pelican;* but afterwards gloried in the designation of the *Golden Hind.* Three of the five survived to enter the Straits of Magellan, which they threaded in the course of sixteen days. This was in the fall of 1578. They found "what they call the Pacific, or Calm Sea," whipped into fury by a tempest. The storm separated the adventurous vessels, and the *Pelican* it drove as far south as the fifty-seventh degree of latitude. Nearly two months she was hurled backwards and forwards about Cape Horn. Drake plainly made out that here the continent was at an end—that the Atlantic and Pacific met. Here, then, was a route, not an inviting one indeed, yet one that ships might take to return from the Pacific towards Europe. It was a discovery of great value, for though by the time he made it a lost one of his own fleet had forced a passage eastward through the Straits of Magellan, he had accepted as true the Spaniard's doctrine that such a thing was scarcely possible; and no wonder, as to this day, for sail-vessels, it is not often deemed practicable.

After waiting duly for his delinquent vessels, Drake pushed northward in the *Golden Hind* alone. Off Arica, in the harbor of Callao, and elsewhere, he plundered ship after ship of its silver, silks, and costly gums. He captured the great galleon and appropriated her treasure, avoided Panama, paused at Acapulco, and refitted during a single day.

But when the *Golden Hind* was getting overburdened with her precious freight, the question grew troublesome, "What should he do with it?" He had no fancy for Cape Horn, though that tedious way had no such terror for mariners a century later, as his name had at that time for all that sailed. He did not doubt if he returned, that he would find a Spanish fleet waiting off the Straits of Magellan to sink him. As he had seen the oceans meet at the South, he believed they must meet, too, at the North. It suited his adventurous spirit to slip away from his enemies by a road they never had heard of, and sail back into some old English bay, laden with a grand discovery, as well as with gold and silver, pearls and spices, from the Orient.

Home, by a northeast passage, then, was his determination, and he soon found himself off the coast of California in exceedingly cold weather. The Rev. Mr. Fletcher, chaplain of the buccaneer's fleet, writes a distressing account of the inclemency of this wretched coast. If it had been his misfortune actually to enter the Arctic Ocean, where our bold whalers now-a-days rather like to summer, and occasionally even winter, he would have suffered from an exhaustion of his vocabulary of freezing adjectives before reaching Behring's Straits.

On the 3d of June, 1579, in latitude forty-two—that is, the southern line of Oregon—the crew complained grievously of "nipping cold;"

the rigging was stiff, the rain was frozen. In latitude forty-four—that is, off Umpqua City—their hands were benumbed, the meat was frozen when it was taken from the fire!

On the 5th of June they ran in shore, and cast anchor in a bad bay, where, when the thick, vile fogs lifted, they were not without danger from violent gusts and flaws of wind. Finding it no place to stay, they got to sea again as soon as possible. It was probably here, if the story which the Spanish historians tell is true, that he left behind him his Spanish pilot, Morera, who afterwards made his way overland down to Mexico; and a hard pedestrian excursion he must have found it—that first white man toiling through thirty-five hundred miles or so of strange territory, the amazement of a land full of savages.

Drake and his companions would seem to have gone as high as forty-eight degrees, and then to have been driven southward by a wind that they could not face. In thirty-eight degrees they found a fit harbor, though there the low hills were covered with snow, entered it, and tarried thirty-six days.

Now it is possible that the *Golden Hind* happened along our coast when our usually charming weather was "not at home." Such mishaps have occurred before now, that a climate has lost reputation because, at just the time when an observer was prepared to note it, both barometer and thermometer agreed to depreciate its average excellence. It may possibly have been a cold June that "the oldest inhabitant" among the natives told of for half a century afterwards.

But another explanation is quite as probable. The *Golden Hind* had been for months loitering in the tropics. To men just emerging from the soft, southern gales, the winds of our temperate zone, though charged with only frost enough to make them bracing and grateful to the acclimated, are rasping. Drake's crew had no relish for the northern passage, no taste for rugged weather, and in their dread they met it half way. Then Shasta and the Oregon mountain peaks, generally capped with snow in early summer, quickened their sensitiveness, and made them verily believe that they had prematurely confronted an Arctic clime.

Fletcher's excessive caution to prevent such a conclusion, itself suggests its probability. He argues the causes of the extreme cold, and anticipates the objection that they felt it the more from their recent arrival from equatorial regions. The general's admirable regimen, he says, secured them from any possible suffering on account of sudden transitions of lines of latitude; and then he speaks contemptuously of your "chamber company, whose teeth in a temperate air do beat in their heads at a cup of cold sack and sugar by the fire." The sprightly chaplain had the whole story to himself: there were no previously written accounts for his to conflict with, and it must be admitted that he made a good apology, and all the more plausible for being indirect, for the abandonment by Drake of his deliberately formed purpose to go home to England by the Straits of Anian.

Those much-talked-of Straits, we know, as happily for our curiosity they did not, lead up to a frozen ocean which, may as well, for all commercial purposes, have no connection with Atlantic waters. Drake troubled his head no more about them, for on leaving the California coast the *Golden Hind* steered for the Philippines, and so, by the way of the Cape of Good Hope, went back to Europe—the first craft that ever made the circuit of the globe with the same commander on board who took her out of port.

Drake named all the land he had seen hereabouts *New Albion*, the white cliffs reminding him of his native coasts, and suggesting the happy compliment that his loyalty seconded. English books after that spoke of New Albion as "Drake's land, back of Canada."

But where is the bay that Captain Drake—it was later that he was knighted and was called Sir

Francis—spent those thirty-six days in? Where is the quiet nook so shielded from raw winds, so free of fogs and gusts, so altogether pleasant and secure that even Chaplain Fletcher, with his bones aching from past cold, has for it no word of abuse?

From time immemorial, until lately, it was presumed to be San Francisco. But Humboldt, in correction of the common belief, remarked that Drake's port was farther north, under the parallel of 38° 10′, and was called by the Spaniards *Puerto de Bodega*. Later writers, in correction of Humboldt, hold that it was a curve in the coast under the lee of Point Reyes, and which, on the modern maps, is marked as Drake's Bay. In support of this theory, it is urged that Drake's Bay is in latitude 37° 59′ 5″, which corresponds within a minute to the statement of Drake's chronicler, who made the latitude 38°; that the cliffs in the vicinity of that bight are white, resembling England's in the neighborhood of Dover, and that if he had really entered San Francisco harbor he would not have been silent as to its excellence.

These reasons would seem quite insufficient to rob San Francisco of the claim to Drake as its discoverer. Its latitude is 37° 59′, to which that given by Drake's chronicler is quite as near as those early navigators, with their comparatively rude instruments, were likely to get.

CHAP. II.
1579.

The cliffs about San Francisco are not remarkably white, even if one notable projection, inside the Gate, is named "Lime Point;" but there are many white mountains, both north and south of it, along the coast; and Drake named the whole land—not his landing-place alone—"New Albion." They did not go into ecstasies about the harbor—they were not hunting harbors, but fortunes in compact form. Harbors, so precious to the Spaniards, who had a commerce in the Pacific to be protected, were of small account to the roving Englishman. But the best possible testimony he could bear as to the harbor's excellence were the thirty-six days that he spent in it.

The probabilities are, then, that it was in San Francisco Bay that Drake made himself at home. As Columbus, failing to give his name to the continent he discovered, was in some small measure set right by the bestowal of his name upon the continent's choicest part, when poetry dealt with the subject, so to Drake, cheated of the honor of naming the finest harbor on the coast, is still left a feeble memorial, in the name of a closely adjoining dent in the coast line.

To the English, then, it may be believed, belongs the credit of finding San Francisco Bay, though the Spanish had long before named and mapped points on the coast farther north. Of this, however, Drake was ignorant, and in Queen Elizabeth's name he took possession of the land, and erected a monument in token of the fact—"a plate nailed upon a faire great poste, whereupon was ingraven her Majestie's name, the day and year of our arrival there, with the free giving up of the province and people into her Majestie's hands; together with her highness' picture and arms, in a piece of five-pence of current English money, under the plate, whereunder was also written the name of our general."

The natives, who were robust, powerful, unsuspecting, and kindly, lived in huts by the water-side, and were found huddled around the fires in their huts, midsummer though it was. The men were naked; the women wore deerskin blankets over their shoulders, and mats of rushes around their bodies. They brought to the Englishmen presents of feathers and tobacco, harangued them with speeches, and, mistaking them for something more than mortals, proposed to worship them. This the visitors declined; and, to show that they too were subjects of a Higher Power, they themselves had divine worship in the presence of the Indians. Then, with much ceremony, with singing and dancing on the part of his attendants, the king of the Indians approached and placed upon the admiral's head a crown of feathers, and made him a present of his whole kingdom; all which the admiral accepted in the name of his sovereign, and in memorial of it, as well as of his visit, erected the monument spoken of above. The narrative proceeds:—

"Our necessarie business being ended, our general, with his companie, travailed up into the countrey to their villages, where we found heardes of deere by 1000 in a companie, being most large and fat of bodie. We found the whole countrey to be a warren of a strange kind of connies. * * * The people do eat their bodies, and make great accompt of their skinnes, for their king's coat was made out of them."—"There is no part of earth here to be taken up wherein there is not a reasonable quantity of gold or silver."

All this is very extraordinary. The deer have not yet vanished from the wooded parts of the land. The squirrels still remain in countless numbers, to annoy the farmers in the valleys. But about the gold?

The Europeans of that day had very contemptuous notions of any portion of the New World which did not sparkle with gold or silver. The chronicler of Drake's voyage remembered that, and wrote: "The earth of the country seemed to promise rich veins of gold and silver; some of the ore being constantly found on digging." It is ungracious to question the veracity of travellers who brought home so many indisputable truths; but it is significant, that the Indians whom they met wore no golden ornaments, as the natives of lands usually do where gold is so very abundant; and none of Drake's successors have had any similar good luck in their explorations of the vicinity that it is supposed he visited.

CHAPTER III.

VISCAINO'S EXPLORATIONS ALONG THE CALIFORNIA COAST.

CHAP. III.
1596.

The time had come, when, unless Spain would consent to let go quietly a vast region that might be a barren desert, or might be an El Dorado—unless she would see her bitterest foe inherit, before her own decay, an immense territory that she had earned by discovery—unless she would see her Indian possessions fronted by her spoiler, the time had come for action. In 1596, Philip II., from Madrid, forwarded a dispatch to Monterey, Viceroy of Mexico, conjuring him to explore and seize California. In accordance with this command, Viscaino, with three ships, sailed from Acapulco, crossed over to the peninsula, established a garrison, built a small church, and out of the branches of trees constructed some rude huts at La Paz—a name given to the bay and the new settlement in token of the peaceful reception that they received from the Indians. But speedily they ran across the misfortunes that seemed to be inseparable from all enterprises in the Gulf, and were compelled to return, abandoning the settlement before the expiration of the year.

Philip III., hearing the result of the attempt, gave orders to survey the ocean side of the peninsula. Viscaino, cheerfully accepting the charge, left Acapulco with three vessels, in the spring of 1602, for an expedition that proved notably successful. The unceasing head-winds made the passage up the coast tedious and slow, but that gave the better opportunity to survey it faithfully. At Barbary Bay (near Cape St. Lucas) he found a well-behaved people, incense-trees, pearly shells, and salt. About Magdalena Bay he found friendly though naked savages, frankincense, and eatable mussels. He stopped at several points before reaching Cerros Island, where there were "affable Indians," some pearls, little wood, and brackish water. On Cerros Island they observed a bald, painted mountain, for its sides were streaked with different-colored veins; and a seaman, who, because he came from Peru, was presumed to be a judge of precious metals, gave his opinion that it was entirely made up of gold and silver! They saw, as they sailed, "ill-smelling but precious amber enough to load a ship."

On the 10th of November they entered the harbor of San Diego, where they saw a forest of tall, straight oaks, shrubs resembling rose-

CHAP. III.
1602.

mary in savor, and many fragrant and wholesome plants. They stopped here ten days, and were delighted with the mildness of the climate, the excellence of the soil, the look of the land, which they accurately surveyed, and the docility of the Indians, who besmeared their bodies with paint and loaded their heads with feathers. The harbor abounded with fish, the flats with shellfish, the woods with game.

At sea again, they saw frequently the smoke of fires burning on the hills, which they interpreted as sure tokens that the country was inhabited, and as invitations for them to land. On the Island of St. Catalina they saw savages who had a temple, and worshipped idols with sacrifices; who sold fish to those who dwelt on the mainland, and were shrewd thieves. When in Santa Barbara Channel, the cazique offered to give the strangers ten wives apiece if they would settle among them. Occasionally they went on shore, and had mass celebrated. The harbor, where they anchored on the 16th of December, 1602, under the Point of Pines, they named Monterey, in honor of the viceroy who managed the fitting out of the expedition. From this point, one ship was sent back to Acapulco to report progress. The others, after a tarry of eighteen days, during which time they had made out that the place furnished fine, large pines fit for masts, and oak excellent for ship-timber, that the harbor was secure against all winds, and that the natives were so docile that their conversion would be easy, pushed still farther northward. Disease, however, had thinned their numbers and weakened most of those who still survived. Sharp pains were continually shooting along their bones. They were painfully sensitive to the keen, cold winds. Purple spots broke out upon their flesh. Their teeth were loosened in their gums, "even so that, unawares, they spit them out." To tell their story in a word, they were sadly afflicted with scurvy.

In twelve days after leaving Monterey, a favorable wind—it was about the only favor of the sort they could boast—carried the flag-ship "past the port of San Francisco;" but, the smaller vessel having been separated from her, the ship put back into that port and waited. The barefooted Carmelite who accompanied and wrote the story of the expedition, clearly states that the flag-ship "put back into the port Francisco," where a ship, that was sent out from the Philippine Islands to survey the California coast, had been driven ashore and lost, eight years before. The pilot of that lost ship was chief pilot of Viscaino's vessel, and he affirmed that, from the wreck, large quantities of wax and several chests of silks had been landed.

The reader is naturally puzzled, at first, on seeing the name used as familiarly as if our matchless harbor were already well known to the Mexicans, especially as the writer speaks of some place in this very vicinity. But there is not the slightest probability that Viscaino entered the harbor of modern San Francisco. "The flag-ship," says the record, "came to anchor behind a point of land called La Punta de los Reyes." Doubtless it was the bight outside and north of the Heads. It is not possible that Viscaino, who was on a hunt for harbors, could have sailed through the Golden Gate into the best harbor north of Acapulco, without making special mention of so perfect a place of safety. He would have felt that his expedition was an entire success, if he had been able to report to the viceroy that, at the very point where the great circle of the trade-winds touched the coast, he had found a good retreat and recruiting-place for the Philippine galleon, where wood and water were easily obtained, and abundant security furnished against every storm. He who had spoken so glowingly of the harbors of San Diego and Monterey, would not have neglected a eulogy on that of San Francisco, if he had ever seen it. He would not have spoken of it only as a place where a ship had been driven ashore by the violence of the wind. Drake may have entered it, and yet not be struck with its capacity to accommodate a fleet, for he was sated with the sight of natural wonders. Gold and adventure were his objects—not safe anchoring-places.

CHAP. III.
1602.

Wherever it was, Viscaino finished his surveys in a day, and moved on again slowly to the northward. On the 12th of January, he made some high, red mountains, and beyond them, farther northwest, some snowy mountains, which he judged to be Cape Mendocino. But here they encountered one of the dragons that had guarded the coast so long. They fell in with a violent gale, accompanied with sleet, and it was intolerably cold. There were but six persons on board able to keep the deck; all the rest were down with scurvy. On the 19th, they saw high mountains, covered with snow, which, from their color, and the fact that they were seen on the eve of St. Sebastian, they called Cape Blanco de San Sebastian.

1603.

The smaller vessel went, probably, as high as the mouth of the Columbia River, where, finding they were beyond the point to which the viceroy's instructions authorized them to sail, and with a sickly crew, the officers put about to return to Acapulco. At the highest point that they reached, they found a large river, its banks covered with ash-trees and willows, whose pleasing appearance tempted

CHAP. III.

1603.

them to land; but, the currents hindering them, they turned toward the south, and sailed for home, firmly believing that the current which they could not stem was the Strait of Anian, through which the fabulous ship had passed from the Atlantic to the Pacific.

The flag-ship, in returning to Acapulco, kept before a favoring wind near enough to shore for the explorers to see that the coasts were covered with verdure, and, from the fires, they judged them to be populous; but the crew were too much thinned and enfeebled to permit the closer examination they had proposed to make on their return.

Viscaino was exceedingly anxious to repeat his expedition, but before doing so it was necessary to obtain the permission of his Spanish Majesty. He went to Spain, and urged the affair at court with great assiduity. He met a courtier's fate. He was promised, and promised again, rebuffed, encouraged, and put off, until, quite disheartened, he returned to Mexico.

In a subsequent letter of Philip III. to his agents in Mexico, we find how much better report Viscaino had made of the Pacific coast than had ever before been given. He represented the country as carpeted with verdure, the climate mild, the land covered with trees, the soil fruitful. The chief subsistence of the people were the spontaneous products of the earth and the plentiful objects of the chase. Their clothing was made of the tanned skins of sea-wolves. They had an abundance of flax, hemp, and cotton. He heard that in the interior there were large towns, silver and gold, and veins of other metals.

The monarch, apparently, labored under the impression that Viscaino visited the coasts of Japan and China, which he evidently thought were but a little distance off. He ordered a search to be made for Viscaino, and, if found, that the command of a new expedition be given to him. The veteran in his retirement heard the news with joy, and prepared with alacrity to engage in fresh enterprises, but, being suddenly overtaken with a fatal illness, the royal commands were never executed.

Worse than that. The charts that Viscaino made with so much difficulty, were carelessly treasured, or, in their transfer to Spain, were lost, and in a few years the results of his costly explorations were forgotten.

It was one hundred and sixty-six years before the harbor of Monterey was visited again, and San Diego, "well watered and well wooded," and its bay, "spacious enough to contain many ships," and the smaller bay contiguous to it, passed as entirely out of mind as if they had never been mapped. Such sorry results could scarcely have come of such grand undertakings if there had been newspapers in those days, to serve up, in popular form, the story of brave adventurers, or print, in solid columns, the official reports of their officers.

CHAPTER IV.

UNSUCCESSFUL ATTEMPT TO COLONIZE THE COUNTRY.

It was a great grief to Spain, when there was leisure between her wars to consider it, that California could not be conquered and peopled. During many succeeding years, traders frequently sent down pearls of great value, obtained on the west coast of the gulf. There were current many stories of inland discoveries to the northward, and of the wealth that adventurers found. Then there were pirates infesting the Pacific, making their head-quarters in the California harbors; and these, though quiet the rest of the year, were sure to sally out when the Philippine galleon was due. Attempts were repeatedly made to re-discover the harbors already described, and bring them into use; but all were in vain.

There was a well-planned effort made for the conquest of California in 1683, which, for a while, promised fairly. It was under the command of Admiral Otondo, though its spiritual government was intrusted to Father Kino by the Jesuits, upon whom it was conferred by

CHAP. IV.
1683.

special warrant from Spain, and with the forlorn hope that, by a joint effort of Church and State, a permanent settlement of the country might be effected. They sailed up the gulf, and once more California was taken possession of in the name of the Spanish Majesty, with the usual imposing ceremonies. The admiral spent his time in coastwise and inland explorations, while the religious members of the company, making La Paz their head-quarters, and having erected a church but three months afterward near San Bruno Bay, set to work learning the languages of the natives. It was very tedious, but the learners were in earnest, and it was not long before they had translated into the Indian tongue the chief articles of the Christian creed.

They did not escape the difficulty always experienced by missionaries in finding native terms to express ideas of which the untutored heathen has no conception. On one occasion they took some flies, and, putting them under water in the presence of the Indians, waited till the insects seemed to be dead; then, placing them on the warm ashes in the sunlight, told the natives to watch until they came to life again. As one after another the flies were restored to vitality, and began to stretch themselves and clean their wings for a flight, the exclamation of the watchers was accepted as the proper word by which to render the idea of resurrection.

But there came a drought of eighteen months' duration. Hardships innumerable followed, and so much sickness, that the most sanguine debated whether the enterprise must not be abandoned. Just then came orders for the vessels to put to sea, to take under convoy the Philippine ship, for which the Dutch privateers were waiting; and so was precipitated the end of an effort which had cost three years of time and large appropriations of the royal revenue.

The viceroy next endeavored to engage the Society of Jesuits to undertake the reduction of California, promising them, as material aid, $40,000 a year, to be paid annually out of the king's treasury. The chapter thanked him for the honor conveyed in the invitation, but foresaw too great inconveniences in taking upon itself such rugged temporal engagements, and declined. It professed a readiness, however, always to supply the necessary missionaries to accompany any future expedition that might be planned.

Thus, after nearly two centuries of repeated, costly efforts, it was resolved on the part of Spain that the projects which Cortez and the kings attempted in vain must be abandoned; and California was left to the unrestrained tenantry of its naked natives; though the most fabulous reports of its wealth were credited, and every year the absolute necessity to the

CHAP. IV.
1683.

East India trade of a good harbor on the coast was made the more apparent.

The mountain system of Upper California, when studied on the modern maps, furnishes much apology for the incompetence of the Spaniards to effect an earlier settlement, and especially for missing the best harbor. A series of mountain ranges lies almost parallel to the coast; indeed, for most of its extent, the surf beats the broadside of a rocky mountain. There is only one perfect, noteworthy fissure in the range, and that, widened by the currents, constitutes the Golden Gate which opens into San Francisco Bay. At the Point of Pines the range strikes the sea. Between that point and the Santa Cruz range the ocean excavates the Bay of Monterey. To the same fact, that the mountain ranges are not exactly parallel with the coast, we are indebted for the roadstead of San Luis Obispo, the Santa Barbara Channel, and the Bay of San Diego. When the old navigators, sailing northward, saw the peaks of a distant range draw nearer and nearer to the sea, they might naturally expect it soon to strike the sea at a sharp angle, and just north of that they would look for anchorage. But at San Francisco the range is abruptly broken. It is an exception to the rule, and they failed to note it. Remember, too, the thick fogs that so often veil the Golden Gate, and it will seem less strange that these early navigators missed it.

The Jesuit historian, in commenting on these repeated failures, sees the hand of Providence, for the glorification of religion, in the fact that not until majesty and power and wealth had exhausted their resources, and confessed their inability to cope with it, was the work done. In the same spirit, the American Christian sees that it is Providence who now will send a succession of earnest, indefatigable, religious men to wrestle with and subdue the land; and after them, a race of quiet, easy, comfortable priests to possess it, tame its wildness, bring to view the mild, serene enjoyments so natural to it, travel unsuspicious over its hoarded wealth, seed and stock it, and plant vineyards in a few favored spots; develop, though feebly, its agricultural resources, and then, with scarcely a struggle, surrender all to another people, of a reformed faith and more progressive practice.

CHAPTER V.

EXPERIMENTS OF THE JESUITS IN CALIFORNIA.

CHAP.
V.
1697.

The Father Kino, or Kühn (as it was in his native German), who attended Otondo in his unsuccessful attempt to plant a colony and a mission at La Paz, was not a man to retreat from a project once undertaken. While holding the professorship of mathematics in a Spanish college, highly esteemed, quietly enjoying a life of leisure, and with a prospect of a large fortune before him, he was taken exceedingly ill. When lying, as he supposed, at the very verge of death, he made a vow to Saint Francis Xavier that if he should recover, that saint should be the model of his life. He did recover, resigned his professorship, and came to Mexico. But before long he grew jealous of the tranquillity of his new career. He embraced with delight the hardships promised in Otondo's expedition, and certainly had no cause for disappointment in that respect. When the barrenness of the land and its utter poverty forced its abandonment, he, if no others, was determined that it should be only temporary. He was inflamed with a desire to conquer California for the Church—an object to which he devoted his life. He travelled widely through Mexico, persuading, pleading, arguing with his Jesuit brethren, to enlist their sympathies with his. That he might the better accomplish his ends, he sought and obtained the appointment of "Superintendent of the Missions of Sonora." Their contiguity to the land which it was his ambition to convert gave him facilities, no other way attainable, for watching over and devising means to subdue the barren Canaan of his hopes. Fortunately, as he travelled on one of his mission tours he met, and infected with his own zeal, Father Juan Maria Salva Tierra, who soon became his equal in enthusiasm. For a while the two struggled in vain. The Society of Jesuits, the Viceroy of Mexico, the King of Spain saw in it nothing but a chimerical experiment, in which, with an empty treasury, there was no temptation to embark. But in 1697, eleven years after Father Kino began to preach his project, Salva Tierra was authorized by the Jesuits to raise contributions for the spiritual conquest of California. He found a valuable colaborer in Father Juan Ugarte, professor of philosophy in the College of Mexico, a shrewd manager of temporal affairs, who undertook to act in Mexico as agent for the conquerors while they were in the field.

It was not long before the funds were pouring in, and when they accumulated sufficiently an expedition was fitted out. There were but two conditions required of the colonists by the royal council: first, that they must not waste any thing belonging to the crown, or draw on the treasury, without the king's express order; second, that they were to take possession of all territory in the king's name. They were empowered to enlist soldiers for their guard at their own expense, and to appoint officers of justice for the land they should conquer.

Salva Tierra and his little company of six soldiers and three Indians crossed the gulf from the mouth of the Yaqui, and pitched their first encampment, which they called Loreto, on the Bay of San Dionysio, thirty miles south of San Bruno. It was a place green with trees and grass, and rich in its convenience to springs of fresh water. The barracks for the garrison were built, and the tents for a chapel set up, before whose door was planted a crucifix, and on it displayed a garland of flowers. On the 25th of October, 1697, possession was taken of the country in the name of the king.

Father Salva Tierra at certain hours of each day read to the Indians, who gathered for the purpose, prayers and parts of the catechism, which he translated to the best of his ability, with the aid of the papers that the missionaries of Otondo's expedition had preserved. Then, in order to learn their language, he wrote down their discourse. The Indians were very much amused with the blunders that he made, but he took their banter kindly, and made fine progress. When these labors of the day were over he distributed to each Indian an allowance of boiled maize, and so teacher and taught made a very good start.

It was scarcely a month, however, before the Indians, who greatly admired the boiled maize, and were even willing to take the catechism to get it, began to pilfer from the corn-sacks, and so improve upon the daily half-bushel allowance. The attempt to prevent this provoked them to plot the murder of the whole company, that they might get all the corn. This calamity being happily averted, the Indians called their brothers from many miles around, to take counsel how to crush out the little colony.

These were tough times with the handful of soldier missionaries. They were obliged to keep constant watch, and they suffered sadly from the intense heat of the sun by day, and still more from the heavy rains at night; against which, being misled by the continued drought that Otondo reported, whence they inferred that it never rained in California, they had made no provision. Still, when the assault came, they were ready for it, and the ten men of the garrison withstood the attack of the five hundred savages. When the enemy retreated, the pious victors saw to their amazement that the pedestal of the cross had caught most of the arrows, while the cross itself and the chapel tent were untouched, and only two of the soldiers were wounded. The Indians, driven back now by force, were afterwards won to friendship by kindness; and Salva Tierra's letters to Mexico were so full of modesty and gratitude for the preservation and success of the mission, that to four of them was accorded the honor of publication!

And now for two years all things went smoothly. The missionaries widened by degrees their circle of influence, and made an occasional tour of exploration into the interior. The next trouble was one that the native doctors or sorcerers stirred up, because their craft was in danger; for they very naturally and correctly suspected, that if the strangers should introduce a new religion, the prophets of the old would find their occupation gone. So thinking, they encouraged a rebellion; but the appetite for boiled maize, of which they could of course get none while hostilities were maintained, brought the rebels to terms again. Once the vessel with supplies from the main failed to arrive before the whole stock was reduced to three sacks of poor meal and three of maggoty maize. Fortunately, the twenty-two soldiers that constituted the camp were "cheerful and devout," and the supplies came before their courage failed.

There was a solitary grumbler in the camp, however, whose letters home did much mischief among the friends of the mission. The worthy captain of the garrison had been compelled by a trouble in his eyes to return to Mexico. His successor felt his subordination to the fathers irksome, and in his correspondence found much fault with their management. His representations might have produced no bad effects, if there had not already grown up in Mexico much jealousy of the Jesuits. Other expeditions, said their enemies, sent home many pearls; this one sends none. Their faithful friends claimed that that fact showed the disinterestedness of the missionaries. Rather, answered the disaffected, it proves that they conceal the treasures which they gather; and, besides, that they are pretty busy at something else than the state's business, one might guess, seeing that no creek or bay or harbor has yet been found by them for the great galleon to seek shelter in.

Meanwhile, no help towards the new conquest came from the civil government. Once

CHAP. V.
1700.

the viceroy and general assembly tendered an appropriation so contemptibly small that Father Ugarte declined to accept it. Philip V., on his accession to the throne of Spain, ordered that six thousand dollars a year be paid towards the object. In 1701, Mary of Savoy expressed her highest admiration of the enterprise. She deemed it already a grand success, for she had learned that for fifty leagues about the Indians were brought to a settled obedience, that four towns had been founded, that they counted six hundred converts and two thousand adult catechumens. But, since the treasury was already exhausted by an expensive effort to conquer Texas, and save Pensacola from falling into the hands of other nations, neither the king's order nor Mary's good wishes brought a dollar to the famishing conquerors of Lower California.

Father Ugarte, despairing at last of state aid, gathered what contributions he could in Mexico, and proceeded in person to the field. This was about the close of the year 1700. He took his station at St. Xavier, in the interior, and henceforth the professor of philosophy dedicated all his energies to the work of teaching and civilizing half-naked savages. There was a little good land about his mission, and he determined to make the most of it. The first thing in the morning, the Indians, young and old, were gathered into church for mass. Then came breakfast of pozoli, and then work.

It was easy working with such a master, for he claimed the hardest task for himself. He was first in the trench with his spade; at felling trees, no one handled the axe so well; at splitting rocks, he was the handiest with the crow. His good-nature infected his company, and when he himself began to tire, he ordered all hands to rest. He was patient as the day was long, but they must not trifle with him out of season. Once, at prayers, he was annoyed at seeing his whole congregation full of merriment, evidently at his expense. He kept on with his duties as if he saw nothing amiss, until he was sure that the cause of the giggling was a stout, full-grown Indian, who was a sort of bully among them. The meek but muscular missionary said nothing, but suddenly catching the stout savage by the hair of the head, swung him to and fro, till the others, thinking their turn might come next, ran frightened out of the church. But when he learned that they had laughed because of his mispronunciation, and the comical misuse of words that the wags of his class led him into, he possessed his soul in patience, and chose more carefully his philological advisers. The savages could not but be charmed with his shrewd and kindly ways.

CHAP. V.
1707.

And he made not only the little patch of rich soil about the mission, but the rough, craggy desert around it too, wave with golden grain and corn, and the vines of his planting yielded a small stock of generous wine. In 1707, while New Spain was suffering with drought, he was eating bread of his own raising. The stock was not enough to last the year, but sufficient to lessen essentially the charges for supplies from abroad. The horses and sheep, brought over from the opposite coast, increased rapidly. He made distaffs, spinning-wheels, and looms, and imported a weaver to teach his Indians the mysteries of that art. "Who," he gayly wrote, "who would have dreamed of any such thing!"

Yet long before Ugarte had eaten bread of his own making, all the missions would have been blotted out but for the untiring zeal of Kino, who, from his Sonora settlements, was sending over continually grain, cattle, furniture—every thing that he could muster to supply their wants. California was his field, and he only tarried in Sonora that, with its fertility, he might relieve the barrenness of the land where his affections lay.

But frequently it occurred that all the surplus proceeds of a harvest, shipped for the California missions, were lost or damaged by the dangerous transit of the gulf. Kino early concluded that the salvation of the California missions, which could not become self-supporting in many years, hinged on this question: whether or not California was joined to the main land. He believed firmly that it was, and in this faith he constantly pushed up his missions to the northward. He gathered the Indians into villages, travelled among them, won their confidence, and slowly extended his peaceful conquests in that direction where he thought— perhaps in the latitude of Monterey, perhaps of Mendocino—he would be able to turn south again, and carry on the chain of Christian settlements, till the last link were established with Loreto and its circle. He met few difficulties in the Indians themselves, but an abundance from his commercial countrymen. The Apaches, at this day such a terror to travellers, gave him no trouble; but avaricious Spaniards were the plague of his life. These fellows studied to keep the Pimos rebels and enemies, that they might have an excuse for making slaves of them. At his earnest solicitation, the Audience of Guadalaxara agreed that none of his converts should be obliged to work in the mines or on the public lands for five years after conversion. Charles V. extended the term of exemption to twenty years. And yet Kino was sadly mortified to see his baptized converts dragged off without mercy to the mines, in spite of the agreement—in violation of the king's explicit order.

CHAP. V.

1700.

But Father Kino knew that in Mexico, and among those who were regarded as authorities, there were many who denied the premises of his reasoning, and were sceptical as to the connection of California with the main land, upon which he presumed. More to satisfy their doubts than any of his own, in the year 1700 he made up a party of friendly Indians, and proceeded to the junction of the Gila and the Colorado, crossed the Gila, where fifteen hundred natives came out in a body to see him, and ascended a mountain, whence he saw nothing but land to the westward. The natives, too, assured him that the first "big water" in a westerly direction was the South Sea.

1701.

1702.

The next year he repeated the journey, accompanied by Salva Tierra, and both were satisfied on the point. The year following, Kino once more took the excursion, and made his own assurance trebly sure that California was not an island, as the maps of that day had it, under the name of *Islas Carolinas*. But the course of our story must wait no longer on the movements of Father Kino, the life as they were of the land to whose spiritual subjugation he was entirely devoted. He abated no jot of his first zeal, remitted no effort that could forward his cause, until, in 1710, he died.

1704.

The seventh year (1704) of the California

missions was near to being their last. The supplies were spoiled on the way. The garrison grew discontented. Matters came to such a strait that Salva Tierra called the fathers together, and plainly put the question whether they should surrender to the impending famine and go home. Not that he for a moment meditated joining himself in any retreat, but it seemed like submitting to a company of men whether or not they would consent to stay and starve. The fathers, with one voice, agreed to take the risks and stay. Nor upon consultation would one of the camp consent to go, unless the fathers would. So Ugarte gathered a force of soldiers and Indians for a raid into the woods; and on the fruits of the forest and the roots that they dug, they managed to subsist until supplies arrived.

This peril passed, Salva Tierra went over to Mexico on business of the mission. There he heard bad news—that he was promoted to be provincial. He sent on at once, asking permission to resign his new post, but meanwhile exerted all the increased influence that the position gave him to forward the California interest. He waited on the viceroy, pleaded the king's warrants, urged the arguments two centuries old, but won only promises. He prepared a bold and earnest memorial to the Assembly, just about to meet, in which he set forth the policy of supporting what was so well begun, and represented the impossibility of continuing the settlements unless a more generous liberality were extended them. For seven and a half years they had been allowed three vessels; now two of them were lost, and one could not answer the purpose. He contrasted the luckless, fruitless, wretchedly misconducted expedition of Otondo, who had the royal treasury at command, with the economy and success of this. He pictured the barrenness of the country. From the time of Cortez the peopling of it was tried in vain; but, the holy Virgin of Loreto aiding, the land was subdued at last and settled. He showed how certainly all would be lost if the fathers had not the power to appoint and displace the commander of the military. He dwelt upon the danger of insurrection if, under any pretence, the Indians were compelled to fish for pearls, and he asked that twenty-five soldiers and a captain be put at the service of the missionaries. The cost of the enterprise to that day was one million two hundred and twenty-five thousand dollars, exclusive of the "foundation" of six missions, which amounted to sixty-eight thousand dollars more. Of these sums the treasury had paid only eighteen thousand dollars. As to the king's suggestion to establish a garrison on the western coast, for the relief of the Philippine ships, he proposed that, without the expense of a new garrison, a subsidy of thirteen thousand dollars be paid to the fathers, which would enable them to push the settlements across to the western coast. As to the condition of the country, he assured them that the sovereign was now possessed of fifty leagues in circuit, where all was so profoundly peaceful that the fathers traversed it alone without a guard. Three routes to the Pacific had been discovered, and a distance of two days' journey along the ocean coast had been surveyed.

But the viceroy, who listened with politeness, meant no relief. His royal master needed all that could be spared from the treasury, for the greater part of Europe was leagued to deprive him of his crown. Perhaps the viceroy was influenced by the common scandal of the time as to the insatiable avarice and wealth of the Jesuits; more probably he thought he made a better case for himself with the king, by remitting money to Spain, than he could by carrying into effect his pious orders, which did not need to be enforced to gain for majesty an abundance of credit. But, whatever his motive, California got no favors from him.

The churlish viceroy died in 1711, and the Duke de Linacres succeeded him. The duke had an hereditary affection for the Jesuits, and would have strained a point to forward their enterprise; but in his official capacity he could do nothing, for all the king's schedules had been so carefully secreted by his predecessor that they could not be found. However, he testified the sincerity of his professions by giving by will one-third of his estates to the California missions, and then, as the climax of his excellent behavior, died in 1717, and gave them an early enjoyment of his bequests.

The missionaries, meanwhile, kept themselves busy; now Father Piccolo was directing all their energies to secure the supplies for their subsistence; now Father Ugarte was laboriously surveying a new route to the ocean; now all were engaged in inducing the Indians at a distance to exchange their wild life for the habits of the settlements, and now founding new missions.

Salva Tierra had at last obtained his discharge from the office of provincial, and returned to share the perils of his brethren. Scarcity of food was the dark shadow that was always approaching, or just behind them, but seldom entirely out of sight. At one time the small-pox made terrible ravages among the natives. The sorcerers whispered that the fathers poisoned the children with the baptismal water, and the adults with extreme unction, and thence came seditions and revolts. Then the vessels were lost. Then again there would be a burst of sunshine; supplies would arrive, and peace follow in the wake of plenty; and so, with alternations of good and bad fortune, things went on until 1717.

In the autumn of that year all the peninsula was visited by a hurricane, which did great damage to the missions. Father Ugarte's house and church were levelled to the ground. A Spanish boy at Loreto was reported as taken up in a whirlwind and never seen more! If (says the chronicler) in former ages such hurricanes were frequent in California, it is not surprising that all its mould was swept away, leaving its rocks bare, and its plains and valleys covered with heaps of stones.

But a more remarkable event than the hurricane notched this year as noticeable. A new viceroy had arrived at Mexico, charged by the minister Alberoni—afterwards cardinal—to lend every encouragement to the Sonora and California missions; to establish garrisons on the South Sea coast at all practicable points, and, if possible, to induce the formation of settlements up the Colorado and Gila Rivers. Alberoni believed that the settlement of California would tend to develop immensely the trade with the Philippines, and that in return that trade, after a nucleus on the coast were once formed, would build up California. His instructions on these points wonderfully foreshadow the destiny of the coast that we are seeing fulfilled to-day, though of course the glory and wealth of Spain were the objects to be attained by all the means that he suggested. The viceroy desired to second with spirit all that was commanded him, and, that he might do so intelligently, sent for Salva Tierra to visit Mexico.

The noble old pioneer, though afflicted with a very painful disorder, and stooping with the weight of years, immediately started. He paused from sheer necessity at Guadalaxara, and was never able to renew his journey. Two months he suffered there the sharpest agony; then, perfectly contented, resigned his breath. The whole city assisted at his burial, and every friend of California mourned her loss in his death.

Jayme Bravo, who attended the good father through his illness, pushed on to Mexico, and answered, a good deal better than was feared, the purposes for which Salva Tierra had been summoned. The viceroy's council and the Assembly, with the greatest generosity, granted, so far as resolutions could do it, all that was asked, but forgot the necessary appropriations; and so the treasurer, who was a very strict economist where his own interests were out of question, declined to pass over any funds. Then Alberoni, being made cardinal, left Spain for a different order of business, and thus his grand scheme for California collapsed.

In 1722 clouds of locusts invaded Lower California, and consumed every green thing. The Indians, being short of food, turned the invaders to account for that purpose, and from this cause, as they alleged, came the general epidemic, of which great numbers of them died. The next year an epidemic dysentery raged with great havoc.

But no opportunity for making explorations was ever omitted. The Pacific coast had been surveyed, from St. Lucas to the latitude of Cerros Island, and three tolerable harbors, with wood and water convenient, had been discovered. Maps, charts, and minute draughts of the result of every tour were forwarded to Spain, but it is doubtful if royal eyes ever vouchsafed a glance at them. Valuable papers of this sort were either treated carelessly and soon lost, or, if deposited in the state archives, it was so difficult to gain access to them, that their information failed to enter into general circulation. So it happened, that during this century there were many important discoveries and re-discoveries; and the country was still, at the end, almost the Unknown Land that it was at the beginning.

As to the insular or peninsular character of California, there was scarcely less diversity of

CHAP. V.
1722.

sentiment than if Father Kino had not three several times during his life established the point. Even Father Ugarte thought there might possibly be some channel between Loreto and the mouth of the Colorado, through which the waters of the Gulf issued into the ocean. The doubt at last bred in him the determination to know the truth. But he had no vessel to make a survey with, no money to purchase one, and no timber at hand to build one. Being in earnest, however, he procured a gang of ship-masters, climbed with them over the mountains, found in a secluded spot trees that they pronounced fit for the purpose, cleared a road into the slough, cut and dragged the timber to the landing, and constructed a vessel, of no great dimensions indeed, but a stancher craft than they were accustomed to see in those parts; and though it about exhausted their provisions and money, it cost less than to have bought her equal in Mexico. This pioneer California coaster was named *The Triumph of the Cross.*

Taking an open boat along as a tender, Father Ugarte and a company of twenty men set sail in the *Triumph*, on an expedition from which they did not return until they had thoroughly explored both sides of the Gulf to the mouth of the Colorado. It proved a voyage full of perils and hair-breadth escapes. As

FATHER UGARTE'S DEATH.

they neared the upper end of the Gulf, the tide rolled impetuously at the flood over an immense extent of flat country, and currents of great strength swept around the rocks. The water was poisonous to their flesh. One day it was as dark at noon as it usually is at midnight! They had thunder and rain, and waves of frightful height. Once they were terrified by the close approach of a water-spout. It was a great comfort to the men, as the fiercest of the gales that they encountered was raging, to see St. Elmo's fire hovering around the cross at the mast-head. Out of all their troubles they were safely delivered, and they returned well satisfied that they had seen the end of the Gulf, and that there was no way for its waters to reach the ocean except southward. As to the people on the shores, they noticed that those on the east were cruel and malignant, but on the west they were gentle, friendly, and just. Father Ugarte made no more expeditions, built no more vessels. In 1730, when seventy years old, after thirty years of missionary life and service, he quietly died.

If he had lived four years longer, he would have thought the sun of a brighter day was rising on his rugged land. For, in 1734, the Philippine galleon for the first time visited it, turning in to St. Lucas with only water enough on board to last two days longer, and her crew down with scurvy. The missions furnished her with water, fresh fruit, and vegetables, and most of the crew were recovered before she resumed her lazy course toward Acapulco.

Here were demonstrated at last the benefits of the mission to East Indian commerce. When the story should reach Mexico, it must commend the policy so long pursued without encouragement, and give a fresh impetus to the work of settling the country.

But it worked precisely an opposite result. The Philippine trade itself was in Jesuit hands. The owners of the cargoes of the galleon were the monks of Manila. They had their enemies in Mexico, and these found now a new reason for frowning on the missions. Their influence was sufficient with the Government to prevent the dispatch of garrisons to protect the later settlements.

The Indians, no longer restrained by moral means, since the fathers had no physical force to make it respectable, rose in rebellion, destroyed the four missions between La Paz and St. Lucas, and gave crowns of martyrdom to Fathers Carranco and Tamaral. The missionaries returned to Loreto, which was the capital of the province, and their settlements for a while ran to waste. The next year's galleon, putting in to St. Lucas, found all desolate that was shortly before so flourishing, and, indeed, thirteen of her men, who went on shore without suspicion, were murdered by the insurgents.

The Yaquis came over from the continent to aid the missionaries, and the Governor of Sinaloa tendered his help. It was not, however, until after he had spent two years in learning that coercion was the only method of dealing with insurgent Indians, that he took the fathers' advice, treated the rebels as enemies, whipped them soundly in battle, and restored peace.

Philip V. assumed the cost of repressing this outbreak for the royal treasury, and he made some spasmodic efforts to complete the reduction of California. Ferdinand VI., with all his power, seconded his father's efforts. He essayed, but without success, to settle the peninsula by means of emigration from Mexico. He ordered that the soldiery be entirely subordinate to the clergy. He suggested to the Jesuits the propriety of doubling the number of their missionaries, and, in accordance with Father Kino's plan, sweeping the circle of their establishments from Pimeria to California. But the provincial replied, that the utter barrenness of the region around the head of the Gulf, and the experience of fifty years, made it quite useless to repeat that attempt. Still, Father Consag, in 1746, explored anew the

CHAP. V.
1746.

Colorado, with a view to the practicability of establishing an overland route from California to Sonora.

Meanwhile, the order remitted no effort to maintain the missions that were established, and found new ones. In 1745 they numbered sixteen. Their signal fires on the mountains guided the annual galleon into St. Lucas Bay, and the products of their thin soil furnished the fresh supplies that her scurvy-stricken crew required.

1758.

In 1758 the Indians, for a tract three hundred leagues northward from St. Lucas, were tamed and converted—that is, they did no harm to the whites, worked a little under the orders of the fathers, and were supported in part or entirely by them.

Life at the missions passed off very quietly, in about this way:—

Every morning the sexton, or catechist, assembled the Indians in the church, where the *Te Deum* was sung, mass said, and catechism rehearsed. Then came a breakfast, for all who were punctual at church, of corn, boiled, bruised, macerated in water, and warmed again—they called the dish *atole*. Then all went to the work of the day, or to the woods. At noon, they who fed at the public table had *pozoli*—simple boiled corn—with meat, and " vegetables in their season." At night, there were devotions again in the church; and, after that, more *atole*. Every Sunday they walked in procession around the village, and then to church, where, besides prayers, catechism, and singing, they heard simple sermons.

The father was head laborer, head cook, school-master, physician, and priest. In every new mission he was attended by a soldier, who was vicegerent in the father's absence; for small faults he whipped, for larger ones he imprisoned the offender, or put him in the stocks. Whipping, from the way it came into vogue, was always very popular. The captain of the garrison at Loreto once detected a thief, and ordered for him a very severe punishment. Just as sentence was about to be executed, Salva Tierra interfered; the captain consented to change the punishment to flogging, and the natives were filled with admiration that so innocent and superficial a substitute could satisfy justice.

The captain of the garrison was also captain of the coast; but in all things he was subordinate to the fathers, which was a grievous offence to the sword. The soldiers and sailors complained about being denied the privilege of diving for pearls, of which every fifth one found was the king's perquisite; but diving, the missionary firmly prohibited. Nothing so much prejudiced the natives as to find the foreigners running off with this source of their wealth;—

nothing would sooner entail scandal on the missions. He encouraged diving by the natives, on their own account; but neither sailors nor soldiers must engage in it.

Everywhere, the children were the first care. Some from all the missions came up to Loreto, where they learned reading, writing, singing, and Spanish; and were promoted, as they earned the honor, to be church-wardens or catechists at home. The priests furnished their parishioners with coarse clothes and blankets. Those who could work were instructed to do so, and the product of their labor was their own, except only the wine, which the father saved for his personal and medicinal uses. But, as the very best of them would waste all they gathered, if left in their hands, the father saved it for them in a common store, distributing it as their necessities demanded, or occasionally helping out some other mission not quite so able. As it was found impossible either to subsist the entire population who would attend service, as was first intended, or to find profitable work for them, the policy adopted was to feed the chief, the aged, the sick, and the children from six to twelve years old, and to give a certain allowance to all the rest, provided once a week they came to receive instruction. This was done to induce them to keep together in villages, rather than to stray about the mountains, drifting hither and thither without any home. Seeing that not the church only, but all the parishioners were to be supported, these missions were very costly experiments to their faithful patrons. When the contributions for their support amounted to $10,000, the sum was invested at home as a "foundation," and the five per cent. interest was transmitted to the missionary as his salary. Afterwards, instead of investing the principal, it was devoted to the purchase of a farm, which was managed for the missions' account. Really, since 1735, there had been no great difficulty as to the finances. The Jesuits had received some large donations, which were administered shrewdly—they purchased some productive real estate, and afterwards added to it mines, factories, and flocks. This property was held sacred to the California enterprise, and was called the "Pious Fund."

Whatever they may have to answer for on other parts of the continent, the Jesuits certainly earned a good name in Lower California. True, none but Jesuits were the historians of their career on the barren peninsula, but their version is confirmed by Indian tradition, and by all the mute witnesses that remain after the workman is gone, and testify of his faithfulness or his treason to his trust.

But King Charles of Spain saw Jesuitism

CHAP. V.

1758.

1767.

CHAP. V.
1767.

steeping in the politics and controlling the interests of the realm; and, to save his throne, he expelled the order from his domain. The decree was instantly enforced in the provinces of Mexico; and the Jesuit establishments in California, and their pious fund, were turned over, in 1767, to the Franciscan monks of the College of San Fernando, at Mexico.

Father Junipero Serra was selected as the president of the missions under the new order. He set out at once for his field, and on the 1st of April of the next year, at Loreto, took possession. In the manuscript records of the Loreto church stands the entry that Serra made on the next day: "We are in the mission and royal presidio of Loreto, capital of this peninsula of California, sixteen religious priests, preachers and apostolic missionaries; * * * the fathers of the Company of Jesus having been expelled, for reasons known to his Majesty."

If thus the Franciscans came in without a compliment to their predecessors, the Jesuits went out saying "the grapes were sour," and wasting no adulations on the land they were quitting. Father Begert, a German, who had spent seventeen years in the land, relieved his mind of a load when he got back to Europe, by publishing at Manheim, in 1773, some "Historical Sketches of the American Peninsula of

California." He pronounced it a miserable land, not worth the trouble of describing—a land of chaparral, thorn-bushes, bare rocks, and sand-hills, with a brutish people, whose Christianity was all on the surface, but whose habits of laziness, lying, and stealing were ingrained. They had no words to express the most homely virtues, yet had so small a share of such virtues that the lack was not annoying to them. Begert's book must have made the bones of Kino and Salva Tierra rattle with indignation in their graves, that a Jesuit should come to speak in such a strain of the poor land and the poorer people whom they offered themselves to save!

The Franciscans girded themselves to their work with enthusiasm, but a rival order, the Dominicans, began to clamor for a share of the field, and at last obtained a royal edict requiring one or two of the missions to be surrendered to them. The Franciscan warden explained how indivisible the interests of the missions were, and proposed, instead, to cede the whole to them; for they had, by this time, another project at heart. So the Dominicans took possession of the Lower California missions, and the Franciscans retired altogether into the unknown land to the northward—our own Upper California.

This concludes our dealings with Lower California. The impatient reader may deem all written on this subject impertinent to a history of California. But really it is an essential part of the story. The bald Pacific coast of California presented a front that Spanish enterprise could not penetrate. The Jesuits were then invoked to flank it with their mission strategy—to approach it gradually, by civilizing the rude tribes of the peninsula, by ascending the Colorado, by subduing the deserts, and planting settlements at convenient distances from Cape St. Lucas northward, until the goodly land described by Viscaino were reached and subjugated. Father Venegas's *History of California*, published at Madrid, 1757, was the record of this grand flanking enterprise. His California was not the peninsula alone, but all the unknown land north of it, though repeated failures led the Jesuits at last to relinquish their long-cherished hopes of going much above the mouth of the Colorado, since every new advance northward separated them farther from their base of supplies.

Accompanying Venegas's History, published at Madrid, 1757, was a curious map, which shows at a glance what the pioneers thought our western world was like. The outlines of Lower California are laid down with general accuracy. The Colorado, a little above the mouth of the Gila, stops short. But the most curious feature is a grand sea—an ocean situated within the continent of North America—stretching from Mexico, in the latitude of Cape St. Sebastian, up to the latitude of the southern point of Greenland, and twenty-five degrees in width. Two straits connect this mediterranean sea with the Pacific, in latitudes forty-three and forty-six. From the course of the Colorado it is evident they thought future discoveries would lead it up to this great sea, which on the northeast, by a river and through two lakes, connects with Hudson's Bay. Midway between Cape Mendocino and Monterey is the Cape of Pines, and behind it, on the north, a deep indentation in the coast—the only thing that looks like San Francisco. Hudson River makes a clean breach across to the St. Lawrence, and New England is an island.

CHAP. V.

1757.

CHAPTER VI.

OCCUPATION OF UPPER CALIFORNIA BY THE FRANCISCANS.

CHAP. VI.
1768.

BEFORE the Franciscans had consented to give up Lower California, José de Galvez, the new visitor-general, and afterwards minister-general for all the Indies, had arrived, bearing an order from the King of Spain to rediscover by sea, and make a settlement at San Diego. Galvez, who seems to have been a man of marked ability and enterprise, at once undertook the execution of the king's design, and he found in Father Junipero Serra a faithful and enthusiastic co-operator. Studying the spirit rather than the letter of his instructions, Galvez with all haste prepared two expeditions, one to go by land, the other by water; and, to make success more sure, he divided each of these in two, to start separately, but all to meet at San Diego. His fleet consisted of two vessels, the *San Carlos*, of not more than two hundred tons, and the *San Antonio*, both of which were brought over from San Blas for the purpose.

The *San Carlos* was the flag-ship. She sailed from La Paz January 9th, 1769, Father Junipero having first blessed the flags, and Galvez delivering a cheering address to the embarking adventurers, who numbered in all sixty-two persons. Her commander was Don Vicente Villa. Among those on board were Friar Fernando Parron, father missionary; Lieutenant Pedro Fages and twenty-five soldiers, a baker, two blacksmiths, a cook, and two tortilla-makers. Her manifest, which is still to be found in the State archives of California, includes Indian corn and flour, crackers, home-made sugar, peas, beans, rice, hams, fish, chocolate (but no coffee or tea), a little brandy and wine, plenty of dried meat, one thousand dollars in small coin, candles for the churches, fish-oil and lamp-wicks for light, and supplies of other sorts sufficient to afford very comfortable living, for both cabin and forecastle, during a long voyage or a tedious delay on a desolate shore. Galvez accompanied the *San Carlos* in a little vessel as far as Cape St. Lucas, and saw her fairly to sea, with the wind in the right quarter, before he turned back.

The next off was the *San Antonio*, which started from Cape St. Lucas on the 15th of February, commended, as her consort had been, to the patronage of St. Joseph. Her commander was Juan Perez, who was born on the

Island of Majorca, and had already won fame as a pilot in the Philippine trade. Among her passengers were two priests. The *San Antonio* had been thoroughly overhauled at St. Lucas, Galvez himself seeing that not a barnacle was left on her, and that her keel was as sound as on the day it was laid. She carried ornaments for the church; all sorts of utensils for tent, house, or field; flower, vegetable, and fruit seeds for the garden and orchard, and grain for the valleys. Indeed, all that was thought necessary for the foundation of at least three missions was dispatched in one or the other of these vessels, or overland.

The land expedition was placed in command of Gaspar de Portalá, who, at the time, was Governor of Lower California, and a captain of dragoons. The next officer in rank was Don Fernando Rivera y Moncada, who was captain of a company of foot-soldiers. Rivera had made the tour of the northern missions in the preceding fall, and collected men, provisions, horses, mules, and two hundred head of cattle, with which to stock the unknown country they were to settle. On the 24th of March he left the frontier mission for the northern wilderness. In his company were Father Juan Crespi, a pilot who undertook to keep an itinerary, twenty-five foot-soldiers who wore leathern bucklers, three muleteers, and an unnumbered host of Christian Indians, from the peninsular missions.

Last of all started Governor Portalá's company, in May,—Father Junipero, though in wretched health for a journey into the desert, being punctually at the rendezvous.

These four detachments reached San Diego, but not precisely in the order of their starting. The first vessel in was the *San Antonio.* The *San Carlos* arrived twenty days behind her, having lost, by scurvy, all of her crew but one sailor and the cook, and several of the soldiers. Rivera's company was in by the 14th of May, and Portalá's, after a pleasant jaunt of forty-six days, at a time of year when the landscape is most charming and the weather most delicious, came in sight on the 1st of July. There was a great time in San Diego on that day, when all who were alive of the two hundred and fifty that made up the total of the four expeditions met again. The vessels fired salutes, the soldiers discharged round after round for joy. The 1st of July, 1769, is marked in the almanacs as the birthday of both Wellington and Napoleon, but it is memorable in our history, as Randolph, in his admirable *Outline of the History of California,* well remarks, for a greater event than either—it was the first day that white men entered Upper California with the purpose to live and die there.

CHAP. VI.

1769.
July 1.

Just as soon as the mutual congratulations were ended, the work of founding a mission commenced. For this the process was to select a suitable spot, and take formal possession of it in the name of Spain. A tent was erected, or an arbor, or booth, or rude log-house constructed for a temporary church, and into it the sacred ornaments were carried. A cross was planted before its entrance, a patron saint was named, a clergyman for the post designated. Then all the premises were sprinkled with holy water, the candles were lighted, mass was said and sung (the soldiers with their fire-arms doing duty for the organ, and the smoke of exploding gunpowder answering for incense), and a sermon was preached. The next task was to draw in the Indians. Presents of cloth and food served to catch the adults, and bits of domestic sugar captivated the children. The natives were to be convinced that the strangers came as friends, to protect them from their enemies and to do them good. As their confidence was gained, they were to be allured away from their idle wandering habits, persuaded to settle in villages near the mission, instructed in farming and the simple arts, taught the elements of the Catholic faith, and, as soon as they consented and seemed disposed to their new life, to be baptized and reckoned converts. Father Junipero considered himself fairly started in this work in a fortnight after his arrival at San Diego.

Leaving him at his labor of love, than which nothing could more delight him, the *San Antonio*, with all the sailors who were able, was dispatched to San Blas with tidings of what had been done, and to fetch up additional supplies. It is a significant intimation of the perils of the coast, and the state of navigation in those times, that, though she made the trip in twenty days, she lost nine men on the way.

Meanwhile, Governor Portalá, with soldiers, priests, muleteers, and Indians, sixty-five persons in all, and a pack train of provisions, started on the 14th of July to rediscover Monterey; for Galvez had charged him to accomplish the never-executed scheme of Philip III., so carefully laid down one hundred and sixty-three years before. Over six months Portalá was gone on this errand. He stopped at Monterey and set up a cross, but never dreamed it was the place he sought.

Pushing still northward, he came upon a land-locked, hill-encompassed bay or lake. Eastward the land rose gently to a lofty range of hills, beyond which peered the blue peak of a far-distant mountain. On the north were mountains; on the west high hills, whose sandy slopes descended even to the water's edge. They said they recognized this as a spot which had been described, though where, or in what, does not appear. That it was a fit place for a mission was clear to them all.

Then the priests remembered that when Galvez had suggested the three names that were to be given to the three missions that they were to found, Father Junipero had exclaimed, with much grief in his countenance, "But is there no mission for Father St. Francis?" and that Galvez had replied, gravely, as if it were not a sudden thought, "If St. Francis wants a mission, let him show us his port, and we will put one there." They accepted the token; good St. Francis had guided their errant steps and brought them to this port, so they named it San Francisco. This is the first unquestioned account of a visit to San Francisco.

That Sir Francis Drake had spent several weeks here, recruiting, has already been shown as probable. That Viscaino did not visit it, has been shown as equally probable; and yet Portalá's company recognized the place from the descriptions, and, curiously enough, before they had made out whether the broad sheet of water at their feet was a lake or a bay!

It seems possible, although this is only a surmise, that the port may have been visited casually by some of the Spanish navigators, whose oral descriptions, coinciding with Francis Drake's written accounts, led them to speak of it as San Francisco—the given name of the discoverer being preserved in a form not offensive to the prejudices of the Spaniards, and calculated to secure a saint's protection; but afterwards, as the minutiæ of their story faded into indistinctness, the glowing accounts still surviving were presumed to refer to the harbor of Monterey. So, much of the eulogy that was originally spoken of San Francisco harbor may have been put to the credit of Monterey; yet, when the former place was revisited, the locality was recognized as already described under the name it now bears.

Portalá and his company returned in about six months, and thrilling news they heard from the little party that had guarded the San Diego Mission. The Indians, coveting the cloth which the missionaries only doled out to them very judiciously, took every opportunity to steal it, and even cut out pieces of the sails of the vessel. Of course the missionaries protected their property by force. On the 15th of August, the Indians came down in full fighting feather and began pillaging. The score of whites and their Christian Indian retainers from Lower California flew to arms, whose explosions soon commanded peace. In the struggle, one of the priests was wounded and a Christian Indian killed. The savages saw the strangers were

CHAP. VI.
1770.
March.

too much for them, and treated them from that time, for a long while, as their kind superiors. But other troubles, and not of Indian origin, awaited the San Diego pioneers. Provisions fell short, and the sad resolution was taken at last, that unless supplies came by the 20th of March, they must abandon all and return home. Providence kindly remembered the dispirited company, for on the very day before the one set for the abandonment of all, the *San Antonio* sailed into the harbor with supplies in abundance.

Portalá now started again northward by land, and this time found Monterey without a question, and was satisfied of the fact.

The *San Antonio*, too, ran up the coast, with Father Junipero on board, and entered Monterey harbor eight days after Portalá, on the 31st of March. Here again they took possession in the name of the king, hung up their bells on the trees, rang them out merrily, builded the chapel, blessed all, said mass, sang the *Veni Creator* and a *Te Deum*.

Portalá, in the *San Antonio*, returned to Mexico, taking with him, or sending overland under Rivera, the whole of the company, except Father Junipero, five priests, Fages, and thirty soldiers. The Indians told those who remained, as they sat under those dark Monterey pines, ghostly stories of how the crosses shined that each white man wore on his breast the first time they had passed through there, not knowing the place; and of the great cross that was planted by Portalá before he knew he was at the spot he coveted; how it would grow at night till its point rested among the stars, glistening the while with a splendor that outshone the sun; that when their superstitious dread of it wore off, they had approached, planted arrows and feathers in the earth around it, and hung strings of sardines, as their choicest offerings, on its arms.

It was like a gala day when Galvez, at the palace of the viceroy, surrounded by distinguished citizens, heard from the mouth of Portalá that Monterey had been discovered, and that three missions were established in Upper California. The bells of the cathedral and of all the churches were rung for joy, and every generous pulse in New Spain beat faster for the glorious news.

Father Junipero did not stay long at Monterey; but, establishing a mission close by on the Carmel River, made that his residence, though he spent much time in travelling about the country, looking up wild Indians, and winning them from their savage ways, establishing missions, watching his converts, and baptizing the little ones. He was the president of all the missions in Upper California until his death.

When a new mission was to be established he would take a couple of priests, an escort of soldiers, and a train of mules, packed with the necessaries for a journey, and the furniture for a church. Then, wandering over the mountains, and peering into all the pleasant valleys, until he found a place to suit, he would hang the bells on the trees, and himself pull lustily the rope, while he shouted, "Hear, hear! O ye Gentiles! come to the holy church." Then, having set up the church tent, blessed and dedicated it, and appointed a pastor, he would go out hunting for parishioners. He lived until the year 1784, when, at his own mission on the Carmel, he died.

This venerable Franciscan pioneer was a man worthy of the work he undertook. He was the son of humble parents, who resided in one of the islands of the Mediterranean, and from his childhood was educated for the church. He showed a wonderful faculty for attaching to himself the affections of the natives, and seemed by his presence to charm them into a new mode of life. It is said that, even before cultivated audiences, he would hammer his breast with a stone, and hold his flesh in the flame of a candle, to show that pain had no terrors in view of the love for Christ that filled him. In travelling, which he usually did on foot, though lame from a chronic ulcer on his leg, he wore sandals and never stockings. The visitor-general's proposal for an expedition to the north of his desolate field in Lower California chimed exactly with his desire, and Galvez himself did not more urgently strive than he to make the undertaking a success. When he came up to Portalá's rendezvous on the Lower California frontier to start for San Diego, he was so lame that he could scarcely mount and dismount from his mule. Portalá gave orders for a litter to be made for his conveyance, but the tender-hearted father would not hear of burdening the Indians to carry him. After a prayer that this cup might be spared him, he called one of the muleteers and asked him what to do for his sore foot and leg; but the muleteer modestly demurred that he was no surgeon, and was only equal to the task of curing the sore backs of beasts. "Then consider me a beast," said the father, "and my limb as his back." The muleteer, under shelter of this fancy, ventured upon the cure, and applied to the ailing limb a salve of mashed herbs and tallow. The next morning the father was in excellent condition and royal spirits. He mounted his mule and rode off, apparently as well as the rest them.

Junipero's life was written by a devoted friend and admirer, Father Francisco Palou, the first priest who had charge of the Mission Dolores, and his book was doubtless the first book written at San Francisco or in Upper California. It was published in Mexico in 1787, and with it a map of the country, which shows the nine missions and the three presidios, and the road between them, all lying near the coast, while to the eastward was a blank.

Before Father Junipero Serra rested from his labors he had founded eight missions. Their location speaks loudly for the judgment and taste of the fathers. They occupy the very choicest valleys that snuggle between the coast ranges. Generally convenient to the sea, or, if not, close by the stream that dries up latest during the long droughts, their vicinity is green when the other plains are parched. The best pasturage, the fattest land, the prettiest valleys to look down upon from the mountain passes, or up toward from the sea, were chosen for mission sites. Perhaps the least desirable of all them for purely mission purposes was the one at San Francisco. Though the Franciscan order owned no richly freighted galleon annually sweeping down the coast, and generally needing a harbor, yet it was so charged with the traditional policy of Spain, that the Bay of San Francisco pleaded for a mission on account of its position. Indeed, Father Junipero long had his eye on the sites of both San Francisco and Santa Clara, and when he went to Mexico to straighten up some other matters, he obtained a promise from the viceroy that they should be founded so soon as communication was opened with them from Monterey by land. Captain Juan Bautista Anza effected that in 1773, reported the fact to the viceroy, and returned with quite a company of families in 1776. Meanwhile the *San Carlos* had gone up the coast, and by actually entering the Golden Gate, or the Gulf of the Farallones, as they called it, in June, 1775, demonstrated that the land-locked bay—whose two arms stretched, one to the north till it met another great bay into which St. Francis river, fed by five other rivers, flowed, and the other southeasterly some fifteen leagues—was open from the Pacific for vessels to sail into it at pleasure.

On the 17th of September, the presidio of San Francisco was founded. An expedition was organized to explore the interior—a portion to go by water up San Pablo Bay, a portion by land. The latter strayed into one of the cañons of the Diablo range and discovered the San Joaquin Valley.

On the 9th of the next month, October, 1776—year ever memorable as the date of American Independence—the mission "De los Dolores de Nuestro Padre San Francisco de Asis" was established. There were several Saints Francisco—Francisco of Paula, Francisco of Sales, and Francisco of Asisis, the founder of the order of Franciscans. This mission was in honor of the sufferings of him of Asisis, and to avoid confusion it soon came to be known as the Mission Dolores, while to the presidio and the fort clung the saint's name. The first site chosen for the mission was near the "lagoon," back of Russian Hill; but the winds were so bitter there that soon it was removed to the spot on the creek where the crumbling old church and some of the houses that surrounded it still stand. It was the sixth in the order of the founding of the Upper California missions, and as late as 1802 was the most northerly of the eighteen then in existence.

The order of the establishment of the twenty-one missions in Upper California was as follows:—

San Diego, July 16, 1769.

San Carlos de Monterey (soon removed from Monterey to the Carmel River), June 3, 1770.

San Antonio de Padua (thirteen leagues from San Miguel), July 14, 1771.

San Gabriel (near Los Angeles), September 8, 1771.

San Luis Obispo, September 1, 1772.

San Francisco (Dolores), October 9, 1776.

San Juan Capistrano (between Los Angeles and San Diego), November 1, 1776.

Santa Clara, January 18, 1777.

San Buenaventura (southeast of and near Santa Barbara), March 31, 1782.

Santa Barbara, December 4, 1786.

La Purisima Concepcion (on the Santa Inez River), December 8, 1787.

Santa Cruz, August 28, 1791.

Soledad (on the Salinas River), October 9, 1791.

San José, June 11, 1797.

San Juan Bautista (on the San Juan River), June 24, 1797.

San Miguel (on the Salinas River), July 25, 1797.

San Fernando Rey (near, and northerly from, Los Angeles), September 8, 1797.

San Luis Rey de Francia (thirteen and a half leagues from San Diego), June 13, 1798.

Santa Inez (twelve leagues from Santa Barbara), September 17, 1804.

San Rafael (north of San Francisco Bay), December 14, 1819.

San Francisco de Solano (Sonoma), August 25, 1823.

CHAPTER VII.

THE ABORIGINES.

WHEN explorers come upon a new land, if they find it heavily timbered, or the intervals rank with wild grass, they know that cultivation will make it yield richly of grains and fruit; but if it bear no trees, or only scraggy and stinted ones, and a thin, scant herbage on the open country, they condemn it as unfit for all farming purposes. Californians have the best of reasons for hoping that the aborigines of a land do not indicate, by the degree of their nobleness or degradation, the style of men that will be produced under civilized auspices upon the same soil; for, of all wretchedly debased and utterly brutal beings, the Indians of California were the farthest fallen below the average Indian type. They were neither brave nor bold, generous nor spirited. They seem to have possessed none of the noble characteristics that, with a slight coloring of romance, make heroes of the red men of the Atlantic slopes, and win for them our ready sympathy. We hear of no orators among them, no bold braves terribly resenting and contesting to the last the usurpations of the whites. They were "Diggers," filthy and cowardly, succumbing without a blow to the rule of foreign masters. As redeeming them from utter brutality, it is refreshing to see occasional glimpses of humor in them, and a disposition to make fun of the missionary when his back was turned. But under the father's eye they cowered like children on the low benches before the old-time pedagogue wielding the ferule. Perhaps the mild, motherly sort of treatment which priests met them with, disarmed them. Perhaps, if they had been subject to the rough handling that the Indian tribes generally received from English settlers, they might have fired up, and displayed some of the violence and savage fury that make us respect the Indians of the East and the North. Perhaps it was in part because they were treated as children, that they grew into simple, childish ways.

They were as contemptible physically as intellectually, and evinced as little traces of conscience as of a reasoning faculty. To Drake's party they showed a disposition to offer sacrifices, thinking the sea-king's jolly tars to be veritable gods. Venegas thought the Lower Californians to be the most stupid and weak, in both body and mind, of all mortals. But the settlers of Upper California, who had seen both, thought the northern natives far inferior to the southern. Humboldt, from all his reading, concluded them as low in the scale of humanity as the inhabitants of Van Diemen's Land. Though in many respects one people, the gibberish they spoke varied widely in different localities. Those about San Diego could not understand a word of the language of those sixty miles north, and every high mountain-range divided dialects. In all their customs, their religious notions, and their habits, the residents of different valleys differed, though not widely. Father Boscana, of the San Juan Capistrano Mission, left a pretty full account of the Acagchemem nation, who constituted his parishioners, and who seem to have been about the best of the whole, though that may be simply because they found a more affectionate historian than did any of their brethren. Mr. Robinson, the translator of Boscana's paper, presumed that the descriptions might be taken as true, with some slight variations, of all the tribes in Upper California. We may take, then, the picture of the tribe that occupied the sea-coast forty or fifty miles below Los Angeles, as representatives of the people whom the missionaries found in Upper California, and whom Father Junipero learned to love as if they were his own flesh.

They held that the inferior regions were once

on a time married, and their children were the sand and soil, rocks, stones, flints for their arrows, trees, herbs, grass, and animals. There was a phantom whom they called Chinigchinich, an orphan from the beginning, who could see in the darkest night as clearly as at noon. This powerful being defended the good and chastised the bad; he was always and everywhere present, but hailed from the stars as his home. Him they regarded as the creator of their race, and as their great Captain. The land where they lived was the first land made—they seemed to believe that there was very little beyond it. The sea was at first but a fresh-water stream, coursing around their little earth; but the fishes, putting their heads together, agreed and managed to break a rock, inside of which was gall; emptying this into the river, the waters grew bitter, and swelled to an ocean, and the thoughtful fishes were rewarded with plenty of room and a wholesome pickle to sport in.

To the great Captain, or god of the long name, they accredited all the precepts of morality that they taught their children, and to his commands they traced their customs and mode of life. He told them to build a temple; so in every town, close by the chief's house, was the oval enclosure, made of the branches of trees and mats, surrounded by stakes of wood driven into the ground, which constituted the temple.

CHAP. VII.
1776.

It was a very sacred spot, within or near which no irreverent act was ever performed; for the god himself was there, in the person of a coyote-skin, stuffed with feathers, claws, talons, and beaks, which doubtless symbolized the strength, swiftness, fierceness, and power of the birds and beasts from which they were taken. They worshipped him with grotesque dances and hideous yells, or sometimes in perfect silence, squatting in most awkward attitudes in his presence, and retaining one position while the ceremony of adoration lasted. His temple was the "city of refuge," where the most outrageous criminal was safe, and after one visit could go free, though the crime might be punished upon the descendants of the offender at once or after the lapse of generations!

The boys were whipped with nettles, and laid upon ants' nests, that the stings of the insects might make them courageous under the infliction of pain. They were branded by burning moxas upon the fleshy part of the arm, to put them above the consideration of trifling ailments. They were forbidden to warm themselves at a fire, lest they came short of the toughness of men; and, until they were heads of families, certain food they must not touch. To violate any of these orders, would let loose the Evil Spirit on them, and provoke the ire of the god.

The girls were trained to work from infancy. At ten, to heighten their beauty, their busts and faces were tattooed, the flesh being pricked with the thorn of the cactus until it bled, and a soft charcoal rubbed in, in lieu of India ink. On arriving at womanhood, they were placed on a bed of branches over some heated stones that were lain in a hole in the ground, and there kept with little or no food for three days, while ancient hags danced around the pile, singing songs well calculated to inspire the wretched, perspiring beauties with a sense of the vast responsibilities that pertained to their new condition. Betrothed by their parents in infancy, they were married with a good deal of ceremony, and divorced without any, at their own or their husbands' will.

A skin thrown over his shoulders constituted the full dress of a gentleman. Mats made of squirrel-skins twisted into rope, sewn together, and tolerably fitted to the person, was a fine lady's common dress. Add a fringe of grass reaching to the knees, hang ornaments of beads and shells upon her neck, and varnish her face with colored mud, and she was dressed for a grand occasion. The San Francisco Indians are said to have used a much more simple style of dress, plastering their whole bodies with mud, especially in the cooler months of the year— though, if this were so, the fashion came in vogue probably after Drake's day, or was reserved for winter.

The men made bows and arrows, baskets, and nets for fishing, killed some small game, and fished a little, when the mood was on; but most of the work was done by the other sex. The women went to the woods, gathered the acorns that were a staple of food, picked the berries, dug the edible roots, gathered the firewood, cooked, kept house, and cared for the children. The acorns they mashed, wet up with water into a dough, and cooked between hot stones. Buckeyes they rubbed down with water into a thin gruel, and boiled by throwing hot stones into the mess. They held it a godsend when a whale was stranded on the coast: it relieved them from the necessity of work for weeks; for, like most gourmands who prefer their game a little high, they thought the blubber improved by moderate age!

Dancing was a very important part of all their entertainments and of their worship. Excepting at a few special feasts, the dances were generally very modest, the sexes dancing apart from each other, though in the same room. Their god was a great admirer of a vigorous dancer; so dancing was a virtue, and this virtue at least was popular. War was never their passion; but if one of a tribe stole a squirrel or an ornament from another tribe, they generally indorsed his theft, and maintained their honor with their arms. The war being ended, the thief was dealt with as he deserved. Yet it appears that they lived very peaceably most of the time, and did very little quarrelling. On occasion of their grand feasts, scalps taken in war were exhibited on a pole planted on a temple. The women and children who were captured in war generally stayed with their captors for life.

Every town had its chief, but he enjoyed very little consideration in the town councils. If he transgressed his authority, they deposed him. His person was held in veneration, although his advice might be treated with sovereign contempt.

Their medical practice was exceedingly simple. Herbs, crushed or bruised, and applied as a poultice, was the treatment for most external diseases. For slight internal ailments they smoked the same herbs, or whipped the part affected with nettles. For serious diseases the cold-water bath was a common remedy; that failing, the patient was laid upon the dry sand, or ashes, and a fire kindled near his feet, which was kept blazing night and day. By his head was placed a cup of water, or some gruel. His friends then sat down by his side, and waited in patience until he recovered or died. Of course, they had their quacks, who per-

CHAP. VII.
1776.

formed wonderful cures through the medium of a perfect faith and the entire control of the patient's imagination — thus swindling him away from under the power of disease. Some writers speak of the sweat-house as the never-failing remedy for the Indian, whether his ailment were little or great. It was supposed to add very largely to the mortality of the tribes; but their ancestors, "the authorities," believed in it, and to the sweat-house they went, whether afflicted with typhus or tooth-ache, a fit of indigestion or the small-pox.

When one died, he was either buried or burned, according as the custom of the locality was. Where burning was the fashion, the corpse was laid upon a pile of fagots, in the presence of the friends, and the bows and arrows, and whatever the deceased cherished as his property, were laid beside him. When the professional burners announced that all was consumed, the friends retired outside the town to do their mourning—the doctor accompanying them, and chanting the story of the fatal sickness, while they wept. After three days and nights, they returned home and cut their hair in token of their loss. If the departed were a distant relative, the rule required that it be cut half its old length; if it were a parent, wife, or child, the head must be shaved close.

They thought Death was a being who took

away a person's breath, and after that there was no more of him forever. The punishments that they feared from their god were almost entirely physical, and pertained to this life. Still, they thought that the heart of a good chief went up, after death, among the stars, to enlighten the earth; hence, that the stars, comets, and meteors, were the hearts of great Indians departed. Common men had no such honor awaiting them, and the chiefs only attained it by virtue of the fact that, after death and before being burned, men who practised a modified cannibalism as a profession came and, with much ceremony, consumed a small portion of their flesh.

CHAPTER VIII.

DETAILS OF THE MISSION SYSTEM.

CHAP. VIII.
1781.

But degraded as was the Indian, the whole theory of the Spanish conquest required, and the first principle of the missions was, that he should be trained in the simple arts, educated in the elements of letters and religion, and be made a citizen. The fathers succeeded in teaching him to plough and plant, to sow and reap, to raise corn, to make wine, to weave cloth, to dress leather, to manufacture soap, brick, and tiles; but they never could bring him out of his stolid ignorance. The project of manufacturing him into a valuable subject of Spain was an utter failure. In other of her Indian possessions this had been done, but in California it could not be. Yet, throughout the career of the missions, throughout the rule of the Church in California, the Indian was always treated as the object of solicitude and kindly care. If he was a slave of the fathers, it was that he might become a subject of the crown.

In the political system of the country, his weakness and wants were scrupulously consulted. The missions were to grow into towns; the presidios were for their defence; and the pueblos were established only when it was found that the Indians were not competent to sustain the missions and the presidios without a heavy draft upon the Government at Mexico. The first grant of land made within California was to a Spanish soldier, in consideration of the fact that he had married a native convert. This care for the Indians, as the prospective subjects and sacred occupants of the soil, was never intermitted until the revolution came that overthrew the missions themselves, and California was distracted with the civil wars that followed its attempt at independence.

How many Indians there were in California when the missions were in their glory, there are no means of knowing: not because they were a floating population, for those near the coast, at least, seldom drifted far beyond the horizon of their birthplace; but they were not reckoned worthy of being counted until converted. They were more valuable than beasts only as they were susceptible of conversion.

The missions were built upon one general plan, though they differed in the expenditures upon them. In the centre was a handsome church, generally built of adobe, whose tinsel

CHAP. VIII.
1781.

and pictures, marble pillars for the altar, and gold and silver plate, must have struck the Indians as exceedingly fine. Close by the church were the residences of the clergy, store-houses, granaries, shops for blacksmiths, weavers, and soap-makers, all of which were built of adobe and roofed with tiles. There were also large gardens, and pens for cattle and horses. Two or three hundred yards away was the "rancheria," sometimes an adobe structure, sometimes a collection of wigwams made of poles, which had this advantage over the adobe house, that when they became altogether filthy, they could be burned down, and new ones put on their site. Close by the rancheria was a building for a garrison of half a dozen soldiers, with their families. About the mission as a centre, the best land of the vicinity, generally a tract of some fifteen miles square, was set apart to it for a farm, where the thousands of sheep and cattle grazed and pastured. But this was not all that the missions claimed. Their boundaries touched each other. From the sea-coast to the mountains, from San Diego to San Francisco, all, with a few exceptions to be hereafter named, was claimed by the priests as mission property, without reference to the number of the establishments.

Over each mission was a presiding father, who had a control of its affairs that was almost absolute, being responsible only to the president of the missions and the college to which he belonged. The ground was tilled, the cattle killed, the cloth woven, the vintage nourished or neglected, as the father dictated. If he were blessed with worldly wisdom, his mission flourished, its Indians were fat and contented, and its treasury full. If he had no mind for such matters, unless indeed his assistant clergy were wiser than he, spiritual and temporal affairs alike went amiss, the Indians suffered from nakedness and hunger, and fumed with discontent; converts were not multiplied; the buildings went to decay; the mission got a bad name.

To give greater protection to the missions, which were mostly inland, four presidios, or military establishments, were planted at as many sea-ports—San Diego in 1769, Monterey in 1770, San Francisco in 1776, and Santa Barbara in 1780. The presidio was an enclosure of from two to three hundred yards square, surrounded by an adobe wall of about twelve feet in height. In this square were a chapel, storehouses, residences for the officers, and barracks for the soldiers. Upon the walls were mounted sundry small cannon. Near the anchoring-ground and aside from the presidio was generally a fort of rude construction, also mounted with cannon. The presidio was, in theory, manned by seventy soldiers, but that maximum was seldom reached; most of the number rated as cavalry, and a small portion as artillery. Their commander had military jurisdiction over a certain number of missions and the pueblos within his limits. Thus the Presidio of San Francisco, as late as 1835, had within its jurisdiction the town of San José and the six missions about the bay. The commandant stood in the place of the viceroy throughout his district. He must assist the missionaries and protect their charge, but in no way interfere with them.

One of the objects of Father Junipero in visiting Mexico was to bring to an issue a dispute concerning the mutual rights and relations of the military and the ecclesiastics. The law of the latter toward the Indians was kindness; the former looked down on the red men with scorn, and abused them accordingly. They made the Indian men work, the squaws carry burdens, the children wait upon them, and punished them all promptly if they tried to avoid work. The priests had complained to the viceroy of the behavior of the soldiers; the military had complained to him that the priests were meddlesome, and in the habit of transcending their powers by dictating to their equals. The viceroy took the priests' part, invoked the military to preserve harmony, to help the fathers cheerfully, to give them aid, escorts, and supplies, and to treat the Indians so kindly that their example would commend their religion. The most explicit advices failing to produce the desired harmony, Junipero went personally to Mexico, and, from the Convent of San Fernando, issued the gravest charges against the soldiers, and Don Pedro Fages, their chief commanding officer. Then Fages was peremptorily ordered by the viceroy to remove any soldier at the demand of a missionary, and to leave the entire management of the Indians to the priests. After that, though there were occasional jealousies, the positions of the two powers were pretty well defined, and there was not much conflict between them.

The commander of a presidio had authority to grant building-lots to the soldiers and other residents within the space of four square leagues of head-quarters, where it could be done without encroaching upon the mission. It is not certain that this right was ever exercised by the captain of the San Francisco presidio, but probably it was at San Diego, Santa Barbara, and Monterey.

There were a few farms set apart for the use of the presidio soldiers, but the military did not take well to farming; and, excepting for grazing purposes, this land was very little used.

The soldiers were an undisciplined, riotous set of fellows, mostly mutineers or deserters from the Mexican army, or felons transported to the wilderness because the prisons of Mexico were crowded. Still, miserably mounted and shockingly equipped as they were, they answered every purpose that was required of them. The timid Indians only needed the shadow of an army to keep them within the bounds of propriety. When the converted Indians were disposed to relapse into heathenism, and ran away, the soldiers went out on a grand hunt and brought them in again, and with them all the wild natives that they could corral. Once, at San Diego, the Indians rose, murdered several persons, and burned the mission-houses. The soldiers, with a few "terrible examples," soon restored tranquillity, and this was the only occasion for any warlike demonstration to quiet insurrection during the early history of the settlements.

At each presidio a certain number of pack-mules were kept for the government service, and four horses stood saddled by day and eight by night, ready to carry dispatches in any direction.

To relieve the Government of Mexico of the heavy burden of supplying the presidios with recruits and rations, there were established, in Father Junipero's day, the pueblos of San José in the north, and of Los Angeles in the south. Later, in 1795, the Marquis of Branciforte ordered a commission to select a pueblo site in the vicinity of San Francisco. The commissioners reported that San Francisco was probably the worst place in all California for the purpose, and so the "Villa of Branciforte" was established near the Santa Cruz Mission. It never grew to any consequence. Portions of its adobe ruins are still pointed out to the visitor to that pleasant sea-side retreat.

These pueblos were reckoned of little account —a necessary evil, whose growth beyond a certain point was to be discouraged. Each pueblo had its common lands, where the cattle were pastured, and whence the fuel was obtained. Each settler was entitled to an inalienable homestead of two hundred varas square, a certain number of cattle, horses, and poultry, a stipulated quantity of agricultural implements, a salary at the outset, and, for five years, exemption from all taxes. In return, he engaged to sell all the products of his lot, beyond what his family required, to the presidios, at a fixed price; to keep a horse, saddle, carbine, and lance, and hold his own person in readiness for the king's service, on demand. After five years' occupation, he must pay an annual rent of a bushel and a quarter of corn.

For the first two years after the establishment of a pueblo, it had an alcalde or judge, and other town officers of the governor's appointment. After that, the officers were elected by the people, subject to the governor's approval. The settlers were mostly soldiers whose term of service had expired. These free towns, which were originally intended to be subservient to the presidios, as the presidios in turn were but the servants of the missions, were naturally eyed with jealousy by the missions; especially, as to them were attracted all straggling foreigners, and the trappers and hunters who wearied of their adventurous life, and were disposed to settle, and end their days in a semi-civilized fashion. Very naturally, there were occasional collisions between the ecclesiastic and the military authorities; and there was a law-suit of tedious length, brought by the college at Mexico to which the priests belonged, before the viceroy, because the pueblo of San José was established nearer the mission of Santa Clara than Father Junipero thought to be wholesome for his Indians.

But here we are verging upon ground that the lawyers of California, and especially of San Francisco, have disputed about too much for any one not of the profession to travel over it without great risks. Early in the career of San Francisco, it became a question of importance, whether or not it was ever a pueblo. The

Supreme Court of the State decided that it was one; and the Federal Court of the district has pronounced a like decision. Long as the litigation lasted, it was not without some redeeming results. The legal investigation of the pueblo question, on which hangs the title of the city as the successor of the alleged pueblo to the greater part of the lands in its suburbs, threw a deal of light upon the system under which California was settled, developed many curious historical facts that were buried in the Spanish documents of the State archives, and explained other things, of which the full records were lost in the bustle of the American occupation. Dwinelle's "Colonial History of San Francisco," published in 1863, was the argument of John W. Dwinelle, in the United States District Court, for the city's pueblo claim for four square leagues of land.

There are those, and Mr. Dwinelle appears to be among them, who hold that the Spanish and Mexican system for settling California contemplated a threefold occupation of the land: by the religious pioneers, building up missions and drawing the natives around them; by the military, making the influence of the presidios meet each other and cover the whole country; and by civilians, congregated in pueblos. On this theory, all three were alike, if not equally, cherished by the Government, as *nuclei* of population and growth into a State. If that were really the theory of those who began the settlement of California, the failure of the Indian to grow into a citizen caused the mission element so early to outgrow the others in importance and influence at Mexico, that very soon the pueblo was deemed an intruder, and the presidio only tolerated as the prop and defender of the missions.

Still, it is clear that the mission was never intended to be a permanent institution under priestly control. Just as soon as the converted Indians were educated up to the capacity for self-government, the missions were to be converted into pueblos. The "religious" priests—that is, priests who had taken the three vows of a "regular order"—vows of chastity, obedience, and poverty, and were consequently held in law as "civilly dead"—were to be succeeded by the "secular clergy," and the mission churches would become parish churches;—in short, the missions were to be secularized. It had been presumed, at first, that ten years would suffice to carry a mission up to the point where it could be secularized; but the priests loved the missions too well, and their Indian converts were too stupid for that. A few missions, forced by the impatience of the Government, struggled into the pueblo state, but soon went to decay. On the other hand, the original pueblos flourished finely, and several presidios grew so rapidly in spite of ecclesiastical objections, that they assumed the rights and privileges of pueblos.

Much confusion has originated in the sometimes loose, sometimes precise meaning of that word *pueblo*. It seems to have worn all the vagueness of our word *town*, and like it to have had also a specific meaning. The same term was applied to a settlement of straggling Indian huts, and to an incorporation with powers precisely defined. Moreover, a pueblo might be aristocratically called a *villa*, like Branciforte, or a *ciudad*, like Los Angeles; but under whatever name, it still was a pueblo, with its privileges determined exclusively by the numbers of its "reasoning" population.

California, when first settled, was a department of the kingdom of Spain, and to the viceroy at Mexico its governor was responsible. In 1776, it became one of the "Internal Provinces," which were ruled by a commandante-general. When, still later, the Internal Provinces were divided into Eastern and Western Provinces, it formed a part of the Western, and then its capital was either at Arispe or Chihuahua. Still later a few years, the old order was restored, and the governor of California, residing at Monterey as the capital, was directly responsible to the viceroy.

Events travelled slowly in those times, and it took many years to furnish a chapter of history. Each subordinate officer was a despot, until his superior's order came. Loyalty was instinctive, and the very distance of the supreme authority added dignity and weight to his behests.

The King of Spain forwarded his order to the viceroy, who sent a copy to each Spanish dependency; so that a command, intended for Peru, came through to California, and was filed here as well as there. Among these old kingly communications preserved in our State archives, Randolph quotes one for the furnishing of the royal park with some of the deer that abounded, as was said in the neighborhood of San Francisco; and another, that would have been more useful in Nicaragua than here, announcing that a certain archbishop had happily discovered that when the jiggers have burrowed into the human flesh, it is sure death to the insect to anoint the part affected with cold olive-oil! So, in every corner of Spanish America this royal remedy against jiggers was heralded. To reach here, it had travelled a long and crooked circuit, from the king to the viceroy, to the commandante-general, to the governor, to the captain of the presidio, to the fathers, who read it aloud to the shivering, dusky crowd, who wondered doubtless what sort of creature this jigger was, that henceforth, in all the dominions of Spain, was to have no chance for his life.

CHAPTER IX.

A CALM HALF CENTURY.

THE Indians accepted their new style of life with apparent cheerfulness. Its restraints were probably balanced in their reckoning by the freedom from any peril of hunger or cold. Though exceedingly lazy, they got through their tasks with ease, and they were apt enough to understand readily the simple arts they were required to learn. They came together to the missions in the morning, at the sound of a bell. Seven hours a day they gave to work, and two to prayer. For their misdemeanors they were whipped—the females in private, the males in public, for the edification of both sexes. Boiled corn was served to them, morning, noon, and night. On saints' days and great occasions they had beef, which some of them preferred unspoiled by cookery. So soon as an Indian was baptized, he was regarded as a member of the community, and entitled to feed at its expense. He was no longer at liberty to return to the gentile Indian village, or to his heathen

CHAP. IX.

1775–1830.

family. He had nothing that he could call his own. He was a slave, under a mastership that was mild enough, so long as he did his day's work complacently, and said his prayers with becoming gravity.

Without disturbance, without bloodshed, with scarcely a ripple on the calm surface of their simple society, these occupants of a wild and unknown portion of the continent drifted through two generations. While America, on her eastern border, was convulsed with a war that was rending from England her thirteen colonies, nothing disturbed the quiet of this priest-ruled region. While Spain was passing through the fire, this, her distant province, was literally occupying a Pacific slope. The old cannons on the presidio walls and in the forts grew rusty for lack of use, or were buried in the rank growth of the sod. The soldiers forgot the art of war, and craved the excitement of the cattle-ranches. The captains of the presidios were sending to the governors of the province the copy-books of the children in their schools. Nearly sixty years this great calm lasted. The Indians grew somewhat skilful in their trades. The fathers waxed fat and patriarchal. To start with, they had little of the consuming zeal and unquenchable thirst for explorations that characterized the Jesuits, and, as their possessions increased, that little vanished.

They were contented with the valley in which they lived. Mountains, rising abruptly from the plain, bounded their horizon; they were not curious to widen it or discover what lay beyond. So the land that was unknown in 1776, was scarcely known in 1830. It was only a fringe, a few miles deep from the sea-coast, that was explored, from San Francisco Bay to San Diego. They knew there were such valleys as the San Joaquin and Sacramento, but they took no steps to possess them.

In 1786, when the missions were ten in number, it was estimated that there were five thousand one hundred and forty-three domesticated Indians in California. In 1790, when there were eleven missions, the population was set down at seven thousand seven hundred and forty-eight; and in 1801, at thirteen thousand six hundred and sixty-eight. Humboldt estimated the population at the close of 1802, of the ruling classes, the *gente de razon*, or rational creatures of the land, among whom were embraced all the whites, mestizoes, and mulattoes in the pueblos, presidios, and missions, at one thousand three hundred; and the converted Indians of the eighteen missions at fifteen thousand five hundred and sixty-two, of which number seven thousand nine hundred and forty-five were females.

The list of missions, in the order of their

CHAP. IX.
1802.

population in 1802, would stand as follows: San Diego, population about one thousand five hundred and sixty; Santa Clara, one thousand three hundred; San Antonio de Padua and San Gabriel, each one thousand and fifty; Santa Barbara, La Purisima Concepcion, and San Juan Capistrano, each one thousand; San Juan Bautista, nine hundred and sixty; San Buenaventura, nine hundred and fifty; San Francisco, eight hundred and twenty; San Luis Obispo and San Carlos de Monterey, each seven hundred; San José, six hundred and thirty; San Miguel, San Fernandino, and San Luis Rey, each six hundred; Soledad, five hundred and seventy; Santa Cruz, four hundred and forty.

The seeds and grains so carefully provided by Galvez, flourished beyond expectation. The cattle thrived and multiplied like Jacob's flocks in Padan-aram. There were plenty of sheep and horses and cattle in the land, an abundance of corn, wheat, beans, and peas, in the fields, and of fruit in the orchards. At the south they had grapes in profusion, and olives of excellent quality.

Commerce, scenting great bargains from afar, sent around the Horn, from Boston and New York, vessels to buy up the surplus hides and tallow. As the settlers had no use for gold or silver, the traders brought in payment such goods as were sure to captivate the whites, and such stout stuffs as were desirable for Indian costume. The hides were rated so low, and the goods they brought sold at so high a figure, that, after the balance on the first venture was struck, the trade was permanently established.

The Yankee visitors took home tales of true Arcadian landscapes; of a climate beyond criticism, where spring was perennial, and flowers bloomed in the open fields every month in the year; of a fat land, where people lived to an extreme old age, and were free, to the verge of their departure, from the infirmities of declining life; of a country civilized, yet of the simplest manners, and where a fortune could be made in a year or two, if one would consent to take it in the shape of lands or hides. These stories generally passed for travellers' tales, but many restless pioneers at the East heard them, who, as they pushed westward before the advancing wave of Western settlement, climbed the Rocky and the Snowy Mountains, and dropped quietly into these valleys before they found the country that matched their ideal; and so, unobserved, there was quite a sprinkling of American settlers through the country before this long calm was disturbed.

But, because there was no political storm, it must not be supposed that the Californians had not their share of grievances. They lived in no little fear of earthquakes, perhaps as much because the land has such an unfinished aspect in many parts, as from any experience of their effects. The Indians said there had always been more or less of them throughout the country, and they early felt tremors enough to make them appreciate the low, modest Mexican style of building.

The adobe houses at San Juan Bautista were severely injured by an earthquake which occurred on the 18th of October, 1800; and the captain of the San Francisco presidio reported to the governor that several occurred early in July, 1808, which did no greater damage simply for want of more material to destroy. Within the four weeks preceding the 17th, twenty-one shocks had been felt, that cracked all the walls of the captain's house, and threatened the entire ruin of the barracks of the fort. On one Sunday of September, 1812, the church of the Mission San Juan Capistrano was destroyed by an earthquake, and thirty persons killed; on the same day the church at Santa Inez was thrown down. In 1818, an earthquake levelled the mission church at Santa Clara.

But, more than earthquakes, from first to last, they feared foreigners. On the 23d of October, 1776, the viceroy wrote to the governor to be on the watch for Captain Cook, and not permit him to enter the ports of California. Information had reached the King of Spain that Cook CHAP. IX. had sailed, with two armed vessels, from London, on a voyage of discovery to the 1776. Southern Ocean and the northern coast of California. But the world-renowned circumnavigator never sought an entrance into the king's inhospitable harbors.

Seventeen years later, Spain felt better to- 1793. ward the land that had the effrontery to give birth to Francis Drake, and orders were received here to treat Vancouver well, if he should arrive. The noise of the French Revolution, and the high doings of "that Lucifer," Bonaparte, had reached this coast, and they made the English seem friendly, by comparison with any thing French. So, when Admiral Vancouver turned into Monterey, in 1793, he was received with distinguished consideration.

In 1790, Governor Fages commanded the 1790. captain of the presidio at San Francisco, that whenever the ship *Columbia*, "said to belong to General Washington, of the American States," which sailed from Boston, 1787, "bound on a voyage of discovery to the Russian establishments on the northern coasts of this peninsula" (the good governor thought California a peninsula yet, all the way up to those mysterious Straits of Anian), should appear, she was to be "examined with caution and delicacy." The *Columbia* was on a nobler errand than that of peering into ports where she would be cautiously examined; she struck the coast farther north, and, by the discovery of the great Western stream, gave her own name to the Columbia River.

On the 1st of August, 1803, " at the hour of evening prayers," two American vessels, the *Alexander*, Captain John Brown, and the *Aser*, Captain Thomas Raben, entered the harbor of San Francisco, dropped anchor, and sent ashore for permission to take in wood and water. The captain of the presidio, finding that Captain Brown was the same man who was there five months before, refused him permission to remain. Next morning the Yankee captain sent in a doleful account of the hard times he had experienced on the northwest coast, and of his severe encounters with the Indians in the Straits of Chatham. At San Juan de Fuca he heard that the ship *Boston* had been captured by the Indians, and burned, and all but two of the crew butchered. The presumption is that this tale, whether entirely true, or not, so moved the captain of the presidio, that the strangers were permitted to supply themselves with wood and water.

The Russians made their first appearance about 1807. The czar's ambassador to Japan, Von Resanoff, after looking at the establishments of the Russian Fur Company, both on the Asiatic and American coasts, and failing in an attempt to enter the Columbia River, came on to San Francisco. His immediate object was to obtain supplies for Sitka; but once here, he attempted to lay the foundations of a regular intercourse between the Russian and California settlements. To cement more surely the national alliance, he proposed to take as his wife the commandante's daughter. The daughter and the father were nothing loth, so the ambassador hastened back to obtain from the Russian and the Spanish courts the requisite authority. On his road through Siberia, he fell from his horse, and died from the effects of the fall. The disappointed lady assumed the habit, if not the formal vows, of a nun, and devoted her life to the consolation of the sick and the education of the young, and we hear no more of the proposed commercial compact. But in 1812 one hundred Russians, and in their company one hundred Kodiak Indians, came down from the north, and squatted on a narrow strip of land in what is now Sonoma County, making Bodega their port. Whether they ever had permission from the Spaniards, or whether indeed they asked it, is not sure; but this is, that they were never regarded otherwise than as intruders of the most unwelcome sort. They maintained themselves by virtue of their forts and many soldiers, and when at their best estate, in 1841, numbered eight hundred Russians, and a great company of Indian stipendiaries. They raised some grain, kept some cattle, hunted on all the coasts, creeks, and inlets, for seals, beavers, and otters, and scoured the country for inland peltry. To circumscribe their influence, the missions were founded at San Rafael and Sonoma.

But, quite regardless of their jealous, priestly observers, they held in undisturbed possession their strip of exclusive territory, trapped wherever they found game, and in their Greek church, among the solemn pines of Fort Ross, worshipped the Christian's God, after a fashion scarcely less offensive to the zealous papists than were the dances of the natives before the stuffed coyote-skins in the savage temples. Without any premonitions, in 1841, they sold all their property to Captain John A. Sutter, a Swiss, who was to be notable in the next twenty years' history of the country; and then, in 1842, after thirty years' quiet occupation, they retired.

CHAPTER X.

CALIFORNIA UNDER MEXICAN RULE.

In 1822, Mexico threw off the yoke of Spain, and established a separate empire. When the news reached California, the governor (Pablo Vicente de Sola), the generals at the four presidios, two militia captains, and one artillery lieutenant, the prelate of the missions, and the proxy of the father president, met according to previous notice at Monterey, and heard the documents read which announced the establishment of the Mexican empire. Then, without a dissenting voice, they resolved that henceforth California was independent of any foreign state, and would render obedience to Mexico alone. The oaths were changed and taken accordingly, and without a struggle the severance of California from Spain was complete.

Father Boscana tells an anecdote illustrative of how the Indians about San Diego were affected by the news that the viceroy had been deposed, and Yturbide proclaimed emperor at Mexico. They had a grand feast in the village, to which all the neighborhood was invited.

CHAP. X.
1822.

The ceremonies were commenced by burning the chief alive. Then they elected another, and after eight days of revelry they dispersed. When the missionaries heard of it, they administered a sharp rebuke to those of their converts who shared in the entertainment. But the Indians replied: "Have you not done the same in Mexico? You say your king was not good, and you killed him. Well, our captain was not good, and we burned him: if the new one should be bad, we will burn him too."

1767–1822.

Governors are governors the world over, and are entitled to honorable mention for their office' sake. So it is a duty to name the governors of California under the Spanish rule, though they governed but a small fraction of the people, and, with some exceptions, really had less hand in shaping the course of events within the province than any one of the fathers. They were the despotic masters of the military, except as at long intervals there came up orders from their superiors at Arispe, Chihuahua, Mexico, or Madrid. But the military and the people of the pueblos were all that they could control. The wild Indians admitted no ruler but their own chiefs; the tame ones looked to the fathers, and the fathers to the college, between which and them no civil or military ruler intervened. These Spanish governors were nine in number. Their residence was at Monterey, the capital. The time of their continuance in office was as follows:—

Gaspar de Portalá	.	1767 to 1771
Felipe de Barri .		1771 to 1774
Felipe de Neve .	.	1774 to 1782
Pedro Fages	.	1782 to 1790
José Antonio Romeu . .	.	1790 to 1792
José J. de Arrillaga (*ad interim*) .	.	1792 to 1794
Diego de Borica . . .	.	1794 to 1800
José J. de Arrillaga . .	.	1800 to 1814
José Arguello (*ad interim*) .	.	1814 to 1815
Pablo Vicente de Sola . .	.	1815 to 1822

CHAP. X.

1777–1822.

In 1824, Mexico lay down the imperial and put on the republican form of government. California accepted the change without protest or the slightest objection. Lacking the quota of population essential to a State, she was constituted a Territory, with the privilege of sending a representative to Congress, who could take part in the debates, but had no vote. The governor, henceforth called the "Political Chief of the Territory," had a council, which was designated the "Territorial Deputation." In the Deputation a proposition was once made to change the name of the Territory from California to "Moctesuma," and to make the coat-of-arms represent, in an oval, an Indian, with a bow and quiver, crossing a strait—an olive and an oak tree on either hand; thus symbolizing the supposed arrival from across the Straits of Anian of the first inhabitants of America. The proposition was not accepted.

1824.

CHAP. X.

1824.

1826.

These successive political revolutions wrought very few social changes among the people. They were still as jealous of strangers as ever, as chary of their good services outside of their own circle. In the archives of the State are preserved many evidences that all strangers were deemed a nuisance, and those who came from the United States of America as especially worthy of suspicion. "These Anglo-Americans will become troublesome," said a long-headed governor of California, in 1805. On the 20th of December, 1826, Jedediah S. Smith, straying from the East too far into the Great Desert, for want of provisions and water to get home with, was compelled to push forward into California. It stands on the record as among the many triumphs of the Smith family, that one of them was the first to make the overland trip from the States to California. Fortunately, Jedediah found here shipmasters from American vessels who vouched for his honest intentions and perfect harmlessness. He had attempted, during the latter part of the preceding winter, to make his way up to the Columbia River, but the snow was so deep on the mountains that he was obliged to return. Being informed by one of the Christian Indians that the father would like to know who he was, Captain Smith wrote a letter to Father Duran, who resided at San José, in which he honestly confessed that he was destitute of clothing and most of the necessaries of life, that his horses had perished for want of food and water, and that his object was to trap for beaver and furs; and in conclusion he signed himself "your strange but real friend and Christian brother."

But it was not Jedediah Smith alone and the Americans who were after the furs. Even the Californians were awaking to the value of peltry, and the government of the Territory had learned to raise no little revenue from the licenses to trap that it was issuing.

California was under Spanish rule fifty-five years, under Mexican but twenty-four; yet for nine Spanish she had thirteen Mexican governors, or rather that was the number of successive administrations. The last governor under Spain was the first under Mexico. The release from European fetters was not a matter that quickened the California pulse. The new masters were greeted as cordially as the old had been, and no more so. The more radical change of Mexico from an empire to a republic did not fret the lazy Californians. They would as lief be Mexican as Spanish, republican as imperial —any thing to keep the peace at home.

The seeds of mischief, however, had been sown before these great political changes were announced. Napoleon's attempt to place his

CHAP. X.
1813.

brother on the throne of Spain, and the wars that grew out of Spain's refusal to be so degraded, rolled a heavy national debt upon her shoulders. Staggering with the burden, she stepped out of the path of her traditional policy. The Cortes ordered lands which hitherto the crown had always retained for itself, to be sold or granted to private parties. It was with the object of benefiting the pueblos, said the preamble of the law; but that was a cloak. The real object was, to provide means to extinguish the great debt, and to pay the soldiers in the Spanish armies. In the same year, 1813, the Cortes expressed the opinion that the missions ought to be secularized.

But if Spain had felt herself compelled to sell the crown's own acres to raise money, and hint impatience with the mission experiment, how much more likely would Mexico be to summon all neglected resources to her aid, while attempting imperial magnificence with prodigality, on a soil naturally so repugnant to every thing of the sort! She did not wait long, though longer than she played at empire.

1824. On the 18th of August, 1824, the Mexican Congress enacted a general colonization act, which is so liberal as to excite a wonder what hidden motive suggested its wiser provisions.

1828. Four years later, Congress ordered the secularization of the missions to proceed, and adopted a system of rules for colonizing the territories, which evince a clear desire to tole strangers in, and make landholders of residents. Governors were authorized to grant vacant lands in limited amounts to contractors, families, or private persons, whether Mexican or foreigners, who properly petitioned for them, and engaged to cultivate and inhabit them a certain portion of time. The grants must not conflict with municipal rights, nor were they valid to contractors who engaged to bring in a number of emigrant families, without the approval of the Supreme Government, nor valid to other parties without the approval of the territorial legislature. The mission lands it was strictly forbidden to grant until it should be determined whose property they were.

Congress was nibbling at the mission property, but was not quite bold enough to seize it. Probably the whole colonization scheme, so far as California was concerned, was but a plan to make the civil outgrow the religious settlements there, after which despoiling the latter would be an easier task. The year before the regulations above named were enacted, the Mexican government seized seventy-eight thousand dollars of the "pious fund," which had reverted to the Franciscans when the Jesuits were suppressed, and which, during the later Spanish régime, had produced a revenue for the

Missionary Association of about fifty thousand dollars a year.

From that time, Mexico never lifted her eye from that pious fund. From 1828 to 1831, the stipends of four hundred dollars each, for the Franciscan monks, failed to be paid with any regularity. In 1832, Congress farmed out the property of the fund for seven years, the proceeds to be paid into the national treasury. In 1836, Congress, ashamed of that decree, placed the fund at the disposal of the president of the missions, to be used according to the intention of its founders. In 1842, Santa Anna took it out of the hands of the bishop of California (Pope Gregory had erected California into a bishopric in 1840), and intrusted it to the chief of the army-staff, to be "administered." A few months later, the final blow came: Santa Anna sold the pious fund to the house of Barrio, and the Rubio Brothers. To convert the missions into money, to stuff that always empty maw, the treasury of Mexico, was a more tedious task.

The fathers foresaw, from their calm retreats, the coming of the storm, from the time their stipends failed in 1828. That had happened before, however. Even under Spain, from 1811 to 1818, they had been received very irregularly, if at all. The cloud might yet blow over.

THE MISSION PROPERTY.

The missions had a little passed the meridian of their highest prosperity in 1834. At that time, according to De Mofras, the French historian of California, the twenty-one missions had thirty thousand six hundred and fifty Indians living in their communities. The horned cattle numbered four hundred and twenty-four thousand; the horses, mules, and asses, besides the wild ones that scoured the plains in troops, numbered sixty-two thousand five hundred; the sheep, goats, and swine, three hundred and twenty-one thousand five hundred; and the corn, wheat, maize, and other grains that they raised, measured one hundred and twenty-two thousand five hundred bushels. The richest in cattle and horses, and the greatest grain producer, was San Gabriel. Next to it in every thing else, and ahead of it in sheep, was San Luis Rey, which also had the most Indians. The Mission Dolores stood low on the list, with its five hundred Indians shivering in the wind and fog, five thousand horned cattle, one thousand six hundred horses and mules, four thousand sheep, goats, and hogs, and two thousand five hundred bushels of grain.

CHAPTER XI.

THE MISSIONS SECULARIZED.

CHAP. XI.
1830.

The trouble that Mexico was preparing for her, came in earnest upon California in 1830. It was during the administration of Governor Echeandia, who was the third of the list under Mexico. Monterey was the capital of the Territory, but the pleasanter air of San Diego induced him, for the sake of his delicate constitution, to reside much of the time at the more southern port. He was contracted in his views, despotic in the exercise of his power, and selfish in his relations with foreigners. Occasionally there was an insurrection to put down, like that of Soliz, which surprised the garrison of Monterey in the night, and overpowered it, the town surrendering without the loss of a drop of blood. Soliz received the moneys in the hands of the commissary, and was elected president of the insurgents, whose manifesto declared the intention not to interfere with foreigners, nor to interrupt the commerce of the country. He had under his command one hundred well-armed men, which was a powerful force for the place and the times, but in the course of a few weeks Echeandia's party defeated them, and the ringleaders were sent to San Blas. An old friar of the San Luis Obispo Mission was found guilty of abetting the treason, and he too was embarked on board a merchant-ship, and sent out of the country.

Echeandia, probably under instructions from Mexico, though others doubt that, undertook to carry into effect the neglected act of the Cortes of 1813, for the secularization of the missions, which the Mexican Congress in 1828 had ordered to be enforced. The devastation of the missions now commenced. The Indians were encouraged in their refusal to labor; their emancipation, for which the act provided, they thought meant freedom from work, and license to indulge in every form of vice.

But the evil day was postponed by the arrival of a successor to Echeandia. Manuel Victoria reached Santa Barbara on the 10th of January, 1831. He was a man of courage, and rather head-strong. He came up unattended, asking no ceremonious reception. He had great faith in his own capacity to rule, and did not conceal his disgust at the loose way in which matters were managed. He set out to reform abuses, without preparing the public for his reforms, or very carefully consulting the constitution, from which he derived all his authority. He had no patience with the slow course of justice. In those days all cases of complaint, civil or criminal, went before the pueblo's ayuntamiento (or town council), or the alcalde, whose duties were those of a mayor and judge combined. But their decisions had to be confirmed by the commander of the presidio before they were binding. In a capital offence, the alcalde held a preliminary examination, and sent up the accused, if found guilty, to the general for trial.

Two Indians had been convicted of cattle-stealing. Victoria ordered them to be publicly shot in the presidio of Monterey. It was a short cut to justice, and it put a stop to cattle-stealing; but it was unconstitutional; it gave his enemies a handle against him, and hastened the outbreak of a revolution. So soon as the reins of government were in his hands, he had taken measures to counteract the policy of his predecessors with regard to the missions. Echeandia had retired to Monterey, and Inspector Pádrez, who had been his evil genius, to San Francisco. Both busied themselves in drawing together the malcontents, who foresaw their fortunes in the destruction of the missions. Pádrez, working his mischief too openly, was dispatched to San Blas.

Victoria had placed all confidence in Portilla,

the commander at San Diego, and in return the commander gave him timely notice that certain persons had met and declared for Echeandia in that extreme southern port. The governor, dreaming of no treachery, started out with a dozen men to meet Portilla and consult with him. As he travelled, he heard that the rebels had marched up to Los Angeles, taken possession of the town, arrested the alcalde, and were pushing on northward, numbering now two hundred men. Victoria pressed on to meet them, his force increased to thirty persons. When they confronted each other, the governor called upon the rebel leader to surrender, and then for the first time discovered that it was his trusted friend Portilla! Instantly the governor's firmest supporter was shot dead by the traitors. Then Victoria, rushing in with "sacred fury," and dealing his blows on every side, routed the rebels like so many sheep, and marched on victorious to the mission of San Gabriel, where the loss of blood compelled him to halt. Portilla's vagabonds, learning that the champion was badly wounded, rallied, gathered about the mission, and demanded the governor's surrender. Victoria, seeing his case hopeless, replied that, if they would leave him to himself, he would resign his command and return to Mexico.

He kept his word. Friends gathered about

him, tendered their services, and pleaded that a promise extorted could be violated with honor; but he adhered to the letter of his. At San Diego he embarked for San Blas, and thence retired to a cloister in Mexico.

The victorious party formed a new government at Los Angeles, and the legislature appointed Don Pio Pico governor. But soon, news came from the north that the new government would not there be recognized. Echeandia, retreating to San Juan Capistrano, gathered about him many Indians, whom his promises enticed from their work at the missions, and inaugurated a series of robberies and murders. Other Indians at distant points, especially at the south, revolted. The Indian was free, and as he staggered along the pathway where he had hitherto been a willing slave, he felt that his freedom entitled him to do any violence that might be convenient. Anarchy ruled throughout the province, and confusion covered the whole country.

It was happy for the distracted land that José Figueroa was the next governor; but his voyage up from Acapulco prefigured the unhappy state in which he was to find his command. The brig in which he sailed, accompanied by his officers, soldiers, and eleven missionaries from the College of Zacatecas, was struck with lightning, while at Mazatlan; but fortunately, the fire was extinguished just before it reached the powder. At Cape St. Lucas the troops revolted, declaring for Santa Anna, who was in arms against the ruling Mexican faction, and compelled the captain to take his vessel to San Blas. The captain returned from that point to St. Lucas, took on the governor, a few faithful friends, and the friars, and landed all safely in California in January, 1833. Figueroa had been ordered to suspend the operation of the secularization act, the Supreme Government, though not opposed to the policy, having entirely disapproved the method of effecting it that Echeandia and Pádrez had attempted. Figueroa published a circular, pardoning all who had taken part in the revolution against Victoria; and Echeandia went down to San Diego, to prepare for returning to Mexico.

About this time, owing to the growing jealousy of whatever reminded of Spain, the jurisdiction of the missions was divided. The establishments north of San Luis Obispo fell to the management of the native Mexican friars from the Franciscan College of Zacatecas, while to the old Spanish Franciscan directors were left the missions of the south.

The Mexican Congress had repeatedly passed acts concerning secularization, and afterwards annulled them again. But now Pádrez, whom Victoria had packed off in disgrace to San Blas, was in favor at the capital, and through his influence the president gave his sanction to an act which Congress had passed (in 1833), ordering the secularization of the missions and the colonization of both the Californias. Hijar was appointed governor and director of colonization, while Pádrez himself was made subdirector. Hijar started for his post, accompanied by a large number of colonists, to whom half a dollar a day was assigned till their arrival, with a free passage, and maintenance during the voyage. In the brig *Natalia* he arrived at San Diego on the 1st of September, 1834, with a part of his colonists, who were of both sexes. Pádrez, with the rest, reached Monterey on the 25th. The *Natalia*—it was the same vessel on which Napoleon had escaped from the island of Elba—reached Monterey on the 14th of October, was beached there in a storm, and utterly wrecked. It came out, during the bitter discussion that followed Hijar's arrival, that the president had authorized the appropriation of fourteen thousand dollars, payable in tallow from the missions, for the purchase of this brig, and that the colonists were organized as a company, with power to monopolize the commerce of the country, making the missions and towns their dépôts, while all their capital was to be squeezed out of the missions.

When the news was fairly bruited through California, the missionaries aroused to a new ambition—an ambition to destroy what they had been so long in building. They saw that the destruction of the missions was a foregone conclusion. Orders were given, and at once obeyed, for the immediate slaughter of the cattle. Of thousands that were slain, nothing but the hides was saved; the carcasses were left to enrich the plains.

Figueroa had been ordered to provide a proper spot for the colonists, and he had selected San Francisco Solano, on the north side of San Francisco harbor, for the purpose. He received Hijar with civility and proper demonstrations of respect, but showed him that his arrival had been anticipated by an overland order to himself, from the secretary of state, not to deliver up to him the civil command—Santa Anna having displaced President Gomez Farias, and assumed the government. Hijar, as simple director of the colony, was reduced to a man of little consequence, unless he could get possession of the missions, of which the prospect grew dimmer daily.

But the colonists at Solano were brewing a revolt. One of their number, who had been chosen as a commissioner to the home Government, proceeded with his friend to Los Angeles, under the pretence of embarking from that point for Mexico with dispatches from Hijar. But they went no farther than Los Angeles. There, on the 7th of March, 1835, these two Solano men, and some fifty others, declared Figueroa unworthy of confidence, appointed the first alcalde provisional governor of the Territory in civil matters, and Portilla in matters military, announced the restoration of the missions to the fathers, declared their plans subject to the approbation of the Supreme Government, and solemnly averred that they would not lay down their arms until all these points had been gained. At three o'clock, the same afternoon, the revolution was ended, in Los Angeles, where it began, their own agent having delivered over to the authorities the ringleaders. But in other places, especially by the colonists, it was for some time regarded as an accomplished revolution. These poor fellows were of all trades and professions, excepting those which would have been useful to them. There were artists and printers, and teachers of music, but never a farmer; there were goldsmiths, where there was no gold in use; blacksmiths, for a country that employed very little iron; carpenters, where adobe and tiles were the principal building materials; painters, for a region where paint was in no demand; shoemakers and tailors, for a people who shod themselves with raw-hides, and wore blankets instead of coats. In their disappointment they talked loudly, and sometimes treasonably, and at last the more restless and least prudent of them were banished to Mexico.

The Mexican scheme of secularization was not offensive to the California politicians. The Territorial legislature at last came round to it. Administrators of the mission property were appointed. These swindled all parties pretty effectually, but at last turned over all the missions to Governor Figueroa. The governor's position was not one to be coveted. The missionaries were his enemies, the Indians were his enemies, the great horde of swindling speculators were his enemies, and all for different reasons. He was harassed and perplexed, sick and disheartened, and at last he died. He was the best governor that California had yet seen. Aiming conscientiously to perform the very delicate duties imposed upon him, he succeeded in what he undertook, but the penalty of success was his death. The "Excellent Deputation" in session at Monterey passed the most extravagantly eulogistic resolutions in his honor. It ordered a portrait of the deceased to be painted, and a monument in his memory to be erected and inscribed with the flattering title, "Father of his Country." Figueroa was forty-three years old when he died, on the 29th of September, 1835. His remains were carried in an American vessel to Santa Barbara, and deposited in a vault of the mission church, minute-guns being fired as they were conveyed from the vessel to the burial-place, and a large procession following them to the grave.

CHAPTER XII.

REBELLION.—SECESSION.—RESTORATION.—PANICS.

AFTER a brief interval, during which José Castro acted as governor, Nicholas Gutierrez succeeded to the command, in accordance with the will of Figueroa, but he held it very briefly, for Mariano Chico was sent up from Mexico to be governor. But Chico's tyranny soon brought him into disgrace; he was expelled from the Territory, and Gutierrez once more assumed the reins. Matters now went quietly enough until there broke out a quarrel between Gutierrez and the custom-house department, which was supposed to have been stimulated by resident foreigners, retired hunters and trappers from the Columbia River and the Rocky Mountain region, and by Mexican adventurers.

The administrator of the customs was Angel Ramirez, a Mexican, and formerly a friar of the Zacatecas College. Next in authority was Juan Bautista Alvarado, a native Californian, who for years had been secretary of the Territorial Deputation. He was a person of some talent, was educated by the missionaries, popular,

CHAP. XII.
1836.

and acquainted with the English language. With this Alvarado, Governor Gutierrez quarrelled on a point of etiquette concerning the posting of guards at the landing-places. The dispute running very high, Alvarado's arrest was ordered, but he escaped from the town, and the warrant was not served. His asylum was the cabin of Isaac Graham, of Santa Cruz, who had crossed the Rocky Mountains from Tennessee and settled among the Santa Cruz Mountains. Alvarado told his story to Graham, and a scheme was concocted on the spot, with the understanding that, if it resulted happily, the independence of California from Mexico should be declared. Graham raised in a few days fifty riflemen, and Alvarado brought to join them a hundred Californians, under José Castro. They entered Monterey at night, having obtained ammunition from American vessels in the harbor, shut up the governor and twice their own number of soldiers in the presidio, and demanded a surrender. Gutierrez hesitating, a ball was fired from a brass four-pounder —the only shot that was fired during the revolution—and it struck the roof of the presidio. This brought him to terms, and the Mexicans surrendered. Castro and Alvarado took possession of the town.

The people of Monterey, of California indeed, were ripe for the change. They wanted the

ALVARADO'S INSURRECTION. 143

Federal Constitution of 1824 restored. As there was no prospect of that until the next *coup d'état*, which, even at the pace of Mexican revolutions, might be a twelvemonth off, the proclamation which followed caused no great offence, though it showed that Alvarado had by unanimous consent been placed at the head of the government, and Guadalupe Vallejo at the head of the military; and that the Territorial Deputation had adopted resolutions declaring California independent, and erecting it into a free and sovereign State, whose religion was to be Roman Catholic without admitting the exercise of any other, though no person was to be molested for his religious opinion. The southern part of the country did not come in quite so heartily to this arrangement, but at the north it was accepted with pleasure. Gutierrez, his officers and soldiers, were expelled from the country, and most of the Mexican officials throughout the Territory were sent home.

It was said at the time, that a flag with a lone star on it was prepared for the new Republic, but the victorious insurgents lacked the courage to use it. With characteristic dread of all changes, except in the one item of governors, they still kept the Mexican banner floating on all their public places.

The Mexican Government fulminated a large quantity of paper proclamations at California

CHAP. XII.
1836.

for its rebellion, and threatened terrible chastisements. But, there coming hot work for the politicians at Mexico, California was allowed to govern herself until there should be peace at the capital; and foreigners, the customs being now diminished one-half, were satisfied. Alvarado sent General Castro down to Santa Barbara, to discover and improve the feeling there towards the new government. As Captain Graham and his fifty riflemen accompanied Castro, all that part of the country was readily persuaded that independence was desirable.

At Los Angeles, a little party proclaimed itself in favor of adherence to Mexico, and grateful Mexico named as the governor to be defended by that party, Carlos Carillo, Alvarado's uncle. Carillo declared war at once, but Alvarado soon captured his uncle and set a guard over him in his house at Santa Barbara, sent off his advisers as prisoners to Sonoma, and dispatched a letter of explanation to Mexico. As they were still busy at the capital, the victorious Alvarado was approved in all his acts, and appointed governor; while, to make matters right with the vanquished, to Carillo was given the little island of Santa Rosa. In return for Mexican generosity, Alvarado recognized Mexico again as the central power, and Upper California was divided into two districts, each representing a State government, with Castro as prefect of the North, and Peña, a Mexican lawyer who had figured briskly in the revolution of independence, prefect of the South, while both were subject to the jurisdiction of Alvarado at Monterey. Meanwhile, the missions were by all parties regarded as fair objects of plunder, and the forts of the presidios were left to fall to ruins.

But, as Alvarado grew easy in his seat, the remembrance that he owed his elevation to foreigners, began to chafe him. There were subjects of his who slapped him on the shoulder, and forgot the dignity that belonged to the executive. Graham, the Tennesseean, was especially obnoxious, for he did not mind telling the governor to his face, that, but for his aid, his excellency would still be simply a clerk. It was at last an absolute necessity to get the Tennesseean out of the way. The nuisance was intolerable, and fortune provided an early excuse for abating it. Graham had challenged all the country to produce a swifter horse on the racecourse than one that he had trained. A Yankee accepted the challenge, and, to make the bargain sure, the terms of the race were drawn up in writing. The spies of Alvarado got a passing glimpse of the document, and construed it into a terrible plot to overthrow all that was stable in California.

Castro was sent with an armed force to arrest Graham, at the dead of night. Other Americans, and some Europeans, about a hundred in all, were seized and taken to Monterey. Some, who were considered the most dangerous, were conducted to Santa Barbara, and afterwards fifteen or twenty of them were embarked, in chains, to San Blas. This event, which was celebrated with a mass and a general thanksgiving, occurred in May, 1840. Two months later, a French ship, and the American man-of-war *St. Louis*, entered the harbor of Monterey. Now was Alvarado in a most unhappy predicament. Vallejo was not present, and Castro had gone to Mexico with the prisoners. Fortunately, in the very nick of time, he heard, or feigned to hear, of a disturbance among the Indians in the interior. He slipped off at once to attend to that, nor did he return till the ships of war, finding no party to get an apology from, had sailed again. Then every thing went on in its old career of quiet dilapidation until 1842.

To the consternation of Alvarado, and the amazement of everybody, in July of that year the exiled foreigners returned to Monterey. They came in a Mexican vessel, were much improved in personal appearance, and admirably armed. In their absence they had been maintained by Government, and now they were sent home at its expense. This extraordinary issue

ARRIVAL OF MICHELTORENA.

of their exile had been accomplished through the urgency of the British consul at Mexico, who succeeded besides in getting the guard of the prisoners themselves imprisoned.

Meanwhile, Vallejo, who had found Alvarado impracticable, from his retirement at Sonoma had begged the General Government to appoint some one as political governor in his stead; and Alvarado had as earnestly solicited a new general in place of Vallejo. Both were gratified. In August, 1842, General Micheltorena arrived suddenly at San Diego. He came empowered to assume both civil and military command. Only a moderate force attended him, but close behind were enough to make all opposition futile.

Micheltorena was already distinguished as a soldier. He had served with Santa Anna in the Texan campaign, and he brought away laurels if no scars. His soldiers were veterans too, veterans in crime if not in war, a hard lot of convicts, who brought their wives and children with them, for they were of the sort who trundle their families around with them—not because they prize their society so much, as because they have no other home than the place where they feed to-day.

The new governor was received with distinguished honors. A series of grand dinners, fandangoes, and bull-fights, was arranged.

Micheltorena was travelling northward like a prince, and being hailed like a true lord, when suddenly word reached him that put fandangoes out of his head and lent wings to his feet. He and his forces dashed back into Los Angeles at a speed quite unbecoming the gubernatorial dignity. The startling news that brought his triumphal entry so suddenly to an end was intelligence well calculated to excite alarm. Commodore Jones, of the United States Navy, had sailed into Monterey harbor with the sloop-of-war *Cyane* and the frigate *United States*, on the 19th of October, 1842, had taken possession of the town (Alvarado gladly surrendering on the 20th to a foreigner rather than to a Mexican), had run up the stars and stripes, and proclaimed the country a portion of the American Union. The people had saluted the new flag with genuine delight. A braver general than Micheltorena would have been pardoned a swift gait to the nearest place of safety.

Next day, Commodore Jones pulled down the stars and stripes again, and handsomely apologized. It was all a mistake. The commodore had "blundered" the seizure. He knew the programme of the politicians, that Texas was to be annexed, that Mexico was to go "on the rampage," that the Americans were to discover unparalleled outrages on the part of Mexico, that finally war was to be proclaimed, and then

California would be fair game for the American squadron in the Pacific. The commodore, knowing so much, misconstrued some rumors that he had heard, did not doubt that war was declared, and so pounced upon Monterey. When he saw his error and had apologized, Micheltorena came up to the capital and assumed control without opposition. That his ammunition might be out of the way of the Yankees in case of another such freak as that of Jones, he stored it with great care at the mission of San Juan.

But Alvarado, deposed, was not idle. He had harmonized again with General Vallejo; and the two, aided by Castro, November, 1844, captured the Mission of San Juan and the governor's ammunition. Micheltorena gave the rebels eight days in which to lay down their arms. When that time was up, the parties met, disagreed upon the terms of peace, and the Californians made ready to attack the capital. Micheltorena called for help on Captain Sutter, whose settlement in the Sacramento Valley had become quite an important power in the State. The captain consented, but before he would start he made a bargain for his friends. Since 1841 he had enjoyed a grant of land for himself, had erected a fort near the junction of the American and the Sacramento Rivers, and, as justice of the peace, ruled the region. He

CHAP. XII.

1844.

asked—and Micheltorena granted this request—that every petition for land on which Sutter as justice had favorably reported should be taken as granted, and that a copy of the general title which the governor then conferred should be regarded no less binding than a formal grant.

Sutter and a hundred men then placed themselves at the service of the governor; but his excellency marched with such deliberation, that a good part of his foreign allies turned back in disgust. On the 21st of February, Castro,

1845.

heading the rebels, pushed out from Los Angeles, and the hostile parties met. As Castro had some fifty foreigners with him, by agreement all the foreigners from both parties withdrew, to allow the Californians and Mexicans to fight out their own quarrel alone.

After a brief and bloodless engagement, that was resumed next day, when, it is said, four persons were killed, Mexico surrendered. The California "Deputation" declared its oldest minister, Pio Pico, governor. Castro was appointed general, and Micheltorena, his officers, and all of his soldiers that had not married in the country, were put on board an American bark and hustled off to San Blas.

In the spring of the following year, Pio Pico still being governor, and Castro busy at the north plotting how to oust him—the bone of contention being the custom-house, which each wanted at

GOVERNORS WHILE UNDER MEXICO.

the place of his residence—there glided in from over the mountains at the east, a young surveyor with a little party of old mountaineers, whose appearance brought all Castro's schemes to a halt, and put a period to the civil wars and the old times in California together.

The following are the names of the Governors of California, after Mexico declared her independence of Spain, and until the American conquest—a term which continued from 1822 to 1846:—

Pablo Vicente de Sola	Nov. 1822 to	1823.
Luis Arguello	1823	to June 1825.
José Maria de Echeandia	June 1825 to Jan.	1831.
Manuel Victoria	Jan. 1831 to Jan.	1832.
Pio Pico	Jan. 1832 to Jan.	1833.
José Figueroa	Jan. 1833 to Aug.	1835.
José Castro	Aug. 1835 to Jan.	1836.
Nicholas Gutierrez,	Jan. 1836 to May	1836.
Mariano Chico	May 1836.	
Nicholas Gutierrez	1836.	
Juan B. Alvarado	1836 to Dec.	1842.
Manuel Micheltorena	Dec. 1842 to Feb.	1845.
Pio Pico	Feb. 1845 to July	1846.

CHAPTER XIII.

THE "NATIVE CALIFORNIANS."

CHAP. XIII.
1846.

Three times the Californians had struck for their independence from Mexico, and won it: in 1832, when they deposed Victoria, and made Pio Pico governor, but in the year of anarchy that followed were glad to welcome Figueroa from Mexico; in 1836, when Alvarado, by the aid of the Tennesseean, expelled Gutierrez, and straightway forgot the independence he had proclaimed, on being recognized by Mexico as governor *ad interim;* and in 1845, when Alvarado, Vallejo, and Castro, expelled Micheltorena, and Pio Pico was again made governor. But they never got much farther than to *declare* independence, to adorn the State with a new set of offices, and appropriate the customs from the shipping. They never fairly claimed the country as their own. The right to grant lands they seemed to consider as solely resident in the home Government, nor do we know that they ever demurred to the right of Mexico, at the treaty of Guadalupe Hidalgo, to stipulate their whole territory away. Yet the leading men, Pico, Alvarado, Castro, were native Californians.

Eleven years had wrought wonders. The priestly rule was entirely overthrown. The Christian Indians had either relapsed into paganism, or, by intermarriages with soldiers and sailors, formed the basis of a mixed race that still survives. It was estimated, by Larkin, that there were fifteen thousand people in Upper California in 1846, exclusive of Indians. Of that number, perhaps two thousand were from the United States. They had come from over the mountains, had tarried from vessels that stopped at the various harbors, or had drifted from the Columbia River region. Trappers retiring from their hardy pursuits had taken up their residence in valleys that suited their fancy, far away from points of contact with the Mexican settlers, and in portions of the country that the missionaries had neglected.

The people that made up the body of the population were dashing and careless, fond of fandangoes, always ready for a dance, making the most of their religious holidays with bullfights and bear-baitings, and almost universally given to gambling. *Monte* was their favorite game, in which all classes, and men and women alike, engaged. They accepted their good fortune without any lively demonstrations of joy, and their losses did not disturb their composure of mind. On Sunday afternoons, devotions being ended, they generally surrendered themselves to some sort of gay festivity.

There were few such riders in the world. Wild horses, though every one had his claimant, scoured the plains in droves, and those that were accounted tame would seem to any other people quite unbroken. When a gentleman set out on a journey, he took a driver and a drove of horses with him. As one animal wearied of the saddle, another was made to bear the burden. In this way a hasty rider would accomplish his hundred miles a day. If a horse gave out on the road, he was turned loose to find his way home at his leisure. His owner's name was branded on his flank; there was little danger of his being lost; but of his being stolen there was great danger, since with the Indian, relapsed into barbarism, horse stealing was a passion.

The child, at a very early age, was taught to ride at a breakneck pace, and with the use of the lariat every one was dexterous.

The saddle was an elaborate piece of workmanship. The stirrups were of wood, and set well back; the skirts were broad, and pierced for strips of raw-hide with which to lash fast the blankets and baggage of the rider. It was fastened very tightly by a wide girth, without the aid of a buckle, and in a manner that made slipping or turning impossible. Over its high pommel was coiled the inevitable lasso. The bridle, like the lasso, was of braided raw hide. To the bit was attached a cruelly long spur, running back upon the beast's tongue, so that the slightest pull at the bridle compelled obedience without much reference to the original intentions of the brute. He soon learned to take his cue from the weight of the rein upon his neck, and the horseman dashed along the highway, generally at full gallop, with loose reins. A poor man might own a dozen horses, but he was rich who was supplied with the complete furniture for one. When overtaken by night on the road, the saddle was his pillow; the blankets, unrolled from the bundles that they were as they dangled from it, were bedding and covering enough in so mild a climate; and the ever-useful lasso limited the range of the horse, as he fed on the wild oats of the valley.

It was not until the Indians discovered how delicate and savory roast horse-flesh was, that the tribe of horse-thieves sprang into existence, but then they grew with astonishing rapidity, till they were the terror of all the country. Their chief haunts were the valleys of the San Joaquin and its tributaries. Temperate writers estimate that from five thousand to ten thousand horses were stolen and eaten in the twenty years between 1827 and 1847. It is impossible to conceive how frightful the nuisance was, unless we bear in mind how large a proportion of the male population jingled immense spurs at their heels perpetually, and that, unhorsed, the Californian considered himself but half a man.

Their houses were one story high, generally built of large unburned bricks, or adobes, floored with clay, and roofed with tiles. The pleasures of the table were not foremost in their thoughts. The supply of flour for the day was ground in hand-mills each morning from the grain. Tortillas—simply thin cakes of meal beaten by hand and baked before the fire—figured at every meal. Beans were a staple article of diet. Red pepper entered into the composition of every cooked dish, and, like onions, were cultivated in every garden. The table-drink was generally water. The use of milk would have implied tame cattle and work, so its presence was rare. The poorest householder had plenty of beef in his pot. The butchered animal was hung up under the shade of the oak, close by the house. In the clear, dry air, there was no risk of its tainting before the knife had cut off, day by day, the tenderer parts for the family, and the tougher for the troops of dogs that stretched themselves lazily in the sun.

The cattle introduced by Governor Portalá and Father Junipero had increased beyond all calculation. They formed the principal wealth of the missions at one time, and for leagues the higher grounds were spotted with bullocks, while the valleys, for acre upon acre, waved with growing grain. There was food enough for all.

Every year all the cattle belonging to one party were gathered to a *rodeo ;* that is, driven together and passed through a corral or pen, where they were branded with the owner's mark, or at least old brands inspected, and other necessary operations were performed upon the calves. It was always a merry occasion, beautifully adapted for the display of horsemanship in capturing and controlling the wild cattle; and, both because of its own charms, and to prevent the branding of other folks' cattle, the neighbors generally came in to share its sports. Every cattle-owner of course had his special brand, and his marking-iron was deposited with the alcalde of the district.

The mission gardens were hedged in with willows—at the south, with rows of the gigantic cactus. Fruit-trees were planted about the missions very generally. Shade-trees in the vicinity of houses were never in favor, but long *alamedas*, or shaded walks for the convenience of distant worshippers along the line of travel from the pueblos to the churches, were pretty features of the landscape.

Both sexes were excessively fond of dress, but they found little opportunity to humor their fancy in that matter. They had few of the luxuries of life, however great their wealth might be. With the extortionate impost duties, few elegancies were imported, but for the finery that did arrive they paid enormous prices.

From Mexican ports they got rice, sugar, silk, scarfs, and woollen shawls, shoes, saddles, and some English and American goods. Before 1822, they exported little except a few hides, some tallow, a trifle of wine, and perhaps some wheat. But in that year a Yankee ship appeared with a cargo of notions, and she proved the pioneer of a trade that made many a Bostonian rich, that bewitched the Californians of both sexes, and put the local authorities in excellent humor, for they taxed customs generously, and seldom or never sent a shilling of what was collected to the Mexican Government.

These Boston traders kept one or two vessels on the coast, which took out a coasting license and sailed from port to port between San Diego, where the hide-houses were, and San Francisco, near which were the most northern missions. They took in any thing that was for sale, but chiefly hides and tallow, and paid for them, from the well-appointed "store" on board, where the more tempting goods were displayed in show-cases. Hats, hoes, shoes, shovels, calico, crockery, ribbons, hardware, groceries, furniture—every thing, in short, that a Californian coveted, or which his taste could be educated to covet—was for sale on board. Two or three times a year the ships dropped down to San Diego and stored their hides. Finally, one of them would be quite loaded and dispatched for Boston, the other continuing the collection until a new ship with fresh supplies of "notions" arrived, to keep her company in coasting until her own time came to be left alone. It was in one of these hide-ships that Richard H. Dana spent his *two years before the mast*, of which he wrote so readable and still popular an account.

The administration of justice was a very simple matter. They had no written statutes. Equity was the law which the magistrates were expected, if honest, to enforce. All minor offences and actions, involving less than one hundred dollars, were examined and determined by the alcalde. If the offence were great or the penalty capital, he made a preliminary examination, and sent the convicted party to the first judge of the district. If an action involved more than one hundred dollars it was tried by the first

CHAP. XIII.

1840.

judge, and carried on appeal to the prefect or governor. Either party might demand a jury, which generally consisted of three or five persons. When honest men were on the bench, they came to the substance of the thing in dispute with great promptness, and the law had no delay. When rogues held the balances, they suited themselves without much interference, and Justice was dumb as well as blind; for it was a trait of California character that when an appeal had been taken to the law, its decisions were borne with patience and in quietness.

The New England whale-ships, famous always for spying out good harbors in queer out-of-the-way places, were early accustomed to look in at San Francisco and Monterey; and not a few fine farms in the country were in the hands of whalers, who had given up their "lay" on board, stopped ashore, taken wives at least half Indian, neglected to learn the Spanish language, and brought up their large families on frijoles and tortillas in adobe houses.

After 1840, immigrants from over the plains had begun to settle in the Sacramento Valley, getting grants for the asking from the Government, or taking, by consent, a slice out of some early settler's broad claim. All these brought with them the impression—and most of the Englishmen in California assumed the same—

that in a few years the region would all be under the flag of the American Union.

They did not, like the Puritans, however, plant first a church, and then a school-house. The church they quite forgot; and the only schools, outside of the decaying missions, were poor apologies for them, and scarcely worth the name, where it was not pretended to teach much beyond reading and writing. Nor were those accomplishments of much account with the natives, or greatly practised by the immigrants.

CHAP XIII.

1846.

CHAPTER XIV.

FREMONT AND THE BEAR-PARTY REVOLUTION.

CHAP. XIV.
1846. March.

We left Castro diverted from all his schemes against the government of Pico, which he had helped to establish, by the apparition of John Charles Fremont from over the plains. This young pathfinder, then a brevet captain in the corps of United States Topographical Engineers, had been dispatched, in the spring of 1845, on a third tour of exploration across the continent, and especially charged to discover a better route from the western base of the Rocky Mountains to the mouth of the Columbia River. He arrived on the frontier of California early in March, 1846, prudently halted his company, then consisting of sixty-two men, some hundred miles away from Monterey, and proceeded alone to General Castro's head-quarters. His errand was, to obtain permission to take his company to the valley of the San Joaquin, where there was game for his men, grass for his horses, and no inhabitants to be molested by his presence.

Castro received him with courtesy, and told him to go wherever he pleased—the whole country was free to him. Fremont suggested that it would be pleasant to have the permission put in writing, but Castro was quite too "sick" for the effort; so he gave "the word of a Mexican soldier, which was his bond." Fremont returned to his men, who at once broke up camp to remove to the San Joaquin Valley.

Castro, upon reflection, seems to have felt that now was the coveted opportunity to distinguish himself with the Government of Mexico, which, smarting under the recent loss of Texas, could have no excess of affection for the Americans. He was speedily in his saddle, and spurring about the country, arousing the Californians to expel the strangers. His work sped bravely; in a few days he had raised a company of three hundred men. He now sent word to Fremont to quit the country at once, adding also a threat that if the orders were not complied with, he would attack his company, and devote every man among them to destruction. For his sudden change of demeanor he had the decency to plead fresh instructions from Mexico.

Fremont was not entirely unprepared for the general's treachery, having been posted from Consul Larkin, of Monterey, as to the value of "the Mexican soldier's word." He sent back an oral message that he would hold no correspondence with a man who had so shamefully broken his faith, and that he should go when he was ready. He then took his position on the "Hawk's Peak," a height overlooking Monterey from a distance of some thirty miles, intrenched it, and raised the American flag.

His men were exhausted with their long tramp through the deserts and over the mountains. They needed repose and refreshment; but if these were not to be had, they were quite ready to defend themselves to the last. Secretary Marcy, in his report to the President, was careful to insist that there was not in the company an officer or soldier of the United States Army. They were scientific explorers, rough, hardy pathfinders—reliable in any emergency—true as steel. Six of the number were Delaware Indians—the leader's body-guard. Kit Carson was there, and others worthy to keep his company. Each was armed with a knife, a tomahawk, two pistols, and a rifle—not a very desirable company to attack, and evidently one not to be frightened out of its self-possession.

Castro manœuvred his dashing cavalry for three days in full sight. He displayed a fair show of infantry, too, and, through their glasses, the Americans saw a body of artillery getting field-pieces in place. He issued repeated bulletins about the "foreign vagabonds," and several times inspired his cavalry to charge: they charged gallantly, but always wheeled before coming within bullet-reach, apparently concluding that, for every rifle before them, there would be an empty saddle in their ranks; and native Californians wisely held that it were a foolish thing for such good riders to be permanently unhorsed. Then Castro himself must have considered that an actual attack would array against him all the foreign settlers of the valley. If numbers and fierce demonstrations would send the adventurers flying out of the country, his purpose would be gained. If not, he could afford to keep on manœuvring and writing proclamations. Perhaps the little band would be foolhardy enough to make an assault upon their persecutors; in that case he could run. So really there was nothing to be lost by Fabianism.

It was dull sport to Fremont, however. He had been charged on leaving home to provoke no hostilities with the Mexicans, and he was impatient at this detention from his legitimate work. So on the fourth day, seeing no increased prospect of an attack, his party broke up their camp and leisurely moved off northward, toward Oregon. Castro, delighted with so easy an opportunity to herald a victory, was careful not to follow.

Fremont had passed the Oregon border, and

by the 9th of May was on the northern shore of the Greater Klamath Lake. Here word was brought him that an officer of the United States Army with dispatches was on his trail. Instantly, with nine men, he turned back upon his track to find the unknown messenger, and fortunately came upon him the next evening. The stranger was Lieutenant Gillespie, of the Army, who had left Washington the November previous, had crossed the continent from Vera Cruz to Mazatlan, arrived at Monterey in a United States sloop-of-war, and thence hastened up the Sacramento Valley to overtake the explorers. If the Mexicans had arrested and searched him, as the threatening relations of the two republics made not unlikely, they would have found no suspicious papers upon his person. All that he bore was a letter from the Secretary of State, commending the bearer to Fremont's good offices, and some private letters from the captain's distant family. There was not a word of politics in them, or of war with Mexico, or of the future of California; but there were some expressions in a letter from Colonel Benton that the old senator's son-in-law studied with extraordinary diligence. No doubt the oral communications of Gillespie helped to draw from them a deeper significance than the words conveyed on the first reading.

At any rate a new resolution was taken before the last of the party had retired for the night.

After the excitement of the day, for in the life of such wanderers there is no such excitement as news from home, the usual vigilance was relaxed, and all slept soundly until awaked by a cry from Kit Carson. The Indians had broken into their camp; Lajeunesse, one of Fremont's most devoted adherents, was uttering his death-groan; and three of his trusty Delawares were killed before the assassins could be driven back and dispersed.

Whether Castro really had tampered with the natives, as was then thought, or whether, as was suspected afterwards, the hot friends of a scheme on foot to give to England the protectorate of California, had stimulated the savages to violence, is not known; but the resolution of the night before was now irrevocable. Fremont determined to become the pursuer rather than the pursued, to turn upon the faithless foe, and revolutionize the Government.

This would have been a hazardous course for the reputation at home of one sent out on a scientific errand, unless, either in his secret instructions before starting, or in the advices conveyed by Lieutenant Gillespie, he was assured that a successful indiscretion of the sort would be acceptable to his Government. As to the precise plan that he adopted, there is no doubt

CHAP. XIV.
1846.

that he consulted his own judgment alone. But there is abundant circumstantial evidence that he was given to understand that any defensible method of gaining California to the Union would be acceptable. President Polk's Administration had taken the position that the northern Oregon boundary was some nine degrees higher than Great Britain conceded. "Fifty-four forty, or fight," was a party watchword for a while; yet when the issue was pressed, the forty-ninth parallel of latitude was accepted as the boundary, and the fighting was deemed unwise. It would atone for this ungracious issue, if by an apparent accident, or at least without any interposition of our Government, the whole of California should tender itself as the next subject of annexation to the growing Republic, whose manifest destiny, as every stump speaker and bar-room politician now clearly saw, required the absorption of all that was southward down to the tropic of Cancer.

A hint was enough for one so ambitious as Fremont, and if he was not instructed, he certainly was most fortunate in his instincts. A different issue to the revolution he inaugurated might have overwhelmed him with reproach. As it resulted, he had the perfect and flattering indorsement of the Secretary of State. The South was delighted with the new area for slavery that the conquest opened, and the North, admiring the gallantry of the conqueror, lay all the blame of "plotting to rob Mexico" on the shoulders of the Administration, whose instructions they contended that he obeyed.

But the country was not conquered yet. There was a deal of proclaiming, manœuvring, marching, and even some fighting to do before the finest country in the world would drop from the impotent hand of "the sick man, Mexico," into the palm of the United American States.

Fremont returned with his party to the Valley of the Sacramento, and encamped at the Buttes, near the mouth of the Feather River. He found the scattered settlers in a state of high alarm. They had put the worst interpretations upon Castro's proclamations, and did not doubt that the time had come when they must either be driven out, or defy the authorities of the land and overawe them.

While the excitement was at its height, an Indian from below told the story that he had seen between two and three hundred armed men advancing up the valley. This alarming tidings was spread to the remotest settlements as fast as the swiftest riders could carry it, and instinctively the settlers rallied to the camp of Fremont. There the foundation of the story that aroused them was soon learned. Castro had ordered Lieutenant De Arce, commandant of the garrison at Sonoma, to remove a large

CHAP. XIV.
1846.

number of Government horses from the Mission of San Rafael, on the north side of San Francisco Bay, to Santa Clara, at its southern extremity. To accomplish this, De Arce, with a guard of fourteen men, ascended the Sacramento Valley to New Helvetia, the nearest point where the horses could safely swim the river. The Indian had seen the horses and the guard, and he presumed the rest. But the bearer of the true version added that he had conversed with De Arce, who told him that Castro wanted the horses to mount a battalion of two hundred men and expel the settlers. It was deemed wise to frustrate this attempt without waiting for any portion of it to be accomplished. Twelve volunteers, under command of Mr. Merritt, the eldest of their number, were dispatched to overtake De Arce. On the 11th of

June. June they surprised the object of their pursuit, gave to each of the guard a horse to ride home with, and charged De Arce to report to Castro that if he wished the rest of the drove he must come and take them. Merritt's party then marched on to Sonoma, and at daybreak of the 15th entered and captured that military post, of which the honest spoils—they took no other—were nine brass cannon and two hundred and fifty stands of arms. They also made prisoners General Vallejo and two other persons of consideration in the province, and sent them off under an escort for safe keeping to Sutter's Fort at New Helvetia.

Eighteen men, under William B. Ide (a native of New England, and then but one year resident in the country), were left in Sonoma as a garrison, but, as the news spread, the force was soon increased to forty.

Castro heard of these presumptuous doings, and on the 17th fulminated a proclamation from his head-quarters at Santa Clara. He called upon his fellow-citizens, in the name of their religion, liberty, and independence, to rise irresistibly for retribution upon the contemptible and daring invaders.

On the following day, Mr. Ide, the garrison consenting, issued his proclamation—crude in its style, and in its allegations quite unsupported by facts, yet commendably explicit and direct—to all persons in the district of Sonoma, requesting them to remain at peace and follow their rightful occupations, without fear of molestation. The insurgents, so the proclamation declared, had been invited to the country under promise of lands to settle on, and a republican government. But these promises (who made them does not appear) were violated. They were denied the privilege of either buying or renting lands. Instead of a republic they were treated to a military despotism, and were threatened with extermination. They had

CHAP. XIV.

1846.
June.

risen for self-protection, and the overthrow of a government that had seized the property of the missions for its individual aggrandizement and "had ruined and shamefully oppressed the laboring people." To assist in establishing and perpetuating a republican government, all peaceable and good citizens of California were invited to repair to the camp at Sonoma without delay.

Ide's proclamation, if not couched in more superb language than Castro's, drew better, and his camp soon had men enough to spare a party to go out and break up a gang of desperadoes, under one Padilla, who had brutally tortured to death two young men captured on their way to Bodega. Lieutenant Ford commanded this expedition, which mustered twenty-one men. He came upon the enemy between Santa Rosa and San Rafael, and found them far stronger than he had anticipated, they having been re-enforced by Captain Te la Torre, and numbering now eighty-six persons. Ford engaged them, killed eight, wounded two, set the rest into precipitate retreat, and, without loss to his own party, returned to Sonoma.

The party at Sonoma seems to have declared an independent State, and some say that Ide was elected governor. Of course a flag was needed, and with such rude appliances as were at hand they produced one whose like had not been seen before. On a sheet of cotton cloth, with a blacking brush and a pot of berry juice, a tolerable likeness of a grizzly bear was painted. This was the "bear flag," and the party that raised it has gone into history as the Bear-Flag party. The rude flag is still preserved as a choice relic by the California Society of Pioneers, and on notable occasions it has been borne in procession by the society.

Meanwhile, Fremont was busy among the settlers organizing a battalion. It was on the 23d of June that he heard at Sutter's Fort that Castro was crossing the bay with two hundred soldiers to fall upon Ide's garrison. Thirty-six hours later he and his ninety riflemen had put eighty miles behind them, and were at Sonoma, but the only enemy north of the Bay of San Francisco was De la Torre's retreating force. No pains were spared to prevent their escape from the peninsula. Once Fremont's scouts fell in with the fugitives, killed or wounded five, and captured nine pieces of artillery. But the main body, coming to Saucelito, had the good fortune to find a boat just arrived. This they seized, and so made good their escape across the bay—notable as the last Mexicans that were on the soil north of the bay, claiming it for any other Government than the American.

Fremont dispatched a party of ten, under R. Semple, to cross to San Francisco, to take prisoner the captain of the port, R. T. Ridley, and convey him to Captain Sutter's residence and fort, which was to serve as a prison. The task was successfully performed. Fremont himself, accompanied by Kit Carson, Lieutenant Gillespie, and half a score of others, crossed in a launch to the old fort near the presidio, spiked its ten guns, and returned to Sonoma. There, on the 5th of July, 1846, he called the whole force together, and recommended an immediate declaration of independence. All present united to make such a declaration, and with the same unanimity intrusted to Fremont the direction of affairs. Thus the bear party was absorbed into the battalion, whose roll-call now showed one hundred and sixty mounted riflemen.

Next day the pursuit of Castro began. He was understood to be intrenched in Santa Clara with four hundred men. To get there it was necessary to ascend the Sacramento and cross at Sutter's Fort. The battalion effected the crossing only to learn that Castro was retreating towards Los Angeles. To Los Angeles then they must follow him, four or five hundred miles distant though it was. As they were just about to move forward, news came that the flag of the United States had been raised by the American naval force at Monterey, and that the American fleet would co-operate in the effort to capture Castro. Down came the flag of independence, up went the stars and stripes, and, rejoicing that they had the law as well as right on their side, on they dashed southward. Leaving Captain Fremont on the gallop, we turn now to the operations on the coast.

CHAP. XIV.

1846. July.

CHAPTER XV.

THE AMERICAN CONQUEST OF CALIFORNIA.

CHAP. XV.

1846. July.

On the 2d of July, 1846, Commodore Sloat arrived, in the United States frigate *Savannah*, at Monterey. In the instructions that Secretary Bancroft had given him, he was charged to be careful to observe the relations of peace, unless they were violated by Mexico; in that case, he was, without further notice, to employ his fleet —all told, it numbered one frigate and five smaller vessels—for hostile purposes. Before he left Mazatlan he had heard of movements that could scarcely fail of precipitating the two republics into war. The annexation of Texas had been several months accomplished; Mexico was boiling with indignation in view of it, and every movement of the American Administration seemed to be hastening the inevitable collision. All this Commodore Sloat knew; but he could not know that President Polk's ambassador, Slidell, had visited Mexico, tendered his offer of money for a peaceable boundary on the Rio Grande and the cession of California, and that the bribe had been spurned; nor that General Zachary Taylor, in obedience to orders, had taken his post at the mouth of the Rio Grande; nor that, on the 11th of the previous May, Mr. Polk had announced to Congress, in special session, that the blood of our own citizens had been shed on our own soil; nor that Congress had promptly responded that war existed by the act of Mexico, and voted men and money accordingly.

Sloat hesitated what to do. Instructions from Secretary Bancroft were then on the way to him (dated May 15, 1846), charging him to take Mazatlan, Monterey, and San Francisco— either or all, as his force would permit; taking them, to hold them at all hazards, encouraging the people to self-government and neutrality; but of all things, when peace should come again, to be sure that the country were found in possession of the United States. Sloat knew well enough that the conquest of California had been predetermined at Washington. But, suppose the war, by some accident, averted, it would be an awkward blunder if, by any act of his, the plans of the Administration should be revealed to the opposition, who were charging, with great effect, at the Northeast, that the President was bent on waging a war of conquest and for the acquisition of territory, in

CHAP. XV.

1846.

contravention of the spirit of American institutions, and in violation of the popular wishes.

Fremont says that Sloat heard of the doings at Sonoma, and of what he had done, and the news determined him. Doubtless it hastened his determination. But there was another urgent reason for speed. In the harbor of San Blas lay Rear-Admiral Sir George Seymour's flag-ship, the *Collingwood*, while the *Savannah* was at Mazatlan, and eight other British naval vessels were on the coast, watching every American movement. It was clear that England suspected the American designs, and counterplotted to make the Californias her own. When the *Savannah* sailed out of Mazatlan, the *Collingwood* sailed from San Blas. Both ships spread every sail, and raced all the way to Monterey. The *Savannah* was the better sailer of the two, and her commander had time to hear the news, weigh it well, and deliberately choose his course, before the duller craft rounded the Point of Pines.

Here, at Monterey, he learned how sped the project for which Mr. Forbes, the British vice-consul, had labored so faithfully, to put California under British protection, where she would lie as an ample security or equivalent for the debt due in Mexico to British subjects.

Mr. Forbes, in April, had had an interview with Governor Pico and Generals Castro and

Vallejo, when the scheme was partially discussed. It contemplated a fresh declaration of the independence of California, and an appeal to Great Britain for protection. A British naval force was to be convenient to respond to the call. Mexico would be easily appeased, for California was but a troublesome province, and her enemy, the United States, would thus be cheated out of the principal prize that made war acceptable to her. Of all this, which was concealed from the American people in California, intimations had reached our Government, through the watchfulness of its consul at Monterey, Thomas O. Larkin. From him Commodore Sloat probably learned that part of the scheme was to plant a colony of Irishmen in the Valley of San Joaquin, and that Macnamara, an Irish Catholic priest, had petitioned the Mexican Government for large grants of lands around the bays of San Francisco and Monterey, at Santa Barbara, and along the San Joaquin. Tempted by the double object of spreading their religion and by possession excluding the Americans, Mexico readily granted, not all that Macnamara asked, but three thousand square leagues in the San Joaquin Valley, which was enough for his purpose. To be perfected, the patent only needed the signature of Governor Pico.

Upon information of these British plots, Mr.

CHAP. XV.
1846.

Marcy, Secretary of War, had given oral instructions, through Lieutenant Gillespie, to Fremont, that made him nothing loth to postpone his scientific explorations when Castro blocked his way, and turn back, as we have seen, from the frontier of Oregon, to assist the menaced American settlers in the Sacramento Valley. George Bancroft, Secretary of the Navy, in possession of the same facts, had charged the commander of the Pacific Squadron not to wait for *official* information of the declaration of war, but at the first news of it to go in and possess California.

July 7.

In view of all these facts, Commodore Sloat, on the 7th of July, sent Captain Mervine and two hundred and fifty marines and seamen on shore to hoist the American flag over Monterey. As the stars and stripes were run up, the troops and the people cheered, and all the shipping in the harbor saluted it with a display of flags and twenty-one guns. A proclamation was then read, of which copies in Spanish and English were posted about the town.

This proclamation declared California henceforth a portion of the United States. The civil and religious rights of such of its inhabitants as chose to remain citizens would be respected and secured. Those who declined the high privileges of United States citizenship might remain, so long as they preserved a strict neutrality ; or they might go, if they chose, after ample time had been afforded them to dispose of their property. The titles to real estate, the administration of justice, the property of the clergy, were to remain just as they were found, and no private property was to be taken for the use of the ships or soldiers, without just compensation.

CHAP. XV.
1846. July.

The day preceding this notable event, Commodore Sloat had dispatched a messenger to San Francisco, requesting Commander Montgomery, of the United States sloop-of-war *Portsmouth*, to raise the flag, if he had force enough to warrant it. On the 8th, Montgomery landed with seventy sailors and marines, took possession of Yerba Buena, and hoisted the Union standard on the plaza.

On the 10th, Montgomery sent an American flag to Sonoma. The revolutionists received it with joy, and, pulling down the bear flag, raised it over the garrison. Sloat had ordered Purser Fauntleroy to organize into a company of dragoons all volunteers from the shipping and the shore, for the purpose of keeping the roads open from port to port in the vicinity. On the 17th this corps left Monterey for the San Juan Mission, thirty miles to the eastward.

Now when Micheltorena had recovered from his fright at the premature seizure of Monterey by Commodore Jones in 1842, he concealed all his spare guns and ammunition at San Juan, lest more Yankees should blunder an invasion and find them. When, in 1844, Vallejo, Castro, and Alvarado declared the independence of California, first of all they made sure of San Juan. But as they brought their revolution to a successful issue without the explosion of much gunpowder, their concealed treasure appears not to have been disturbed. To secure these hidden arms was Purser Fauntleroy's errand. He made good time on his excursion, and was soon at San Juan, but the treasure was claimed by another party. An hour before his arrival, Fremont and his battalion, riding down from Sutter's, had dashed into the mission, taken possession without one movement of opposition, and dragged to light nine pieces of cannon, two hundred old muskets, twenty kegs of powder, and sixty thousand pounds of cannon shot.

The purser had conveyed from Sloat a request to Fremont that he would report himself. So next day both parties marched into Monterey, and Fremont and Gillespie early presented themselves on board the *Savannah*. The commodore was not in the best of humor, for he had taken a responsibility. He had a misgiving that he had been re-enacting Jones's blunder of 1842. He had been sixteen days in port; why had not Fremont reported to him at once? Fremont had known of his raising the flag six days before: why had he not conferred with him at the earliest possible moment? "I want to know," said he, "by what authority you are acting. Mr. Gillespie has told me nothing. He came to Mazatlan, and I sent him to Monterey; but I know nothing. I want to know by what authority you are acting."

The answer that he got was not of a nature to compose the commodore's spirits. Fremont said he was acting on his own authority. "And I have acted," said the commodore, "upon the faith of your operations in the north. I would rather suffer from doing too much than too little." And the worthy commodore suffered sadly at the moment, suspecting that he had done a good deal too much. If he had known the nature of a dispatch that would be on the way to him in less than a month, from Secretary Bancroft— a dispatch recalling him because he had not acted long before—he would have felt relieved.

Fremont might have taken the commodore to the quarter-deck and pointed to the *Collingwood*, which arrived but the day before. He might have recalled to his attention the fact that Great Britain had never before so large a squadron in the Pacific as now; that Macnamara, the priest, had resided at Mexico, in the house of a British official, and had been taken by the British sloop-of-war *Juno* up to Santa Barbara in June; that the scheme for the British occupation of the country was well concocted, and about ripe; and that America's chance would have slipped irrevocably, if somebody had not taken the responsibility before Admiral Seymour arrived.

It is doubtful if the argument would have comforted the commodore much. It might have accounted for the ambitious young captain's zeal, but there was a mystery still that annoyed him. The captain was a topographical engineer, not an army officer, and Gillespie but a lieutenant of marines. Yet the lieutenant of marines had been sent past him, at Mazatlan, without a message for *his* eye, to whisper an oral message to the young engineer, and all the while, he, Sloat, a faithful officer of the navy, long in service, commander of the squadron, left to take his cue from a younger man! The commodore was sick, disgusted, and fully resolved to return homeward as soon as he could be relieved.

But there was the battalion of one hundred and sixty men, panting for the work of crushing Castro and finishing the job that had been taken in hand. Would the commodore accept their services? By no means. He had no service for them. He intended to tarry in Monterey; there was no war of his making to be prosecuted.

On the 15th of July, Commodore Stockton arrived at Monterey, in the United States frigate *Congress*. He had left Norfolk, Virginia, nine months before, with sealed orders, which were to be opened only after passing Hatteras. The orders directed him to repair first to the Sandwich Islands, and thence to Monterey and deliver dispatches to Consul Larkin, and then to report to his superior officer. Stockton obeyed his order to the letter. Sloat at once expressed his intention to return to the East, leaving Stockton in command of the squadron.

CHAP. XV.

1846. July.

Fremont and Gillespie, after Sloat's refusal to have any thing to do with their battalion, had a conference with Stockton. The New Jersey commodore took a different view of things from that of his superior officer. He was suffering no grievance, had not been overlooked by the Administration, was young yet, enjoyed a good digestion, did not despise the credit nor shrink from the perils of being a conqueror.

He asked, and Sloat granted him permission to assume command at once of the land forces. Then he invited Fremont and Gillespie to take service under him with their battalion. Fremont was at the head of the popular movement, and in a branch of the service that owed no duty to a naval officer; but he was glad to accept, and so settle cheaply all questions of the irregularity of his late proceedings. Gillespie was in the navy, but he was now detailed to a special duty by the President. So his acceptance was entirely voluntary, and it was cheerful. The battalion was satisfied with any thing that promised work. Thus the reorganization was completed instantly. Stockton commissioned Fremont as major, and Gillespie as captain of what thereafter was to be called in the official documents the "California Battalion of Mounted Riflemen," but in common parlance, the "Navy Battalion."

On the 23d, Commodore Sloat sailed for home in the *Levant*, and the same day Stockton, now in full command, dispatched the *Cyane*, Commodore Dupont, to convey Major Fremont and his battalion to San Diego. A week later, Stockton himself sailed on the *Congress* for San Pedro. At Monterey was left the *Savannah*, and at San Francisco the *Portsmouth*.

Before he left Monterey, Stockton issued a proclamation, announcing that he would "immediately march against the boasting and abusive chiefs, who had not only violated every principle of national hospitality and good faith towards Captain Fremont, but who, unless driven out, would keep this beautiful country in a constant state of revolution and bloodshed, as well as against all others who might be found in arms aiding and abetting General Castro."

There was not wanting a certain Mexican

flavor in this, but the commodore proceeded with great dispatch to carry his promises into effect, which was a very un-Mexican procedure.

The *Congress*, on her way down the coast, touched at Santa Barbara. Stockton went on shore and took possession unhindered; then, leaving a small detachment to hold the place, he sailed on to San Pedro. Here, on the 6th of August, he disembarked, inquired for the enemy, and learned that Castro and Pico were at Los Angeles, with, as was reported, fifteen hundred men. He learned, too, that Fremont had safely reached San Diego, but, as he had found it exceedingly difficult to obtain horses to mount his men, there was little reason to hope that the battalion would traverse the hundred and thirty miles between San Diego and Los Angeles in time to help capture Castro.

Stockton had six small guns, borrowed from the shipping, and they probably of no very belligerent antecedents, but now mounted on rude carriages for use. Without horses, however, of what service would they be? With the little force at his command he could not strike a heavy blow, but he determined it should be a swift one. His marines and all the sailors that could be spared from the ship were landed and set to practising the artillery drill. The tars knew very well that, once on shore, they might have to find their way back to Monterey overland, for the harbor of San Pedro was never to be trusted in case of a storm. The drill was all Greek to them, but they were apt scholars, and soon were fit to be trusted to march.

While they were in the camp of instruction, there came in commissioners from Castro with a flag of truce, proposing that all active operations should cease, and each party hold the possessions it had until terms of peace could be negotiated. Stockton doubted whether he could trust Castro's promises, but did not doubt that the commissioners were really spies. So he met them with studied sternness, and bade them carry back word that no terms would be accepted. "Tell Castro he must unconditionally surrender, or experience my vengeance." Meanwhile he occupied the opportunity by skilfully parading his men at distant points of view, so as to convey the impression that they were a mighty multitude. To impress the commissioners with the terrible nature of the engines of his warfare, he so arranged a huge mortar, enveloping it in skins, except its mouth, that they did not doubt that they beheld a cannon of more power and greater calibre than ever had been displayed on the coast before. In a few days other commissioners appeared, to assure the commodore that at every sacrifice his intentions should be opposed. These were sent back with much the same lesson fastened in their minds as their predecessors had borne away. On the 11th of August, five days after landing, Stockton took up the line of march with his three hundred. Los Angeles was reached that night—the cattle, besides which they had no other provisions, being driven with them in a hollow square, and the six guns dragged by hand. Castro's skirmishers were in sight much of the time, but they acted simply as scouts, who bore to Castro tidings of the progress of the invaders.

As they neared the intrenched camp, a courier from Castro came out, kindly to warn them that the town would prove their grave if they entered it. Stockton hastened the courier back with word to the general to have the bells tolled at eight in the morning, for at that time he should enter. He kept his word, but Castro did not wait to superintend any funeral ceremonies. Breaking up his camp, he disbanded his forces and fled to the province of Sonora.

Stockton at once took possession of Los Angeles, where he was soon after joined by Fremont and his battalion. Having received official notice of the existence of the war with Mexico, Stockton proclaimed California a territory of the United States, organized a territorial government, reserved for himself the duties of governor, appointed trusty men to certain official stations that could not well be left vacant, and invited the people to meet on the 15th of September and elect officers of their own. He left fifty men, under Captain Gillespie, to garrison Los Angeles; others, under Lieutenant Talbot, to hold Santa Barbara, and others to hold San Diego. With the rest of his force he returned to Monterey. Hearing there that a thousand Walla-Wallas were threatening the inhabitants of the Sacramento Valley, he sailed for Yerba Buena with the intention of engaging this new enemy, but learned upon arrival that the report was without foundation.

The hundred or two inhabitants of Yerba Buena and the people of the neighboring country gave Governor Stockton a public reception, going down in procession to the landing-place to meet him. They had music, a ride, a dinner, with toasts and speeches, and the festivities closed with a ball. In lack of any thing more to do, Stockton conceived the project, and set Fremont to the work of executing it, of embarking a force of volunteers to Mazatlan or Acapulco, and thence to cross the country and meet General Taylor at the city of Mexico.

But there was more work to be done at home

before the conquest of California was completed. Among the persons of rank who surrendered as prisoners of war at Los Angeles, and were permitted to go at large on their parole of honor, was General Jose M. Flores. No sooner had Stockton withdrawn from Los Angeles than Flores began to rally the disbanded troops and organize a new opposition. On the 23d of September, his troops invested the garrison, and Captain Gillespie, seeing nothing else to be done, capitulated on the 30th, and retired with his riflemen to Monterey. The insurgents next besieged the garrison of Santa Barbara. Talbot would not surrender to the overwhelming numbers that presented themselves, but safely escaped with all his men.

Then Flores and his conspirators issued a proclamation to the people. They attributed the defeat of the former army to the cowardice of the authorities. They called upon the Californians to rally for the expulsion of the "North Americans," and to re-establish the Department of California as a member of the great Mexican nation. They declared all Mexican citizens between the ages of fifteen and sixty, who refused to take up arms, traitors, incurring the penalty of death. The North Americans, who had directly or indirectly aided the enemy, were to be removed, and their property confiscated. This proclamation was indorsed by more than three hundred persons, all swearing never to lay down arms till the Americans were expelled from Mexican territory.

CHAPTER XVI.

CALIFORNIA'S THREE CONQUERORS AND FIRST THREE AMERICAN GOVERNORS.

So the American conquest was to be repeated. Stockton heard the news from Gillespie, and sent immediately the *Savannah* to San Pedro, with three hundred and twenty men, under the command of Captain Mervine. They landed, attacked a large number of mounted Californians some twelve miles from San Pedro, and were repulsed, losing five men killed and six wounded. Fremont he ordered, with one hundred and sixty volunteers, to proceed to Santa Barbara, there to mount his men, and meet the commander-in-chief, who had sailed in the *Congress* for San Pedro, at Los Angeles.

Stockton effected his landing on the 23d of October, in the face of eight hundred of the enemy; but, on account of the impossibility of procuring supplies, re-embarked for San Diego. Attempting to enter that harbor, the *Congress* grounded on the bar, and just then the enemy attacked the town. Stockton landed all the men that could be spared from the ship, defeated the enemy, and saved the town.

Though victorious, it was any thing but a pleasant prospect that the commodore found there before him. There were no cattle or horses, for the enemy had taken the precaution to drive them into the interior. He sent out messengers to the south to procure some, who, after much labor, returned with one hundred and forty wretched horses and five hundred cattle. Meanwhile he heard from Fremont, who, utterly failing to procure horses at Santa Barbara, had gone up to Monterey to see what could be done there.

Stockton established a camp, built a fort, set his men to constructing bridles, saddles, and shoes, and trained them in their tactics. While thus busily engaged, on the 3d of December, a messenger arrived, announcing that Brigadier-General Kearny was approaching from the East, and desirous of opening communication with him. The same evening the commander sent off Captain Gillespie, with thirty-five men, to meet the general. Three days later another messenger came, saying that General Kearny had been defeated at San Pasqual, with the loss of eighteen men killed and as many more wounded, and the capture of one of his howitzers. He was even then surrounded by the enemy, who threatened every hour an attack.

Stockton instantly prepared, bad as was his condition for the march, to proceed with all his force to aid Kearny; but as still other messengers came in, telling a better story of the general's strength, he contented himself with sending Lieutenant Grey and two hundred and fifty men to his relief.

CHAP. XVI.

1846. Dec.

How Kearny came into this position is thus explained: He had left St. Louis under orders from the War Department to cross the continent to New Mexico and California, and, if he should conquer, to establish a civil government over them. New Mexico fell readily before his force. As he was about to move onward thence, he met Kit Carson, with letters from Stockton and Fremont, announcing that the conquest of California was already achieved. So, turning back the greater part of his troops, he proceeded with only a small detachment of dragoons as a body-guard.

At the mouth of the Gila, Lieutenant Emory, of his party, captured a horseman with the California mail for Sonora. From letters that it bore, he read that the south had risen on the conquerors, and retaken the lower country. Kearny gave little credence to the tale, though it was true enough. Still, when near San Pasqual, thirty-six miles from San Diego, he thought it prudent, in his wearied, travel-worn state, to halt until he could hear from Stockton. Mr.

Stokes, the Englishman who owned the rancho where he halted, conveyed to San Diego the message that brought Lieutenant Gillespie, on the 5th, to Kearny's camp.

Before the dawn of the next day, Kearny and Gillespie moved forward; but the Californians were up equally early, and gave them a warm reception. The Americans maintained their position; but in the conflict they lost eighteen killed and thirteen wounded, and, among the latter, both Kearny and Gillespie. They buried their dead that night, and next morning again took up their march. Encumbered as they were with their wounded, they charged upon the Californians, who came out to dispute their way, and drove them from the field. On the following morning, December 8th, the Americans found the desolate hill of San Fernando, which they occupied, besieged on all sides. They were out of supplies, sick, wounded, foot-sore. Fortunately, they obtained water on digging for it, and so were not utterly hopeless. They must have perished but for the heroism of Kit Carson, whom Kearny had turned back from the errand with which Stockton and Fremont had sent him eastward, and reserved for his guide through the desert. Carson, Lieutenant Beale, and an Indian volunteered to pierce the circle of the enemy, and convey intelligence to Stockton of their perilous situation. The desperate attempt succeeded, and on the night of the 10th, Lieutenant Grey and his dragoons came dashing up to San Fernando, at the sound of whose advance the besieging force fled, and troubled them no more.

Two days later, Kearny's party were in San Diego. The commodore received the general graciously, and tendered him the chief command. This Kearny politely declined, though he expressed his desire to command under Stockton, which, of course, was permitted him. On the 29th of December the march was commenced through the sands and over the rugged mountains that make up the hundred and thirty miles of distance between San Diego and Los Angeles; and about the same time commenced the quarrel between Kearny and Stockton, which was removed afterwards to Washington, was thoroughly ventilated on the court-martial of Fremont, and for a long time arrayed against each other the friends of these distinguished citizens. The disagreement tinges all their after proceedings on the Pacific coast, but led to no serious collision until the reconquest was completed.

The advancing forces consisted of Captain Tilghman's company of artillery, a detachment of the first regiment of dragoons, Companies A and B of the California battalion of mounted riflemen, and a detachment of sailors and ma-

CHAP. XVI.
1846.
Dec.

rines from the frigates *Congress* and *Savannah* and the ship *Portsmouth*. The horses were in such wretched condition, that Captain Turner, of the dragoons, preferred to go without them. The men wore canvas shoes of their own manufacture, and were otherwise but miserably equipped. It was in the midst of the rainy season, and whenever the line of march led them out of the sand, it took them into mud ankle deep. The draught-horses gave out so fast that half the work of dragging the guns, ammunition, and provision wagons devolved upon the men. Kit Carson and a corps of scouts kept ahead of the main body, engaging in frequent skirmishes.

1847.
Jan.

From San Luis Rey, Stockton sent a messenger to announce to Fremont his advance, and to caution him against risking an action before their forces could be joined. This messenger was dispatched on the 3d of January, but he did not reach Fremont until the 9th. Several times runners came from Flores, proposing compromises; but they were all rejected, and word sent back that if he, or any one else, who, like him, had broken his parole, should be caught, he would surely be shot.

On the 7th of January it was discovered that the enemy, apparently a thousand or twelve hundred in number, and mostly cavalry, were drawn up on the bank of the river San Gabriel, in position to command the ford. Next morning, Stockton advanced, and, when within a quarter of a mile of the river, formed his men into line, and gave orders not to fire a gun until all had crossed. The order was obeyed, though the enemy did not intermit their brisk but ineffectual discharges. As they were crossing, Kearny sent word to Stockton that the bed of the river, in which there was about four feet of water, consisted of quicksands, and that the guns could not be safely transported. "Quicksands or no quicksands," said Stockton, "the guns shall pass over," and hurried to the head of his column, took his place at the ropes, and himself assisted to drag the guns across. All over, the line of battle was again formed. Kearny charged up the bank, while Stockton gave his attention to repelling an assault upon his flank, with which the enemy, descending to the bank of the river, had visited him. The assault was repelled, and, the enemy retreating, Stockton with his artillery pushed up the declivity after them. Arrived on the heights, he found the enemy drawn up in battle array, with their artillery in front, but his well-aimed fire soon scattered them. A portion of their right wing came upon the rear of the Americans, who were guarding the baggage and cattle, but Captain Gillespie handsomely repulsed them, and drove them across the river. The main body

CHAP. XVI.
1847.
Jan.

fled towards Los Angeles, stopping occasionally to renew the defence, but always without success.

The next day, Stockton came upon them again, well posted on the plains. Here the Californians redeemed their reputation for valor. They charged gallantly upon Stockton's army, but were met with a disastrous fire. The second attack was made upon three sides of the square at once, yet it met with the same result. The third time they returned to the charge, and a third time were repulsed with loss, after which they fled in confusion.

On the 10th of January, Stockton marched into Los Angeles, and raised again the very flag that Gillespie had been compelled through the treachery of Flores to strike some three months before.

Meanwhile, Fremont from Monterey, where he was trying to get horses for his battalion, had sent news to Sutter's Fort of the disasters at the south, and begged for re-enforcements from among the settlers. Edwin Bryant and some friends scoured the country for volunteers,

1846.
Nov.

and not without success. On the 29th of November, these recruits from the north joined Fremont near San Juan Bautista, where he had gone in pursuit of a party of Californians which had taken Consul Larkin prisoner, though before his arrival the consul had been rescued.

Fremont's battalion now numbered, including Indians and servants, four hundred and twenty-eight. Excepting his original exploring party, they consisted of volunteers from the American settlements, and newly arrived emigrants, who were expert with the rifle, a few Walla-Wallas from Oregon, and some native Californians. Each man had in his leathern girdle a hunter's and a bowie knife. Each carried a rifle, holster pistols, and sometimes a brace of pocket pistols besides. The best equipped wore trousers and moccasons of buckskin, and broad-brimmed hats; the worst-supplied made blue flannel answer in place of buckskin.

The battalion was organized into eight companies of cavalry, and one of artillery which Louis McLane commanded. They drove five or six hundred mules with them, besides pack-mules loaded with baggage and provisions. They began their march southward on the 30th of November, but halted the next two days, while a party returned to the mission and brought back a hundred head of cattle, which the troops drove before them, confining them in a movable corral at night, and slaughtering from the herd as they were needed.

The rainy season had rendered the travelling

exceedingly bad, and the ground was so washed by the rains that it furnished little fodder for the cattle. The half-starved horses frequently gave out on the march, and they seldom made more than fifteen miles a day. Their cattle corral was soon empty; but happily they found sheep in plenty at the Missions of San Miguel and San Luis Obispo, whose fine cactus-hedged enclosures lay on their route.

They captured a few prisoners as they proceeded. Among these was Jesus Pico, a distinguished citizen, who had been released by Stockton on his parole, and had afterwards violated the terms of his release. For this offence he was tried by a court-martial and sentenced to be shot. The women came in procession at San Luis to intercede for his pardon, and not in vain. Colonel Fremont, with impressive deliberation, granted the pardon, and thereby, as he said on his own court-martial, won the hearts of the people.

On Christmas Day the battalion was dragging its weary way up the difficult pass of the St. Ynez Mountain. The wind was a gale, and the rain poured down. Descending the southern slope of the mountain, many horses fell into the ravines and were swept away by the flood. Others tumbled over the precipices and were killed. It was late at night before the drenched and wretched party straggled down to the foot of the mountain, and encamped on ground so saturated that all efforts to kindle a fire were useless. Next day the castaway baggage was brought down, and some of the stray animals; but there were not horses enough to left mount the men.

They entered Santa Barbara on the 27th, and remained there in camp for a week. They resumed the march on the 5th of January, 1847, and next day effected, without seeing an enemy, the narrow pass of the Rincon, where they confidently expected that the way would be disputed, as it might have been by a very small force. On the 6th, when some seven miles from the Mission of Buena Ventura, they saw sixty or seventy mounted Californians drawn up in order, but they disappeared as the battalion advanced. A little later the courier from Stockton met them, announcing that the commodore and Kearny were on the way from St. Diego to Los Angeles. On the 11th, approaching San Fernando, they met Californians, who told them that Stockton and Kearny were in Los Angeles.

Here too suddenly swarmed about them the enemy, apparently in strong force. Fremont sent them a summons to surrender. Though they would not obey that order, they did not seem indisposed to parley. So the colonel and Don Jesus Pico, his pardoned captive, and now fast friend, went out to meet their chiefs. Fremont did not know that Stockton had previously and repeatedly refused all terms to these same men. They professed to admire Fremont's clemency towards Pico, and flattered him by assurances that to him and him alone they would capitulate. Commissioners were speedily appointed from each side to negotiate, and the result of their labors was the Treaty of Couenga. By its articles the Californians agreed to surrender their artillery and public arms, to return to their homes, and assist in maintaining the public peace. The Americans agreed to protect the life and property of all Californian or Mexican officers and privates, whether they took up arms while on parole or otherwise. Equal rights were guaranteed citizens of California and of the United States. All paroles were cancelled, and their conditions annulled, and all prisoners of both parties released. The oath of allegiance was not to be required of any Mexican or Californian until a treaty of peace between Mexico and the United States was signed, and if any such Mexican or Californian desired to leave the country, he could do so without let or hindrance. The treaty, signed by Major P. B. Reading, Captain Louis McLane, and Colonel Wm. H. Russell for the Americans; and by José Antonio Carrillo and Augustin Olivera for the Californians, was approved, January 16th, by Fremont, as "Military Commandant of California," and by Andres Pico, "Commandant of Squadron and Chief of the National Forces of California." It was instantly proclaimed, as needing no further ratification, and the war was ended.

The Treaty of Couenga brought peace to the contending armies and the people, but trouble enough to the three chief agents in the conquest of the country. Fortunately, Flores, when his forces dissolved before Stockton, fled to Sonora. If he had remained it is doubtful if the commodore would have assented to the terms of the treaty. It was very natural that he should prefer to make his own stipulations with an enemy whom he had defeated. Still there the treaty was, signed, proclaimed, and under its grateful shade the late belligerents were at peace. Kearny urged its recognition, and Stockton was too shrewd to object. In fact, neither could afford just at that time to quarrel with the man who made it.

Fremont perceived the gravity of the next matter that claimed his attention, and moved deliberately. Halting still at the Couenga rancho, he sent Colonel Russell to Los Angeles to discover who was chief in command there, and to report to him. Kearny was his superior officer in the army, to a department of which he belonged. But to Stockton he was owing the authority under which he had raised his battalion and written "Military Commandant" after his name. It was a delicate matter for him to decide, and he proposed to leave it for their decision.

The messenger, returning, reported that Stockton was acting as chief, but that Kearny claimed for himself superiority. Both commanders were exceedingly complacent towards him, both tendered desirable positions, but Stockton's bid was rather the most tempting. Stockton had previously arranged to leave the country soon, and he had transmitted to Washington his intention to make Fremont governor on leaving. Kearny held that he was endowed with the functions of governor by his orders from Washington; but, if Fremont should report to him, he proposed to make him his successor at some future day.

Fremont knew that Kearny was authorized to establish a civil government in California, provided he should conquer it, as he had done in New Mexico. But Stockton and Fremont insisted that the conquest was accomplished before he crossed the plains. Or if the conquest was not complete, as these later troubles showed, it was with a bad grace that he set up to be its conqueror, who was shut up at San Pasqual, and might have starved there but for the relief that Stockton sent him.

FREMONT AS GOVERNOR. 207

To Stockton, then, Fremont reported, when on the 14th he entered Los Angeles, and by that act, as it gave him the command of the four hundred effective troops of the battalion, the commodore won the field from the general. A military tribunal has since reversed the decision, and held Fremont to blame for his choice.

Two days later, Fremont received from Stockton his commission as governor. Kearny still kindly remonstrated; but when he found his dissuasion quite in vain, he determined to arrest and punish the offender. For a little season the general's wrath was quite impotent. But, repairing to San Diego, he found that the Mormon battalion, part of the re-enforcements for Kearny's "Army of the West," which Stirling Price had brought to Santa Fé, had arrived, under Colonel St. George Cooke. Cooke reported to Kearny, who thence proceeded by sea to Monterey.

Scarcely was Kearny gone from Los Angeles, when Stockton also departed. At San Pedro he re-embarked his marines, and sailed for the Mexican coast.

So Fremont was left alone as governor. He resided in the mansion where several California governors before him had lived. His battalion he sent to San Gabriel for quarters. He enjoyed the friendship of the first families of the land. He was honored for his position, his achievements, his gentlemanly bearing. He was at peace with all men, and throughout the length and breadth of the land order prevailed. It lasted some seven weeks, and then a storm!

At Monterey Kearny found Commodore Shubrick in the *Independence,* and the two, perhaps disgusted that so young a man as Fremont should be leading so merry a life, while his elders were neither governors nor popularly regarded as conquerors, harmonized in a course that plucked the roses from his path, and strewed it with thorns. First, they sent him the copy of a proclamation, dated March 1st, 1847, signed jointly by the two, declaring that President Polk had assigned to the naval commander—that was Shubrick—the regulating of port charges; and to the military commander—that was Kearny—the functions of governor. Second, there came to him a proclamation, bearing the same date, signed by Kearny alone, telling the old story of his authority, and how he came by it, announcing the entire annexation of California to the United States, absolving all Californians from allegiance to Mexico, and continuing the Mexican laws in operation, and the existing civil officers in their offices, provided they would swear to support the Constitution of the United States.

It was not Fremont alone who was startled

by this unheralded proclamation. It abrogated the Treaty of Couenga, without so much as naming it. Californians found their citizenship transferred without the courtesy of a question asked. The man whom they had accepted at the hands of the American authorities, as their governor, after valiantly declining him, and being honorably compelled to succumb, and with whom now they were well pleased, was utterly ignored. With him went the terms of their capitulation. What next would the Americans do? Perhaps annex them to the Chinese Empire! perhaps proclaim them an integral part of the Cannibal Islands! The whole procedure seemed to them a gratuitous insult, and an incomprehensible piece of insolence, that a word from Fremont would have tempted them to repudiate.

But Fremont, though mortified beyond measure, was reasonably prudent. On the 11th of March he received orders through Kearny, which discovered to him that the Administration at Washington would side against Stockton and himself. These orders required him to muster the California battalion into the regular service, or, if they were unwilling to be so disposed of, to conduct them to San Francisco and discharge them. Moreover, he was assured that Colonel Cooke was made commandant of the southern district, with his Mormon battalion to back his authority. Here was a pretty position for a governor in good and regular standing!

Fremont was military man enough to know how to obey, though every item of these orders was a cruel stab at his authority, his pride, his self-respect. His battalion, moreover, claimed to have a will of its own. Officers and men refused to be mustered. They would be disbanded if there were no help for it, but they would like their pay for past services before even that were done.

Fremont ordered the officers to keep things as they were until his return, and then, with Jesus Pico and a solitary servant, mounted for a ride to Monterey. In three days and a half he had put some four hundred miles between him and Los Angeles. He called on General Kearny, but was refused permission to see him, except in the presence of Colonel Mason, who had arrived with instructions to relieve General Kearny, and allow Colonel Fremont to join his regiment or to pursue his intermitted explorations, as he chose. Fremont's errand was to consult with Kearny as to the payment of the battalion, but Kearny was in no consulting mood. He demanded to know if Fremont would obey him. Fremont answered that he would. "Then send those of the battalion, who refuse to be mustered, to Monterey, and come yourself by land," said his chief.

FREMONT DISOBEYS ORDERS. 211

Swiftly as he had come, Fremont returned to Los Angeles to learn that Colonel Cooke had been there in his absence, to demand the ordnance of the battalion, which, according to their orders, the officers had refused to surrender. Close on his heels came Colonel, *alias* Governor Mason, ordering Governor Fremont to embark his men for Monterey, and himself appear there twelve days afterwards.

Fremont proposed to mount his original party, with the intention of joining the regiment, of which he was a lieutenant-colonel, in Mexico. But the twelve days, the whole month of April passed, and he still lingered.

Kearny meanwhile had received new accessions to his forces. Colonel Jonathan D. Stevenson's New York Regiment of Volunteers arrived by way of Cape Horn, in four transport ships, the *Thomas H. Perkins*, *Loo-Choo*, *Susan Drew*, and *Brutus*. The three first named left New York September 26th, 1846; the *Brutus* left later. The first to arrive was the *Perkins*, March 6th, 1847.

This regiment was composed of men selected with reference to their willingness to tarry in the country, if they found it what they expected; artisans of all sorts, men versed in the arts of peace, but bearing arms, and retaining their military organization till the close of the war. Except two companies, which were sent

CHAP. XVI.

1847.
April.

to La Paz to take possession of Lower California, the regiment was distributed throughout California to garrison its chief points. They did good service as soldiers, and afterwards as civilians reflected no discredit on their origin.

Early in May, Kearny went to Los Angeles, to hasten the proceedings of his tardy subordinate. He refused Fremont permission to join his regiment, sold the horses he had collected, and ordered him instantly to repair to Monterey. There he compelled him to turn over his exploring instruments to another party. When at last Kearny was ready to go East, Fremont was obliged to keep him company, with orders to encamp at night in the rear of the Mormon guard, and never more than a mile away from the general; at Fort Leavenworth he was arrested; at Fortress Monroe, a court-martial found him guilty of mutiny, disobedience, and disorderly conduct, and sentenced him to forfeit his commission.

On this trial Fremont behaved with spirit, and pleaded his cause with an eloquence that made the people of the States reverse the decision so soon as they read the proceedings. The court recommended him to the clemency of the President, on the grounds of his past services, and the peculiar position in which he was placed when the alleged disobedience took place. Mr. Polk was not sure that the mutiny was proven, though the other charges were, and they were enough to warrant the sentence. So he approved the court's decision, discharged the culprit from arrest, and directed him to report for duty. Fremont spurned the mercy of the President, and retired from the army. The people—to them these cases go for final adjudication—pronounced it superlatively mean to visit the consequences of an irrepressible conflict between two senior officers upon a junior, who could not possibly side with both parties, and had the manliness to take the responsibility of reporting to the one he thought best entitled to his services. They saw merits in their hero that probably never would have struck them if he had not been shamefully maltreated. If he had been left quietly in California, until superseded in a regular way, probably Stockton would have been regarded as the foremost man in the conquest. But when spite dogged Fremont home, and jealousy attempted to crush him, the people pronounced him the genuine "conqueror of California," and only narrowly missed, a few years later, making him President of the United States.

CHAPTER XVII.

SAN FRANCISCO AMERICANIZED.

CHAP. XVII.
1847.

CALIFORNIA is to be congratulated on its narrow escape from a Mormon element in its population, at a time when every ship-load of people told with great power upon the shaping character of the State. A company of Mormons, from New York, under the leadership of Samuel Brannan, arrived at Yerba Buena on the 31st of July, 1846, pitched their tents at the foot of the sand-hills, and fortunately fell soon to quarrelling. Their dissensions ran so high that many of their leaders seceded. Then followed a lawsuit and a jury-trial (the first in the Territory), of which Brannan, who had been much reviled for alleged misdeeds in the office of president of the association, was the winner. These proceedings prevented the settlement of the Mormons as a community in the neighborhood. The ties that bound them together were broken. Some of them joined Fremont's battalion; some of them went into trade. Afterwards, most who retained their Mormon faith were seduced over the Sierras by the news of gold discoveries about the Salt Lake, and so California escaped the curse of Mormonism.

This little town of Yerba Buena, as people persisted in calling it until January, 1847, had, by that time, grown to be a post of three hundred inhabitants and about fifty adobe houses, and was indulging in a weekly newspaper, the *California Star*, published by Mr. Brannan, and edited by Dr. E. P. Jones. Three months later it had a second paper, Messrs. Colton and Semple's *Californian*, which was the pioneer in the country (having started at Monterey, August 15, 1846), being transferred to the more thrifty settlement.

That change of name, from *Yerba Buena* (good herb), which was balmy and unhackneyed and unique, to *San Francisco*, which was common and significant of nothing peculiar, was the fruit of an ordinance promulgated by its first alcalde; and one of its effects was to compel Mr. Larkin and Mr. Semple, who had laid out a city on the Straits of Carquinez, in expectation that it would eventually prove the chief city about the bay, to change its name from *Francisca* to *Benicia*, in honor of General Vallejo's wife.

An alcalde had a perfect right to change the name, or, indeed, to do almost any thing else that he could persuade the people to approve. He could make grants of building lots to intending settlers, with very uncertain restrictions, order affairs to suit himself, and administer justice according to his own notions of equity. He was the chief magistrate under the Mexican laws, and as yet the country enjoyed no other than Mexican laws. The first alcalde of San Francisco was Washington A. Bartlett, who did not long hold the office, being soon needed on board the naval vessel to which he was attached as lieutenant. During his administration he had Jasper O'Farrell survey and plan the city. Bartlett's temporary successor as alcalde was George Hyde, who, to judge from the court records of later times, must have been constantly occupied in making grants to applicants. After him came Edwin Bryant, appointed by General Kearny. Bryant had crossed the Plains the year before, and materially aided Fremont in raising his battalion for the conquest. He continued briefly in office, returning in June, with Kearny's party, to the States, and publishing a valuable book of his travels, entitled *What I saw in California*. The succeeding alcaldes were George Hyde (again), Dr. J. Townsend, Dr. T. M. Leavenworth, and Colonel J. W. Geary, who, as he was the last alcalde, was his own successor and the first mayor under the Americanized city charter.

It was during Hyde's second term that, because the town business grew so heavy, an ayuntamiento or town council was established, to aid in conducting it, and, once established, it continued until the boards of aldermen and assistant aldermen took its place.

The San Franciscans were chiefly Americans, and they began, before 1847 was ended, to do as all Americans do—to talk politics, to celebrate Fourth of July, observe Thanksgiving, have a steamboat on the bay, and take measures for establishing a public school. They were fond of public meetings and of uttering their sentiments in the form of resolutions. One of the earliest occasions for such a meeting during the year was notable for its object, and most creditable for its spirit and results. We condense the story from the narrative of Mr. Bryant in his book before alluded to.

Of the overland emigration to California in 1846, about eighty wagons took a new route, from Fort Bridger around the south end of Great Salt Lake. The pioneers of the party arrived in good season over the mountains; but Mr. Reed's and Mr. Donner's companies opened a new route through the desert, lost a month's time by their explorations, and reached the foot of the Truckee Pass, in the Sierra Nevada, on the 31st of October, instead of the 1st, as they had intended. The snow began to fall on the mountains two or three weeks earlier than usual that year, and was already so piled up in the

Pass that they could not proceed. They attempted it repeatedly, but were as often forced to return. One party built their cabins near Truckee Lake, killed their cattle, and went into winter-quarters. The other (Donner's) party still believed that they could thread the pass, and so failed to build their cabins before more snow came and buried their cattle alive. Of course these were soon utterly destitute of food, for they could not tell where their cattle were buried, and there was no hope of game on a desert so piled with snow that nothing without wings could move. The number of those who were thus storm-stayed, at the very threshold of the land whose winters are one long spring, was eighty, of whom thirty were females, and several children. The Mr. Donner who had charge of one company was an Illinoisian, sixty years of age, a man of high respectability and abundant means. His wife was a woman of education and refinement, and much younger than he.

During November it snowed thirteen days; during December and January, eight days in each. Much of the time the tops of the cabins were below the snow level.

It was six weeks after the halt was made that a party of fifteen, including five women and two Indians who acted as guides, set out on snow-shoes to cross the mountains, and give notice to the people of the California settlements of the condition of their friends. At first the snow was so light and feathery that even in snow-shoes they sank nearly a foot at every step. On the second day they crossed the "divide," finding the snow at the summit twelve feet deep. Pushing forward with the courage of despair, they made from four to eight miles a day.

Within a week they got entirely out of provisions, and three of them, succumbing to cold, weariness, and starvation, had died. Then a heavy snow-storm came on, which compelled them to lie still, buried between their blankets under the snow, for thirty-six hours. By the evening of the tenth day three more had died, and the living had been four days without food. The horrid alternative was accepted—they took the flesh from the bones of their dead, remained in camp two days to dry it, and then pushed on.

On New Year's, the sixteenth day since leaving Truckee Lake, they were toiling up a steep mountain. Their feet were frozen. Every step was marked with blood. On the second of January their food again gave out. On the third, they had nothing to eat but the strings of their snow-shoes. On the fourth, the Indians eloped, justly suspicious that they might be sacrificed for food. On the fifth, they shot a deer, and that day one of their number died.

CHAP. XVII.
1847.

Soon three others died, and every death now eked out the existence of the survivors. On the seventeenth all gave out, and concluded their wanderings useless, except one. He, guided by two stray, friendly Indians, dragged himself on till he reached a settlement on Bear River. By midnight the settlers had found and were treating with all Christian kindness what remained of the little company that, after more than a month of the most terrible sufferings, had that morning halted to die.

The story that there were emigrants perishing on the other side of the snowy barrier ran swiftly down the Sacramento Valley to New Helvetia, and Captain Sutter, at his own expense, fitted out an expedition of men and of mules laden with provisions, to cross the mountains and relieve them. It ran on to San Francisco, and the people, rallying in public meeting, raised fifteen hundred dollars, and with it fitted out another expedition. The naval commandant of the port fitted out still others.

The first of the relief parties reached Truckee Lake on the 19th of February. Ten of the people in the nearest camp were dead. For four weeks those who were still alive had fed only on bullocks' hides. At Donner's camp they had but one hide remaining. The visitors left a small supply of provisions with the twenty-nine whom they could not take with them, and started back with the remainder. Four of the children they carried on their backs.

Another of the relief parties reached Truckee Lake on the 1st of March. They immediately started back with seventeen of the sufferers, but, a heavy snow-storm overtaking them, they left all, except three of the children, on the road. Another party went after those who were left on the way, found three of them dead, and the rest sustaining life by feeding on the flesh of the dead.

The last relief party reached Donner's camp late in April, when the snows had melted so much that the earth appeared in spots. The main cabin was empty, but some miles distant they found the last survivor of all, lying on the cabin-floor smoking his pipe. He was ferocious in aspect, savage and repulsive in manner. His camp-kettle was over the fire, and in it his meal of human flesh preparing. The stripped bones of his fellow-sufferers lay around him. He refused to return with the party, and only consented when he saw that there was no escape.

Mrs. Donner was the last to die. Her husband's body, carefully laid out and wrapped in a sheet, was found at his tent. Circumstances led to the suspicion that the survivor had killed Mrs. Donner for her flesh and her money, and when he was threatened with hanging, and the rope tightened around his neck, he produced over five hundred dollars in gold, which probably he had appropriated from her store.

When General Kearny returned to the East, in June, 1847, he halted at the scene of these terrible sufferings. By his orders the mummied remains of the dead were buried, and all the relics of the cabins gathered and burned. Of the eighty who were thus arrested at the eastern foot of the Truckee Pass, forty-four were saved, of whom twenty-two were females. Thirty-six perished.

Another subject which a public meeting was called in San Francisco to consider was the dethroned idol of the populace, Fremont. That distinguished ex-governor left a people behind him divided as to his merits. It was presumed that California would soon be erected by Congress into a territory of the United States, and a petition was in circulation asking the President to appoint Fremont as its governor. This petition had been numerously signed at the South, for there he was popular. His treaty of Couenga, the easy terms he had allowed to those who broke their parole, all his intercourse with the first families of the country, made him a favorite.

But when the petition came North it was the signal for an angry controversy. Fremont's most bitter enemies were his lately devoted soldiers, the disbanded battalion of mounted riflemen, and those whom he had favored with contracts. He was in arrears to the latter for his army outfit and supplies, and to the volunteers for their pay. Personally, he had no funds to draw upon. Kearny would not strain a point to relieve the embarrassment of one who had denied his authority, nor would Mason either employ the ample resources of the country to pay debts contracted before his day, or without the previous sanction of Congress grant-warrants upon the Treasury. Kearny's repudiation of him, and Mason's refusal to recognize the authority of "the Pathfinder," led the malcontents to feel that he was not simply a penniless debtor, but a swindler as well. So they called a public meeting— there is no surer sign that they were thoroughly Americanized—and expressed their indignation. The meeting appointed a committee to investigate and publish all reliable instances of his misconduct, and by resolution protested against his appointment as governor.

Meanwhile the subject of all this indignation, dispirited and unhappy, was about a month on his way across the plains, whose pathless deserts and difficult passes he had done more than any other man to describe and map. He who had always been foremost of his company, rode now behind and in disgrace.

San Francisco was fast outgrowing in importance the older towns of the coast. In March, 1848, its population numbered over eight hundred. Two wharves were being constructed. A public school had been opened.' The unoccupied fifty-vara lots, into which O'Farrell's survey divided the land north of Market Street, were granted by the alcalde to any who petitioned for them and paid, including the cost of recording, sixteen dollars a lot; while those southerly of Market Street, each by the survey one hundred varas square, cost to the petitioner twenty-nine dollars. The city, on the maps, embraced Telegraph and Rincon Hills, the land between, and the area westward to about two miles from the waterfront. Yet really it nestled along the beach, and encroached very little either on the sandhills or the rocky heights that overhang the bay. But there was already about it the busy hum of an American town. All felt that its rapid growth was predestined. It must soon become a notable mart. Every week added to its population. Its thrift was the theme of every day's discourse.

Suddenly its streets were deserted, its business stopped, its infant commerce was paralyzed. The desertion was as instant and complete as if a pestilence had swept over the peninsula— and not in San Francisco alone, but every little village in the province shared the sudden depopulation. The people were all flying eastward and northward, to the foot-hills of the Sierra Nevada!

The *Californian* issued an extra, apologizing for the non-appearance of its regular edition. "The whole country," said its editor in his farewell, "from San Francisco to Los Angeles, resounds with the sordid cry of 'Gold.'" The *California Star* held out a fortnight longer, when, everybody in his office having deserted him, the editor announced that he must stop its issue.

15

CHAPTER XVIII.

THE DISCOVERY OF GOLD.

CHAP.
XVIII.
1848.
Jan. 19

Gold was discovered at Coloma, on the American River, January 19th, 1848, and the most skeptical and phlegmatic, by the middle of the following spring, were yielding to its attractions. Governor Mason left Monterey on the 17th of June to visit the place, and the account that he wrote home to the War Department created a great sensation.

He alleged that the land was full of gold. "I have no hesitation in saying," he wrote, " that there is more gold in the country drained by the Sacramento and San Joaquin Rivers, than will pay the costs of the late war in Mexico a hundred times over. Nearly all the Mormons," he added, " are leaving California to go to Salt Lake, and this they surely would not do unless they were sure of finding gold there in the same abundance as they now do on the Sacramento."

This was remarked as if quite incidentally; but to many people at the East, the governor knew that the departure of the Mormons out of the land would be scarcely less welcome news than the mineral discoveries. Again, but not as if the matter much affected him, Governor Mason mentioned a visit to the New Almaden quicksilver mine of Alexander Forbes, the British Consul. The mining world appreciated the point, and observed that quicksilver, so necessary to every gold-miner, was produced abundantly within easy reach of the gold-fields. Finally, the governor said, "No capital is required to obtain the gold, as the laboring-man wants nothing but his pick and shovel, and tin pan, with which to dig and wash the gravel, and many frequently pick gold out of the crevices of rocks with their butcher-knives, in pieces of from one to six ounces!"

The party in the States which had opposed the Administration of Mr. Polk in the Mexican war, ridiculed mercilessly the whole story of the gold discovery. This last statement, they thought, must break the back of the camel credulity. It was too much like reproducing one of De Foe's imaginary adventures in South America, to be for one moment believed by sober men on the Atlantic slope.

Yet it was substantially and literally true. Let us follow the governor on his tour, as detailed in his letter to the War Department:—

He found San Francisco deserted of nearly

CHAP. VIII.

1848. June.

all its male inhabitants, and even females were very scarce there. Between Sonoma and Sutter's Fort the mills were idle; the fields of wheat open to cattle; the houses vacant; the farms going to waste. At Sutter's there was much life and bustle. Flour was selling at thirty-six dollars a barrel, and the captain was carefully gathering his crops of wheat, estimated at forty thousand bushels. Several stores had been established, and a hotel erected. Cargoes were being discharged at the river-side, and carts were hauling goods to the fort. The captain had two mechanics in his employ, to each of whom he paid ten dollars a day. A two-story house in the fort was rented as a hotel, at five hundred dollars a month.

July.

On the 5th of July he pushed up the American fork of the Sacramento some twenty-five miles, where he found a mining camp in full operation. Canvas tents and arbors of bushes strewed the hill-side. There was a store opened, and several shanties were used as boarding-houses. The sun poured down its rays with intense heat upon two hundred miners working for gold, some using tin pans, some Indian baskets, and some rude cradles. Going farther up the American, he reached the spot, fifty miles above Sutter's Fort, where the gold was first found.

The people at work there were averaging

from one to three ounces of gold a day. At eight miles above Weber's Creek, the governor was shown a small gutter where two men had taken out seventeen thousand dollars worth of gold. At the end of one week's work they had paid off their party of hired men and found ten thousand dollars worth left in their hands. He saw a small ravine out of which twelve thousand dollars had been taken. "Hundreds of similar ravines, to all appearances, were as yet untouched." Men who were getting fifty dollars a day were leaving because they could do better at other places. Three miles above Sutter's, on the American, he met a Mr. Sinclair, who employed fifty Indians for five weeks, and showed, as his net proceeds, gold to the value of sixteen thousand dollars: the last week's results were fourteen pounds avoirdupois of gold. A soldier got a furlough of twenty days from the artillery company to which he belonged. He spent most of it in travelling, but one week in mining, during which week he made fifteen hundred dollars—more than all his pay, clothes, and rations for the five years of his enlistment.

All prices were enormous, of course, yet the treasure was so plenty that even Indians could sport gaudily-colored dresses. The most moderate estimate that the governor could obtain was, that four thousand men were working in the gold district, more than half of whom were Indians, and that from thirty thousand to fifty thousand dollars worth of gold were taken out daily. Astonishing to relate, crime was infrequent in the mines. There were no thefts or robberies, though all lived in tents or bush arbors, or in the open air, and the workmen frequently had thousands of dollars worth of dust about their persons.

Such statements as these, coming from an official source, and presented to Congress with the report of the Secretary of War, could not but stir the country to its remotest corners.

In Hakluyt's account of Drake's visit to the California coast, in 1579, occurs the following statement concerning its mineral wealth:— "There is no part of the earth here to be taken up wherein there is not a reasonable quantity of gold and silver." There is little reason to believe that this assertion was based upon any knowledge of the fact averred. Yet the Spaniards and Mexicans who visited the Californias saw the indications of gold in the soil. In the vicinity of the Colorado they found the precious metal itself. So, though they did not find it in paying quantities, the impression went abroad that it was a mineral region, and a vague suspicion of the truth perhaps crossed the minds of American politicians who plotted and log-rolled to annex a slice of Mexico to the Union. Indeed, President Polk, in his Message of 1848, said that it was known that mines of precious metals existed to a considerable extent in California at the time of its acquisition.

But Alexander Forbes, in 1835, wrote, "No minerals of particular importance have yet been found in Upper California, nor any ores of metals;" and speaking of Hijar's emigrants who arrived in 1833, he said there were among them "goldsmiths, proceeding to a country where no gold existed."

There are reports that silver was discovered in Alizal, Monterey County, in 1802, and gold in San Isidro, San Diego County, in 1828. A place on the San Francisquito Cañon, forty-five miles northward from Los Angeles, discovered in 1838, was worked till 1848, yielding an average of six thousand dollars a year. These meagre hints of the presence of precious metals were only sufficient to warm the fancy of sanguine prophets of the future of the land, but they did not affect the popular sentiment or excite general attention.

The wonder is now that the discovery was not earlier made. Emigrants, settlers, hunters, practical miners, scientific exploring parties had camped on, settled in, hunted through, dug in, and explored the region, and could not see it. Professor Dana, the geologist of Wilkes's exploring expedition, did say that gold rocks and veins of quartz were observed by him in 1842, near the Umpqua River in Oregon, and pebbles from similar rocks were met with along the shores of the Sacramento; and when speaking of places where gold was to be found, he mentions "California, between the Sierra Nevada and the Sacramento and San Joaquin Rivers." But it is very doubtful whether it occurred to Professor Dana that there was gold to be found here in quantities that would ever get into more practical use than to lie as rare specimens behind plate-glass doors in the mineralogical cabinets of the colleges.

The discovery was entirely accidental. Captain Sutter had contracted with James W. Marshall, in September, 1847, for the construction of a saw-mill at Coloma. In the course of the winter a dam and race were made, but when the water was let on, the tail-race was too narrow. To widen and deepen it, Marshall let a strong current of water directly into the race, which bore a large body of mud and gravel to the foot.

On the 19th of January, 1840, Marshall observed some glittering particles in the race, which he was curious enough to examine. He called five carpenters who were at work on the mill to see them, but though they talked over the possibility of its being gold, the vision did not inflame them. Peter L. Weimar claims that he was with Marshall when the first piece of the "yellow stuff" was picked up. It was a pebble weighing six pennyweights and eleven grains. Marshall gave it to Mrs. Weimar, and asked her to boil it in saleratus water and see what came of it. As she was making soap at the time, she pitched it into the soap-kettle. About twenty-four hours afterwards it was fished out and found all the brighter for its boiling.

Marshall, two or three weeks later, took the specimens below, and gave them to Sutter to have them tested. Before Sutter had quite satisfied himself as to their nature, he went up to the mill, and with Marshall made a treaty with the Indians, buying of them their titles to the region round about, for a certain amount of goods. There was an effort made to keep the secret inside the little circle that knew it, but it soon leaked out. They had many misgivings and much discussion whether they were not making themselves ridiculous, yet by common consent all began to hunt, though with no great spirit, for the "yellow stuff" that might prove such a prize.

In February, one of the party went to Yerba Buena, taking some of the dust with him. Fortunately he stumbled upon Isaac Humphrey, an old Georgian gold-miner, who, at the first look at the specimens, said they were gold, and that the diggings must be rich. Humphrey tried to induce some of his friends to go up with him to the mill, but they thought it a crazy expedition, and left him to go alone. He reached there on the 7th of March. A few were hunting for gold, but rather lazily, and the work on the mill went on as usual. Next day he began "prospecting," and soon satisfied himself that he had struck a rich placer. He made a rocker, and then commenced work in earnest.

A few days later a Frenchman, Baptiste, formerly a miner in Mexico, left the lumber he was sawing for Sutter at Weber's, ten miles east of Coloma, and came to the mill. He agreed with Humphrey that the region was rich, and like him took to the pan and the rocker. These two men were the competent practical teachers of the crowd that flocked in to see how they did it. The lesson was easy, the process simple. An hour's observation fitted the least experienced for working to advantage.

CHAPTER XIX.

GRAND RUSH TO CALIFORNIA.

About a month after the gold discovery, but before it was much bruited, an armistice between the United States and Mexico was agreed upon. The treaty of peace which followed was ratified by the United States in March, by Mexico in May.

CHAP. XIX.
1848. Feb.

The news reached California late in the summer, and was honored with illuminations, the explosion of some gunpowder, and processions. The terms of the treaty were satisfactory to the war party. In consideration of the assumption by the United States of the Mexican debt to American subjects, and of fifteen millions of money, the free navigation of the Colorado, from the mouth of the Gila to the Gulf, and of the Gulf itself, and all right and title to Texas, New Mexico and Upper California were ceded to the United States. Lower California, much to the disgust of Captain Halleck and other military men, who had been at pains to hold it while the war lasted, was left with Mexico. It was despised as an arid, barren, worthless peninsula.

Aug.

CHAP. XIX.
1848.

The opponents of the Administration held the treaty to be a very fit conclusion for a demoralizing and unnecessary war. It paid an enormous price, they said, for what we were a great deal better without. It annexed an immense territory that we did not need, and, worst feature of all, that territory was populous with Indians, of whom we had more on our hands than we had yet learned to take care of, and with drowsy Mexicans, who never could be worked over into American citizens, or brought into harmony with American ideas. If they knew it, they gave little heed to the fact that there were already from twelve to fifteen thousand whites in California, and there was no seer to foretell the revolution that was about to sweep through every settlement in the Union, when the news should reach it of how those whites in California were employing themselves.

The story of the great gold discoveries in California crept slowly into the faith of the people of the Union, but once there, the whole lump was soon leavened. The President indorsed, in a measure, the truth of the reports of army and navy officers on the Pacific coast, by sending them with the documents accompanying his message to Congress. They were printed in the newspapers, and became the topic of Congressional debate, and soon every rural district was echoing those debates. Specimens of the gold were exhibited in the cities, inflaming the imagination of the coolest. The whole land experienced a new sensation.

Some of the New York papers said the gold was mica; but as an offset to these opinions was the announcement of Director Patterson, of the Philadelphia Mint, that the first deposits of gold from California were worth eighteen dollars and five and a half cents per ounce. Colonel Benton said in the Senate: "I am a friend to a gold currency, but not to gold mining... I regret that we have these mines in California, but they are there, and I am for getting rid of them as soon as possible." Again he said, "The gold in these washings is a temporary crop—a mine is one thing, a wash is another." The gold washings of California, or *placers* —called so, he said, from the Latin *placere*, to please, because there was a very lively short-lived pleasure experienced when a man finds one of them—were marvellously rich, yet not so rich as those of Brazil, a hundred years ago, which were exhausted so long since that all memory of them is lost.

But soon the California fever was raging like an epidemic in every section—even in those rare spots where migration was discouraged by the example of a couple of centuries, it swept through like an influenza. High and low, rich

CHAP. XIX.
1848–1849.

and poor took it. They could actually pick the gold out from the crevices of the rocks with their knives! Then it required no more capital to get all the gold that a modest man ought to wish, than one's passage-money and his bare living at the mines! Had a family man the right to plod all his life, and die at last leaving those dependent on him with a mere pittance, when a little energy, or a year or two of "roughing it in the mines," would give him, and those he lived for, a competency?

Before such considerations as these, the conservatism of the most stable bent. Men of small means, whose tastes inclined them to keep out of all hazardous schemes and uncertain enterprises, thought they saw duty beckoning them around the Horn, or across the plains. In many a family circle, where nothing but the strictest economy could make the two ends of the year meet, there were long and anxious consultations, which resulted in selling off a piece of the homestead or of the woodland, or the choicest of the stock, to fit out one sturdy representative to make a fortune for the family. Hundreds of farms were mortgaged to buy tickets to the land of gold. Some insured their lives and pledged their policies for an outfit. The wild boy was packed off hopefully. The black sheep of the flock was dismissed with a blessing, and the forlorn hope that, with a change of skies, there might be a change of manners. The stay of the happy household said, "Good-by, but only for a year or two," to his charge. Unhappy husbands availed themselves cheerfully of this cheap and reputable method of divorce, trusting time to mend or mar matters in their absence. Here was a chance to begin life anew. Whoever had begun it badly, or made slow headway on the right course, might start again in a region where Fortune had not learned to coquette with and dupe her wooers.

CHAP. XIX. 1849.

The adventurers generally formed companies, expecting to go overland or by sea to the mines, and to dissolve partnership only after a first trial of luck together in the "diggings." In the Eastern and Middle States they would buy up an old whaling-ship, just ready to be condemned to the wreckers, put in a cargo of such stuff as they must need themselves, and provisions, tools, or goods, that must be sure to bring returns enough to make the venture profitable. Of course, the whole fleet rushing in together through the Golden Gate, made most of these ventures profitless, even when the guess was happy as to the kind of supplies needed by the Californians. It can hardly be believed what sieves of ships started, and how many of them actually made the voyage. Little river-steamers, that had scarcely tasted salt water before, were fitted out to thread the Straits of Magellan, and these were welcomed to the bays and rivers of California, whose waters some of them ploughed and vexed busily for years afterwards.

Then steamers, as well as all manner of sailing vessels, began to be advertised to run to the Isthmus; and they generally went crowded to excess with passengers, some of whom were fortunate enough, after the toilsome ascent of the Chagres River, and the descent either on mules or on foot to Panama, not to be detained more than a month waiting for the crafts that had rounded the Horn, and by which they were ticketed to proceed to San Francisco. But hundreds broke down under the horrors of the voyage in the steerage, contracted on the Isthmus the low typhoid fevers incident to tropical marshy regions, and died.

The overland emigrants, unless they came too late in the season to the Sierras, seldom suffered as much, as they had no great variation of climate on their route. They had this advantage, too, that the mines lay at the end of their long road, while the sea faring, when they landed, had still a weary journey before them. Few tarried longer at San Francisco than was necessary to learn how utterly useless were the curious patent mining contrivances they had brought, and to replace them with the pick, shovel, pan, and cradle. If any one found himself destitute of funds to go farther, there was work enough to raise them by. Labor was honorable, and the daintiest dandy, if he were honest, could not resist the temptation to work where wages were so high, pay so prompt, and employers so flush.

There were not lacking in San Francisco grumblers who had tried the mines and satisfied themselves that it cost about a dollar's worth of sweat and time, and living exclusively on bacon, beans, and "slap-jacks," to pick a dollar's worth of gold out of rock, or river-bed, or dry ground; but they confessed that the good luck which they never enjoyed, abode with others. Then the display of dust, slugs, and bars of gold in the public gambling-places—the sight of men arriving every day freighted with belts full, which they parted with so freely as men only can when they have got it easily—the testimony of the miniature rocks—the solid nuggets brought down from above every few days, whose size and value rumor multiplied according to the number of her tongues—the talk day and night unceasingly and exclusively of "gold, easy to get and hard to hold," inflamed all new-comers with the desire to hurry on and share the chances. They chafed at the necessary detentions. They nervously feared that all would be gone before they should arrive.

The prevalent impression was, that the placers would give out in a year or two. Then it behooved him who expected to gain much to be among the earliest on the ground. Where experiment was so fresh in the field, one theory was about as good as another. An hypothesis that lured men perpetually farther up the gorges of the foot-hills, and to explore the cañons of the mountains, was this: that the gold which had been found in the beds of rivers, or in gulches, through which streams once ran, must have been washed down from the places of original deposits farther up the mountains. The higher up the gold-hunter went, then, the nearer he approached the source of supply.

To reach the mines from San Francisco, the course lay up San Pablo and Suisun Bays, and the Sacramento, not then as now a yellow, muddy stream, but a river pellucid and deep, to the landing for Sutter's Fort; and they who made the voyage in sailing vessels thought Mount Diablo significantly named, so long it kept them company and swung its shadow over their path. From Sutter's, the most common route was across the broad, fertile valley to the foot-hills, and up the American or some one of its tributaries; or, ascending the Sacramento to the Feather and the Yuba, the company staked off a claim, pitched its tent or constructed a cabin, and set up its rocker, or began to oust the river from a portion of its bed. Good luck might hold the impatient adventurers for a whole season on one bar; bad luck scattered them always farther up.

So it was not gradually, but almost simultaneously, that the settlement of the northern mining region was effected. The great trouble was the excess of water in the winter, and its deficiency in the summer. But the mountains where the branches of the San Joaquin rise being farther south, are covered with a thinner mantle of snow than those that feed the Sacramento, and consequently those southern rivers never rage with such tumultuous floods. It required but a year's experience to discover that the mines of the south could be best worked during the wet weather, when the northern ones were impracticable. So, though the more sober and persevering stuck by the bars that paid them, and spent the months when they could not get out gold, in constructing flumes and dams that would put the water henceforth under their control, the fluctuating population alternated like a tide between the northern mines in the summer and the southern in the winter.

Roads sought the mining camps, which did not stop to study roads. Traders came in to supply the camps, and, not very fast, but still to some extent, mechanics and farmers to sup-

CHAP. XIX.
1849.

ply both traders and miners; so, as if by magic, within a year or two after the rush began, the map of the country was written thick with the names of settlements.

Some of these were the nuclei of towns that now flourish and promise to continue as long as the State is peopled. Others, in districts where the placers were soon exhausted, were deserted almost as hastily as they were begun, and now no traces remain of them except the short chimney-stack, the broken surface of the ground, heaps of cobble-stones, rotting half-buried sluice-boxes, empty whiskey bottles, scattered playing-cards, and rusty cans.

1849–1850.

The "fall of '49 and spring of '50" is the era of California history, which the pioneer always speaks of with warmth. It was the free-and-easy age, when everybody was flush, and fortune, if not in the palm, was only just beyond the grasp of all. Men lived chiefly in tents, or in cabins scarcely more durable, and behaved themselves like a generation of bachelors. The family was beyond the mountains; the restraints of society had not yet arrived. Men threw off the masks they had lived behind, and appeared out in their true character. A few did not discharge the consciences and convictions they brought with them. More rollicked in a perfect freedom from those bonds which good men cheerfully assume in settled society for the good of the greater number. Some afterwards resumed their temperate and steady habits; but hosts were wrecked before the period of their license expired.

Very rarely did men on their arrival in the country begin to work at their old trade or profession. To the mines first. If fortune favored, they soon quit for more congenial employments. If she frowned, they might depart disgusted, if they were able; but oftener, from sheer inability to leave the business, they kept on, drifting from bar to bar, living fast, reckless, improvident, half-civilized lives; comparatively rich to-day, poor to-morrow; tormented with rheumatisms and agues; remembering dimly the joys of the old homestead; nearly weaned from the friends at home, who, because they were never heard from, soon became like dead men in their memory; seeing little of women, and nothing of churches; self-reliant, yet satisfied that there was nowhere any "show" for them; full of enterprise in the direct line of their business, and utterly lost on the threshold of any other; genial companions, morbidly craving after newspapers; good fellows, but short-lived. In fifteen years almost the whole generation of pioneer miners who remained in that business has passed away, and the survivors feel like old men among the crowds of new-comers, who may be just as old, but lack their long, strange chapter of adventures.

This heterogeneous mixture of men was either without law, or were the makers and executors of their own law. Most of the companies that left the East together quarrelled and dissolved partnership, but they had very little litigation about it. Generally equity ruled in the division, for all men claimed equality, and public sentiment was sharp for the right. Theft was a crime little known, but, when discovered, the penalty was as swift as it was terrible. Lynch-law was substantially the criminal code of the mines. Its severity held crime in check, but some frightful mistakes were made as to the objects of its stern sentences.

As to civil law, the country was utterly at sea. It had a governor in the person of the commandant of the military district it belonged to, but no government. The authority by which the governor held his power was doubtful and anomalous. While the war lasted, California, as a conquered province, expected to be governed by military officers, who, by virtue of their command of the Department, bore sway over all the territory that their Department embraced. But after peace had come, and the succession of military governors was not abated, a people who had been in the habit of governing themselves under the same flag and the same constitution, chafed that a simple change of longitude should deprive them of their inalienable rights.

General Persifer F. Smith, who assumed command on arriving by the *California*, the first steamship that reached San Francisco (February 28th, 1849), and General Riley, who succeeded him (April 13th, 1849), would have been acceptable governors enough, if the people could have discovered anywhere in the Constitution that the President had power to govern a territory by a simple order to the commandant of a military department. The power was obvious in time of war, but in peace it was unprecedented. Left entirely to themselves, the people could have organized a squatter sovereignty, as Oregon had done, and the way into the sisterhood of States was clear.

They felt that they had cause for complaint, but in truth they were quite too busy to nurse their grievance and make much of it. To some extent they formed local governments, and had unimportant collisions with the military. But busy as they were, and expecting to return home soon, they humored their contempt for politics, and left public matters to be shaped at Washington. Nor was that so unwise a course under the circumstances, for the thing that had hindered Congress from giving them a legitimate constitutional government was the ever-present snag in the current of American political history, the author of most of our woes, the great mother of mischief on the Western continent—Slavery.

CHAPTER XX.

CONGRESS FAILS TO PROVIDE A GOVERNMENT.

President Polk had asked the Twenty-ninth Congress to place at his disposal three millions of dollars to be used in negotiating for a boundary which would give to the United States additional territory. To a bill granting him a portion of that sum, David Wilmot moved his famous "proviso," that no part of the territory to be acquired should be open to the introduction of slavery. The proviso was adopted in the House, and that killed the bill itself in the Senate. Giddings said, "We sought to extend and perpetuate slavery in a peaceful manner by the annexation of Texas; now we are about to effect that object by war and conquest." They said Giddings could see slavery where nobody else dreamed of it, but none were so blind as not to see that the slavery question was the substance and spirit of the whole controversy about acquiring California and other territory from Mexico.

At the next session (1847), the three millions were appropriated. Thomas Corwin notified the Senate that they were paying dear for California. If the war terminated in any thing short of a mere wanton waste of blood and money, it must end in the acquisition of territory to which the slavery controversy must attach. "Should we prosecute this war another moment, or expend one dollar in the purchase or conquest of a single acre of Mexican land, the North and the South would be brought into collision on a point where neither would yield."

Calhoun attempted to meet the case with a new dogma. He moved resolutions declaring in effect that Congress had no right to prohibit slavery in a territory, and that the exercise of such a power was a breach of the Constitution leading to the subversion of the Union. "Your dogma admitted," said Colonel Benton, "the Free Soilers have nothing to fear, and the Slave Soilers nothing to fear from the admission of California. By a fundamental law of the Mexican Republic slavery is prohibited throughout its political jurisdiction. The prohibition was proclaimed by President Guerrero in 1829. An act of the Mexican Congress declared slavery abolished in 1837, and in 1844 the Constitution forbade it forever. Then if you take California for a part of your territory, you take her free, and if Congress, as you say, has no power to legislate upon slavery in the territories, the slavery question has nothing to do with the question of acquiring land."

Calhoun's resolutions never came to a vote. He and his party soon chose a different ground, and the battle between the giants of the Senate was set with California as the guerdon. California with slavery would have been welcomed to the Union by the South. Without slavery, she was coveted by the North. Change the terms, and neither would consent to receive her. Indeed, there was a small minority, mostly composed of conservative Whigs, who cherished the Grecian statesman's advice—"You have a Sparta—improve it,"—and they protested that to enlarge our boundaries in any direction, or at any price, would be a damage to the commonwealth.

As the prospects of making California a Slave State faded, Calhoun asked, "Is there any man here who would give for her fifteen millions of money?" Benton thought better of this land, of which he knew more. Dix appreciated its value to American commerce; but was sure the North would spurn it if slavery were to be introduced by American law upon soil rendered forever free by Mexican law. None dreamed that the region about which they haggled so long would be producing and exporting, within a few years, gold enough to pay the price, which Calhoun thought so extravagant, twice over every twelve months. The negro question effectually closed the golden gate that year, and Congress adjourned without taking any steps towards opening it.

In the spring of 1848 the treaty of peace was signed by which California was annexed to the United States. How to govern this new territory sorely exercised Congress; and the debate on the subject raged with violence until the 12th of July, when Senator Clayton moved a committee of eight—half Northerners, half Southerners, half Whigs, half Democrats—to consider all the measures proposed. The resolution prevailed, and the committee was appointed—Clayton, chairman; Calhoun, Bright, Clark of Rhode Island, Atchison, Phelps, D. S. Dickinson, and Underwood of Kentucky. In committee, the South favored extending the Missouri Compromise line to the Pacific; but the North opposed it. The chairman was finally ordered to draft a compromise bill establishing the territorial governments of Oregon, California, and New Mexico, and submitting all questions as to the rightful existence or extension of slavery in these territories to the decision of the United States Supreme Court. The bill was reported, argued, urged, fought, and finally ordered engrossed by *ayes* thirty-three, *noes* twenty-two—Dix, Hale, Hamlin, and Corwin voting *no*. This victory for the South was accomplished by means of a memorable session of twenty hours, the majority achieving its purpose, and the Senate adjourning at seven minutes of eight o'clock on Thursday morning, July 27th.

But the victory was barren. The House, receiving the bill, tabled it by a vote of one hundred and twelve to ninety-seven—three-fourths of those voting to kill the bill by tabling it being Northern men.

Meanwhile President Polk had, by message, called the attention of Congress to the ample indemnity that California gave for the past. He had dwelt on the value of the public lands of California, on the safety of her harbors, on the rich Eastern commerce that she insured, on the new markets she would furnish, on the increased tonnage she would require, and the enhanced revenue that she must return.

When Congress adjourned without taking a step for the government of the newly acquired territory, President Polk, through his Secretary of State, James Buchanan, dispatched a letter to the Pacific coast to assure the people how matters stood. The Administration's doctrine was, that the Californians had a government *de facto*. To that they were advised to submit. Their consent to it would be presumed so long as they submitted, and there need be no question by what authority the officers of the army were governing them.

Now, Colonel Benton held that the right to issue letters expository and of advice was not exclusively with Secretaries of State or Presidents; so he, too, wrote a letter to the Californians, and sent it by the hands of Colonel Fremont. He assured them that by the treaty they were United States citizens, competent to govern themselves. He pronounced the edicts of Governors Mason and Kearny, "each an ignoramus," null and void. He warmly recommended that they call a convention and provide themselves with a governor, with judges, and with peace and militia officers.

President Polk's message to Congress, on its reassembling, December, 1848, recommended the establishment of a mint at San Francisco, and called attention again to the necessity of erecting some form of government for the country.

Senator Douglas sprang to the work so eagerly, and persisted in it so well, that it was said of him, by way of ridicule, that he had a special mission to give California a government. On the very first day of the session he gave notice that he would introduce a bill for the admission of California as a State. On the seventh the bill was forthcoming. He despaired, he said, of making it a Territory—three several bills to that effect having failed during the preceding session. Now, he proposed that all the region acquired by treaty from Mexico be admitted as one State, with two judicial districts, Congress reserving the right to receive other States out of that portion of it east of the Sierra Nevada. Afterwards, he proposed an amendment, authorizing the judges to lay off the land into districts, and provide for the election of delegates to a constitutional convention.

This bill was referred to the Judiciary Committee, which—Mr. Downs, of Louisiana, alone dissenting—reported adversely upon it. The report argued that the Constitution provided only for the admission, not for the creation of States; that the proviso that Congress should reserve the right to carve out from a State, once admitted, other States, was void, and the bill would inevitably lead to litigation between Texas and California, which the Supreme Court must eventually decide, with all the delay incident to such investigations. The committee recommended that, instead of one State, the newly acquired region be erected into two territories.

Mr. Douglas, foiled by the Judiciary, managed to get his bill referred to a select committee, composed of Senators Johnson, Jones, Clayton, Jefferson Davis, Badger, and Niles, with himself as chairman, which promptly reported a bill erecting the territory into the two States of California and New Mexico.

CHAP. XX.
1849.

In the course of the discussions that arose upon these several bills, some notable things were said. Mr. Downs urged that California should be brought into the Union at once, lest, delaying, she might never come in. Mr. Butler pictured the surprise these Californians would feel, waking up and finding themselves a sovereign State, without asking for it.

Mr. Dayton objected that there was not population enough, nor were the people of the right sort to be admitted with safety. The substratum of population consisted of some twelve or fifteen thousand people of Spanish origin, retired officers, retired soldiers, the remnants of the old Franciscan missions. Not as many more were on their way thither by sea and a few overland, who did not propose to stay. They were heterogeneous, crazy about gold, indifferent to government. "You would have to lasso your members to get them to a constitutional convention. My word for it," said he,

in the course of one or two years your ships will return laden with more gold-diggers than gold-dust."

Mr. Webster said they could do little more there than keep the peace; it was impracticable to administer revenue laws. A military government there for the present would be the best for the people, and the only safe course for the whole country.

But all the efforts of the "Little Giant" of Illinois to push his bill forward were in vain. In the House, a territorial bill for California passed, and Washington Hunt reported, from the Finance Committee, a bill to extend the United States revenue laws over Upper California; but that failed. Then, almost in despair, attempts were made to attach amendments, that would secure a lawful collection of the revenue at San Francisco, to the army bill, and to the civil and diplomatic appropriation bills. At one time, Robert C. Schenck, a Whig, from Ohio, proposed to cede back to Mexico all California and New Mexico, if she would allow us twelve millions of dollars on account; though if she would permit us to keep San Francisco, three millions of dollars were at her service as remuneration for the gift. This astonishing proposal, having been amended somewhat, actually passed the committee of the whole House —*ayes* eighty-five, *noes* eighty-one. When it was reported to the House, however, and the ayes and noes called, it was rejected by eleven *ayes* to one hundred and ninety-four *noes*.

In the Senate, again General Dix, of New York, regretted the necessity of discussing so grave a question in the form of an amendment to an appropriation bill. He was opposed to the admission; he held that the inhabitants of California were mostly Indians, or Mexicans of mixed blood, uneducated, not familiar with the business of self-government, not speaking our language, not intelligent or cultivated to the standard of the American citizen. These objections he considered insuperable to the immediate admission. He wanted to see the population that was pouring in from every quarter of the globe pass through the process of fermentation and settle before permitting it to participate in the administration of the government. He held that a territorial government should be organized for California and New Mexico, the bill to contain a prohibition of slavery, which, he said, would be agreeable to the wishes of the people of his State, New York. He grieved over the news that he heard from the country. Said he, "In the recent discovery of gold, there is much to be deplored; let us hope that it will soon become exhausted, and that the steady pursuits of agricultural, commercial, and mechanical industry, by which alone nations are made prosperous, may constitute the sole objects of application."

For several days senators battled over the constitutional questions involved. Webster and Calhoun wrestled on this point—whether the Constitution of the United States extends over all its territories, as the latter argued, or cannot, by legislation, be extended an inch beyond the States' borders, as the former insisted. The

A STORMY SUNDAY SESSION.

civil and diplomatic appropriation bill, which had passed the House, halted on its passage for these logicians to decide abstract propositions which had no natural connection with any item in the bill, but were incident to the territorial questions that had been grafted on it by the Senate, rather than have them utterly ignored.

The 4th of March came that year (1849) on Sunday. President Taylor was to be inaugurated on the 5th, and Congress had no legal existence after the session of Saturday, the 3d, should end. Unless this appropriation bill passed, the wheels of government would stop; yet midnight came and the two houses still disagreed as to these foreign amendments. Mr. Cass said the term of the session was ended; he could not vote on any motion. Mr. Webster insisted that the legislative day terminated only with the adjournment of the day's session, without regard to clocks.

Mr. Foote raged and raved. He denied the right of the body to take any further action. About four o'clock Sunday morning he protested that nothing was in order; that the chair could not put a question, because the body did not exist. When he made a motion, he said it was not made in the Senate of the United States, but in a town meeting, four hours after the term of several senators had expired. Occasionally he was sharply rebuked by some earnest man who could keep silence no longer. Sometimes his brother senators hissed and groaned at him. Oftener they bit their lips and muttered their disgust; but checked themselves even in that, lest it should provoke new delays and fresh obstacles. In the course of the night Mr. Cameron and Mr. Berrian were nearly betrayed into a personal collision.

Jefferson Davis said, strike out of the bill all concerning California, and save the appropriations. Mr. Douglas preferred to lose the appropriation bill and save California. Finally, the Senate receded from its amendments (which the House would only agree to on condition that other amendments were added), and the appropriation bill passed with but seven dissenting votes—Mr. Douglas voting with the *noes*. Instantly a House bill, which Mr. Dix had in the morning reported, was called up and passed, and the two houses, after a terribly stormy all-night session, adjourned at seven o'clock Sunday morning, March 4th.

This Sunday-morning bill extended the revenue laws of the United States over all the territory ceded by the treaty of peace with Mexico. It made San Francisco a port of entry, and San Diego, Monterey, and a point near the junction of the rivers Gila and Colorado ports of delivery. It authorized the President to appoint a collector of customs, and that collector to appoint three deputies. It provided amply for obtaining revenue from California, but did not even promise at some future day the government that she coveted.

It imposed no new burdens on the people, but it legalized the course that Governor Mason was already pursuing; for, on hearing of the treaty of peace, the governor had taken the responsibility of collecting the revenues under the tariff of 1846. His collections had been without law, yet as there were laws forbidding goods to be landed until the duties were paid, and as the goods were demanded, he assumed that it was his plain duty to encourage the landing of the goods, and raise a revenue from them.

CHAPTER XXI.

THE CONSTITUTIONAL CONVENTION.

CHAP. XXI.

1849.

The Californians were not surprised at the failure of Congress to give them a government. In anticipation of such an issue, they had called public meetings at San José, San Francisco, Sonoma, and Monterey, and discussed their position. They had gone so far as to set the day for the election of delegates to a constitutional convention, but they had neglected such a concert of action as insures success.

When, however, Brigadier-General Bennett Riley (who succeeded General Persifer S. Smith, the successor of Mason as governor) learned positively that Congress had adjourned and done nothing, he issued a proclamation by the advice, he said, of the President and Secretaries of State and of War, which was at once a call for a convention, and an official exposition of the Administration's theory of the anomalous relations of California and the Union. He strove to correct the prevailing impression that California was held under a military government. That was ended with the war. What remained was the civil government recognized by the existing laws of California. Those laws vested the government of the country in a governor appointed by the supreme government, or, in default of such appointment, the office was vested in the commanding military officer of the department, a secretary, a departmental or territorial legislature, a superior court with four judges, a prefect and sub-prefect and a judge of the first instance for each district, alcaldes, local justices of the peace, and ayuntamientos or town councils. Several of these offices were vacant; he advised that they be filled by the people, and named the first of August as the day for the election.

Moreover, he advised the election of delegates to a convention to adopt either a State or territorial constitution, which, if the people ratified, might be submitted to Congress for its approval. The territory, for election purposes, he divided into ten districts. Every male inhabitant of the country, who was twenty-one years of age, was at liberty to vote in the district of his residence, and the delegates so elected were ordered to convene at Monterey on the first of September. The whole number of delegates was fixed at thirty-seven, of which San Francisco was to send five. In the rapidly-shifting state of society, and because no one could pretend to say how the population of the State was distributed, supernumerary delegates could be elected where it was deemed desirable, and the convention would exercise its discretion about admitting them.

There was a little natural repugnance on the part of the people to accepting the dictation of their governor by military position; but as they had once postponed the time that had been set for the election, and as the proclamation really commanded about what they desired, they consented, after relieving their minds by a public meeting or two, to obey it.

The election came off on the appointed day, and a vote so alarmingly small was polled, that those interested hesitated whether to confess that they had greatly overrated the population, or that the masses cared very little about politics. Still, the prophecy of Senator Dayton was not fulfilled, that they would have to lasso the members to get them to a constitutional convention.

The convention met as ordered, at Monterey, on the 1st of September, 1849, assembling in Colton Hall, a large two-story stone building, named in honor of Walter Colton, author of *Ship and Shore*, who, while alcalde of the place, had urged its erection with the proceeds of the sale of city lots. On Monday, the 3d, a quorum was found present, and the first session was opened with prayer by the Rev. S. H. Willey, a Presbyterian clergyman, who had been sent out by the American Home Missionary Society in 1848, before the gold discovery was bruited. They got early to work, and had a lively session of six weeks.

On the roll of members were the names of several who had been already identified with the history of the country, and who have since taken a large share in its fate. Among them were Captain H. W. Halleck, then Riley's secretary of state, and since then known to all the nation as General-in-Chief of the United States Army; John A. Sutter, the pioneer, who kept open house in the Sacramento Valley when the valley, now so busy, was a solitude; John McDougal, the second governor of the State; Thomas O. Larkin, the first and last American consul in California, and before 1848 the confidential agent of the American State Department; Charles T. Botts, afterwards editor of a Democratic paper published at Sacramento; Mariano de Guadalupe Vallejo, who had figured in the civil wars of the province, and had greeted with welcome the Americans at the beginning of their career in the land; and Dr. Gwin, one of the first United States senators elected by the legislature of the organized State.

Enough of the supernumerary delegates were

admitted to make the Convention number forty-seven members. They represented seventeen States of the Union, and five foreign countries. Seven of them were native Californians; ten had not been more than one year in the territory; and ten more had not been residents over two years. Dr. Gwin, who took a very important part in the proceedings, had been there but four months. Eight were merchants; eleven farmers; thirteen lawyers; one gave his profession as "elegant leisure." Several of them did not understand the English language; they addressed the house through an interpreter, and important resolutions were interpreted to them.

When the Convention was permanently organized, Robert Semple, of Sonoma, was its president; W. E. P. Hartwell its interpreter; William G. Marcy its secretary; Caleb Lyon and J. G. Field its assistant secretaries; and J. Ross Brown its official reporter.

There was not at first entire unanimity as to the policy of forming a State government, though the idea that the native Californians were generally opposed to it was denied on the floor. Dr. Gwin had taken the precaution to have some copies of the constitution of Iowa printed, and because that was the only document of the sort to which they had easy access at first, it seemed for a while as if Iowa were to furnish California with her organic law. But as the session advanced, the constitution of New York was oftener consulted, and when the convention finished its labors their perfected instrument resembled more that of the Empire State than of any other. When the preamble was under discussion, McDougal expressed his fervent desire to see a few lines of the delegates' own manufacture. Mr. McCarver said if they sat there much longer they would have a resolution in to annex New York, constitution and all. Botts complained that the standing committee of twenty (of which Gwin and Myron Norton were leading members) had gathered up a constitution out of all sorts of constitutions, without any regard to the circumstances of California.

Delegates complained that they felt the awkwardness of having so few books of reference. Mr. Botts believed there were not fifty law-books in Monterey. Yet the debates exhibit a remarkable degree of ability. The speeches, as reported, were generally brief, pertinent, and exhaustive of the topics discussed. Their freedom from verbiage, repetition, and irrelevant matter would be surprising, if we did not suspect that the reputation of the speech-makers was mercifully spared, and their credit enhanced by the elegant and critical pen of the reporter.

The first article of the constitution is entitled

CHAP. XXI.
1849.

a "Declaration of Rights." When this article was reported from the committee, it provided in general terms that no member of the State should be disfranchised unless by the law of the land or the judgment of his peers. This was not up to the standard of public sentiment. It was finally amended to declare that "all men are, by nature, free and independent, and have certain inalienable rights, among which are those of enjoying and defending life and liberty." Lest that should be at some future day construed into a "glittering generality," Mr. Shannon, an Irishman by birth, who had emigrated three years before from New York, moved, as an additional section to the article, the following: "Neither slavery nor involuntary servitude, unless for the punishment of crime, shall ever be tolerated in this State."

Considering how the territory of California was acquired by the United States; considering the composition of the Convention, and the antecedents of some of its prominent members, this ought to have raised a great storm. But it did not; the text which never failed before to produce a debate, failed utterly here. There was a little talk about what part of the constitution to put that provision in, and then the section was adopted in committee of the whole unanimously. This was done on the tenth day after the Convention assembled, which shows that the action was suggested by the well-understood sentiment of the people, and not bred of the policy developed within the Convention itself.

After so handsome an achievement in the interest of freedom, accomplished with scarce a struggle, it was quite natural that the Convention, in the good nature that follows victory, should be almost betrayed into an action that would have reflected very seriously upon its sagacity. A desperate effort was made to prohibit the emigration of free negroes into the State. This was strenuously advocated by Mr. McCarver, a Kentuckian; Mr. Semple, also from Kentucky by the way of Missouri; Dr. Wozencraft, from Ohio, *via* Louisiana; Mr. Tefft, from New York, and Mr. Steuart, from Maryland. They argued that free negroes were bad members of society, and unless they were strictly prohibited from entering the State, California would be overrun with them, and their labor be brought into competition with white labor in the mines. They said the owners of slaves had already discovered that, by bringing their negroes here and freeing them under indentures, binding them to dig gold for a while, they could get as much profit out of them in three years as during a life-time on the plantations, besides saving the expense of taking care of them when old and valueless as property.

CHAP. XXI.
1849.

Mr. Dimmick, of New York, replied, that few masters could afford to bring their slaves here, especially in view of the extreme probability that they would run away the day they set foot on California free soil.

Mr. Shannon, of New York, said the Slave States might very properly prohibit free negroes from crossing their borders, for their presence was injurious to the slave system; but the Free States had no excuse for such illiberality, and only one of them, Illinois, had practised it. There, the Convention refused to put the prohibitory clause into the constitution; but leaving it to the people, they, by a popular vote, inserted it. He contended, moreover, that the free blacks are not a bad people, and if this illiberal provision should be inserted, it would damage the prospects of the constitution in Congress.

Mr. Gilbert, from New York, though confessing to a fashionable degree of repugnance to the blacks, opposed the prohibition. He held that color was not a crime. The free negro, in the spirit and meaning of the Constitution of the United States, was a citizen, and that Constitution provides that the citizens of each State shall be entitled to all the privileges and immunities of the several States. To insert the proposed section would jeopardize the success of all their labors.

This debate occurred in committee of the

whole, nine days after the unanimous adoption of the section excluding slavery forever from the State. When the vote was taken the proposed section was adopted. It was as follows: "The Legislature shall, at its first session, pass such laws as will effectually prohibit free persons of color from immigrating to, and settling in this State, and to effectually prevent the owners of slaves from bringing them into this State for the purpose of setting them free."

But that dark stigma was not to be indelible. A fortnight afterward the subject came up again, the question being on the adoption of the report of the committee of the whole. Mr. Norton opposed the prohibitory clause on constitutional grounds. He alleged that when Missouri was admitted to the Union it was with the express condition imposed by Congress, that she should strike out a similar clause from her constitution. The subject was discussed again freely, and when the question was taken the whole section was rejected, by *ayes* 8, *noes* 31.

But the negro question was not quite yet disposed of. It reappeared as the principal feature of the long discussion concerning the boundaries of the State. That California should be declared to be bounded on the west by the ocean, on the north by Oregon, and on the south by Mexico, was acceded to so soon as

CHAP. XXI.
1849.

July.

proposed. But where should the eastern line be drawn? The committee had reported in favor of placing it on the one hundred and sixteenth parallel of longitude. This would have included within California the whole of modern Nevada. Mr. McDougal proposed the one hundred and fifth parallel of longitude, which would have taken in portions of Kansas and Nebraska. Mr. Semple preferred to make the Sierra Nevada the eastern boundary. Dr. Gwin wanted to follow the line of separation between California and New Mexico, as laid down on Fremont's map, which would include the Mormon settlements about Salt Lake. Captain Halleck favored that, with a proviso authorizing the legislature to assent to a proposition, if Congress should make one, for the erection of all east of the Sierras into either a Territory or a separate State. Mr. Shannon proposed nearly the boundaries that were finally adopted. He objected to all schemes or proposals that left the territorial question open, for that left the slavery question open. The usual arguments for and against a large State were urged and answered. The dignity of imperial dimensions, the pride of size, the fact that there was no neighbor on the east to object to the widest scope proposed, the humanity of extending State law over the deserts which were beginning to be populous along certain lines of approach and which Congress had failed to shield with any law, the doctrine that the California of Mexico included all and more than the committee recommended, and that it was not becoming for the convention, unasked, to dismember or reject any portion of her—these were the considerations urged at first for making the State embrace all the area possible. On the other hand, it was argued that it was wasting political power to give to so vast a territory no more United States senators than little Delaware is entitled to; the desert east of the Sierras was worth no State's possessing; the expense of sustaining a State government over so broad a field would be burdensome; to take in Utah would be simply to stipulate for a Mormon trouble; to be modest would look well in Congress, and cost the sacrifice of not an acre that was really worth owning. Of course no one dreamed then that within twenty years the desert east of the Sierras would be ringing with the clatter of mills, populous with permanent inhabitants, and famous the world over for the products of its mines.

But the specious arguments that men advance are seldom the ones that govern their votes in deliberative bodies. The boundary question was settled by considerations connected with slavery. One party said, we have prohibited slavery from our State; now, for humanity's sake, let us make the State as large as possible. Do you suppose, asked the Chivalry, that the South is so blind as not to see that? and will they let you in at all, when for such a purpose you ask so much? Ask modestly, said a third party, and ask for a fixed, unalterable line, and Congress will not be tempted to debate your admission all next term. Mr. Semple quoted T. Butler King, as begging very emphatically, "Leave us no territory to legislate upon in Congress." Mr. Shannon understood it now—the Cabinet was divided about the Wilmot Proviso, and the President had sent out T. Butler King to induce the convention to put all the loose territory west of the Rocky Mountains within California, and take that bone of contention, the "Wilmot Proviso," out of Congress.

Whether that was literally true or not, there is no doubt that the most comprehensive boundaries were advocated, with the hope that the action of the convention would be taken as final, and relieve the Administration of a troublesome question that it did not care to encounter. In committee of the whole this policy prevailed, and the Gwin-Halleck proposition was adopted by *ayes* 19, *noes* 4.

That did not end the discussion, however, which was resumed in the House and maintained with energy, amendment after amendment being voted down. When, at last, three days before the Convention adjourned, the report of the committee of the whole was concurred in by *aye*s 29 to *noes* 22, there was great confusion and excitement. Mr. McCarver moved to adjourn *sine die*—they had done mischief enough. "Your constitution is gone—is gone!" exclaimed Mr. Snyder. "I will sign it under protest." "All is lost," and cries of "Order," rang through the hall. Afterwards the matter was reconsidered, and, as a compromise, the line accepted which forms the present eastern boundary—a line drawn north and south from the forty-second to the thirty-ninth parallel on the one hundred and twentieth degree of longitude, thence southeasterly to the Colorado; thence along the channel of that river to the Mexican line. This left the Mormons out, took in all that was supposed to be of any earthly value of the territory that Mexico ever treated as California, and gave to the new State an area of one hundred and eighty-eight thousand nine hundred and eighty-one square miles.

Other topics gently exercised the Convention, but no other one excited it. The freedom of the press was guarded by a provision that in criminal prosecutions for libel, the truth of the alleged libel might be pleaded, and if good motives for the publication appeared, the accused should be acquitted. The right of suffrage was extended to white male citizens of the United States, and to white male citizens of Mexico, who elected to become citizens of the United States under the treaty of peace. The Legislature was prohibited from granting divorces.

Lotteries were prohibited. Mr. Price believed lotteries a necessary evil; they could be made to defray the expenses of the Legislature until a system of taxes were devised. He contended that the people of California were essentially a gambling people. Every public house had its monte and faro tables licensed by law, where there was a law. Lotteries were less offensive to public morals; he would tax them for the sake of revenue. Mr. Halleck reminded gentlemen of the famous case of Yates and McIntyre, which involved not only many individuals in ruin, but so embarrassed the finances of New York State that the convention of 1846 felt called on to prohibit lotteries. Mr. Dimmick denied the truth of Mr. Price's charge, that California was a community of gamblers. It was not applicable to his constituency, the people of San José. The prohibition was not seriously contested further.

Fighting a duel, or sending or accepting a challenge, or acting as a second in a duel, after the adoption of the Constitution, made the party so offending ineligible to any office of profit, and disfranchised him. Dr. Gwin earnestly contended for this clause. He pleaded his observation in Mississippi and Tennessee in evidence that this remnant of the dark ages, which the greatest cowards cling to, can be put down by law.

Provision was ordered for a system of common schools, to be supported in every district for three months in the year; but they were not required to be absolutely free. The rights of women to a separate property were recognized. Banks of circulation were forbidden, and, after a long discussion, hard money was made the exclusive currency. Mr. Botts struggled hard to make the State treasury a bank of deposit of gold and silver, with power to issue certificates of deposit. "You want a mint," said he, "but you cannot have one—not in three years; nor at all!—the expense of labor required to conduct it would be too great in this country;" in which prediction, happily, he made a mistake.

They fixed the capital at San José; but they left it optional for the Legislature, by a twothirds vote of each house, to remove it at any time.

The expenses of the Convention, General Riley gave them to understand, that he would take care of, out of the proceeds of the anomalously collected revenues. They allowed to their secretary twenty-eight dollars *per diem;* to the assistant secretaries and engrossing clerk they paid twenty-three dollars each, daily; to the copying clerk, sixteen dollars; to the door-keeper, twelve dollars. The sessions were opened with prayer, either by the Rev. Mr. Willey, Presbyterian, or the Rev. Father Ramirez, Catholic; for this, sixteen dollars a day was paid. The reporter, J. Ross Browne, engaged to deliver a certain number of printed copies of the proceedings; he was paid ten thousand dollars. These seem like liberal salaries—heavy ones, they all confessed when they lugged them off at the close of the session, paid mostly in silver coin; but they were not out of proportion to the wages that men were making in the field, the shop, and the counting-room.

Only one design for a great seal of state and coat of arms was offered to the committee that took that matter in charge. It was presented by Caleb Lyon, of Lyonsdale, as with harmless affectation the eccentric first assistant secretary loved to designate himself. After it was accepted, some members claimed the original design of it for Major Garnett, who, however, had expressed to Mr. Lyon a desire that he alone should be known as its author. Mr. Lyon was authorized to have it engraved, and to furnish a press and necessary appendages, and the Convention paid him one thousand dollars for it. The seal is thus explained by its designer:—

"Around the bend of the ring are represented thirty-one stars, being the number of the States of which the Union will consist upon the admission of California. The foreground figure represents the goddess Minerva, having sprung full grown from the brain of Jupiter. She is introduced as a type of the political birth of the State of California, without having gone through the probation of a Territory.' At her feet crouches a grizzly bear, feeding upon the clusters from a grape-vine, emblematic of the peculiar characteristics of the country. A miner is engaged, with his rocker and bowl at his side, illustrating the golden wealth of the Sacramento, upon whose waters are seen shipping, typical of commercial greatness; and the snow-clad peaks of the Sierra Nevada make up the background, while above is the Greek motto, 'Eureka' (I have found), applying either to the principle involved in the admission of the State, or the success of the miner at work."

Dr. Wozencraft tried to have the gold-digger and the bear struck out; and General Vallejo wanted the bear removed, or else fastened by a lasso in the hands of a vaquero; but the original suited the majority, and it was not altered.

The Convention had been in session six weeks.

CHAP. XXI.
1849.

Though members had indulged in some personalities, had always very freely criticised each other, and once Mr. Tefft and Mr. Jones had mutually rasped each other until the experts in affairs of honor interfered and gently forced them to make the proper apologies inside the House, harmony had generally prevailed, and their work was crowned with good feeling. They had met as strangers; they parted as friends. Of all parties, they had, to an astonishing degree, ignored party. Representing all sections of the Union, they had, to a wonderful extent, laid aside sectional prejudices, and given to the new State a constitution fully up to the standard of the times, and defaced with but few of those innovations (like the popularly elected judiciary) which have crowded themselves in among the improvements of the age, and, for a season, passed for such.

Oct. 13.

On Saturday, October 13th, the Convention adopted a brief address to the people, thanked General Riley for his courtesy, and voted that he ought to have ten thousand dollars a year for his salary while governor; named six thousand dollars as a proper salary for Captain Halleck, as secretary of state; paid Lieutenant Hamilton, for engrossing the Constitution on parchment, five hundred dollars; signed the engrossed copy, Colton Hall meanwhile trembling and the hills around the bay echoing the salute of thirty-one guns fired from the fort, and adjourned *sine die*.

The members then went in a body to call on General Riley at his house. Captain Sutter expressed the Convention's thanks for his aid in creating a State government. General Riley replied that he never made a speech in his life; but it was a prouder day than when his soldiers cheered him on the field of Contreras. He handsomely complimented the people who selected such able delegates. The members gracefully turned the compliment back with three cheers for the Governor of California, and three more for "the gallant soldier worthy of his country's glory." "I have but one thing more to add," said the general, weathering the cheers. "My success in the affairs of California is mainly owing to the efficient aid rendered me by Captain Halleck, the secretary of state. He has stood by me in all emergencies; to him I have always appealed when at a loss myself, and he has never failed me." Monterey was gay with American flags that day, and the few people throughout the State, who had given any attention to public affairs, were happy over a good job completed.

It required swift work to publish the Constitution in English and Spanish, and spread it over so broad a territory in those roadless days, so that it could be fairly canvassed in town and country, on the ranches of the valleys, and in the mining camps far up the mountain-sides, by the 13th of November, which day General Riley had appointed for the election to ratify or reject it, and to choose the Congressmen and State officers that it called for. Whether it was well or illy done, appearances were kept up, and on the day set the election came off.

The people adopted the Constitution by a vote of twelve thousand and sixty-four for it, to eight hundred and eleven against it; there being, besides, over twelve hundred ballots that were treated as blanks, because of an informality in the printing. Peter H. Burnett was chosen governor, getting six thousand seven hundred and sixteen votes, while his competitors, W. Scott Sherwood, received three thousand one hundred and eighty-eight; J. W. Geary, one thousand four hundred and seventy-five; John A. Sutter, two thousand two hundred and one; and William M. Stewart, six hundred and nineteen. John McDougal was elected lieutenant-governor; and George W. Wright and Edward Gilbert, getting between five thousand and six thousand votes each, were elected to Congress.

These were small figures for a State claiming, six weeks later, to have one hundred and seven thousand inhabitants. Those most interested felt ashamed of the returns, and were thankful that they could plead a drenching rain and unusual storm upon election-day throughout the country. The day had been set early, in hopes to anticipate the rainy season, but not early enough by a week, as the event showed.

CHAP. XXI.

1849. Nov.

CHAPTER XXII.

THE FIRST STATE LEGISLATURE.

CHAP. XXII.

1849. Dec.

There was a stronger reason than that, however, in the fact that the vast majority looked upon politics as a matter of small account, in the midst of such a harvest of gold, especially as they expected to return soon to their old homes, taking their fortunes with them, and leaving the State and its politics for others of different tastes and more modest expectations, to regulate.

A month after election, the first Legislature met at San José. The Senate consisted of sixteen members, of whom San Francisco sent two, and the Sacramento and San Joaquin districts four each. The Assembly had thirty-six members. Their pay was sixteen dollars a day, and sixteen dollars mileage for every twenty miles travelled in going to or returning from the capital.

Governor Riley kept the promise he had made (conditioned upon receiving no orders to the contrary from Washington), surrendered the administration of civil affairs into the hands of Governor Burnett, and turned over to the

THE FIRST LEGISLATURE.

new government the books, papers, and archives of the territory.

In his message, Governor Burnett advised that without a doubt they had a right to proceed at once to the business of legislation. Missouri and Michigan had started on their State career long before they were admitted to the Union, and their right had not been seriously questioned. The Legislature never hesitated a moment in adopting the course recommended. On the sixth day of the session they went into joint convention for the election of two United States senators. On the first call of the roll John C. Fremont received twenty-nine votes, and was elected. On the third, William M. Gwin received twenty-four votes, and he was elected, his unsuccessful competitors being H. W. Halleck, who had eighteen votes, and T. J. Henley, T. Butler King, and J. W. Geary dividing between them the remainder.

The Legislature continued in session four months. The wits of the day called it "The Legislature of a Thousand Drinks." The appellation may have been fairly won. Members, whose families were the width of a continent away, found it a thirstier land than it ever has been since. But if they drank well, they worked well too. They enacted one hundred and forty laws, most of which were of a general

CHAP. XXII.

1849.

1850.

CHAP. XXII.
1850.

and important character, though some were pretty nearly transcripts of the laws of other States, that have needed very thorough revision since to suit them to the peculiar wants of California.

They created the offices required by the Constitution. They established a judiciary, and required the Supreme Court, after its first two regular terms, which were to be held in San Francisco, to sit at the seat of government. To each of the district judges they appointed a salary of seventy-five hundred dollars a year; to the county judges, from one thousand to six thousand. They fixed the legal rate of interest at ten per cent. per annum, in case no express contract were made; but if it were agreed to beforehand, any rate of interest became legal, and the interest, on failure to pay it promptly, could be added to the principal, and itself draw interest—a law which was early found to tend to the ruin both of borrowers and lenders. They required foreigners not naturalized to pay a license before being allowed to work the mines—a policy which, on trial, failed to raise any considerable revenue, and met with serious opposition in the mining districts.

They would not prohibit the immigration of people of color into the State, but they so far catered to the prejudices of the Chivalry, as to bar from the courts the testimony of any black, mulatto, or Indian, either for or against a white man—a piece of unjust and foolish legislation, which it took thirteen years to erase from the statute-book. They made some meagre provision for common schools, and authorized the Supreme Court to incorporate colleges whenever they could show an endowment of twenty thousand dollars. For murder, and nothing else, they established the death penalty. To send or accept a challenge to a duel they declared a crime, and affixed as a penalty imprisonment for from one to three years, and a fine not to exceed one thousand dollars. They adopted the common law, so far as it was not repugnant to the Constitution of the State or United States, and showed their confidence that nothing of importance was left undone, by abolishing, with a few exceptions, all laws then in force but those of their own enactment.

Early in January two delegates appeared at San José with a curious petition, purporting to come from the people of the "new State of Deseret." The residents in the Great Salt Lake basin had, in March, 1849, met in convention and formed a State Constitution, which afterwards was approved by the popular vote. But, hearing that California was about to hold a convention, they chose two delegates to attend it, and urge that Deseret be included for a time within California. The delegates, arriving, found that the Convention had adjourned. They then modestly asked California to call another convention, throw aside its adopted constitution, and agree on boundaries which should embrace temporarily the Great Basin. This done, they would unite in recommending Congress to reject without discussion or debate both the State constitutions already adopted. They professed to have authority to vote against permitting slavery, and urged that only in this way could the slavery question in the territories be set at rest; for Congress, owing to the division of parties, could not handle it. Reject these terms, and Deseret, "with her twenty thousand inhabitants, and thirty thousand more on the way to settle within her borders," would insist before Congress upon her separate admission, with boundaries stretching from the Rocky Mountains to the Sierras, and a wide strip from the southern end of California, to give her access to the Pacific. Of course, Governor Burnett recommended the Legislature not to accede to the proposition, and it was soon forgotten.

They authorized the incorporation of towns out of any settlement containing over two hundred people, and not embracing more than three square miles; and the incorporation as cities, of places containing two thousand people. They also, by special act, in spite of one veto of the Governor, who insisted that special legislation was not needed for the purpose, incorporated nine cities—San Francisco, Sacramento, San José, Monterey, Los Angeles, San Diego, Benicia, Sonoma, and Santa Barbara.

CHAP. XXII.

1850.

San Francisco was at that time a brisk, noisy, enterprising place, of from twenty thousand to forty thousand inhabitants, full of troubles about land titles, much given to mass meetings and other American ways; with three daily papers—the *Alta, Journal of Commerce*, and *Pacific News*—which advertised seven places of worship open every Sunday, and two theatres; with a prison brig; with steamers on the bay running to Sacramento, and charging "reduced rates," namely, twenty dollars to carry a passenger there, or thirty-five to take him to Yuba or Marysville; running to Alviso also, which town Governor Burnett and Mr. Hoppy were just starting, at the southern extremity of the bay, and charging for passage through to San José thirty-five dollars; and running wherever else freight or passage-money offered inducements enough to tempt them.

Ap'l 15

The city had achieved most of its importance within two years. Though the Mission Dolores was indeed founded in 1776, there was no sign of settlement on the beach of Yerba Buena Cove before 1835, when Captain W. A. Richardson, who had received the appointment

1835.

of master of the harbor, put up the first dwelling, a rude structure with a sail-cloth roof. On the 4th of July, 1836, Jacob P. Leese finished a frame house adjoining Richardson's (its site was the southwest corner of Clay and Dupont streets, where the St. Francis Hotel yet stands) in time for a house-warming and celebration of Independence Day by some sixty guests invited from the first families in all the region. On the 15th of April, 1838, the first child was born in Yerba Buena, Rosalie Leese, whose father was the pioneer American merchant, and her mother a sister of General Vallejo. Leese erected, as the requirements of trade required it, a store on the beach, where now is the crossing of Commercial and Montgomery Streets; for the waterfront, which is now thrust six blocks to the eastward, at that time swept in on the line of Washington Street as far as Montgomery, and crossed Market Street at the intersection of Battery and First Streets. In 1839, Governor Alvarado ordered a survey of the plain and cove; and Captain Juan Vioget made the survey, which included the region between Pacific and Sacramento, Dupont and Montgomery streets. In 1841, Leese transferred his property to the Hudson's Bay Company, and removed to Sonoma. That company did most of the business of the place till 1846, when it sold out and left.

The American conquest quickened a new growth on the narrow, sandy plain that skirted the base of Telegraph, Rincon, and Russian hills. In January, 1847, it had a population of three hundred and a weekly newspaper. In April following, it contained seventy-nine buildings, of which twenty-six were adobe, thirty-one frame, and the rest shanties. In June, with a population of four hundred, it boasted its second weekly paper. On the 30th of January it dropped its old name, and took a new and less fragrant one. On the 20th of July, the lots between high and low water marks, from Fort Montgomery (Clark's Point) to Rincon Point, were sold at auction under orders of General Kearny and Alcalde Bryant. The first steamboat, an importation from Sitka, made its trial trip on the bay November 15th.

By the middle of March, 1848, San Francisco had two hundred houses and eight hundred and fifty people. On the 3d of April the first public school was opened—a delay that would have been a reproach if the population had not been to so great a degree an adult one. In May and June came the rush to the interior which followed the announcement of the gold discovery, when the shipping was deserted, stores shut up, shops abandoned, papers stopped, because of the hegira to the mines. By November the gold-hunters were in good part back again, business resumed, school reopened, the presses running again; and the Rev. J. D. Hunt (chosen "Protestant chaplain," at a yearly salary of twenty-five hundred dollars, to be raised by subscription) had begun a regular Sunday service in the school-house on Portsmouth Square. The year showed a million dollars worth of goods imported, and as much in value of coin, but two millions of gold-dust had been exported.

On New Year's Day of 1849, San Francisco claimed to have a population of two thousand, and rejoiced in her new Broadway wharf. The two weeklies on the 4th merged into the *Alta California*. The people had showed some little interest in a convention scheme, but far more in the election of town councils or ayuntamientos, of which at one time they had three in existence, each claiming to be exclusively the legal one. On the last day of February the pioneer of the ocean steamships, the *California*, arrived from New York, with General Persifer F. Smith on board, to take command of the Pacific department. A month later the steamship *Oregon* arrived from New York with three hundred and fifty passengers, including Colonel Geary, who had a commission to act as postmaster for the city and postal agent for the coast. On the 13th of April, General Bennett Riley came, relieving Smith of the military command, and charged, also, to administer civil affairs. By the end of July there were two hundred square-rigged vessels in the harbor.

This summer the affair of "the Hounds" came off. A gang of desperadoes, organized originally, as they professed, for mutual protection in the mining districts, against the cheap labor of foreigners of Spanish extraction, began to practise their outrages openly. They had their head-quarters and their officers, and claimed to be "regulators" of society. On the slightest pretence they would tear down the tents of the Chilians, rob them of their valuables, and divide among themselves the plunder. On one of their expeditions a youth, who happened to be in their company, was fatally wounded by a foreigner. On Sunday, the 15th of July, returning from an excursion to Contra Costa, they paraded the streets openly, and proceeding to the Chilian quarter, tore down tents, beat their occupants, plundered them, and repeatedly fired into their midst. Next day, when the news spread through the town, the public was warm with indignation. They waited on the alcalde, and urged him to take steps to punish the offenders. The alcalde, by proclamation, summoned a public meeting, which assembled at three o'clock on Portsmouth Square. Samuel Brannan addressed the crowd. A generous subscription was made

CHAP. XXII.
1849.

for the relief of the sufferers, and two hundred and thirty persons enrolled themselves as special constables. They were soon provided with muskets, and had elected a commander and six captains. Before night twenty of the rioters had been arrested and lodged for safe keeping on board the United States ship *Warren*. At another meeting on the square, Dr. Gwin and James C. Ward were chosen judges, to be associated with Alcalde Leavenworth for the trial of the rioters; Horace Hawes was appointed district attorney, and Hall McAllister his associate. On Tuesday, twenty-four citizens, acting as a grand-jury, found a true bill against Samuel Roberts and nineteen other "Hounds," on various charges. On Wednesday the trials began, and were conducted in all calmness, but with dispatch. Francis J. Lippett and Frank Turk assisted Hawes and McAllister as counsel for the people, and P. Barry and Myron Norton defended the accused. Twelve jurors, among whom were John Sime and Frederick Teschmacker, found ten of the accused guilty of one or all of the counts of the indictment, and the convicted were sentenced to different terms of imprisonment. These sentences were never enforced; but the "Hounds" were broken up, and those who had been foremost in the gang quit the city.

On the 5th of August the first Protestant

church in California—the property of the First Baptist Society—was dedicated.

In October, steamers began to make regular trips to Sacramento. The *Pioneer*, a little iron vessel brought out piecemeal from Boston; the *Mint*, also of iron; the propeller *McKim*, and soon the *Senator*, went into that line.

The first large Democratic meeting in California assembled October 25th on Portsmouth Square, "the plaza," Colonel Geary acting as president; O. P. Sutton and Annis Merrill being among the vice-presidents, and J. Ross Brown and John A. McGlynn figuring among the secretaries. On the 13th of November, amidst a heavy rain, the State Constitution was approved—two thousand and fifty-one voting for, and five against it, in San Francisco.

By the end of the year there were twenty thousand people in town. The unfenced plaza, as we have said, was the place of general resort on great public occasions. There were between three and four hundred square-rigged vessels in the bay, very many of which, for lack of sailors, never went to sea again. The expenses of the local government were not great, for the streets were not yet improved, and for a while ample funds had been raised to defray them from the proceeds of the sale of water-lots or of uplands. Later, however, they had raised quite a revenue by licenses, which were required of almost every trade and profession. They had no town-house, no safe jail, no adequate police, no hospital, no public burying-ground.

Collector Collier wrote to Secretary Meredith, November 13th, 1849: "I am perfectly astounded at the amount of business done at this (San Francisco) office." Six hundred and ninety-seven vessels had arrived within seven and a half months. Board, he said, was five dollars a day, without a room. A small room with a single bed rented for one hundred and fifty dollars a month; wood cost forty dollars a cord; flour, forty dollars a barrel; pork, sixty dollars. In lack of stores, nineteen vessels were employed as warehouses. Commercially, the port was already equal to Philadelphia!

Such was the rude but promising town to which the first Legislature gave a city charter, which the people approved by vote, May 1st, 1850. The charter extended the city limits on the west to a line parallel to Kearny Street, two miles from the plaza. The county had separate boundaries, embracing what afterwards was made San Mateo County, and on the west, going some distance into the ocean.

Sacramento was the legitimate successor of Sutter's "New Helvetia;" the site of the new town being originally the embarcadero of the Swiss captain's settlement. The rush to the mines had stimulated it into a promising trading-place. Here the miners landed from the boats in which they ascended the river, and here the returning tide from the mountains first struck navigable water. In October, 1848, there was advertised a sale of town lots in Sacramento—the name then first appearing as the designation of a settlement. In January, 1849, the first frame house was built on the bank of the river, and before that year ended, the settlement about the fort moved down. A school was started, but children were scarce, and it languished. By the spring of 1850, the permanent population was twelve thousand. A grove of fine old buttonwoods shaded the plain and tempered the excessive heat of summer. The Sierras, covered till late in the spring with snow, loomed up on the eastern horizon, and Mount Diablo, like a grand pyramid, lifted its peak on the south. The site of the city, which at once promised to exceed in its growth all the inland cities of the State, was but fifteen feet above low-water mark. The settlers soon found what a mistake they had made concerning the grade, for before January of 1850 was passed, the place was flooded by the rise of the river.

As to the other cities that year incorporated, it was natural to suppose that San José, in a prolific valley on the road to the great quicksilver mine, would grow rapidly; and that Monterey, Santa Barbara, Los Angeles, and San Diego would slowly, at least, justify the wisdom of their Spanish founders. General Riley, it was said, had expressed the opinion that Benicia, with its bold water-front and level upland, enjoyed a position far superior to San Francisco for a large city. Sonoma was solely a city of the future and of the imagination.

This first Legislature also subdivided the State into twenty-seven counties. General Vallejo was chairman of a committee appointed to report the derivation and meaning of their names. The General entered into the task with spirit, and in his report embodied a good deal of useful and curious information, of which we condense all that suits our present purpose.

San Diego (St. James) takes the name of its chief town, which lies three miles distant from the harbor discovered by Viscaino in 1602. The town had its name from the first mission established in Upper California, July 16th, 1769.

Los Angeles, the City " of the Angels," founded by order of the Viceroy of New Spain in 1781.

Santa Barbara was named after the little town established in 1780, about midway between San Diego and Monterey, to protect the five missions that occupied the choice spots of that pleasant region.

San Luis Obispo after its principal town, the site of the mission established September 1st, 1772, by Junipero Serra and José Cavaller.

Monterey: when Viscaino, in 1602, discovered the harbor cut in the coast where one of two parallel coast ranges of mountains strikes the sea; he named it Monterey, after the count, with perhaps an allusion to the pines—" king of the forests "—that still blacken the southern point that shoots out to make the indentation a harbor. It was the official residence of fourteen governors, and generally the capital of the province.

Santa Cruz, the "Holy Cross," from the mission on the north side of Monterey Bay.

San Francisco: Father Junipero Serra was a Franciscan monk, and he named the Mission Dolores, established in 1776, of which he had the immediate superintendence, after the founder of his order. The presidio, established the same year, and the magnificent bay took the same name, and the little village of Yerba Buena, finding itself no longer an obscure hide port, but a stirring American town, assumed it also.

Santa Clara, from the mission established in January, 1777.

Contra Costa, "opposite coast," was the natural designation of the county across the bay, eastward from San Francisco. Yet it had a narrow escape of being profanely christened *Diablo*, after the noble mountain that rises from its very centre and keeps guard over a wonderful expanse of valley and inland sea. In 1806 a military expedition marched against the tribe Bolgeres, then encamped at the western foot of the mountain. At the moment that victory was inclining to the Indians, a mysterious stranger, dressed in extraordinary costume, suddenly appeared, indulged in some curious antics, and disappeared up the mountain. The defeated soldiers were told that the stranger made his appearance there daily, and the Indians called him "Puy," or Evil Spirit. Several legislators thought the mountain entitled to name the county, but the Puy got his full dues in the naming of the mountain, and the county a very creditable designation in Contra Costa.

Marin was the chief of a troublesome tribe of Indians which a military exploring expedition encountered in 1815. Marin was taken prisoner, but he escaped from San Francisco, rallied his tribe, and harassed the troops continually. Being closely pursued, he took refuge in the little islands at the mouth of San Rafael Inlet, which were hence called the Marin Islands. In 1824, Marin was again carried captive to San Francisco. When he was set at liberty he retired to the San Rafael

Mission, and there died in 1834. His prowess and the islets that befriended him named the county.

Sonoma (the "Valley of the Moon") is the Indian designation of the Arcadian region, at whose chief settlement the bear flag was raised in 1846. The Chocuyens possessed the valley when the missionaries visited it and founded there a mission. They called the chief Sonoma, and the tribe (dependants on Marin) adopted that as their tribal name.

Solano: The great chief of the Suisunes, on receiving baptism, gave up his heathen title, Sem-Yeto (fierce hand), and accepted that of Solano, in honor of Francisco Solano, the missionary. The county, embracing the fine arable land and marshes which the Suisunes claimed, not unnaturally was given his name.

Yolo is a corruption of the Indian *Yoloy*, which signified a region thick with rushes, and was the name of the tribe owning the tule lands west of the Sacramento and bordering on Cache Creek.

Napa was the name of the brave tribe that occupied that most charming of valleys which stretches from San Pablo Bay to Mount St. Helen's. The tribe was very numerous and troublesome until 1838, when the small-pox almost swept it out of existence.

Mendocino assumed the name of the westernmost cape of the coast, discovered in 1543, and named after Mendoza, the viceroy of New Spain and the author of the expedition.

Sacramento (the Sacrament). Lieutenant Moraga gave the great river which bears this name the designation of "Jesus Maria," and to its principal branch that of "Sacramento." But before the American conquest the great river had assumed the name of the Sacramento, and the branch was called the Feather. The river named the county.

El Dorado: The county within whose limits the first discovery of gold in paying quantities was found fairly earned the name of El Dorado.

Sutter: John Augustus Sutter, a native of Switzerland, and formerly a military officer under Charles X., emigrated to California in 1839, proposing to found a colony. He obtained a grant from the Mexican Government, fixed the site of his colony on the east side of the Sacramento, and south of the American Fork, named it New Helvetia, built and manned a fort, and by his ever-open hospitality made his home the rallying and recruiting place of emigrants from over the mountains. To name a county after him was but simple justice.

Yuba is a misspelling of Uva, a name that an exploring party in 1824 gave to a tributary of the Feather, on whose banks they found growing immense quantities of wild grape-vines.

Butte is the common French term for mound,

and the symmetrical mounds that rise without foot-hills out of the plain to a mountain height, east of the Sacramento, were named "The Buttes" in 1829 by a detachment of hunters, headed by Michael Laframbeau, of the Hudson Bay Company. Those peaks name the county.

Colusa is an Indian word of unknown origin, the appellation of a once numerous tribe on the west side of the Sacramento.

Shasta was the name of a tribe of Indians that resided at the foot of the noblest mountain in California.

Trinity drew its name from Trinity Bay, discovered on the anniversary of Trinity festival.

Calaveras: An immense number of skulls were found by Captain Moraga in the vicinity of a creek, which, from that circumstance, was called Calaveras, or the river of Skulls. The story was, that the tribes from the Sierras came down to the valley to fish for salmon. To this the valley Indians objected, and, as the conflict was irrepressible, a bloody battle was fought, and three thousand dead bodies were left to whiten the banks with their bones. The county in which the river rises assumed its name.

San Joaquin: In 1813, Lieutenant Gabriel Moraga explored the valley of rushes, and named a rivulet, which rises in the Sierras and empties into Lake Buena Vista, San Joaquin, after the legendary father of the Virgin. The

CHAP. XXII.
1850.

rivulet named the great river; the river named the valley and the county.

Tuolumne: A corruption from the Indian word *talmalaume*, meaning a cluster of stone wigwams.

Mariposa signifies butterfly. A hunting party of Californians, in 1807, observed the trees about the river, where they pitched their tents, gorgeous with butterflies. They named the river Mariposa, and the river named the county.

It is a curious comment on the small importance attached to politics in those times, that there was really danger lest the first Legislature should be dissolved for lack of a quorum. Two senators and three assemblymen, including the speaker, early resigned, though some of them did it to take other offices to which they were elected. One assemblyman never appeared to claim his seat. Many were absent most of the time. Many talked of the great sacrifices they made in staying. In the quiet seclusion of San José, they fancied that, with the return of spring and the end of the rains, business would revive with great energy: they repented their dabbling in politics. A sharp rebuke, administered by a joint committee, shamed members into more attention.

After the speaker deserted his post, John Bigler was elected to occupy it. After Nathaniel Bennet resigned his senatorship to accept the position of Associate Justice of the Supreme Court, David C. Broderick, of San Francisco, was elected to his place by twenty-five hundred and eight out of only twenty-six hundred and nine votes cast in his district. This was the first appearance in State politics of a man who was destined to exert an extraordinary influence on the political future of the State. He was born in Washington, in the year 1819, the son of a stone-cutter. He removed in 1825 to New York City, with his parents, who soon after died. He was a rough, honest, self-reliant boy. He was connected with the Fire Department, kept a drinking-place, and meddled with local politics. In 1845 he was elected to preside over a convention for securing a new city charter. In 1846 he was nominated for Congress, and was defeated. In 1849 he sailed for California. Without education, without flattering antecedents, he determined to become a power in the State. For this he educated himself; to this devoted all his time and his extraordinary energies. He soon made his mark in the Legislature, and controlled the apparent executive. But it was the politics rather than the laws of California that he shaped; he aimed to manage men rather than municipal measures.

CHAPTER XXIII.

WAITING ON CONGRESS FOR ADMISSION TO THE UNION.

CHAP. XXIII.

1849.

So California was fairly launched and started on her career as a State. Will Congress admit her to the sisterhood of States, or keep her out?—a State by the voice of her people, and in all constitutional forms, yet without a State's representation in the Senate, or a State's voice among the Representatives.

The Thirty-first Congress met at Washington on the 3d of December, 1849; but the House could not organize until the 22d, when, after adopting the plurality rule, Howell Cobb, of Georgia, received one hundred and two votes, and was elected Speaker, over Robert C. Winthrop, who received one hundred—the remaining twenty being scattered. President Zachary Taylor then sent in his first annual Message—the one that contained the famous passage which made the critics of the world so merry: "We are at peace with all the world, and seek to maintain our cherished relations of amity with the rest of mankind."

Referring to the affairs of California, he said that as no civil government had been provided for it by Congress, the people, impelled by the necessities of their political condition, had met in convention, and the latest advices gave him reason to suppose they had formed a constitution and State government. It was believed they would shortly apply for the admission of California into the Union as a sovereign State. Should such be the case, and should their constitution be conformable to the requisitions of the Constitution of the United States, he recommended their application to a favorable consideration. By awaiting the action of the people of the territory, who would lay the foundation of a republican form of government in such principles and organize its power in such form as would seem to them most likely to effect their safety and happiness, all uneasiness might be avoided, and confidence and kind feeling preserved. "With a view of maintaining the harmony and tranquillity so dear to all," said he, "we should abstain from the introduction of those exciting topics of a sectional character which have hitherto produced painful apprehensions in the public mind; and I repeat the solemn warning of the first and most illustrious of my predecessors against furnishing any ground for characterizing parties by geographical discriminations."

CHAP. XXIII.
1849.

It was excellent advice, but nobody took it. The President informed Congress that a collector had been appointed for San Francisco under the act extending the revenue laws over California. He advised the confirmation of the collections made there under military authority, and that the avails be expended within the territory, or paid into the treasury to meet appropriations for the improvement of its harbors and rivers. Arrangements for determining the sites of light-houses on the coast had been made, and, appreciating the mineral wealth of California, and its advantages by position, he proposed reconnoissances of several routes for railroads to the Pacific.

1850. Jan.

General Sam Houston, of Texas, on the 4th of January, introduced a proposition which, while conceding that Congress had no power over the subject of negro slavery within the limits of the United States, either to prohibit, interfere with, or establish it in any State or Territory, for the sake of harmony affirmed that if the people in the newly-acquired Territories south of the parallel of thirty-six degrees thirty minutes north latitude [the Missouri Compromise line, and nearly the latitude of Monterey] should establish negro slavery in the formation of their State governments, it should be deemed no objection to their admission into the Union.

On the 21st of January, General Taylor, in answer to a resolution of inquiry, stated frankly that he had urged the formation of State governments in California and New Mexico. For this purpose he had sent out T. Butler King as bearer of dispatches, with a salary of eight dollars a day and expenses. He had not hesitated to express to the people of the territories his desire that they form a plan of State government, and submit it to Congress, with a prayer to be admitted, but he had authorized no Government agent to influence any election or convention, or to interfere as to the provisions or restrictions of the constitution. The officers sent to California by his predecessor were instructed to promote measures leading to the same end. His motive had been a simple desire to afford Congress an opportunity to avoid a bitter dissension.

Eight days afterwards, Henry Clay presented a series of compromise propositions to the Senate. The first proposed to admit California to the Union, with suitable boundaries, and without any restriction by Congress as to the exclusion or introduction of slavery within her boundaries. The second affirmed that Congress ought to establish Territorial governments for all the rest of the territory acquired from Mexico, without adopting any restriction or condition on the subject of slavery. Another de-

CHAP. XXIII.
1850.

clared it inexpedient to abolish slavery in the District of Columbia, while slavery existed in Maryland, without the consent of the people of Maryland and of the District, and without compensation to the slave-owners. Another declared it expedient to prohibit the slave-trade in the District. Others announced that more effectual provision ought to be made for the restitution and delivery of fugitive slaves, and that Congress had no power to prohibit the trade in slaves between the States.

The debate that followed upon these propositions engrossed the attention of the Senate almost exclusively for nearly two months, and they were not finally disposed of until September. Mr. Foote, of Mississippi, saw no objection to admitting all of California above the line of thirty-six degrees thirty minutes, as a Free State, providing another Slave State could be carved out of Texas, so as to preserve the equiponderance between the Slave and Free States of the Union.

Mr. Mason, of Virginia, deeply regretted Mr Clay's admission that by law slavery was already abolished in New Mexico and California—a doctrine never assented to, so far as he knew, until then, by any senator representing one of the slaveholding States.

"Never," said Jefferson Davis, of Mississippi, "will I take less than the Missouri Compromise line extended to the Pacific Ocean, with the specific recognition of the right to hold slaves in the territory below that line, and that before such Territories are admitted into the Union as States, slaves may be taken there from any of the United States, at the option of the owners."

To which Mr. Clay nobly replied: "Coming from a Slave State, as I do, I owe it to myself, I owe it to truth, I owe it to the subject to state, that no earthly power could induce me to vote for a specific measure for the introduction of slavery where it had not before existed, either south or north of that (Missouri Compromise) line. Coming, as I do, from a Slave State, it is my solemn, deliberate, and well-matured determination that no power—no earthly power—shall compel me to vote for the positive introduction of slavery, either south or north of that line. If the citizens of those territories (California and New Mexico) choose to establish slavery, I am for admitting them with such provisions in their constitutions; but then it will be their work, and not ours, and their posterity will have to reproach them, and not us, for forming constitutions allowing the institution of slavery to exist among them."

William R. King, of Alabama, objected to California's mode of procedure. He preferred to train people through a Territorial government for the exercise and enjoyment of our institutions.

CHAP. XXIII.

1850. Feb.

On the 13th of February, President Taylor apprised Congress by message, that California had organized a State Government, and through her senators and representatives was applying for admission into the Union.

Mar. 4.

It was upon the motion to refer this message to the Committee on Territories, that Mr. Calhoun, already prostrated with his last sickness, prepared his speech, which was read to the Senate on the 4th of March by Senator Mason. He asked what was to be done with California if she should not be admitted? and himself answered that she must be remanded back to the territorial condition, as was done in the case of Tennessee. The irregularities in her case, he said, were immeasurably greater and offered much stronger reasons for pursuing that course than did those of Tennessee. "But," said he, "California may not submit. That is not probable; but if she should not, when she refuses, it will be time for us to decide what is to be done." Mr. Calhoun held that the individuals in California who formed the constitution of a State without first receiving the authority of Congress so to do, usurped the sovereignty of a State, and acted in open defiance of the authority of Congress; what they did was revolutionary and rebellious in its character, and anarchical in its tendency. If General Riley had ordered the election of delegates to the constitutional convention without authority, he ought to be tried, or at least reprimanded, and his acts disavowed. As the Government had done neither, he presumed that his course was approved. "If you admit California," said he, "you exclude us from the acquired territories with the intention of destroying irretrievably the equilibrium between the two sections."

Three days later, Daniel Webster addressed the Senate on Mr. Clay's resolutions. He reiterated his previous expressions that we had territory enough; that we should follow the Spartan maxim—Improve, adorn what you have, seek no further. He held slavery to be excluded from California by the law of nature. He would not vote to put any prohibition into any act providing a Territorial government. He "would not take pains to reaffirm an ordinance of nature, nor to re-enact the will of God." In this speech he uttered his remarkable sentence concerning peaceable secession.

William H. Seward said: "Let California come in." "California, that comes from the clime where the west dies away into the rising east—California, which bounds at once the empire and the continent—California, the youthful queen of the Pacific, in the robes of freedom gorgeously inlaid with gold, is doubly welcome.

She stands justified for all the irregularities in her method of coming." He praised her that she would not remain in the condition of a military colony. The irregularities of her method of coming, of which so much complaint was made, were the following: She came unceremoniously, without a preliminary consent of Congress; she assigned her own boundaries without the previous authority of Congress; she was too large; no census had been taken; no laws prescribed the qualifications of suffrage before her constitutional convention was held; she came constrained by executive influence to come as a Free State and to come at once. Of these last charges the first clause was denied, the second clause was admitted, nor was it a serious usurpation in the executive to recommend that a State relieve itself and him from the exercise of military authority. Mr. Seward believed that the perpetual unity of our empire hung on the decision of that day. He urged that the consent of Congress be granted at once—they would never agree if not then. " Nor," said he, " will California abide delay. I do not say she contemplates independence, because she does not anticipate rejection." "Either the stars and stripes must wave over her ports, or she must raise aloft a standard for herself." He asked if it would be a mean ambition to set up within fifty years monuments like those which two hundred years had established on the Atlantic coasts? As to her ability to become independent, he reminded the Senate that she was farther away than England, out of the reach of railroads or unbroken steam navigation; the prairie, and mountain, and desert, an isthmus of foreign jurisdiction, and a cape of storms interposed between her and the armies of the Union. "You may send a navy there; but she has only to open her mines and she can seduce your navies and appropriate your floating bulwarks to her own defence." If she went, he intimated that Oregon would go also, and then the Pacific coast was lost. So, with an argument which few Californians would have used, Mr. Seward insisted upon the immediate admission, while he opposed any compromise.

CHAP. XXIII.
1850.
March 11.

Mr. Seward showed how earnest he was, by a confession which brought Senator Foote to his feet for an explanation, and startled not a little his anti-slavery friends. Repugnant to his wishes as such a necessity would be, he said that even if California had come seeking admission as a Slave State, in view of the extraordinary circumstances of her coming, and of the consequences of the dismemberment of the empire consequent upon her rejection, he would have voted for her admission. It was in this famous speech of Mr. Seward's that the sentence occurred which made him the best-abused man in the country for ten years following: "There is a higher law than the Constitution." He replied to a point which Mr. Webster had made, that there is no just human enactment which is not a re-enactment of the law of God. He could not rely on climate to exclude slavery, for he was born in a land where slavery existed, though it was a land all north of the fortieth parallel of latitude.

While the debate was pending, John Bell, of Tennessee, had submitted a series of compromise resolutions, the sixth of which accepted the constitution of California, and admitted the State on an equal footing in all respects with the original States. Stephen A. Douglas, of Illinois, from the Committee on Territories, doubting the fate of the proposed compromise, introduced two bills for a settlement without a compromise—one to admit California, the other to establish territorial governments for Utah and New Mexico. Both had their second reading, and then Mr. Benton's proposition to consider the California Bill was, on Mr. Clay's motion, tabled—*ayes*, twenty-seven; *noes*, twenty-five. So it was determined that there should be some compromise before the question was settled.

Mr. Foote now moved the reference of Mr. Bell's resolutions to a committee of thirteen, without instructions. Mr. Benton opposed "making an omnibus" of the resolutions, and urged the impropriety of causing the passage of one important bill to depend upon the adoption or rejection of any other bill. His motion to keep the California question separate from all others was lost—*ayes,* twenty-three ; *noes,* twenty-eight.

Mr. Foote's motion, so amended as to refer Mr. Clay's as well as Mr. Bell's resolutions to a select committee, was adopted. The committee of thirteen was selected by ballot as follows: Henry Clay of Kentucky, Chairman ; Mr. Dickinson of New York, Mr. Phelps of Vermont, Mr. Bell of Tennessee, Mr. Cass of Michigan, Mr. Webster of Massachusetts, Mr. Berrien of Georgia, Mr. Cooper of Pennsylvania, Mr. Downs of Louisiana, Mr. King of Alabama, Mr. Mangum of North Carolina, Mr. Mason of Virginia, and Mr. Bright of Indiana—seven from Slave States, six from Free States.

Early in May, Mr. Clay reported, and among the propositions of his report was one admitting California forthwith as a State, with the boundaries adopted in her constitution. These compromise resolutions, and the "Omnibus Bill" which embraced their principal provisions, were vigorously debated for the next four months.

Mr. Soulé, of Louisiana, moved that all south of the parallel of thirty-six degrees thirty minutes be cut off from California, and formed into a Territory to be called *South California*, which should be admitted as a State when it were able and willing, with or without slavery, as its people might desire. This was rejected by nineteen *ayes* (all Southern votes) and thirty-six *noes*. Mr. King moved that the parallel of thirty-five degrees thirty minutes be the southern boundary of the State of California; rejected, *ayes* twenty, *noes* thirty-seven. Mr. Davis, of Mississippi, moved that thirty-six degrees thirty minutes be the boundary; lost, *ayes* twenty-three, *noes* thirty-two. Mr. Turney moved that the people of California be enabled to form a new constitution; lost, *ayes* nineteen, *noes* thirty-three. Mr. Yulee moved to remand California to a territorial condition, and limit her southern boundary; lost, *ayes* twelve, *noes* thirty-five. Mr. Foote moved to erect all that part of California that lies south of the thirty-six-thirtieth parallel into the "Territory of Colorado;" lost, *ayes* thirteen, *noes* twenty-nine. Mr. Turney moved to fix the southern boundary by the line of thirty-six thirty; lost, *ayes* twenty, *noes* thirty. On the 12th of August, the Southern members, having exhausted all parliamentary tactics to stave it off, the question was put on ordering the California Bill engrossed for its third reading, for by this time the several measures of the Compromise Bill had been severed and brought forward in distinct bills. It prevailed, *ayes* thirty-three (all the Free State senators and Mr. Bell, Mr. Benton, Mr. Houston, Mr. Spruance, Mr. Wales, and Mr. Underwood voting *aye*); *noes* nineteen (all from Slave States). Next day the bill had its third reading, and passed, *ayes* thirty-four, *noes* eighteen.

Immediately Senators Mason and Hunter of Virginia, Butler and Rhett of South Carolina, Turney of Tennessee, Jefferson Davis of Mississippi, Atchison of Missouri, and Morton and Yulee of Florida, entered their protest against it. They thought it due to themselves, the people of their care, and their posterity, to leave an enduring memorial of their opposition to the measure. They wished to place upon record the reason of their opposition to a bill whose consequences might be so durable and portentous as to make it an object of deep interest to all who came after them. This reason, reiterated in several forms, was, that the admission of California made an odious discrimination against the property of fifteen slaveholding States. It denied those States a right to the equal enjoyment of the territory of the Union. The Government, they said, had in effect declared that the exclusion of slavery from the territory of the United States was an object so high and important as to justify a disregard, not only to all the principles of sound policy, but also of the institution itself. "Against this conclusion we must now and forever protest, as it is destructive of the safety and liberties of those whose rights have been committed to our care, fatal to the peace and equality of the States which we represent, and must lead, if persisted in, to the dissolution of that confederacy in which the slaveholding States have never sought more than equality, and in which they will not be content to remain with less."

In this protest the abandoned dogma of Mr. Calhoun, that the Constitution of the United States carries slavery with it, into whatever territory it extends, is assumed as a true doctrine. Afterwards it was announced by Judge Taney, in the Dred Scott decision, from the bench of the Supreme Court. The hint at secession on the admission of California as a Free State, and the consequent destruction of the balance in the Senate between the Slave and Free States, was regarded at the time as little more than a very common threat. Afterwards, it was remembered as significant that even then the great rebellion was in contemplation.

The California Bill went to the House of Representatives, and was read twice and committed on the 28th of August. On the 7th of September it came up, and Mr. Boyd, of Kentucky, moved to append the bill organizing the Territory of New Mexico. Mr. Vinton, of Ohio, objected to that, as out of order. Speaker Cobb overruled the objection, but the House refusing to sustain his decision, the amendment was not considered. Jacob Thompson, of Mississippi, moved to cut off from California all below the line of thirty-six forty, which was rejected — *ayes*, seventy-six; *noes*, one hundred and sixty-one. Then the bill was ordered to its third reading and passed—*ayes*, one hundred and fifty; *noes*, fifty-six, all Southerners.

The bill went to the President for his signature, and, on the 9th of September, Millard Fillmore, who, by the death of General Taylor, had succeeded to the Presidential chair, signed it, and California was admitted the thirty-first State of the American Union.

Senators Fremont and Gwin were admitted to their seats as representatives from the new State in time to give a vote upon one or two of the Compromise measures. All the propositions of Mr. Clay's Omnibus, though severed from each other, and presented in separate bills, and two of them, afterwards reunited, were adopted. So the joy over California's admission was not unalloyed at the North, nor the sorrow at the South without compensation. She was admitted as a Free State only on condition of leaving New Mexico and Utah open to slavery, the concession of perpetual slavery in the District of Columbia, the passage of a law for the recapture of fugitive slaves, which grievously offended the North, and a stipulation that the subject of slavery should never again be agitated in either chamber of Congress.

These compromises, which were so distasteful to both sections, really seemed for a time to bring repose to the public mind. The National Democratic Convention of June, 1852, which nominated Franklin Pierce for President, resolved that the Democratic Party would abide by and adhere to a faithful execution of the compromises of 1850. The Whig National Convention of June, 1852, which nominated Winfield Scott for President, recommended and acquiesced in them by a vote of three hundred and twelve *ayes* to seventy *noes*. These two great parties embraced the vast majority of the voters of the Union.

There was outside of these parties a vigilant and restless minority, which never ceased agitating the slavery question, and it was making rapid inroads into both parties; yet the repose might have remained much longer unbroken, but for the fact that they who most deprecated agitation, startled the political world four years later with the doctrine that the compromises of 1850 made inoperative and void the Missouri

Compromise, and insisted on putting that doctrine into the Kansas-Nebraska Bill. After which there was no more "repose," and the compromises, by virtue of which California struggled into the Union, were treated as no longer binding beyond the letter of the laws that embraced them.

CHAPTER XXIV.

"*THE FALL OF '49 AND THE SPRING OF '50.*"

CHAP. XXIV.
1850.
Oct.

News of the admission of the State into the Union reached San Francisco on the 18th of October, 1850, by the steamer *Oregon*. Of course it could create no surprise; the event had been looked on as foreordained ever since the conquest. The people claimed it as a right, and had never contemplated the possibility of its being denied. Notwithstanding, it was a great thing to have the seal of national authority put on their State proceedings; it was a grand thing to be recognized as part of the American Union; and so the *Oregon's* tidings were greeted with high enthusiasm. The 29th was set aside in San Francisco as a day of celebration over the event. A procession, of which the Chinese were a striking feature, an oration by Judge Nathaniel Bennett on the plaza, the recitation of an ode written by a lady, the firing of guns, the discharge of artillery, the display of fireworks, and the illumination by bonfires, made the day and the night memorable.

From the fall of 1849 to the fall of 1850 was the tent era of California—the strange, flush times of the young State. Most of the population felt themselves pilgrims in the land, temporary residents, enduring merrily severe privations for the sake of a future of plenty and enjoyment in a distant home. Property was changing hands, fortune changing favorites, with astonishing rapidity. The poor man of yesterday was the rich man of to-day. The servant, running away from his master, tarried a month or two in the mines, and returned with gold enough to buy his master out. Social distinctions were nearly rubbed out. Almost all men felt that, whether they were born so or not, they had become free and equal.

The average wages made by miners in 1849 were, perhaps, twenty to thirty dollars a day; yet in rich diggings an average of from three hundred to five hundred a week was not uncommon for weeks together. The abundance of gold in the hands of people not used to it made them lavish. There was very little sitting down and calculating how to economize, and there was no "Poor Richard" pleading frugality, and pointing out the penury that must follow thriftlessness. And if there was any shrewd Yankee still following the precepts of his early education, and in an open-handed generation trying to remember that it is not what a man makes, but what he saves, that determines him rich or poor, his daily memorandum of expenses must have seemed very shocking.

If he breakfasted at a restaurant in San Francisco he had a dollar to pay for a beefsteak and a cup of coffee. For fresh eggs he must pay from seventy-five cents to a dollar each. His dinner would cost him from a dollar and a half to five dollars, according to his appetite. A "square meal" at a cleanly tavern cost from two dollars upward. Washing was eight dollars for the dozen pieces; it even happened, they say, that some sent their dirty clothes to China to be washed.

The great body of immigrants were adult males. The lack of refined and virtuous women gave society a rough, unpolished aspect. The fame of the gold placers had tempted a rush of all sorts of men, and it must be confessed that for a while it seemed that the doubtful and dangerous classes were in excess over the orderly. The lightest drift of the floating population of the world washed up here. Not only the restless characters of Christendom, but of heathen countries also, obeyed the strong attraction. Some middle-aged good men came, impelled by a sense of duty to try one chance more of acquiring for their dependent families the competence that they had failed to command at home. Some

left their families, because it was no cross to
leave them. Others came because enterprise
spurred them, and there was nothing to hold
them back. Others came with motives of ambition;
they were conscious of having failed in
the old country—in a new one they would try
life over again. They had counted the offices
to be filled, and came on to serve their country,
and be maintained at the public expense.
There were a few, a very few, who had faith in
the future of the region; who intelligently appreciated
the geographical and commercial position
of California, and came with a sincere desire
to see its foundations laid in justice and its
walls squared by Christian principle. Altogether,
and chiefly, it was not the best material
out of which to construct a model society; but
it was strong, enterprising, swift, and positive.
It might become either noble or infamous. It
was only incapable of mediocrity.

On landing at San Francisco, which early
became the principal port of debarkation, or on
arriving over the Sierras, almost all dashed first
into the mines. Placer mining could be learned
in a day; any one who could shovel dirt, stand
up to his knees in running water, and shake a
pan, knew the art. It indeed required skill to
" prospect " successfully ; but if one doubted
his ability in that matter, he had only to follow
the multitude, and do as they did, or take up

the deserted claim which a company, hearing of better "finds," had quit.

A few weeks' or months' experience satisfied the multitude that mining was not their forte, and they retreated from it, providing they had the money to get off with. If a man knew any trade, he could make more than the miner's average by work he had learned to love. If accustomed to farming, he could raise potatoes or beans or corn in some rich nook close by the miner's camp, and be more sure of a liberal profit than the miner whom he fed. Any body could keep a store. Any one who could erect a cabin, and get a barrel of whiskey safely into it, could keep a hotel. The miners pioneered the farmers, mechanics, and tradesmen; and wherever they stopped for a few months on a bar or in a cañon, a village, perhaps a city, sprang up as if by magic. Still, all the while, there was a strong tide of successful or disgusted miners setting back to San Francisco.

The currency was gold-dust—that is, small scales, globules, or nuggets of gold. At first they rudely measured it; then as rudely weighed it—a silver dollar's weight, the weight of a jack-knife, the weight of an ounce avoirdupois. Then they began to melt the dust into bars, ingots, or slugs, stamping the initials of the assayer to give credit to its designated weight where scales were not accessible. Not till 1854, when the United States gave them a Branch Mint at San Francisco, was the currency regulated with any satisfaction.

The cheapness of gold raised the value of every thing else. Silver was scarce; no change under a quarter of a dollar was given or taken. What was worth buying was surely worth a quarter. Wages were exceedingly high: rough labor at San Francisco brought eight dollars a day; carmen earned from fifteen to twenty dollars a day; "help" was scarce at one hundred to two hundred dollars a month.

While labor was in such demand, and so well paid, it could not be deemed degrading. For carrying a trunk a mile a man would get a week's wages at Eastern rates. So, few scrupled to do for money whatever offered. There were the most astonishing changes in employments. Persons who had been preachers or doctors or lawyers at home, shouldered baggage, did street-work, drove drays, if they could muster the capital to buy a horse and cart, blacked boots, served at table, and were not ashamed.

Almost every company that bought a ship at the East, and came around the Horn in her, put in a full freight of eatables, thinking that if they only were not perishable, they could scarcely fail to find a profitable market. So the market was glutted with certain articles, while others no money would buy. Potatoes were dumped into the bay by the ton, not commanding a price sufficient to pay for boating them to the shore. Word would go East by steamer that the market was bare of butter or tobacco, or some style of dry goods for which a day or two of hot weather made some inquiry. The five or six sharp Eastern merchants who were favored with the news, would give quick dispatch to half a score of clippers, freighted with the articles desired. The first one in would make the fortune of the shippers, the tardy ones find no market. In the spring of 1850 such quantities of tobacco had arrived at San Francisco, for which there was no demand, that rather than pay the exorbitant prices of storage, the full chests were used to pave the muddy street-crossings. The resident merchants generally sold on commission, so the ruin was on the parties abroad for whom they acted as agents. The Eastern merchants then tried assorting cargoes; if one article had to be cast into the street, some other one might cover all losses, and secure a handsome profit on the whole venture. Sometimes it would seem as if they fancied that whatever was not wanted at home would be in demand here, and San Francisco was heaped and piled with odd, impracticable, useless goods, cramming the sparse warehouses, and overflowing them.

Houses framed and ready to be put together without the aid of any tool but an axe and a hammer, were sent out, some fine specimens of which still survive, wearing a pleasant, homely look, very noticeable for a fashion which never prevailed here. When there began to be a panic about fires, corrugated iron plates were shipped in considerable quantities. Some houses built of this material still remain, very rusty and leaky; and the materials of some that have been torn down to make room for brick buildings furnish a more durable than sightly fence for the suburban gardens.

The winter of 1849 and 1850 proved to be a very wet one—the "wettest one," the pioneers insisted, until 1861–62. The fact that the streets were without pavements, and the people chiefly domiciled in tents, no doubt enhanced the discomforts of the season, and contributed to give it a bad name. When a man has nothing but a piece of canvas over him, and cannot set foot into the street without sinking to the ankle in mud, and especially when he has no family in his wretched lodging-place, and has to "find himself," a tolerably moderate rainy season goes inevitably for a "horrid winter." With the opening of that spring, all who were

CHAP. XXIV.
1849–1850.

able, and expected to stay on the coast, prepared more respectable house-accommodations.

Among the curious consignments of the early days were omnibuses, which, because the streets were not easily traversed by heavy-wheeled vehicles, were planted and employed as restaurants. Old ships, which never could get hands enough to go to sea again, were beached at high tide. They served for enviable boarding-houses. As streets were laid out and constructed into the bay, many of these were left standing. As the sand-hills were wheeled down to the flats, and the grades raised, these grew firm in the foundations of the city. Upon more than one such was built up a superstructure in the form of a house. If it was a hotel, it still retained the name of the ship which was its foundation. The ship *Apollo* was used as a store; the *Euphemia* as a prison, while moored in the bay. Still others, beached in more slowly-growing parts of the town, were left to rot for years, unused. But as boats, sloops, and schooners were needed, and the price of labor declined, their timbers and old iron were got out and saved. Some of the best craft in the fleet of coastwise and river vessels that a dozen years later vexed the harbors and navigable streams of California were made out of the skeletons of ships originally built on the New England coast.

The saw-mill was soon at work, splitting the

redwoods, which crowned innumerable heights, into boards, shingles, and joists. Then wooden houses were run up almost in a day. The joists were set in the ground, and a floor laid, the uprights erected, and the frail structure grew story by story. Cloth answered for partitions and ceilings, and paper for paint. These combustible shells brought the rent of substantial houses. If the roof would shed water in winter, and the flimsy walls stand up against the winds of summer, it was enough. Throw a spark of fire into such materials, and unless a pail of water were at hand to quench it, it was of little use to ring the fire-bells. Nothing but a wide vacant space could stop the ravages of the conflagration.

Four great fires San Francisco suffered during this memorable term. The first broke out in Dennison's Exchange, a grand gambling-saloon on the south side of the Plaza, on the morning of the 24th of December, 1849. It burned over half the block, and destroyed more than a million dollars worth of property. Before the ruins had stopped smoking, much of the ground was rebuilt and occupied again. On the 4th of May, 1850, at four o'clock in the morning, fire again broke out near the same site. This time it swept over three blocks, from Montgomery to Kearny Street, and from Clay to Jackson Street, destroying three million dollars worth of property. In ten days, more than half the burnt district was rebuilt. On the 14th of June, 1850, another fire laid in ashes the district bounded by Kearny, Clay, and California streets and the bay, and the damages were estimated at four million dollars. On the morning of September 17th, 1850, a fourth fire consumed the buildings, mostly of wood, and but one story high, on the tract bounded by Dupont and Montgomery, Washington and Pacific streets. The damage was variously estimated at from a quarter to half a million of dollars.

Men grew credulous because there were so many unquestionable marvels as to the occasional finding of gold in nuggets, or lying loose in "pockets" of rocks. Early in 1850, two nuggets of gold were found, weighing about twenty-three pounds each. Others of not quite such astonishing size were brought to light in 1849. Every such case set half wild the miners who were toiling at a claim that paid less than at first, or whose early promise had not been kept. Very soon they were sorely given to "rushes."

In June, 1849, a mountaineer named Greenwood told the miners at Coloma that he had seen gold in abundance at Truckee Lake. The news spread swiftly, though noiselessly, and hundreds left good diggings to try their luck at Truckee Lake. They returned soon after thoroughly destitute. They found the place, but no color of gold there.

In May of 1850, the Gold Lake fever broke out. Two miners were overheard by a third talking of a lake on whose shores the gold lay loose like pebbles. The third man guessed that the wonderful region was Gold Lake, a little sheet of water not far from Downieville. He began at once preparations to go to it, talking freely meanwhile of what he had seen there. The story was whispered from one to another, and thousands of men deserted claims where they were making from twenty to forty dollars a day, and dashed off to the secluded pond—whence they returned a few months later without any thing to show for their pains.

It seems strange now that practical men were so often and easily deluded. But it must be remembered that the majority labored under the impression that they came to California just one trip too late, and they did not choose to lose the second chance at a fortune by tardiness. Besides, the true tales that were told and illustrated by the full belts of gold buckled about the waists of the narrators, were scarcely less astonishing to the inexperienced than the wildest fable that was poured into the ears of the experienced, whose credulity thrived on what they had seen.

These rushes afterwards became so common

CHAP. XXIV.

1849–1850.

that no year passed without one or more of them. Those who went and saw for themselves, were, on their return, instead of being the butt of their companions, regarded with admiration. They had "seen the elephant"— had experienced the joy of waking out of a delusion on the very spot where the charm was to work its wonders. It grew into a habit with some to take every fever, and join in every rush. At heart they thought fortune must favor those who took all the chances; but they professed an unconquerable desire to see the end of every humbug. Doubtless there are some in the State who have personally explored the truth or falsity of every grand mining story that has excited the public since the first stampede for Coloma.

Land, of course, acquired a high value about the centres of population, and troubles sprang up between the squatters, who claimed by preemption or actual possession, and the claimants under Spanish or Mexican grants. In August, 1850, there were serious riots at Sacramento. Most of the land there was claimed under conveyances from Sutter, yet it was sprinkled with squatters. The Sutter claimants got favorable decisions from the courts; but the squatters pulled out their pistols and refused to be ousted. Several of them were arrested and imprisoned. Their friends rushed, armed, to the rescue, and a collision occurred between them and the sheriff's *posse*. Several squatters were killed. Of the sheriff's party, one was killed and others wounded.

The gamblers of the world met here; the foremost of that desperate and wretched class swarmed to San Francisco like vultures to the carcass. The recklessness with which money was squandered made it their paradise. The homelessness of the people furnished them victims in abundance. The absence of municipal law, or the neglect of its officers, left them without restraint to indulge their career.

Soon the choicest business locations in town were occupied as gambling saloons. The plaza was surrounded by them. The Parker House rented for one hundred and ten thousand dollars a year; more than half the amount was paid by gamblers. The "El Dorado," while a tent, fifteen by twenty-five feet on the ground, rented for forty thousand dollars a year to gamblers.

These saloons were fitted up with all the attractions of gilded mirrors, pictures more costly than chaste, and plaster statuary. The gold was heaped upon the tables in piles that made the richest feel poor as they gaped at them. The miner, who had filled his buckskin pouch with gold and his bones with rheumatism after months of toil, dropping down to the

CHAP. XXIV.

1849-1850.

city on business or pleasure, or on his way East, could scarcely pass by the open doors, where so many thronged, without entering from curiosity. He saw there men pocketing by a lucky throw of the dice more money than his pouch held. Possibly he saw a man whom at home he had regarded as a model of morality, staking his whole substance on the chance of a card. The foolish fellow must needs try his luck too, is "dead broke" by the experiment, and now must, of course, hurry back to the mines to begin the world again. Men gambled who did not know a card when they came into the place; some from mere love of the excitement; some hopefully to snatch the means of getting back to their families, unquiet, anxious, and sick with hope deferred; some recklessly, because they were alone in the world, and none would suffer with their loss.

Without law, there was an unwritten law taken for granted, that dealt justice to rich and poor alike with rigid exactness. In the mines, where every thing depended on the good faith of man to man, theft was the mortal sin, and the eighth commandment was deemed altogether the most important of the decalogue. Men frequently wore their gold in belts about them; still, a very successful miner must have some sort of deposit for what he could not lug about his person. So he buried it under his cabin-floor, or by the roots of some privately marked tree, or in some other equally secret spot, where a spying neighbor would be very likely to catch him hiding it. But, woe to the thief who despoiled him! When a robbery was committed, they rallied from all the camps about, to hunt the culprit, and, when found, to try him, Judge Lynch presiding. The jury were intolerant of long trials. The examinations were sharp and brief, the questions apt to be leading. When the jury found a verdict of *guilty*, the miserable prisoner was run up by the neck to a limb of the nearest tree. The very swiftness of Justice saved her from being called into frequent requisition. Lynch law knew no delays, and made some terrible blunders, which, while they scared evil-doers none the less, brought this border law into disrepute.

About the meanest class that cursed the community was a brood of unprincipled, labor-hating, professional politicians, who gathered from all corners of the States, fetching with them the worst vices peculiar to the political system of the locality they had relieved by leaving. Some had found politics unprofitable at home; but, in their pursuit, had acquired habits that unfitted them for any less exciting employment. There were others who had been educated to believe that offices were made for their enjoyment. To demand one as much entitled them to places at the public crib, as more modest folks, by work, entitled themselves to a living. These were the "chivalry," whose touchstone was devotion to slavery. If they came from the South, they spoke with contemptuous oaths of the "Yankees;" if from the North, they out-heroded Herod in their abuse of "abolitionists," and knew no service too menial to render to the "gentlemen of the South."

There were a few who saved politics from utter degradation; men who in the midst of their business had studied the theory of our government, and were statesmen undeveloped to the public; others, also, who had been intrusted with power and position at home, but either because their influence waned, or hoping to rise faster in a new State, brought their talent and their experience to this market.

The Democratic party introduced California to the circle of territories, but the Whigs were in power when she was admitted as a State, and had they managed with shrewdness, they might have taken the cream of that advantage. They lacked sagacity in the selection of agents to represent them. They lost the favor of the miners by advising the sale of the mineral lands which the cosmopolitan crowd claimed to belong, without distinction of color, or nation, or language, or religion, to those who would work them.

Then the calculations of those who made the question of slavery paramount were all frustrated. The very method of the settlement of the country was a nail in the skull of slavery. The expectation of the war party had been that the climate "would draw to it mostly a Southern population." Probably that would have proved true but for the sudden violence with which the gold fever burst upon the States. Many early immigrants from the South brought their slaves with them. But if the penalty of death would not deter soldiers from deserting from camps, where there was nothing to do, to the mines—if wages treble any ever offered to sailors before would not keep Jack on board ship when sailing in any direction was homeward, it was certainly no wonder that the most trusty slave deserted his master, in a land where a few weeks' work made all men equal, and where there was every shade of color to mollify the prejudice that it excites. In every laborer the fugitive found a friend; for the freeman feels degraded to have a slave labor by his side. So the fugitive never came back, and most of the slave ventures into California were perfect failures.

Very soon it was obvious that men of Northern and Western birth outnumbered the Southerners. Now it happened, as we have shown, that Southern notions concerning labor were early unpopular. Still the old Democratic party training had been very thorough, which treated every thing of Southern origin as almost sacred. So here, as elsewhere, the South blustered and assumed every thing, while the North and the West succumbed, partly from habit, and partly because they had not come on a political errand, and did not expect to stay.

A curious anomaly was the result. The State with a marvellous unanimity declared against the chosen and peculiar institution of the South; yet Southern men bullied and ruled the community in every other respect, at their sovereign will.

Some strong conservative influences, some powerful elements of improvement, were at work in this motley mass. The accumulation of property by a man of any character made him a better friend of law and order; for property is always a stringent conservator. The newspapers, not so much by any bold denunciation of wrong as by simply exposing it, were doing a good work. They ventilated crime, and that is often enough to check its growth, which craves darkness and secrecy. Then there were eccentric men who made the circuit of the mining camps, preaching in quaint, unstudied language, summoning men to repentance at the risk of all abuse and insult. In the cities they gathered their meetings on the plazas, or at the doors of the most thronged gambling-saloons, whose inmates, very likely in a fit of sudden respect for religion, would pass around the hat for the preacher's benefit. These earnest, humor-loving, quick-witted street-preachers consorted well with the earnest, excited, rollicking times, and they did more good than at first might be supposed. Their exhortations, heard by fragments amid the oaths and the din of the gambling-table, may have summoned many a conscience, that seemed dead, to life again.

But of less doubtful power, of a force to which society soon responded unmistakably, was the influence of the undemonstrative Christian men sprinkled through the mass of immigrants—men who never lost the memory of home, who cherished the early truths that inspired their fathers, who were true to early vows, and faithful to their religion. Such, among the distant foot-hills, in the wildest settlements, and in all the cities, gathered the scattered children into Sabbath-schools, and formed the nuclei of religious associations that have since built churches, started good schools, rescued the Sabbath, and given to society its wholesome, healthful tone.

Good men, who felt at all at home here,

CHAP. XXIV.
1849–1850.

regarded the magnificent proportions of the State with pride. It enjoyed a far wider range of climate than its bounding parallels of latitude would suggest; yet few places on the globe are favored with so equable a temperature the year through as its commercial and popular capital. The mines clearly were to be the State's first source of wealth; if they held out as they promised, they could not fail to attract a vast emigration. The few experiments upon its soil showed that at an early future day there would be no need of importing supplies of food to feed all that would come. As population increased, wages must diminish, and then no condition would be lacking to encourage manufactures and the arts.

Then the grand position! Seated by the sea, midway between Europe and Asia, on the road that Atlantic sails most naturally take to reach China or Japan, with a harbor not surpassed on the globe, and that without any considerable rival on the coast through a stretch of latitude greater than from Newfoundland to Cuba; midway between the climates which it enjoyed so mixed, that apples and figs, wheat and olives ripened side by side, and summer and winter require a little difference of clothing; midway between "the peoples," who, meeting here, made the metropolis cosmopolitan, and in the same mining-camp conferred in

half-a-dozen languages; midway of the marts
and harvest-fields of the world, it required no
enthusiasm to make the dullest inquirer of her
destiny anticipate a wonderful future for California.

CHAPTER XXV.

AFTER THE ADMISSION.

CHAP. XXV.

1850–1856.

It is next proposed to sketch the growth of the State from the date of its admission (1850), until a great uprising of the people, constituting a thorough radical reformation of politics and morals, once more arrested general attention, and set older communities to speculating upon the future of California — in short, until the Vigilance rule in San Francisco, of 1856.

As a whole, during these six years, the course of the people was upward: the State grew in population, in wealth, in improvements. But in one respect there was no visible growth. Justice fell into bad company. Shameless men managed public affairs, especially in the cities, and society did not keep pace with commerce and mining. Or rather, the conservative element was so overlaid that it was hidden; yet it was growing all the while, and when the burden became too heavy to be borne, it emancipated itself.

The mines did not give out. The croakers had said they would — had prophesied that in five years they would be exhausted, and then the population would vanish as it had come. Sir Roderick Murchison, in September, 1850, endeavored, in an article in the *Quarterly Review*, to show that in all probability the gold washings of California would soon be exhausted at the rapid rate they were being worked, and he laid down the proposition that no gold-bearing veins in the solid rock could be wrought with profit. Fortunately for his fame, that distinguished geologist did not make very definite his prediction. The placers yielded more abundantly in 1851 and 1852 than they did in 1850.

The entire gold-yield, from 1848 to 1856 inclusive, has been variously estimated at from four hundred and fifty to six hundred millions of dollars. Hittell, who thinks the lower estimate the more nearly correct, distributes the yield among these years as follows:—

In 1848, ten millions of dollars; in 1849, forty millions; in 1850, fifty millions; in 1851, fifty-five millions; in 1852, sixty millions; in 1853, sixty-five millions; in 1854, sixty millions; in 1855, fifty-five millions; in 1856, fifty-five millions. The same author holds that in 1850 there were fifty thousand miners at work; if so, each could have averaged but one thousand dollars for that year—which, considering the cost of living and of travel, was scarcely the fortune that the eager emigrant bargained for when he left his home.

At first, the gold was mostly taken from the bars of the rivers, which constituted the "wet diggings," or the ravines which were known as "dry diggings." But in summer, many of the rivers shrank to mere threads, and by degrees the gold was traced far away from their banks. Yet water was essential in the process of separating the metal from the dirt, and either the auriferous soil and gravel must be brought to the river, or the river brought to them. The enterprising miners thought the latter the cheaper plan, so many a river was turned out of its bed, and conveyed in canals to the spot where it was wanted. High up on the mountain-sides dams were built, and the waters, as they gushed from the springs, imprisoned in reservoirs. Thence they were led by gentle declivities across the slopes of the foot-hills, over deep ravines and river-beds, in flumes sustained on trestle-work bridges. They were distributed by branching ditches in all directions, and afforded at a fixed price for the inch in an abundant supply to the miners; thus annihilating the distinction between wet and dry diggings, and substituting for the cradle and rocker the "long tom," and for that, in turn, the sluice-box. These canals, and the long skeleton bridges supporting their aqueducts at immense heights, added a new and curious feature to the landscape, and gave an impression of improvement not justified by the wildness everywhere discernible on a closer look. Nor was the amazement of the traveller abated when he learned that these costly enterprises, valued, at the close of 1856, at eleven millions of dollars, were built with the miners' own money, and almost exclusively without the employment of foreign capital.

The general extension of the system of water ditches made way for another improvement. In 1852, Edward E. Mattison, of Nevada County, and formerly of Connecticut, revolutionized the whole business, and restored great value to many an abandoned field by introducing the hydraulic hose. This was the application of a stream of water conveyed from a height through strong pipes and a flexible hose, and directed upon the face of hills in which the gold was scattered in minute particles. Before this hydraulic force, large hills were entirely broken down and the lighter débris washed away through sluice-boxes, where riffles detained and quicksilver caught the precious metal.

It was early discovered that in a certain white quartz, very abundant in Tuolumne and Mariposa counties, especially on the tract bought by Fremont from Alvarado, in 1846, there was gold plainly visible to the naked eye. The placer miners looked covetously on the sparkling points or seams, but generally pronounced it too tightly locked in its stony safes to be come at with profit. Capital made the attempt, however.

In 1851 the first quartz-crushing mill was erected; others quickly followed, the stamps being worked in some cases by horse-power, in some by water, and in others by steam. Soon there was a rage, especially among foreigners, for quartz. Many Englishmen bought up gold-bearing quartz veins by the map, sent out costly machinery, gave theorizing superintendents exorbitant salaries, paid enormous travelling fees, lavished their money, and looked for returns that would startle the world. Sometimes their agents on arriving could not find the purchased veins; sometimes the veins were all right, but no water was to be had; sometimes, where all the other conditions were satisfactory, the agents failed in practical experience to make unquestionably rich mines pay. Most of the machinery was found useless for the purposes intended. Operations had been commenced when freights and the prices of provisions, materials, and labor were very high. Full two millions of English capital, and not a little American, was squandered, and then quartz-crushing at a profit was pronounced impracticable, and was generally abandoned. Two or three years later that business revived again. In 1855 the quartz on

Alison's ranch, near Grass Valley, which had long been known as very rich, was carefully tested. The result brought quartz-crushing again into favor, started the idle mills, and caused others with improved machinery to be erected. By the end of 1856 there were one hundred and thirty-eight quartz-mills in the State, valued at one million seven hundred and sixty-three thousand dollars, of which forty-eight were driven by steam. There were innumerable shafts and adits and tunnels which sometimes pierced quite through the hills. The hydraulic hose had washed down immense hills, and sadly marred the natural beauty of the mining region. There were more than forty-four hundred miles of artificial watercourses widening the area of the miners' operations, and though the number of miners had not increased, and more and more of the gold was detained in California, her annual export of treasure was maintained without much variation, from 1851 to 1856 inclusive, at about fifty millions of dollars.

CHAP. XXV. 1856.

But although the mines were the strong magnet that drew immigration, they did not furnish the principal occupation of those who arrived. The early immigrants generally tried them long enough to learn that digging gold was after all quite as hard work as digging potatoes. The unrestrained liberty of camp-

CHAP. XXV.

1850–1856.

life soon parted with its first fine flavor, there was so much drudgery mixed with it. Its excitements early lost their charm, and the calmer sort pined for a steadier kind of employment. Every mining camp made a market for vegetables, and the cost of transporting them tempted those who knew the art to "tickle the earth" with hoe and spade, and see if she would "laugh with harvests" of root crops. The great valleys were already famous for their yield of grains; but the Americans had been here for three or four years before it was generally conceded that there were over a few hundred acres of "vegetable land" in the State. Experiment settled the question satisfactorily, and then agriculture soon populated the fertile nooks near the mines, planted the sheltered slopes of the foot-hills with gardens and orchards, and brought into cultivation the great valleys. Money was made more easily, fortunes were built up more surely, and scarcely less rapidly, by catering to the wants of settlers than by hunting for gold.

The census of 1852 reported the wheat crop of the State at two hundred and seventy-one thousand seven hundred and sixty-three bushels. The crop of 1856 was nearly thirteen times as great.

The potato crop of 1852 was quite equal to the demand, the average price being one and a half dollars per bushel. But in the supply and prices of farm produce and garden truck, there continued great fluctuations. The onion-fields of 1851 and 1852 made their owners rich; the same fields in 1853 and 1854, with excellent crops, ruined their owners. The average price of two hundred pounds of wheat flour at San Francisco was, in January, 1851, sixteen dollars; of 1852, eleven dollars; of 1853, twenty-six dollars; of 1854, ten and a quarter dollars; of 1855, nine dollars; of 1856, eight dollars and sixty-two cents. Attention was early attracted to the facilities of the southern and central parts of the State for producing wine. The census of 1850 reported fifty-eight thousand and fifty-five gallons of wine made in California, and no other State in the Union made as much. The number of vines was quadrupled in 1856. The land available for cultivation, aside from swamp and overflowed regions, was estimated at forty-one and a half millions of acres. Of these, one in every three hundred and seventy-six was under cultivation in 1852; and one in every seventy in 1856. Of animal food, from the beginning there was plenty; but as late as 1856 none of the great staple, cereal, or root crops were equal to the demand; yet the conclusion had been reached by intelligent observers that California, considering her limited amount of arable land, was without a rival in her capacity

CHAP. XXV.

1850–1856.

of grain production—that she produced wheat and the other small grains "in larger quantities to the acre, of better quality, with more certainty and less labor, than any other country in the known world."

The high prices of labor kept back manufactures, and only those were developed which populous new lands summon into existence. The saw-mill, herald and pioneer of most settlements, lagged behind population here. In 1856 there were three hundred and seventy-three of them in the State, erected at a cost of two and a half millions of dollars, cutting into lumber the exhaustless forests of the coast range and Sierra Nevada. There were one hundred and thirty-one grist-mills, fourteen iron foundries, and eighteen tanneries. Ship-building was as yet in its infancy.

Commerce reaped a splendid harvest from California during this period. Almost every thing eaten or worn here was imported until 1851. In 1852 the vessels arriving at and departing from San Francisco averaged more than seven a day. In 1853 the imports of San Francisco were valued at thirty-five millions of dollars. The flour and meal bill of this importing people was five millions of dollars; its butter bill four millions, and its lumber bill the same. Its exports were a few hides and over fifty-seven million dollars worth of gold. The vessels arriving and departing that year registered one million one hundred and sixty-seven thousand four hundred and thirty-three tons—greater than the tonnage of Boston three years later.

Indeed, commerce overdid itself that year. It was considerably less in 1854; still less in 1855; and less yet in 1856; and still San Francisco, at the last date named, was fourth in the list of American cities for its tonnage. New York, Boston, and New Orleans only exceeded it; Philadelphia could not claim half its amount. It must be remembered, however, that this vast fleet was not, nor any considerable portion of it, owned here.

The Bay of San Francisco was lively in those days. Long wharves thrust themselves over the flats towards deep water. Their construction had cost a million and a half of dollars as early as 1850, and fair facilities were furnished for tolerably quick dispatch—the great lack being fire-proof store-houses. Vessels propelled by steam ploughed the bay and rivers, and plied up and down the coast. Fortnightly steamers arrived and left in 1853, carrying the mails and bringing crowds of passengers and such freight as could afford to pay the high transportation charges of the Isthmus.

A passion possessed the merchants of the Eastern cities to take California ventures. Cargoes were bought up and sent out to be sold on commission so quietly that none but the sharpest could keep posted on trade movements. Bostonians, New Yorkers, Philadelphians would not be convinced that the high prices of 1849 and 1850 might not suddenly rage again on a day's notice, and they poured in their miscellaneous assortments in spite of the protests of correspondents. Money was plenty, but goods were plentier. Almost every thing was sold on commission or at auction, for rents were too high to permit unmarketable articles to be stored long. Soon it was clear that the race was to the swift. If an article was growing scarce, the first ship that could get around the Horn with it won the market. So, fleet clippers came into fashion, and it was held simple madness to freight a slow sailer.

Throughout the great part of 1852 high prices ruled for the necessaries of life. Flour, from eight dollars a barrel in March, ran up to forty dollars a barrel in November. Storms kept the clippers back. Of some things the supply was quite exhausted, and the shifts to which people were put, were very amusing to disinterested observers. The *Alta* newspaper, in July, suddenly came down from a broad, handsome sheet to a small folio, with a page fourteen by ten inches in dimensions. The *Herald* was forced to use brown wrapping-paper for its issues.

POPULATION OF THE STATE.

This occasional barrenness of markets did something towards stimulating home manufactures; but not much, on account of the rates of wages, and the fact that money commanded so high an interest.

The population of California was estimated in 1831 at little over twenty-three thousand; in January of 1849, at thirty-six thousand, of whom thirteen thousand were natives, eight thousand from the United States, and five thousand from other foreign countries. The national census of 1850 reported one hundred and seventeen thousand five hundred and thirty-eight inhabitants in the new State. In 1851, twenty-seven thousand people arrived by sea, and more than half of them by way of the Isthmus or the Nicaragua route; yet the steamers carried back more than they brought. If the State grew, it was chiefly by means of the large overland emigration. In 1852, the State census showed a population of two hundred and sixty-four thousand, four hundred and thirty-five. Immigration was double that of the preceding year; about one-third the number that arrived departed. Fewer were "going home" to stay. In 1853 there arrived fifteen thousand by land, and thirty-four thousand by sea. The departures were, exclusively by sea, thirty-one thousand. This was pushing ahead—a gain from abroad of eighteen thousand. It was estimated

CHAP. XXV.

1850–1856.

that but one-fifth the whole population were women, and but one-tenth children. By the close of 1856 the State contained, by estimate, over half a million inhabitants.

Though the Indians were left out in the usual business calculations of the people, they played no inconsiderable part in the country during this period. They made some trouble, required much legislation, and were the innocent means of pumping much money out of the General Government.

After the spell of the Fathers was dissolved, many of the tame ones relapsed into heathenism, carrying back with them a more positive laziness than their ancestors possessed, and a surer instinct for thieving. They shrunk into retirement during the conquest, and were seldom thought of. Domesticated representatives of their race were housed among the pioneers, and gangs of them, for wages, hunted for gold.

The Legislature, at its first session, complimented them with an act. It had no trace of an admission of their title to the land. Their villages must not be disturbed, but their rights were only those of a tenant. Minor Indians, with the permission of their parents, might be adopted by the whites. If the Indians were abused, they could complain to the justice of the peace, but no white person on their testimony could be convicted. The justice must tell them what the law was, and, if they violated it, must punish their head men by reprimand, fine, or reasonable chastisement. For stealing they incurred a fine of two hundred dollars, or "twenty-five lashes laid on without cruelty." Able-bodied Indians found begging, strolling, or loitering about places where liquor was to be sold, could be hired out for four months to the highest bidder. To sell them liquor incurred a fine of twenty dollars, or five days' imprisonment. The money that was paid as fines by Indians, or by whites on Indian account, and the wages earned while hired out on account of vagrancy, was to go to a mythical "Indian fund" of the town. So it will be seen that the Indian was treated with a kind of consideration, and as possessed of rights that white men were bound to respect—white men being judges. Considering the state of the typographical art of that day, it is not at all significant that the compiled statutes of the first three years of California legislation scrupulously spelled the word Indian with a little *i*.

Before the Americans came, there was scarcely such a thing known in California as an Indian war. Occasionally, when game and fish, grasshoppers, acorns and pine-nuts were scarce, the hungry Diggers would swoop down upon the ranches of the tame Indians, and make off with their cattle, which led to arms and a hunt.

CHAP. XXV.
1850.

But with the admission into the Union, the Indians assumed the condition which appears to be normal for them in all new frontier States— that is, of frequent hostility.

Some Americans attempting in 1849 to penetrate the country to the head of the rivers, were killed by them. They drove back a party of explorers from the Trinity River region, and attacked parties going to and from Oregon. In 1850, there were hostile movements in Mariposa and Fresno Counties, and some thefts and murders committed. Not that the Indians had combined, but, as Governor Burnett stated it, being impelled by the same causes, they were without combination placed in an attitude of hostility. They saw the lands, for which the General Government showed no haste to treat, passing out of their possession; a people that had no sympathy for them crowding into their choice places; diseases thinning their tribes: they accepted the notion that they were a doomed race. Discouraged and moody, they failed to provide for their wants, and that failure in the presence of the whites was far more serious than while they had the range of the woods, the valleys, the bays, and the rivers. A prospect of starvation followed, and to avert it came thefts from the settlers. The whites were not slow to punish the thieves, nor the Indians to avenge their wrongs with murder. Volunteer companies organized expeditions to quell the disturbance; they failing, the militia were called out, and then there was a pretty bill of expenses on "Indian war account." Twice during 1850 the Governor authorized expeditions at the State's expense, because of formidable attacks at points where the emigrant trains entered the State.

At the confluence of the Gila and Colorado, the savages on the 23d of April surprised and murdered a Mr. Glanton and eleven other men, who had established a ferry across the Colorado. The southern counties, though called on, manifested no great desire to form an expedition to the scene of slaughter. General Morehead raised a party of seventy-five men, conducted them to the southeast corner of the State, waited a month, and then, by order of the Governor, disbanded it, as there were no evidences of its being needed longer.

William Rogers was authorized by the Executive, in October, to arm two hundred men, and proceed along the trail that leads from Salt Lake into El Dorado County, where the Indians had killed several miners, and robbed and wounded a number of emigrants. The expedition went out, did some skirmishing, lost three men, killed sixteen of the Indians, and so restored peace.

There were repeated troubles, too, in Mari-

CHAP. XXV.

1850–1856.

posa and Fresno Counties, near the head of the San Joaquin. Miners were murdered, their cattle, stock, and movables carried off, their cabins burned. Sheriff Burney raised a company of seventy-four volunteers, pursued the insurgents, overtook them, killed forty or fifty of their number, and burned their village, losing eight of his own party.

Indeed, along the whole eight hundred miles of wild mountainous frontier, there was a feverish expectation of trouble kept up by rumors, not always false, of Indian depredations. When, by the resignation of Governor Burnett, John McDougall became chief Executive in January of 1851, he took an early occasion to inform the Senate "of the actual existence of an Indian war within our borders."

1852.

In the spring of 1852, J. W. Denver, and other members of the Legislature, represented to the Executive that the Pitt River Indians and other Northern tribes were constantly in a state of hostility to the whites. They reported that in the counties of Shasta, Trinity, Klamath, and Siskiyou, since the winter of 1849 and 1850, two hundred and forty thousand dollars worth of property had been destroyed, and one hundred and thirty persons murdered by Indians.

This memorial Governor Bigler transmitted to the commander of the Pacific Department of the

United States army, complaining that the General Government was not doing its duty to the coast.

General Hitchcock stated in reply that few instances of late Indian depredations had come to his knowledge. Since Major Kearny, in June, 1851, chastised the Rogue River Indians, he had heard of no trouble until a story was published of eight men killed on the Coquilla. He instantly sent out a force which killed some of the alleged perpetrators of the murders, dispelled the rest, and destroyed their supplies of fish. Afterwards it appeared that the white men, who were reported murdered, had escaped alive into Oregon, and that the conflict arose from their own imprudence. In December, 1851, he was informed of an outbreak in the southern part of the State. Major Heintzelman, with a body of troops, marched against the Indians, met, fought, beat them, secured the immediate authors of the war, punished them, and restored perfect peace. He was not aware that troops were needed in any particular section of California, though he very well knew that isolated cases of robbery and murder had occurred. He reminded the Governor that the country was not settled from the coast gradually towards the interior, but every part of it was suddenly penetrated and explored, bringing the two races into close proximity over the whole area, and not along a frontier line alone. If there had really been any delay in sending troops to the coast, it was only because the peculiar temptations to desertion made it almost impossible to keep troops together.

But Redick McKee, U. S. Indian Agent for Northern California, used a different tone in addressing the Governor. He was informed, he said, that in February two men were murdered, and their house robbed, on the north side of the Eel River, some fifteen or twenty miles from Humboldt. When the settlers heard of it they jumped to the conclusion that the murderers were Indians. They organized a hunt, and shot down fifteen or twenty defenceless natives, whom they had no occasion to suspect. A week or two later they shot four others on suspicion. In the same month an Indian boy was deliberately shot by a Missourian, at Happy Camp, on the Klamath. The Indian friends of the boy charged a certain white man with being concerned in the murder. Alarmed for his safety, the white man collected a party, who went up to the Indian village, shot all the men and a number of the women, and burned their houses. Proceeding two miles up the river to Indian Flat, they treated that village and its inhabitants in the same way, except that here one man escaped to tell the agent the story. In all, between thirty and forty Indians were thus coolly slaughtered. He submitted it to the Governor, whether some measures could not be adopted to vindicate the laws of the country and of humanity, and bring such desperadoes to punishment. Governor Bigler, in reply, called attention to the discrepancies between the statement of Senator Denver and the account of Mr. McKee, some of whose reflections he thought "an imputation on the character of American citizens." "As a private intercessor," said the Governor, "between American citizens and their savage enemies, consanguinity, and the sentiments which it inspires, would incline me to favor the cause of my countrymen; and, as a public magistrate chosen by American citizens, I cannot yield my approbation to any imputations upon their intelligence or patriotism." Mr. McKee assured the Governor that he fully concurred in his remarks touching the progress of civilization—"many of them were familiar truisms very prettily expressed"—still, he must remember that if a pack-train were robbed, or a corral broken open, the first red-skins that appeared were made to pay the penalty, and he cited several cases where "consanguinity" had led the whites to punish Indians for outrages with which it was afterwards clearly proven that none of their race had any thing to do. A sharp letter from the Governor, "with renewed assurances," and so forth, concluded this suggestive correspondence.

"Indian Wars" were not popular in the cities, but they were in the lobby of the Legislature, where the men gathered who furnished supplies for expeditions to quell disturbances, as well as in the wild regions where the Indians occupied choice land that the whites coveted.

It was a snug bill that was run up on account of the raids that punished the Indians, and not a whit the less because it was presumed that the General Government would pay it finally. The "War Debt," by New Year's of 1853, was seven hundred and seventy-one thousand one hundred and ninety dollars; after that it grew only by the addition of interest. The trust in the General Government's generosity was not disappointed, for Congress, at the session of 1854, authorized the Secretary of War to ascertain the amount expended by the State, and appropriated nine hundred and twenty-four thousand two hundred and fifty-nine dollars to pay it. There was a hitch about the interest due after the date of adjustment, and the money was not paid for some time. The State debated a good deal, wanting more money, and legislated some in hopes to get more; then a commission was sent to Congress, but no new action was taken by that body, which already had dealt very liberally

THE INDIAN RESERVATIONS. 367

in the matter. From that time onward, the General Government with its own troops quelled all Indian disturbances, and found but few to quell.

Its early agents made treaties with the Indians, as if they had a title to the land, but the United States Senate rejected them, and, as Mexico and Spain had done, ignored the Indian claim. That, moreover, was the Government's general policy with all savages who, like those of California, had lost their tribal character. Soon it was urged that their hunting-grounds were destroyed, the rivers ruined for salmon-fishing, by the miners, and the forests, with their store of acorns and nuts, cut down. It was pleaded that, for humanity's sake, they should be gathered upon reservations. So military posts were established with farming lands around each, and the Government agents were authorized to gather them in. The Tehon Reservation was established in 1853, in Los Angeles County; Nome Lackee, in 1854, in Tehama County; Klamath, in 1855; Mendocino, in 1856—each containing twenty-five thousand acres; Fresno and King's River Farms, of two thousand acres, in 1854, and Nome Cult Farm, of five thousand acres, in Tehama County. Farming was the chief employment on all of them; at Mendocino, fishing also was extensively practised.

CHAP.
XXV.

1850–
1856.

The Reservation system was a costly, and not very successful experiment; to collect the Indians was not the easiest part of it. The tame or Mission Indians still loitered in considerable numbers at the south, about the sites of the old missions. They lived in families and villages by themselves, and were the willing helpers of the whites, for small wages harvesting their crops and treading their wine-presses. Others engaged as servants of the native Californians, or hired out as miners, and were welcome help to companies that had capital and lacked laborers. Then the wild Indians, who, unless very hungry, or maddened by the attempts of the whites to steal their children, were almost equally harmless, even if willing to go to the Reservations during the famine months, pined for their freedom when the forests and the rivers abounded with food, and were apt to take it. The more restless and bold sometimes drifted as far east as the Sierras, or even beyond, then swayed back again to the midst of the settlements. Perhaps this frequent shifting of location accounts in part for the extraordinary discrepancies concerning their numbers, which Colonel Henley estimated, in 1856, as high as sixty-one thousand six hundred; yet not more than ten thousand were gathered at the Reservations.

The Chinese figured largely in the politics

of the State, though they had no vote, and no standing as citizens. Tempted by gold out of their "Central Kingdom," whose records give them a national and imperial existence contemporary with the Prophet Isaiah, they began to arrive, but not very numerously, in 1850. By the spring of 1852 there were ten thousand of them (almost exclusively males) in the State; and by the close of that year, perhaps eighteen thousand. Most of them went to the mines; but there were also laborers, peddlers, launderers, and merchants in their number, who stayed by the cities. A few came as coolies, but that system of servitude was found unprofitable, and soon abandoned.

At first they were welcomed as a picturesque addition to the peculiarities of the country. The barbaric feature they contributed was a source of pride to the people. Rich or poor, they adhered to their own costume. Their long braided queues, their blue frocks, red sashes, and wooden shoes, the jingling anklets of plated silver worn by their females, the Americans were proud to point out to strangers as tokens that the wealth of their land was arousing even the drowsy Asiatics. Besides, every Chinaman was a silent witness that the Indies were just to the west, and that this was the highway for their wealth from the East of the ancients to the true East of the moderns. The cleanliness,

CHAP. XXV.

1850–1856.

politeness, and unobtrusive good behavior of the Chinese were in every pioneer's mouth. The Chinese restaurants were commended for their fresh and novel delicacies, as well as for their scrupulous neatness. But this did not last long. The miners early took a fright. These pagan strangers were happy and content on three or four dollars a month, and the free passage to and from the country. Even such small wages were princely, compared with any they had at home, and the "honest miners" of European descent feared that Asia would disgorge such a horde upon their gold-fields that the original possessors would be starved out.

Governor Bigler, who was quick to take a hint from a controlling class of voters, sounded the alarm in a message to the Legislature of 1852. He submitted that measures must be adopted to check the tide of immigration from Asia, and keep away "coolies," who intended to take away all they made. He suggested a tax on Chinamen, and that Congress be memorialized for a law prohibiting their working in the mines.

Though the Legislature did not respond to the Governor's suggestion, its effect was a sudden and almost entire cessation of immigration and of importation of goods from China. In the following year the subject was again early before the Legislature. The Committee on

Mines, to which it was referred, had an interview with leading Chinese merchants, who advised that a tax be laid upon their countrymen in the mines, and promised to exert their influence to make its collection easy, arguing that such a tax would be productive enough to make their presence desirable in the several counties. They explained the organization that had been established here for the benefit of their countrymen. All but a score or two of the Chinese in the State were from the province of which Canton is the capital. They divided the province into departments, and for each department a house was built in San Francisco, and presided over by two "heads," who were elected by the Chinese from that department. The house was a hotel, a hospital, a post-office, and assembly-room, all in one. A committee of merchants, elected by the people, served without pay, as advisers to the heads, and decided matters in dispute between them and the members. On arriving in port, the immigrants go to the house of the department from which they come, are registered by the clerk, pay each a tax of ten dollars, and then are entitled to all the benefits of the association. The houses lend money to their poor, send the sick back to China, if they wish it, and see that none return without having paid their debts. The clerks keep a registry of the names and residence of members, and gather up their votes for company officers through messengers. The merchants assured the committee that (contrary to the prevailing opinion), although at first some came under contracts with employers in China, the custom was abandoned as unprofitable. Most came now, they said, their own masters, and with their own means. Some had hired money to come with, and pledged their property or their wages, for a certain time, as security, or pledged their children as slaves in the event of non-payment.

The legislation of the year resulted in an amendment to the law " for the protection of foreigners," which required a license of four dollars a month to entitle any person not a citizen (except California Indians) to work in the mines, the proceeds to be divided between the State and county treasuries.

The law was enforced only on the Chinese. They showed no haste to buy the license, but, when fairly caught, paid the fee with meekness. It was not long before the county tax-payers discovered that there was a compensation in the unwelcome presence of the Chinese, since what they contributed saved several counties from bankruptcy. Then the candid confessed that, with their pans and rockers, and hustled out of any good claim they were lucky enough to find by the covetous whites, these strangers worked principally the tailings, and abandoned claims on which Americans could not make a living. Though their countrymen imported much of their food, they spent their money pretty freely, and so added to the wealth of the State in more ways than one or two.

The politicians set their faces against the Johns, but the people generally treated them kindly, and they must have sent home fair reports, for the immigration rather increased, and at the end of 1856 their numbers in the State were estimated at over thirty-eight thousand. The Supreme Court having decided that they were "colored," their testimony against white men was not taken, and they were isolated in the midst of the multitude. As a class, they had no reputation to spare for truth-telling. Believing in no God but their ancestors, and doubtful if even they were not annihilated by death, it was difficult to shape an oath solemn enough to bind them when they testified concerning each other. On very important occasions a sort of creed, printed on tissue-paper in Chinese characters, was burned as they lifted the right hand, and then, if ever, it was thought they might be trusted to some extent.

They erected a temple in San Francisco, and set up an idol, hideous with bright paint and brazen ornaments; but if strangers handled his apparel or his person they manifested no of-

CHAP.
XXV.

1850–
1856.

fence. On New Year's Day they made a terrible din with gongs, drums, and bells in the temple, and set tables in their houses for such "gods" as there might be, over against the tables of refreshment for guests. They observed no Sabbath, and any thing like religious worship the closest observation failed to discover. They were inordinate gamblers for very trifling stakes, and excessively fond of theatrical entertainments. The appointments of their stage were of the rudest kind, the acting, whether of tragedy or comedy, equally farcical in foreign eyes, the singing nasal, the orchestra deafening with lamentable monotones from gongs, reeds, stringed instruments, and anvils of hard wood. They puffed at their long, shallow-bowled reed pipes incessantly when at leisure, sipped tea night and day when in-doors and awake, and walked single file the streets, giving just half the walk to those they met. A cheery man, meeting them in desolate places, saluted with "How are you, John?" and the unvarying reply was, with a jerking nod, "How are you, John?" They were polite, not obsequious, unobtrusive, and quietly enjoyed their rights without giving offence in the manner. They had little dealings with the whites, purchasing of them, however, whenever they could make a good bargain for their simple wants. Their merchants had the respect of the trade. Their fishmongers competed only with a few Genoese and Maltese in San Francisco. Their purifiers of dirty linen interfered mostly with machine-washers. As house-servants the Irish girls soon drove them from the kitchen. In the country a few were employed on farms and in gardens on wages. But the great body "created values out of nothing," in the "exhausted" placers, on their own account, or ministered to the wants of their own people as petty tradesmen.

When they died, they were buried, after funeral feasts and ceremonies more or less imposing, according to their position and wealth. When the flesh of their dead bodies was decayed, their bones were gathered up by the agents of the companies, polished, preserved in compact form, and in due time returned to rest in Chinese soil.

In 1855, Governor Bigler argued to the Legislature the right of the State to prohibit their landing on its shore; he was shivering yet at the spectacle he had evoked of an overwhelming eruption from Asia. But the treaty stipulations of the United States with China were too well known to the people, and California was spared any such disgraceful legislation as he proposed.

Generally, they lived in peace and harmony with each other. A notable exception occurred on a bar of the Stanislaus, in the fall of 1850, where two mining companies quarrelled about a claim. After one collision, both parties rallied their friends, and one of them ordered up one hundred and fifty muskets with bayonets and cartridges from San Francisco. Not knowing how to use them, when they came, they hired some white men to teach them, whom they afterwards said they understood were sent up by the Governor to make sure of fair play, and to prevent interference by the whites. All things being ready, the party with the muskets, nine hundred strong, assailed the enemy, who were twelve hundred strong and armed with Chinese weapons. The bold assailants fired and ran; and the enemy, panic-stricken, ran the other way. Two were killed and two wounded. The sheriff intervened, and the war ended, costing, during its brief continuance, very much less money, probably, than the newspapers of the day reported.

The negro, though the staple topic of Congressional legislation, did not much trouble that of California. Governor Burnett, in 1851, advised the exclusion of colored persons from the State. The people were wiser than their Governor, and would consent to no such folly. However, they sacrificed to the fuming Chivalry so far as to deny their citizenship and prohibit them from bearing testimony concerning whites in the courts. This last was a cruel wrong to humanity, and the jealous whites suffered their share of its evil; for, though a negro saw a man, white or black, murdered by a negro, his lips were sealed in the witness-box, and justice cheated of her penalty.

At the legislative session of 1853, W. C. Meredith, a Democrat, from Tuolumne, presented a memorial to the Assembly, signed by negroes, asking the repeal of the clause prohibiting colored persons to testify. Instantly one member moved to throw the memorial out of the window. Another did not want the journals "tarnished with such an infamous document." The chairman reluctantly ruled the motion out of order, and an appeal was taken. Finally, in the greatest excitement, the petition was unanimously rejected, and the clerk instructed not to file it. The tempest was too large for the teapot, and the storm was not entirely subdued for several days.

As to the other classes of population, the native Californians early retired into obscurity. Some few allied themselves with American families, yet gradually lost their influence in public affairs; and, annoyed by squatters and defrauded of their lands, grew poorer and poorer, till nothing but the shadow of their old possessions remained. Mexico, and many parts of South America, were thickly represented, but owing to their Spanish tongue, they did not much mix with the rest, except in the mines.

The Europeans and white Americans fraternized in business and in general interests, and were soon scarcely distinguishable, except by their pronunciation of the common English language. These produced the gold, made the valleys bow and wave with grain, beckoned commerce from every sea, set the busy wheels of mills to humming, neglected public affairs till they grew desperate, summoned wealth to their hands like genii, and spent it like princes, built magnificent wagon-roads over the mountains, and forced that wondrous crop of towns and cities, some of which grew up with amazing rapidity, while others blossomed with a name and straightway died.

CHAPTER XXVI.

GROWTH AND HINDRANCES OF THE CITIES AND TOWNS.

SAN FRANCISCO had outgrown the anticipations of the most sanguine. In 1856 it wore the aspect of a hurriedly-built city, whose people had faith in its noble destiny. It had many miles of graded streets, a fair system of sewerage planned and partly put into use, many substantial store-houses of brick, wharves sufficient to meet the demand of commerce, churches, school-houses, and the comfortable homes of families thoroughly satisfied to spend their lives in California. Its eastern front had extended half a dozen blocks' width into the bay, and the principal business was conducted on ground made by the transfer of the sand-hills to the flats, or by piling and bridging far beyond the original beach—a necessity imposed by the closeness with which the hills of rock crowded the bay.

The city had reached its condition of prosperity through very severe trials and in spite of thick difficulties.

A great deal of trouble was caused by the

CHAP. XXVI.
1851.

desperate, reckless villains who flocked to the city from all parts of the world. Many of the best citizens formed themselves into a Committee of Vigilance, and, because the courts could not or would not punish crime, undertook themselves to administer justice. On the 11th of June, 1851, between one and two o'clock in the morning, they executed John Jenkins, by hanging him to the cross-beam of the old adobe building on the plaza. Jenkins had robbed a store, and had been tried and found guilty by the committee. On the 11th of July they executed James Stuart, who murdered the sheriff of Auburn, and attacked and robbed a man in his own store on Montgomery Street. On the 24th of August they recaptured and hung Whittaker and McKenzie, who had been taken from them, after trial, by the authorities, and lodged in jail. Two weeks later, believing that they had taught incendiaries, robbers, and murderers a lesson that they would not dare to forget, the committee, without disbanding, suspended operations and left justice to the courts.

Besides these social disturbances, fires, negligent municipal officers, and swindling schemers had done mischief enough to destroy a place less tenacious of life. It was estimated that sixteen million dollars worth of property was consumed by five fires within eighteen months, while the population numbered but thirty thousand. The most disastrous of these conflagrations occurred May 4th, 1851, the anniversary of a great fire the preceding year. The first stroke of the fire-bell aroused the whole city, for wherever, in the compact business blocks, the ravager began, few felt their light, combustible buildings safe. The foremost men in the town organized themselves into fire companies.

On the ruins of these conflagrations buildings rose again before the ashes were fairly cold, each time a little better than the preceding, and with more careful precautions to render them proof against fire. The immense amount of business to be attended to gave the people an elasticity of spirit that made them recover courage with surprising haste, after apparently crushing misfortunes.

Real estate kept rising in value till 1854. Then many causes combined to make it fall and continue falling till the summer of 1858. The speculators had glutted the market with goods, and money grew scarce. Wages fell, rents fell, and real estate tumbled with the rest. The increasing uncertainty of land titles, the exorbitant taxes, and the unsatisfactory condition of state and city finances, kept the latter from rising again. Claims of astonishing absurdity were set up for property that had been in the quiet possession of occupants who never dreamed of a flaw in their titles.

CHAP. XXVI.

1853.

Gigantic for their impudence as well as their extravagance were the claims of José Yves Limantour, a Frenchman by birth, that were presented to the Board of Land Commissioners in 1853. He claimed that when trading on the coast ten years before, he had advanced to Governor Micheltorena merchandise and money for the use of the Departmental Government. For these considerations he professed that the Governor had granted to him four square leagues of land on the San Francisco peninsula, embracing about half of what had become the most valuable part of the city; also Alcatraz and Yerba Buena Islands and the Farralones, and lands lying elsewhere in the State, covering in all more than a hundred square leagues.

The Board of Commissioners confirmed the claims. The incensed people saw the gloomy prospect, and doubted if it were not the most hazardous of all investments to purchase real estate in San Francisco.

An appeal was taken to the United States District Court, where counsel for the United States contended that all the documents on which the claimant relied were false, forged, and fraudulently fabricated long after the pretended dates, and after the acquisition of California by the United States. Judge Hoffman rendered

1858. his decision (1858), reversing the Board's decree, and rejecting the claims that were still pressed, as invalid. He added that the proofs of fraud were as conclusive and irresistible as the attempted fraud itself was flagrant and audacious. Following is a quotation from his opinion, from which may be inferred what a grievous nuisance was abated when the claims were rejected:—

"Whether we consider the enormous extent or the extraordinary character of the alleged concessions to Limantour, the official positions and the distinguished antecedents of the principal witnesses who have testified in support of them, or the conclusive and unanswerable proofs by which their falsehood has been exposed—whether we consider the unscrupulous and pertinacious obstinacy with which the claims now before the court have been persisted in—although six others presented to the Board have long since been abandoned—or the large sums extorted from property-owners in this city as the price of the relinquishment of these fraudulent pretensions; or, finally, the conclusive and irresistible proofs by which the perjuries by which they have been attempted to be maintained have been exposed, and their true character demonstrated, it may safely be affirmed that these cases are without a parallel in the judicial history of the country."

Exorbitant taxes for State and city purposes were paid, and with a feeling that, in spite of the taxes, the city was nearing insolvency. The expenditures of the double county and city government for the five years following the city's incorporation were more than seven and a half million dollars; and the worst of it was, that they had nothing to show for it all in the way of public buildings, or other than the most elementary improvements. The city's actual debt, in 1856, was more than three and a half million dollars—nineteen hundred thousand of which was funded at six, seven, and ten per cent. interest.

The State, in 1851, had ceded to the city the beach and water lots, and confirmed the sales made in virtue of General Kearny's grant, so that, with its pueblo inheritance, it had ample means to pay all debts, if the land-stealers would but let it alone, and its official guardians save it from waste.

In the early times, large amounts were raised for ordinary expenses, on scrip which never bore less interest than three per cent. a month. As all work for the public was liable to be paid in this carelessly issued paper, every thing that the city ordered done or purchased was charged at enormous rates.

One of the city's creditors, Dr. Peter Smith, on an account for taking care of its indigent sick, declining to exchange his scrip for the ten per cent. stock, into which the Legislature

(1851) had authorized the floating debt to be converted, recovered judgment against the city, and to defray the amount its wharves and certain upland lots were sold by the sheriff. They brought scarcely a twentieth part of their value, the belief being that the sales were illegal and void. As the sum realized by the sale failed to satisfy the judgment, a second and a third sale was made of other city property, of an immense value even then, and of incalculable prospective value. For the same reason as before, this property brought merely nominal prices. Dr. Smith, or parties holding the scrip paid him by the city, subsequently obtained other judgments, and the sheriff sold still other upland and water lots to satisfy them; the Commissioners of the Funded Debt meanwhile, under the advice of their counsel, Judge Heydenfelt, protesting that the city could give no title to the lots offered for sale, since they had been conveyed, by ordinance of the Common Council, to the Commissioners in trust for the benefit of the city's creditors. The protest prevented competition, but did not avert the sale. At one sale (January 30th, 1862) the sheriff sold two thousand acres of land within the city limits at just such ruinous prices as before, to pay Peter Smith judgments.

An inexplicable muddle came of it. The sales were regarded as farces at first, but soon they suggested serious thoughts. When the Commissioners of the Funded Debt attempted to raise money on the land of their trust, this Peter Smith title, like a poisonous shadow, floated over it, clouding their title and depreciating the market value of the land. Suit followed suit, and litigation thickened over the whole matter in a confused web. Every attempt to remedy the evil, as all efforts to prevent it had, only plunged the subject into a deeper chaos. The end is not even yet reached, though this was early demonstrated—that San Francisco was fast being stripped of the choicest of her resources. Plunged to the eyes in debt, her means almost wasted, yet her citizens cheerful, thriving, and getting rich, San Francisco was rushing along like a tough, stanch, but very foul ship, with officers who would bear a great deal of watching, and some very rough and suspicious passengers; yet with tide favorable and a strong wind filling all her canvas.

Sacramento, the second city in the State, was prospering notably under quite as rugged treatment. After the experience of 1850, when the place was overflowed by the river, its people raised the grade of the streets five feet, and built a levee along both river fronts. On the 3d of November, 1852, a fire destroyed six hundred houses, causing from four to five million dollars damage. From December 20th,

1852, to January 24th, 1853, the city was again under water, and still again in April, 1853. It was made the permanent capital of the State in 1854. In July of that year another fire swept off five hundred thousand dollars worth of property. Spite of this variety and excess of calamities, the city increased with a rapid, wholesome growth under the constant stimulus of its great trade with the northern mines. It had its grievous land troubles, too, its oppressive taxation, and its debt, amounting, in the fall of 1856, to over a million and a half of dollars.

Marysville, laid out in December, 1849 (at the junction of the Yuba and Feather Rivers, where one Cordua, a German, in 1842 had put up an adobe building, naming the place New Mecklenburg, and afterwards establishing there a trading post), had assumed the aspect of a busy New England village, with population enough to cast nineteen hundred votes at the November election in 1856. Its principal streets were lined with substantial brick buildings, which secured a remarkable immunity from fires, though a very destructive one visited it on the 31st of August, 1850. Its site had been flooded in 1850, but that warning was not heeded, and in the spring of 1852 the whole business part of the town was under water again. The grade of the streets was then raised one foot above the highest mark of the flood, and the whole city brought to one level. A crop of paper cities sprang up around it, competing for its trade — Plumas, Eliza, Veazie City, Hamilton, Linda, Featherston, and Yaleston, all which the best maps fail to show, and which only local antiquarians are able to indicate as they pass them.

Nearly every business house in Nevada was burned down March 11th, 1851, destroying half a million dollars worth of property. Again, on September 7th, 1852, it was scourged with fire. In December of that year the heavy rains so hindered the transportation from below that the place was threatened with famine. Flour was sold at forty dollars a hundred-weight, and beef at forty cents a pound. But it was the centre of a rich mining vicinity, and flourished maugre all its afflictions. By 1853 it was in telegraphic communication with Sacramento, and in 1855 with Downieville. At the November election of 1856 it cast a larger vote (2,081) than any city in the State, except San Francisco and Sacramento. On the 19th of July, 1856, came a conflagration that consumed four hundred wooden and twenty-two brick houses, causing a damage of a million of dollars, and the lives of ten persons who trusted to the brick buildings as fire-proof. A month later, and two hundred and fifty wooden houses were erected on the burned ground, and twenty-five brick ones were begun.

Grass Valley—so called because some overland emigrants, in 1849, found there the cattle that had strayed from them as they rested after their tedious journey across the Plains and the Sierras, luxuriating in excellent pasture—had, on New Year's of 1851, only three or four cabins in it. Before the year ended it was one of the busiest places in the mountains. It escaped fires till September, 1855, when one visited it, inflicting damage to the extent of three hundred and fifty thousand dollars. The famous Alison's Ranch quartz mine is three miles from the place. In 1855 the men who owned this lead offered to sell it for a thousand dollars, but found no purchaser. The first eighteen tons of rock taken from it produced twenty-three thousand dollars. From October 6th, 1856, to 1861, the deposits of gold from this mine in the mint at San Francisco were nearly a million of dollars.

Placerville—known in early times as "Hangtown," in memory of the lynching there of three men who were arrested for highway robbery and two of them identified as the persons guilty of a murder—owed the beginning of its prosperity to the rich gold surface diggings in its vicinity; and its second growth to the fact that it was on the most travelled road from the bay to Washoe. A fire, on the 15th of April, 1856, consumed the lower part of the town, and another on the 6th of July almost destroyed it.

A fire in Weaverville (March 7th, 1853) damaged that town one hundred thousand dollars; and another (September 7th, 1855), two hundred thousand. Yankee Jim's, in Placer County, was burned down in June, 1852, and Ophir, July 12th, of the same year. This last place, as was often the case with mining villages where the surface diggings were becoming poor, and no other resource presented itself, failed to recover from the shock. A fire in Stockton (February 21st, 1855) did fifty thousand dollars damage; and one in Columbia (July 10th, 1854) was figured up at a loss of half a million dollars. It was estimated, not very accurately, perhaps, that during the three years preceding 1853, the losses to California by fire amounted to sixty-six millions of dollars; yet, as the imperfect list cited above shows, very destructive fires were numerous after that date.

The towns of the southern coast shared little in the general growth, for they were away from the main avenues of travel and trade. They suffered little, too, from either fire or flood, for they were mostly built at leisure, of adobe, and under the direction of those who held the traditions of the fathers and the Indians concerning old-time floods.

It was inevitable that these conflagrations and drownings should ruin many men financially; but those who escaped were generous, and cheerfully helped up the prostrated, and set them on their feet, and many overtook fortune again early. But where so few had family ties to bind them to a spot, every fire or other calamity that put business into confusion increased the tendency to drift from town to town, from bar to bar, and to "rush" to any new diggings that were spoken of in flattering terms.

The Legislature fairly represented this drifting habit of the times in the way it kept the capital of the State trundling about. The first two sessions were held at San José, though early in 1850 the project of removal was agitated. Monterey tendered land enough and all its public buildings to the State for the boon of the capital. San José sent in several liberal propositions, and among the rest the donation of a block of a hundred and sixty-eight building lots. Colonel Stephenson and a business partner offered to erect, free of expense to the State, public buildings worth a hundred thousand dollars, under the direction of a legislative committee, if the Legislature would make "New York of the Pacific" the capital. But General Vallejo's offer was the one of most princely aspect, as viewed on paper. It was a tender of one hundred and fifty-six acres of land on the Straits of Carquines for the sites of public buildings, and three hundred and seventy thousand dollars towards their erection, the money to be paid in two years. Senator Broderick, of the committee, reported in favor of accepting Vallejo's offer, and the Legislature so far concurred as to submit the subject of removal to the people.

The people clearly cared very little about it. On election day there were in nineteen counties reported but twelve thousand two hundred and ninety-two votes cast on the question, of which nearly nine thousand were for removing to Vallejo's site. So the third session met (January 5, 1852) at Vallejo; and because there was no accommodation for the members, it adjourned a week afterwards to Sacramento. The next session (1853) met at Vallejo, and after a month adjourned to Benicia. The fifth session (1854) met at Benicia, but before March removed to Sacramento, to be removed no more, except temporarily, in 1862, when the flood made it impossible to transact business in the drowned city, and San Francisco enjoyed for a season the legislative presence.

CHAPTER XXVII.

FILLIBUSTERISM.

In those days there was a great deal said about the "manifest destiny" of the nation to swallow up by annexation all of the continent between the Gulf of Mexico and the Isthmus, and even to include the Sandwich Islands. It was an Atlantic idea, of Southern origin; but it ran like an epidemic through the North and West. There its most remarkable effect was the curious change of sentiment it developed in conservative circles—the feeling having grown up that, whatever the territory annexed, in a fair race slavery would lag, and the new country come into the Union free. When the "manifest destiny" dogma in its career reached the Pacific coast, it bred a perfect rage for practical fillibusterism in the restless classes. Politics had little to do with the matter, but there were mines on territory that did not belong to us, and that was reason enough for annexing it.

A leader was at hand, who proved to be one of the most notable fillibusters of the century. William Walker was born in 1824, at Nashville, Tennessee. He studied medicine, and graduated in it both at home and in Paris, but never practised. He studied law, went to New Orleans, connected himself with the *Crescent* newspaper, moved to California in 1850, and became an assistant editor of the San Francisco *Herald*, in which capacity he offended Judge Levi Parsons, of the District Court, who fined him five hundred dollars for contempt of court in an article he had written. Walker refused to pay the fine, and was sent to prison. The people held an indignation meeting, expressed their trust in the press, and resolved that it should not be put down for any imaginary contempt of "courts which cannot be reduced much lower than they have reduced themselves," and went in a body to console the prisoner. By a writ of *habeas corpus* he was discharged. The Legislature took up the matter, and a committee recommended Parsons' impeachment, but soon the subject was dropped. Walker afterwards practised law for a short time in Marysville, and then took to fillibustering.

The province of Sonora was well known to be rich in minerals, and to wear very loosely the robe of Mexican rule. A scheme was concocted, in 1853, for its conquest. Money was raised by the issue of scrip to be redeemed by the first proceeds of the new Government, and a vessel procured and fitted out as the pioneer in the unlawful enterprise. General Hitchcock, who commanded the United States troops on the coast, ordered the vessel seized. It was done, but the prosecution was pushed with so little zeal that she was soon released, much to the general's disgust.

Meanwhile the bark *Caroline* was fitted out, and in her Walker and forty-six men sailed on the 16th of October. Landing at La Paz, on the peninsula of Lower California, the adventurers kidnapped the governor, hoisted a flag of their own, and proclaimed Lower California an independent republic. They afterwards had a slight brush with the natives, but the natives suffered all the loss. Walker was now formally elected president by his handful of followers, and he appointed a goodly number of them cabinet members and to other high offices. Then retiring in their vessel to Magdalena Bay, they disappeared for three weeks from view. Next they were heard from at Encinada, a little south of the California boundary line, in Lower California, whence they sent flaming accounts of their conquests to San Diego.

The news made a great sensation in San Francisco among the shiftless, impatient classes; and the "dead broke" and desperate came down from the mines in greater numbers than could be accepted to volunteer as recruits. After

General Hitchcock's late experience he did not feel called upon to meddle, the other authorities were glad to get rid of some who were going, the newspapers rejoiced in the sensation and kept their peace about the morality or legality of the expedition, and the people laughed at it as a very good joke. On the 13th of December, the bark *Anita* sailed with a hundred and fifty men or more. Arriving at Encinada, Walker by proclamation abolished the republic of Lower California, and announced that of Sonora, with boundaries embracing both provinces. He took the presidency himself, and gave the vice-presidency to Colonel Watkins of the *Anita*.

But with all the cattle and corn they bought with Sonora scrip or confiscated, the president could not feed his followers to their taste. Some half a hundred of them deserted and tried to make their way to San Diego. A few were caught, of whom Walker had two flogged and expelled, and two others shot for example's sake. With about a hundred still faithful to him, he set out in March, 1854, overland for Sonora, but, harassed by the natives out of all supplies, very hungry and quite dispirited, they gave that up, and, turning northward, surrendered themselves as prisoners to the United States troops. Taken to San Francisco, most of them were set at liberty on their parole.

Meanwhile, Vice-President Watkins, having preceded them to San Francisco, had been arraigned before the United States District Court, Judge Hoffman presiding, and found guilty of setting on foot a military expedition against Mexico. He was condemned to pay a fine of fifteen hundred dollars. Frederick Emory, Walker's secretary of state, pleaded guilty to the same charge, and was fined to the same amount. Walker himself was afterwards tried and acquitted.

Trouble springing up in Nicaragua, he gathered some sixty or seventy followers, and left in May, 1855, to assist the revolutionary faction. They landed at Realejo, and success soon smiled on the side they espoused. Then Walker began to use his power as a dictator. He revoked the charter under which the Vanderbilt Steamship Company sent its passengers across Nicaragua, appointed E. J. C. Kewen and two others commissioners to wind up the affairs of the company, and gave to Edmund Randolph a new charter for twenty-five years' time. Hitherto he was but generalissimo of the forces; now he caused himself to be elected president of the republic, and he abrogated the decree by which slavery had for thirty-two years been prohibited. An insurrection took place, fomented by the Vanderbilt Company, and joined by several Central American States.

CHAP. XXVII.
1857.

1860.

Walker, being hard pushed, surrendered himself in May, 1857, with sixteen of his officers, to the United States authorities. Returning again in November to Nicaragua, Commodore Paulding, of the United States Navy, compelled him and one hundred and thirty-two of his followers to surrender. President Buchanan had, in his message, denounced Walker's fillibustering expedition, but he condemned Paulding for landing his force on foreign soil to extinguish it. Walker, freed again, raised more followers in the United States, and proceeded to Honduras. There he was captured, condemned by court-martial, and shot at Truxillo on the 3d of September, 1860.

Personally, Walker was a small man, slow in his speech, reserved, gray-eyed, freckled, unattractive, heartless. His confederates in California were men of very opposite traits and principles; nor is it easy to judge from their character what the arch-fillibuster's motive was. Some hot ambition fired his cold nature. He wished to make a position and a name, not in the vulgar way. Indifferent to slavery or freedom, he was willing to use either as it would promote his end. Perhaps he dreamed of a Southern empire, with slavery as its cornerstone, anticipating the attempt of Jefferson Davis and his fellow-traitors. It is hardly probable that the conspirators took him into their counsels. More likely, believing that the American Union would soon embrace all north of the Isthmus, he aspired to shape the destinies of whatever land he could conquer by proclamation or his sword, in such fashion that when the time for annexation should come, he would be the Sam Houston of the new State, entitled to its first senatorial honors, with a prestige that might, perhaps, in time, make him chief magistrate of the Union. His reward was an early death, and such fame as a pirate wins. However, he gave a cheap reputation to some very small men who never would have been heard of but for him, and some men of character were seriously compromised by their connection with him.

Interlacing with the trials of Walker and his men were those of the Mexican and French consuls at San Francisco, which produced still more excitement. The Pacific Military Division was commanded by General John E. Wool, who was determined to put down fillibustering. The Mexican consul, Mr. Del Valle, under instructions from his Government, prevailed upon some five or six hundred persons, mostly French or Germans, to join an expedition, with a purpose not very clearly explained, to the province of Sonora. When they were about to embark in the British ship *Challenge*, General Wool ordered that vessel seized. She was released,

CHAP. XXVII.
1854.

however, in a day or two, and permitted to depart; but the general had Consul Del Valle arrested on a charge of enlisting soldiers for a foreign power on United States territory. The trial that followed was tedious and imbittering. It became necessary, in the course of it, to have the French consul, Mr. Dillon, in court as a witness; but that gentleman stood on his consular dignity, declined the invitation, and ignored the summons that followed. The marshal finally brought him into court, where Judge Hoffman allowed the justice of his claim for exemption. But Dillon held that France had been insulted by his arrest, and so pulled down his consular flag. The trial of Del Valle proceeded, and he was found guilty.

Dillon was next arrested, charged with aiding the Mexican consul in his unlawful enterprise. He pleaded, as Del Valle had done, that the *Challenge* expeditionists went, not as fillibusters, but to put down fillibusters, and especially the Count Raousset de Boulbon; who, failing to find the Arizona silver mine he sought, and goaded by persecution, had turned to political schemings. The jury disagreed, and the prosecution was abandoned. Further proceedings against Del Valle, too, who had not yet been sentenced, were suspended. In November of

1855, Mr. Dillon raised his flag again as a French war-vessel entered the harbor, which was saluted with apologetic guns, and the consular trouble was happily ended.

CHAPTER XXVIII.

A FINANCIAL STORM.

CHAP. XXVIII.
1855.

A GREAT financial storm passed over the State early in 1855. The Constitution prohibited incorporations for banking purposes, and forbade the issue of any paper currency. In the early times men deposited their spare gold-dust with such merchants as had safes or vaults. As business increased, houses were established in all the principal towns with the special purpose of exchanging coin for the dust of the miners, of receiving deposits, furnishing exchange, and, in short, of doing a general banking business, always excepting that they could utter no bank-bills.

It happened that the winter of 1854–5 was very chary of its rains, and, in consequence, the mines could not be worked extensively. Hence, the miners, who were generally cash customers, wanted credit with the mountain merchants; these wanted it of the jobbers; these of the consignees and importers; and these of the Eastern shippers. Meanwhile the Eastern merchants were pouring goods into the already overstocked market. At auction their consignments found a sale, because they were so cheap, and the gold kept flowing Eastward to pay for them. Most gold-shipments were made through the banks, which were drained fearfully low of their treasure.

At this critical time, news arrived that the house of Page & Bacon, of St. Louis, had got into trouble through its advances to the Ohio and Mississippi Railroad. At once began a run upon the leading bank in California (Page, Bacon & Co.'s), which was in close business relations with the St. Louis firm. The bank stood it for a few days, and then, on February 22d, Washington's birthday, it suspended. A panic seized the town, and soon affected the whole State. The house of Adams & Co., which had grown from an express business into a large banking business, also suspended next day, and their books, notes, dust, coin, and so forth were turned over, at least so the public supposed, to Alfred A. Cohen, as receiver. Wells, Fargo & Co. followed, and Henry M. Naglee was appointed their receiver. They resumed soon after, and continue yet, with an express business added to their banking, whose ramifications may be traced throughout the States and in Europe. Dr. Wright's Savings Bank and some others in San Francisco closed. In the interior, besides the branch offices of the large city houses, many smaller banks shut up, and the crash among the merchants swiftly followed.

All the suspending banks—there were a few, some of which are still in operation, that weathered the gale—insisted that it was solely a lack of coin that compelled their closing, and that they had abundant assets if they only could be given a little time to make them available. Many of the leading merchants, to whom Page, Bacon & Co. were largely indebted, were so well satisfied that time alone was wanting in their case, that they guaranteed the time-certificates of the house, and Page, Bacon & Co. soon started again; but only to stumble deeper into the mire. The gentlemen who guaranteed their certificates were helped out of their liability by a decision of the Supreme Court, that a discrepancy of dates on some of the certificates and their bond was fatal to the validity of the former.

Nine years afterwards, when it was represented that all that either the San Francisco or the St. Louis house had relied on to make good their promises was gone, William T. Coleman, a brother-in-law of Mr. Bacon, stated to a meeting of the creditors of the California house, that the remaining total indebtedness in this State was about half a million of dollars, aside from interest, which was as much more. He proposed to pay ten per cent. on the principal, if creditors would accept it, for the sake of releasing Bacon. But the creditors thought five per cent. on paper that they had carried nine years was scarcely worth accepting, and the meeting dissolved, agreeing to nothing.

For Adams & Co. there was a stormy future. The bitterness of the indignation of their creditors is scarcely yet out of their mouths. They began in San Francisco in 1850, soon came into an immense business, were universally confided in, and were never suspected of unsoundness until after their failure. The public very soon after that event began to fancy that there was some collusion in the appointment of Cohen as receiver, who deposited at least a portion of the funds turned over to him with Palmer, Cook & Co., his sureties, a notable firm of bankers, which had gone through the panic of February without harm. The creditors, thoroughly aroused, at last obtained the appointment of H. M. Naglee as receiver, in place of Cohen; but, though they had the shrewd counsel of Trenor W. Park, it was not an easy task to make Cohen surrender the assets he had received to his successor. So much of them as Palmer, Cook & Co. held on deposit that firm refused to give up. Suit followed suit, and Mr. Jones, one of the partners, was imprisoned for contempt of the Fourth District (Judge Hager's) Court. Relenting at last, Jones handed over so much as he had, and was released.

Cohen was of more stubborn stuff, or else the ignorance that he professed was genuine. He too was imprisoned for contempt, and one question that was asked—what became of a certain amount of money that was removed on a particular night, from Alsop & Company's vaults—is not to this day answered. The books would tell, thought the creditors; but on search they were missing. One day a bag of books was found floating in the bay, near North Beach, by some Irishmen, who, on being assured that they were the missing accounts of Adams & Co., caught the infection of the times, and asked thirty thousand dollars for them. The officers of the law searched the vicinity of the finders' homes, and at last discovered the books, wet and water-soiled, between two mattresses. But the important leaves detailing the expenditures and receipts of February 21st and 22d were wanting.

Cohen, still persisting that the books were never in his possession, and that he had told all he knew, was allowed to lie in jail. He was prosecuted for embezzlement, and the jury found that two hundred and sixty-nine thousand dollars had gone into his hands, for which no account was made. But suddenly, when Judge Hager had gone East, and while Park was away, application was made to the Supreme Court for his release, and it was granted.

It was a mystery why the prosecution of Cohen should so suddenly cease, and the intimate relations soon after found to exist between Park and Cohen's sureties, Palmer, Cook & Co., and the connection of both with Fremont and the Mariposa mine during the Presidential campaign of 1856, caused some scandal, but it remained a mystery until the subject was forgotten.

Meanwhile, Isaiah C. Woods, the resident partner and manager of the house of Adams & Co., slipped off for Australia, and although in a card he said he was going for the benefit of creditors, he has not yet returned. The Supreme Court decided his proceedings in insolvency void, and further raised the hopes of creditors by determining that those who had taken out attachments must fare precisely as the rest; but nothing was saved from the wreck.

Among the bankers ruined by this financial storm was "James King, of William." Born in Virginia, he went to California in 1848. When he failed he reserved nothing of the handsome fortune he had made as a banker, and refused to avail himself of the insolvency act, for which scores eagerly applied. He became a clerk with Adams & Co., but soon perceived practices repugnant to his nature. Before he had decided that it was right to leave, seeing that many of his old customers had followed him to that house, came its failure.

Now, entirely out of employment, and believing that an independent press might shed light enough on the wretched state of society to compel its reform, he associated himself with C. O. Gerberding, and began (October 8th, 1855) the publication of the daily *Evening Bulletin*. It was a small sheet, and its editor's inexperience in his new profession was marked in the first as in many a succeeding number. But it was from the start a power and a terror to evildoers. Intimately acquainted with the villany of men in a rank that too often is not amenable to law or even to public sentiment, he began at once to apply the lash to their shoulders. He had not much to say about sin, but sinners he flayed alive. Into Palmer, Cook & Co., Broderick, Cohen, into city officials derelict in duty, into courts that shielded crime with law, into lawyers almost as a class, but specifically enough, into ballot-box stuffers and ward colonists, into politicians of all schools, into anybody that seemed to him to be injuring society, sapping its virtue, or defending its criminals, he thrust his weapon with all his might.

He was exceedingly careful of his facts. The thought of libel suits never disturbed him. He gave early notice that he would not fight a duel, and that for assassins he went prepared. The people rallied to his support as if Justice had come down to edit a paper. He told secrets that made rich villains wince and detectives wonder how he learned them. The Richmond of his heaviest siege was "Palmer, Cook & Co." He claimed that they were doing a general banking business, and so were amenable to honest criticism. He charged them with heinous political crimes; he alleged that they furnished the funds for Broderick to make his successful fight against Gwin, and compelled Gwin (whose defeat was no cause for regret) to confess that Palmer kept him out of the Senate; they were kings of the lobby. He said they compelled office-holders to engage them as sureties that they might finger the funds. He showed that while they were on Cohen's bonds for a million dollars, they were on the bonds of State, city, and county officers for half a million, and of other persons and officers enough more to make the total of their obligations of that sort over two million dollars. He charged them with financial unsoundness and political corruption, with debauching public officers, controlling elections, and buying judicial decisions.

About vulgar criminals he made less noise, but when Cora, the murderer of Marshal Richardson, was supposed to be rather loosely held

CHAP.
XXVIII.
1856.

by the sheriff, he exclaimed in his paper, "If Mr. Sheriff Scannell does not remove Billy Mulligan from his present post as keeper of the county jail, and Mulligan lets Cora escape—hang Billy Mulligan; and if necessary to get rid of the sheriff, hang him—hang the sheriff!"

The price that James King paid for this independence, these bold, unusual utterances, which the disjointed times demanded, will appear in a future chapter.

The finances of the State were coming into a very bad way. Prohibited by the Constitution from creating a debt of over three hundred thousand dollars, except under circumstances that did not then exist, a debt of ten times that amount had been contracted. At the close of the year 1856, the aggregated city, county, and State debts amounted to twelve million one hundred and sixty-three thousand dollars. The State owned the tide lands, but early gave away to the several cities most of those portions of them from which a revenue might have been raised. It owned the swamp land, donated to it by Congress for purposes of reclamation, on which it raised something by sales. It owned several millions of acres more, given it by Congress, and by the terms of the gift or by local legislation devoted to school purposes. Besides these resources, it had great expectations that Congress would refund the customs collected at

San Francisco while California was neither a Territory nor a State; but they were never realized. To raise money, then, for current expenses, the chief reliable resort was taxation. Real and personal property were taxed at a high rate; poll-taxes were levied, and all proprietors of theatres and shows, all bankers, brokers, foreign miners, merchants, tavern-keepers, and the officers of incorporations for gain were required to take out licenses; but the tax-collectors were not quick enough to catch the shifting population, and high rates brought small returns.

The Legislature began to be eyed suspiciously, especially from San Francisco. It was always plotting some scheme that disturbed the temper of citizens. Session after session it attempted to extend the city's water-front in a manner that would enrich a few at the expense of the many and of commerce. In 1853, a bill to extend the front at some points six hundred feet into the bay, passed the Assembly The five San Francisco members who opposed it— John Sime was of the number—resigned their seats, and were re-elected on that issue by an immense majority. In the Senate the bill was defeated only by the casting vote of Lieutenant-Governor Purdy. Governor Bigler advised in his next message another effort at extension, pleading the necessities of the State, which sadly wanted the revenue that the water-lots would fetch, but happily, though backed by a horde of hungry speculators, the city was saved the infliction.

The lobby, which early became a formidable power at the capital, devised schemes for obtaining valuable franchises for toll-roads leading out of the cities and over the mountains, and for bridges; but Governor Bigler was sound on that question; he vetoed most that came before him, and the franchise-hunters tarried till a later day for their harvest.

The Federal courts commanded respect at all times; but the Supreme Court of the State had only a tolerable reputation. The personal character of some of the judges was bad. If there was ability, spotless integrity did not always accompany it; if honesty, it was not always well mixed with wisdom.

CHAPTER XXIX.

POLITICS.

POLITICS had grown to be a profession, and its professors were not eminently the salt of the earth. The honest, order-loving people were blamable for leaving their local and State policy to be controlled so entirely by persons too idle to labor, and too fond of office and the spoils of party to be trusted safely. They suffered for their neglect, in pocket, in reputation, in the peace of community.

A Democratic Administration had acquired the country; but a Whig Administration first enjoyed it. Certainly it might have managed its inheritance better. It succeeded early in making every department of Federal rule offensive to the people. It persisted in collecting customs on the basis of the war levy long after peace had been restored. It left the country without the existence of either a Territorial or State Government. It was not slow to furnish postal facilities; but the rates of postage were maintained at an intolerably high figure. President Fillmore advised that the mines be held

CHAP. XXIX.
1850–1856.

as United States property, and that they be made to contribute to the Federal revenue, than which nothing could be devised to set the miners more stubbornly against the party in power.

For these and other reasons, the Whigs, notwithstanding all their patronage, gained nothing for their party in California, and never carried the State. The first Governor elected by the people (1849) was Peter H. Burnett, a Democrat. The total number of votes cast was but fourteen thousand one hundred and seventeen. John A. Sutter received two thousand two hundred and one; John W. Geary, fourteen hundred and seventy-five; W. M. Stewart, six hundred and nineteen; W. S. Sherwood, three thousand one hundred and eighty-eight; and Burnett, six thousand six hundred and thirty-four. The first Legislature was of like politics as the Governor. After a single year's service, Burnett resigned, and John McDougall, the Democratic Lieutenant-Governor, succeeded to his chair—David C. Broderick being elected President of the Senate to fill the vacancy thus created.

In the fall of 1851 the people elected again. John Bigler (a Pennsylvania Democrat, whose familiarity with parliamentary rules made him Speaker *pro tem.* of the Assembly in 1850, and permanent Speaker in 1851) received twenty-three thousand seven hundred and seventy-four votes for Governor, while Reading, his Whig opponent, got twenty-two thousand seven hundred and thirty-three.

In this contest Bigler had the aid of the squatters, who were becoming a power in the State. He was democratic in his manners—the "hale fellow" of all he met. His opponent was a gentleman of more genteel bearing, and owned much land. Bigler was kind-hearted, unambitious, landless, and always mindful of his friends. He urged economy in his messages; but found it hard to prevent an office being made for a friend. It was his pet project to unite the Southern and Western men of his party, and let the Free-soilers shift for themselves; but it is not in that direction that party cleavage runs. The Southerners scorned the alliance. They were "high-toned," and looked down upon a Missourian as little better than a man from Massachusetts. The Governor's project would not work. He carried water on both shoulders, and spilt very little on either side. Though a man of positive opinions, and bold in the expression of them, he managed to make his party grow, as was shown at the Presidential election in 1852, when Franklin Pierce received forty thousand four hundred and twenty-nine votes in California, and General Scott thirty-five thousand seven hundred and sixty. Indeed, he was a devoted partisan. In judging of his Administration it must be remembered that he fell on evil times, when men gambled a great deal, had not their families with them, were rough, money-making, and extravagant. At his first nomination, Broderick was against him; but after Weller went to the United States Senate, the stone-cutter's son took a different view of things, and brought his powerful aid to secure him the nomination for a second term.

Successful in convention, Bigler was successful again before the people, who (in 1853) re-elected him Governor by a majority of fourteen hundred and sixty-seven over Waldo, his Whig opponent.

Hitherto the Democracy, quarrel as much as they might in caucus and convention, had managed to present an unbroken front on election-day. Now the feud was too hot for concealment. The party was split into factions—the Northern (Tammany) wing under the lead of Broderick, and the Southern, or Chivalry, under Dr. Gwin. Broderick struggled in the Legislature of 1854 to bring on the election of United States Senator at once; hence his party was known at the time as "Electionists." Gwin, with equal vigor, girded himself to stave off the election, and his wing were "Anti-Electionists." Broderick was chairman of the State Central Committee. A State convention was called to meet at Sacramento, in the First Baptist Church, on the 18th of July, 1854. The building was kept closed until a few minutes of the time; the doors were then unlocked, and a great crowd dashed into the little building. Broderick called the excited assembly to order, and asked nominations for a temporary president. A Gwin man named ex-Governor McDougall, and a Broderick man almost simultaneously named Edward McGowan. Broderick recognized the last-named, and put the vote. A storm of *ayes* and *noes* was thundered out, and McDougall and McGowan both started for the chair. They reached it together, and both proceeded with business, professing to ignore each other's presence. There were double sets of officers, double speeches, double reports. At one time a collision occurred, and a pistol was discharged, probably by accident. The trustees of the church gave notice that they could not occupy the building any longer—it was not calculated to bear the strain of a double convention. At last a double motion to adjourn was carried, and the two chairmen left the church arm-in-arm.

Next day the factions met in separate halls. The Chivalry nominated J. W. Denver and Philip Herbert for Congress. The Tammany wing nominated General James McDougall and James Churchman of Nevada.

A week later the Whigs had a State convention at Sacramento, which was marked with all the harmony peculiar to hopeless minorities. J. Neely Johnson presided. Resolutions were adopted, invoking the people to help reduce taxes, unshackle commerce, remove restrictions on trade, restore the purity of the ballot-box, and make secure life, liberty, and property. For Congressmen, they nominated Calhoun Benham and G. W. Bowie.'

At the election the Gwin Congressmen won, getting some thirty-seven thousand five hundred votes; the Broderick candidates had little over ten thousand; while the Whigs had thirty-five thousand.

It is curious to note here the future of some of these worthies. McGowan, Broderick's chairman, at the outbreak of the great rebellion, presented himself in Washington, claiming to represent Arizona, and threatening to take that Territory out of the Union if Southern claims were not respected. Herbert, while in Congress, murdered an Irish waiter at Willard's Hotel, and fell into disgrace, even with his party. Denver became a Brigadier-General of Volunteers, and fought for the Union, until he was shelved quietly. Calhoun Benham became Buchanan's District Attorney for California, and prophesied that grass would grow in the streets of New York if Lincoln should be elected. After the war broke out he was arrested by General Sumner, in company with Dr. Gwin, in Panama harbor, and for a brief time occupied an apartment in Fort Lafayette.

In 1855, Bigler was renominated for a third term as Governor. Some of Gwin's friends urged Milton S. Latham, but they were a minority in convention. Bigler obtained forty-six thousand two hundred and twenty votes, the full strength of his party, but he failed of re-election. The Whigs merged into the new Know Nothing party, which gave fifty-one thousand one hundred and fifty-seven votes to J. Neely Johnson, and made him Governor. The politicians of the day said that Bigler, in despair of carrying any longer the friendship of Estill, who had the obnoxious State Prison contract, threw him off, and Estill, changing over to the Know Nothings, with a party strong enough to turn the balance of power, revenged himself on his old friend. But the governorship was never deemed the highest political prize in California. Far above it shone the United States senatorship, and the attainment of that from an early date taxed heavily the energies of faction and the purse of the aspirant. At the first session of the Legislature (held at San José, December, 1849) parties were not organized, and the senatorial election was soon over.

The nominees for Senator were John C. Fremont, William M. Gwin, Captain H. W. Halleck (since General-in-Chief,) T. Butler King, Thomas J. Henley, Robert Semple, Colonel Jonathan D. Stevenson (but Edmund Randolph hastened to withdraw the colonel), and Colonel (now General) J. W. Geary. On the first ballot Fremont had twenty-nine (which elected him), Gwin twenty-two, Halleck fourteen, King ten, Henley nine, Geary five, Semple three. On the third ballot Gwin had two majority. So Fremont and Gwin were California's first Senators. Halleck's highest vote was eighteen on the third ballot. Fremont drew the short term, and his seat became vacant on the 3d of March, 1851.

The Legislature desperately essayed, early in 1851, to elect a successor to Fremont, but all in vain. After sundry efforts to appoint a day for a joint convention, the 17th of February was agreed on. When twelve o'clock arrived the Assembly was still in session, engaged in a call of the House, and the Senate took a recess of ten minutes, to give the officers time to prepare seats for the other branch in the Senate chamber, on the first floor; for, seeing how great the crowd was, it was deemed imprudent to meet in the Assembly chamber, on the second floor. When order was called in the Senate again, Mr. Broderick stated that several members of the Assembly were absent from their seats in the Assembly, and could not be found. He said, moreover, that there was a rumor on the street that one member had been drugged the night before, to prevent his voting for a Senator. He moved to postpone the joint convention, and, though while the vote was being taken the Assembly was at the door, the vote was carried—*ayes* nine, *noes* six; and the astounded Assembly was in a quandary, with a joint convention on its hands, and no Senate to help adjourn it. However, the joint convention met soon after, and on the first ballot forty-nine votes were cast. Twenty-five were necessary to a choice, and no one had near that number. Fremont had eight; Heydenfeldt, whose brother was a Whig member of the State Senate, had sixteen, King had fifteen, Geary four, Weller four, Collier two. Seven days were spent in ineffectual efforts to elect. On the sixty-sixth ballot Fremont had eleven, King nineteen, Heydenfeldt fifteen, Geary one, and George B. Tingley two. On the 27th of February the one hundred and forty-first ballot was taken, when Fremont had fourteen, King eighteen, Heydenfeldt fifteen, Bennet one. Heydenfeldt was now withdrawn, and John B. Weller nominated. Next day the one hundred and forty-

CHAP. XXIX.
1852.

second ballot was taken, resulting as follows: Fremont nine, King twenty, Weller eighteen, Geary one. Then, satisfied they could never agree, the joint convention adjourned to January 1st, 1852. The letter-writers of that day represent San José as black with the lobby, and the candidates giving suppers to their friends with the most profuse hospitality.

The Legislature of 1852 met at Vallejo, but finding no accommodations for remaining, removed to Sacramento. By this time the Democratic party, which was largely in the majority, had perfectly organized. The seventy-two Democrats went into caucus, and on the first ballot Weller had twenty-one votes, Broderick sixteen. The joint convention, however, did not wait on caucus. At its first balloting Weller had twenty-three, G. B. Tingley sixteen, Broderick fifteen, William Smith nine, Alexander Anderson nine, W. McLane seven, and ten scattering. Caucus tried it again, and on the fifth ballot Weller had two majority over Broderick. Next day, in joint convention, John B. Weller had seventy-one, P. B. Reading seventeen. So Weller was elected the successor of John C. Fremont in the United States Senate.

1854.

In 1853 there was rest from Senator-making; but in 1854 the campaign reopened. Gwin's term of office was not to expire until March 4th, 1855. But Broderick doubted if he would soon again get so favorable a Legislature, and determined to bring on an election. The Whigs having nothing to lose by delay, united with the Gwin faction in the employment of every means to postpone the election. At one time Broderick needed but a single vote more to carry his point and secure his election. The Legislature adjourned mid-session from Benicia to Sacramento—it was said to win a Sacramento vote—but the ruse was unsuccessful, and the election could not be ordered. Hence the bitterness and obstinacy with which the factions struggled for the advantage in the State Convention of the following fall.

In 1855, Gwin started with a majority in the Legislature, but not enough to control the election. They balloted fifty times, and from the 17th of January to the 16th of February. On the first ballot Gwin had forty-two, Broderick twelve, Philip L. Edwards thirty-six, Joseph W. McCorkle fourteen, James A. McDougall two, Frederick Billings one, Solomon Heydenfeldt one, Frank Soulé one, and R. T. Sprague one. On the fiftieth ballot, Broderick had twelve, Gwin forty-one, Edwards thirty-six, Roman fifteen; and then the joint convention adjourned *sine die*, and from the 4th of March of that year there was a vacancy in the State's senatorial representation at Washington. To prevent accidents in case the next Legislature should be of some other than the Democratic party, a law was enacted, requiring all regular elections for United States Senator to be held after the 1st of January next preceding the commencement of the senatorial term—a precaution necessary to keep Weller's seat open for a Democrat.

Neely Johnson was inaugurated Governor in January, 1856. He was supported by a Know Nothing Legislature, which came within one vote of electing Henry S. Foote, formerly of Mississippi (and since then a member of the Confederate Senate in Richmond), but at that time a resident of California. Wilson Flint, one of the senators, though a Know Nothing, sturdily refused to vote for Foote, believing that he was a pro-slavery man and a carpet-bag politician, whose sole errand to the State was to gain this prize. Great was the wrath of the party, but Flint was stubborn, and without his vote no progress could be made. His life was threatened, but his friends guarded well his ways, and no harm came to him. Foote's party competitor was Henry A. Crabb, who afterwards withdrew in favor of W. J. Ferguson, of Sacramento. The party lacking discipline, and its members distrusting its lease of power, each faction felt that compromises were useless, and present success all that was worth struggling for. The Democrats did not doubt that next year they would have the Legislature again, and as then Weller's term as well as Gwin's would be out, there would be a place for each faction. So they harmonized in view of the spoils, and with a very little Know Nothing aid, got a resolution through the Senate, declaring it inexpedient and contrary to the wishes of the people to fill the existing vacancy, and postponed all action on the subject to January 1st, 1857. The two Houses did not go into joint convention.

The Presidential election came on that fall. James Buchanan obtained the electoral vote of the State. His popular vote was fifty-three thousand three hundred and sixty-five. Millard Fillmore, the American candidate, received thirty-six thousand one hundred and sixty-five votes; and Fremont, who now claimed a residence in New York, from the State which delighted almost unanimously to make him her first Senator, received twenty thousand six hundred and ninety-three.

The candidates for Congress that year were Joseph McKibben and Charles Scott (Democrats), who were elected; Whitman and Dibble, Americans, and Ira P. Rankin and Mr. Turner, Republicans, who ran far enough ahead of Fremont to mark the unpopularity of the young Pathfinder in the region of which he was the reputed conqueror.

CHAP. XXIX.
1851-1856.

San Francisco had come by degrees to stand at variance with the State on politics. In 1851, it gave a majority to the Whig nominee for Governor. In 1853, Bigler had but five majority there over Waldo. In 1854, it gave a plurality for the Whig Congressmen, and to the Broderick wing from three hundred and fifty to four hundred votes more than to the Gwin faction. In 1855, the united Democracy got nearly two thousand majority over the Know Nothings. In 1856, it gave Buchanan a plurality, but to Fremont more than three to one for Fillmore. San Francisco, generally, tended to the side of the minority.

In Sacramento the Whigs were in the majority in 1852, 1853, and 1854; the Know Nothings in 1855; and the Democrats in 1856. As between Broderick and Gwin in 1854, it inclined to the former. The strongholds of the Chivalry were in the mining region.

But the real "ruling classes" do not come to light in these statistics. The dregs of society —swindlers, thieves, and gamblers—dictated to the party dictators, and ruled the State with a tyranny that conventions dare not meddle with. The party in power had to bear the odium of the wretched condition of affairs; probably it would have been all the same whether Whigs or Democrats, Tammanyites or "Chivs" occupied the public places. The better classes had despised politics, and the worst classes picked up the reins and were driving fast to ruin. Good men, who were elevated to power by parties that they could not think of controlling, were ashamed, disgusted, mortified by the power that used them. The judiciary fell into disrepute. The course of regular justice was obstructed. Criminals enjoyed an alarming immunity from punishment. Violence ruled in city and country. Then Judge Lynch crowded the slow judge (whom the people elected) off the bench. The legal executioner could not learn his business for lack of practice; yet in many a quiet nook among the mountains, the thief or murderer, or the party pronounced to be such after a hurried trial, was hung by the neck to the limb of a tree—the trial beginning in the morning, the hanging over before noon!

Here are some examples which occurred long after the organization of the courts was completed for every settled section of the State: Two Mexican horse-thieves were lynched near Martinez in April, 1853. A bar-keeper was, in the same month, hung on the very day that he shot a citizen of Whiskey Creek, near Shasta. In July, a Mexican was hung at Jackson for horse-stealing. At Volcano, in December, 1854, one Macy stabbed an old man. In less than half an hour the assassin was swinging lifeless

—having been executed by the mob. The same month, one Johnson stabbed a man named Montgomery, at Iowa Hill; he attempted to escape, but was captured, and was hung the next day. As the wounded man gave signs of recovery afterwards, a revulsion in the public sentiment took place, and a suspicion got out that perhaps the avengers had been in too much haste. Three men, convicted of murder, lay in jail together at Los Angeles, under sentence of death. An order went down from the Supreme Court granting a stay of proceedings in the cases of Brown and Lee, leaving Alvitre to his fate. The people insisted that Brown should suffer death the same day with Alvitre. The mayor of the city made a speech, urging the justice of that course. On the 12th of January, 1855, Alvitre was executed according to law. The mayor resigned his office and joined the mob, which demanded Brown from the sheriff. They took Brown forcibly out of the jail and hung him, in spite of the Supreme Court, by the side of his fellow in crime. On the 18th of the same month, Mr. Heslep, the acting treasurer of Tuolumne County, was murdered. The supposed murderer was caught and lynched on the 19th. Three cattle-thieves were captured one Sunday of February, 1855, in Contra Costa County, and hung by the mob on the Monday following. The same month, some unknown persons took a horse-thief out of the Oakland jail, carried him to Clinton Bridge, and hung him to the bough of a tree. In August, 1855, six Americans were murdered by a gang of Mexicans, not far from Jackson, in Amador County. The people turned out and caught thirty-six of the Mexicans. It was proposed to hang them together. But that was thought too irresponsible a method. So a jury was selected, several of the captives tried, and three of them hung on the same tree together.

Robbers infested the highways, of the Southern counties especially. There is a long chapter of violence that may remain unwritten, where the criminals were not caught. Sometimes these cases created an excitement far beyond the immediate vicinity where the crime was committed. In November, 1855, Isaac B. Wall, ex-Speaker of Assembly, and Collector of Monterey, and T. S. Williamson, a county officer of Monterey, when on the road between their home and San Luis Obispo, were assassinated. The same month, William H. Richardson, United States Marshal, was shot fatally by Charles Cora on Clay Street in San Francisco, a few doors below Montgomery Street, by daylight. Cora was arrested.

There was no assurance that conviction would follow arrest, no matter how many witnesses. The county jails were seldom very secure at the best, even if there had not been conniving sheriffs. The State's Prison at San Quentin was a sieve. In December, 1854, thirty convicts escaped from it on the same day.

The sudden rise of the Know Nothing or American party into power was not owing so much to any outburst of exclusively American feeling as to the determination to adopt anything new, with the hope that an unhackneyed party and fresh men might dam the flood that had swept away the social reputation of the State, and threatened to wreck its financial character. That party's equally sudden collapse was due to the discovery that unprincipled persons had got control of that organization too, and were handling it as all others had been.

Things came at last to a pitch beyond endurance. There were some good men in office, but so hampered and hedged that they might as well have been out; there were some good judges on the bench, but generally they were powerless to punish crime or protect innocence against the tide of false swearing that set in the hour it was wanted to shield criminals or convict the guiltless. There were bad men in office, too, who had things very much their own way: corrupt judges, who fingered bribes, as the public believed; sheriffs, and constables, and jailers, to whom detected criminals ran for

DESPERATE SOCIAL CONDITION.

refuge. San Franciscans, after dark, instinctively avoided a crowd; and if they had occasion to go into the sandy or chaparal-covered suburbs after nightfall, they felt that they neglected their duty to themselves and their families unless they took a revolver.

Ballot-box stuffing was as regular as the arrival of election-day. Voters felt it a farce to spend their time at the polls, when rowdies, gamblers, state-prison convicts, and "Sydney ducks" could, in ten minutes after the polls were closed, make any majority for their side that was wanted. It was a condition of affairs that American citizens could not long endure.

CHAPTER XXX.

THE VIGILANCE COMMITTEE OF 1856.

The explosion occurred in 1856, at San Francisco, but the whole State felt the shock. A correspondent of the *Bulletin*, signing himself "A Purifier," had spoken of one Bagley, who had been indicted for attempting the life of James P. Casey, as an objectionable appointee to the Custom-House, which Collector Latham was busily reforming. James King, in an editorial, on the 14th of May, used the following language:—

"It does not matter how bad a man Casey had been, nor how much benefit it might be to the public to have him out of the way; we cannot accord to any one citizen the right to kill him, or even beat him, without justifiable, personal provocation. The fact that Casey has been the inmate of Sing Sing Prison is no offence against the laws of this State; nor is the fact of his having stuffed himself through the ballot-box as elected to the Board of Supervisors from a district where it is said he was not even a candidate, any justification for Mr.

Bagley to shoot Casey, however richly the latter may deserve to have his neck stretched for such a fraud on the people."

CHAP. XXX.

1856. May.

The *Bulletin* was issued about three o'clock in the afternoon. At four o'clock, Supervisor Casey, the subject of the above "disparaging allusion," entered the editorial room of the *Bulletin*, which was on the second story of a building on Merchant Street, near Montgomery. King was seated at his desk. Casey asked him what he meant by the article in the *Bulletin* just issued; King asked him to what article he referred.

"To that," said Casey, "which says that I was formerly an inmate of Sing Sing Prison."

"Is not that true?" asked King.

"That is not the question," replied Casey; "I don't wish my past acts raised up; on that I am sensitive."

"Are you done?" asked King. "There's the door—go! Never show your face here again."

Casey moved off immediately. Passing out of the door, he said, "I'll say in my paper what I please;"—he was editor of a weekly sheet—the Sunday *Times*.

"You have a perfect right to do as you please," answered King; "I'll never notice your paper." Casey, without another word, departed.

King left his office soon after five o'clock, as usual, to go to his dinner. He passed up Merchant Street, up Montgomery to Washington Street, and began to cross it to the west side of Montgomery. Casey, who was on the west side of Montgomery Street, waiting, threw off his cloak, and presenting a revolver when they were a few feet apart, and saying, "Come on," or something to that effect, fired. The shot entered King's left breast and passed out under the shoulder-blade. King staggered into the Pacific Express Company's office, on the northwest corner of Washington and Montgomery Streets. The wound bled freely. He was got to bed, and slept somewhat during the night.

Casey, so soon as he had fired, was hurried off to the station-house by his friends, and thence to the jail on Broadway, as to a place of refuge.

Fearful of an attack upon the jail, the military were ordered out, and they promptly responded. A hundred of them, more or less, took their position on the roof, ready to fire on the crowd in case of emergency. At half-past six P. M., Mayor Van Ness attempted from the front of the jail to address the crowd. He advised them to disperse quietly—"the prisoner was safe"—"it was best to let the law take its course and justice be done." He was interrupted with cries of "Where is the law in Cora's case?"—"There is too much law and too little justice in California."—"Down with such justice!" The Mayor, seeing his efforts useless, retired. The crowd tarried about the jail till a late hour, and then dispersed.

But all night there was a great assemblage before the Pacific Express Company's office, waiting to learn the fate of Mr. King. Ropes were placed across the street to prevent the friendly crowd from entering the building and disturbing the wounded man's repose.

The old Vigilance Committee of 1851 met during the evening, but deferred definite action until the next day.

That next day was one of profound excitement in San Francisco. The *Herald* spoke of the attempted assassination as "an affray between James P. Casey and James King, of William." "Motives of delicacy, needless to explain, force us to abstain from commenting on this affair," said the editor. He confessed that in times past he had sustained the Vigilance Committee, but now "justice was regularly administered," and there existed "no necessity for such an association."

The *Sun* and the *Globe* abstained from editorial comments. The *Chronicle* called for justice. "Let reason and law—nay, *make* reason and law vindicate the outraged laws and peace of society." It almost suggested, but did not quite, that the people assume the functions that the officers of the courts had so long neglected to employ. The *Alta* spoke out decidedly that the time to stop such outrages had come. The *Bulletin* appeared that evening with a blank column in place of a leader. It narrated the story of the assassination minutely, and its correspondence teemed with calls for instant popular organization. On Friday it received over a hundred letters, most of which advocated speedy action by a Vigilance Committee. The *Pacific* (a religious paper edited by a Congregational clergyman) said, "Casey ought to be hung. Believe it who will," that, left to the courts, he will be; "we do not." Said the *Christian Advocate* (the Methodist organ), "Providence is a farce and justice a lie, or the doom of the ungodly in this city is at hand." The other papers spoke freely, and nearly to the same point.

If the newspapers reflected the public sentiment—and probably nowhere else in the world are the papers more generally read, or do they more truly speak for the whole people—there was a very strong majority demanding the formation of a vigilance committee, and thorough radical work by it. The *Globe* spoke out, like most of the other papers, on the second day. The *Herald* consistently opposed the Vigilance Committee; but its course cost it dear. It had been the leading commercial and news journal of the coast. The day that "motives of delicacy" led it to treat of the attempted assassination of King as "an affray," subscribers to the number of two hundred and twelve stopped their paper. Two hundred and fifty importers, merchants, and jobbers notified the auctioneers, who had, as a body, used it as their advertising medium, that they should not longer subscribe for it. So the auctioneers took their advertising over to the *Alta*, which waxed strong at once on the patronage; for in those days the paper that had the auctioneers' advertisements was necessarily the leading commercial organ. The *Herald* shrank in its dimensions next morning, and never regained its former prestige. The *Sun* soon ranged itself with the *Herald* in the opposition. It was a political sheet, of Democratic faith—for Bigler and Buchanan, and against Broderick. It was temperate but firm in its opposition, and made light of its lack of support—presenting, some days, under regular advertising heads, whole or half columns of blanks, as much as to say, "We reserve vacant and in order the space that our patrons will be sure to want so soon as this little flurry is over."

But it was no "little flurry." The Vigilance Committee—to this day it is hard to say how it started and was organized—was in session from nine in the morning until a late hour in the evening of the 15th. It was said, that

CHAP. within thirty hours after King was shot, they
XXX. had twenty-five hundred names enrolled on
1856. their books, of men who pledged themselves to
work together for the purging of the city of its
late "ruling classes," the gamblers, ballot-box
stuffers, jury packers, foreign convicts, swindlers,
thieves high and low, and of villains generally.
Hundreds were waiting their turn, all day, to
register themselves.

May 18. The meetings of the committee were held
with closed doors. The secrecy of its operations terrified the guilty, and large numbers of
suspicious characters departed up the river, or
scattered over the stage routes into the country.
Some bolder ones attempted to get inside of
the organization. Perhaps some of these succeeded; but if they did, they did not tarry
long, for "the all-seeing eye" that was printed
on the committee's official paper looked inside
as well as out of the committee.

Mayor Van Ness telegraphed to the Governor
that his presence was required. His Excellency
hastened down from Sacramento, had an interview with leading citizens and the city authorities, and by his advice Sheriff Scannell admitted some twenty persons, as a delegation of
the Vigilance Committee, into the jail, to keep
guard over Casey.

King still lingered; sometimes improving a
little; then again giving signs that his wound

was fatal. Bulletins were posted about the town, detailing his condition, which were consulted by crowds.

Sunday was a day of gloom and sadness. The churches were perhaps more thronged than usual. The Rev. Mr. Lacy (Congregationalist), according to previous announcement, took for his subject, *Law and Religion*. The Rev. Mr. Cutler (Unitarian) dwelt on the exciting topics of the week. The Rev. Mr. Brierly, at the Baptist church, discussed the matter that engrossed all thoughts. Indeed, the Protestant pulpit throughout the State very generally availed itself of the great overshadowing event, to make research for the principles that lie at the base of all substantial human governments. The Rev. J. A. Benton (Congregationalist), at Sacramento, said: "A people can be justified in recalling delegated power and resuming its exercise"—guarding his statement with the further remark, that "like every such remedy and resort, it must be reserved for rare occasions and the most trying emergencies."

But while, in San Francisco, a portion of the community were listening with the closest attention to sermons on what filled every man's thoughts, a larger portion were in the streets. The members of the Vigilance Committee, or so many of them as had received the hasty notice, issuing from their places of rendezvous, armed with muskets, rifles, or revolvers, and noiseless, except as their tramp rang out from the pavement, marched through the most public thoroughfares to the jail on Broadway. There were twenty-four companies represented. Perhaps half the complement of each (which was one hundred) were in the procession.

Soon a brass cannon was placed in the street, facing the jail door, and the roofs of the neighboring houses were covered with riflemen. A committee from this armed and noiseless crowd waited upon Sheriff Scannell, and demanded the surrender of Casey. With scarcely a minute's parley the jail door was thrown open. Casey at first remonstrated, and expressed some indignation that "Scannell too had deserted" him. But he was shown how vain opposition would be. Casey drew a concealed knife, and said that no person should put irons on his limbs. He was told that the committee would have him dead or alive. Thereupon he submitted to be handcuffed, and was taken to a carriage, which, under guard of two hundred men, was driven to the committee's head-quarters in Sacramento Street.

After Casey had been driven off, the special committee returned to the jail, and demanded Cora, the murderer of Marshal Richardson. There was a little delay about this, but in about an hour he too was produced, and put in a close carriage, which three members of the committee entered. Two other carriages, filled with members, followed, and, with a company of guards marching on either side, they proceeded to head-quarters. All this was done so quietly that the people in the churches knew nothing of it until services ended.

A little after noon of the 20th of May, six days after he was shot, James King, of William, died. It was known instantly upon the street, and the tolling of nearly all the bells conveyed the intelligence to every part of the city. By telegraph the event was known before night throughout the State. Merchants closed their stores, mechanics their shops; laborers stopped work at once. Very soon Montgomery Street was lined with crape. Men appeared with crape on their arms and on their hats. The bell-handles of many houses were trimmed with crape. A stranger would have thought a plague was raging.

There was a general hastening of men to the Vigilance Committee rooms. The expectation was prevalent that Casey would not many minutes outlive his victim. But they learned that the assassin was on trial, which would be calmly conducted, and that no step would be rashly taken.

From five o'clock until late in the evening, King's body lay in state in a room on Montgomery Block, and the throng seeking admittance to where it lay stretched down the sidewalks of Montgomery Street for two blocks. Not in San Francisco alone, but in many other places throughout the State, the emblems of sorrow were assumed by the people, and the bells tolled as if a public calamity had occurred.

On the 22d, the funeral of King took place. More generally than upon the Sabbath, all places of business were closed. The body was taken to the Unitarian Church. The Rev. Mr. Cutler made a brief address, the Rev. Mr. Taylor read appropriate passages of Scripture, and the Rev. Mr. Lacy followed with some details of conversations that he had held with the deceased during his last sickness, wherein he had expressed himself assured of the truths of the Christian religion. The whole house was affected to tears.

Then came the procession to Lone Mountain. First in the line were the representatives of seven Lodges of the Masonic Order, in full regalia; then the Society of Pioneers; next the Sacramento Guard; then every company of the Fire Department, except Crescent, No. 10, of which Casey was once the foreman; then two hundred and fifty mounted draymen; then one hundred and forty-two stevedores; then the Turners in costume; then a deputation from a colored society; then a long line of mourners in carriages. In all, the procession numbered thousands of people. Many bands of music accompanied it, but in silence, their mute instruments draped in mourning. To Lone Mountain, with Masonic honors, the body was resigned. The spot is marked by a fine monument that was erected by the citizens.

The bereaved people of the State cheerfully accepted as their charge the support of the widow and orphans of their champion. Contributions in money poured in generously from all quarters for their benefit. The proceeds, amounting to over thirty-one thousand dollars, were profitably invested by the trustees of the fund and the guardians of the children.

The same day—and those who rode most swiftly back from the cemetery were too late to witness the extraordinary sight—both Casey and Cora were hanged in Sacramento Street, near Davis, in front of the head-quarters of the Vigilance Committee. The hour, one and a half P. M., was chosen as the time when there would be the least crowd.

The murderers had been tried by the committee and found guilty. A trap had been constructed from the second-story window of the committee's building; the condemned were placed upon it, and they were asked if they had any thing to say.

James Casey was thirty-nine years of age.

CHAP.
XXX.

1856.
May 22.

He had formerly lived in New York, was tried there in 1849 for grand larceny, was found guilty, and condemned to two years' imprisonment in Sing Sing. He served out his time, inserted a "P." in his name, emigrated to California, and soon became a most valuable assistant of the "ruling classes," as an expert at manufacturing election returns. When, in the fall of 1855, his purposes required that he should enter the Board of Supervisors as a member, he scorned the slow methods of most politicians, he neglected the "primary elections" on which others set such store, and yet he was elected, to the astonishment of his district, whose foremost men did not know that he was running until the vote was announced. "If," said the *News* of that day, "if the eleven thousand voters are satisfied with this, if there is not a gallows in the land at the service of such wretches, so let it remain." Casey had visited the editor after this passage appeared in it, but Mr. Bartlett was amply prepared, and there was no collision. Casey had found the gallows, and now stood under it.

He had been told the day before that he must die, and by the invitation of the committee, Archbishop Alemany had visited him. He had property worth some thirty or forty thousand dollars; he appointed Charles Gallagher as his executor. The Grand Jury of the

City and County had on the preceding day indicted Casey, Edward McGowan, and Peter Wightman, for the murder of King; but that fact gave him little concern. Justice was swifter than Law, and was in no mood to wait for her tardy companion.

Casey was asked if he had any thing to say. With pinioned arms he addressed the vast congregation that stood before him. He charged that no one of all he saw, and especially the newspaper men, should call him a murderer. His faults, he said, were those of his education. He had been taught that it was his province to resent a wrong—he had done so now. He spoke of his aged mother—it was her pain that he felt. He pardoned those who took his life—he asked pardon of God for the guilt of his life. With another exclamation concerning his poor mother he seemed to faint. Those who were near sustained him, and Father Gallagher pressed to his lips the cross, which he kissed.

By the side of Casey stood Cora, three hours a bridegroom, having been married that morning to a public woman, who had lavished money not in vain for his defence before the court, and in all his troubles shown constant devotion. He desired to say nothing. He only pressed the cross to his lips repeatedly, and waited, without emotion, until, at twenty minutes past one o'clock, the cord that held the outer ends of the platforms was cut, and the two miserable men were suspended lifeless.

Thousands of people witnessed from the streets and the house-tops this terrible spectacle. Many steamers from bay and river towns had come in with delegations to attend Mr. King's funeral. After the services in the church, and the procession in carriages and on horseback had started for the cemetery, hundreds had bent their way towards the committee's headquarters, though without any definite idea of what would occur. A dead silence reigned over the whole assemblage when they perceived what was proceeding.

As if to deepen still more the gloom of the day, while the procession was moving and the scaffold was being constructed, the *Golden Age* steamed up the bay, bringing the news that on the 15th of April more than one hundred of the natives on the Isthmus had assaulted the California-bound passengers from the *Illinois*, and the passengers from the *Cortes*, bound eastward, and had massacred twenty, and severely wounded fifty or sixty more. Nothing was lacking to make the day thoroughly memorable.

The bodies of Casey and Cora were given over to the coroner. His jury held an inquest, and found a verdict to the effect that they " came to their death by hanging by the neck, which hanging was done by a body of men styling themselves a Vigilance Committee of San Francisco." Cora was buried on Saturday, followed to the grave by a few friends.

CHAP. XXX.
1856.

Casey's body was given to the engine company of which he was once foreman. On the following Sunday the funeral took place, when a large procession followed the body to the Mission Dolores Cemetery. Not long after, a tasteful graystone monument was erected over his remains, and it is to-day one of the most noticeable structures in the old churchyard, as you ride along the Mission road. On one side of it was cut the following: "Erected by the Members of Crescent Engine Company, No. Ten, as a tribute of respect and esteem." On another side, cut in a white marble slab, was the following: "Sacred to the memory of James P. Casey, who departed this life May 22d, 1856, aged twenty-seven years. May God forgive my persecutors. Requiescat in pace."

The day after the burial of King, movements about the head-quarters gave token that the Vigilance Committee meant to continue, for a while at least, the work it had so vigorously commenced. A large cooking stove, and cartloads of bedding, were added to the appointments of the upper rooms of the United States Appraiser's store, which they occupied. A heavy triangle was suspended from a frame on the roof, a signal stroke on which brought every

May 23

Vigilant to his feet, and several cells were fitted up for the confinement of prisoners. Before night, an armed detachment brought in to occupy the cells, besides other notables, Billy Mulligan, one of the sheriff's deputies, Martin Gallagher, who had achieved renown as a ballot-box stuffer, and "Yankee Sullivan." Although James Sullivan was one of the judges of the election which stuffed Casey into the Board of Supervisors, in this emergency he remembered that he was not an American citizen, and appealed to the British Consul, but in vain. Born in Ireland, he was transported to Sydney for felony, and escaped thence, leaving his true name, Francis Murray, behind him, but bringing to Sag Harbor, Long Island, the reputation of a prize-fighter. Very soon Sullivan removed to New York, where he kept, on Division Street, the "Sawdust House," and extended his fighting fame. He got the name of "Yankee" from the fact that he went into the ring, at one of his fights, with the American flag wrapped about his loins. In 1849, at Rock Island, Maryland, he was whipped by Tom Hyer in seventeen minutes, the stakes being ten thousand dollars. In 1853, at Boston Corners, he fought with John Morrissey. In 1850 he came to California, but tarried only a short time. In 1854 he came again to the State, and plunged into the career of vice for which his previous life had educated him.

From the hour that he was taken prisoner, mortal fear seemed to possess him. He expressed deep penitence, and promised, if his life were spared, to reform. He was told that he need not fear being hanged, for the committee would not execute any man for crimes that were not capital in the eyes of the law. He begged, that if they banished him, he might be sent away separate from his companions, who he said would kill him for what he had divulged. He wrote a long confession, chiefly regarding his election frauds, which implicated many parties.

Early on the morning after the eighth night of his confinement, he suddenly shouted for a glass of water, and, when it was brought him, he told the guard his dream. He had stood under the gallows, the fatal rope was around his neck, the drop was falling, when he woke strangling, calling for water, and in a cold sweat. The guard told him that he was not to suffer the extreme penalty, that he would only be banished. He knew it, he said, but the crimes of his life haunted him, and he deserved to die. The guard took breakfast to him a few hours later, but Sullivan was dead. With a dull case-knife he had sawn a terrible gash in his arm, and thus severed an artery, from which he bled to death.

The day before this new horror was added to the history of the times, Judge Terry, of the Supreme Court of the State, issued a writ of *habeas corpus* for the person of Billy Mulligan. But the sheriff who attempted to serve it could not give the pass-word to enter the building, and the Executive Committee paid no attention to the writ. The rumor prevailed that Governor Johnson was about to issue a proclamation, and that he had applied to General Wool, commandant of the Pacific Department, for arms, and to the commander of the United States ship-of-war *John Adams*, then in the harbor. To prevent a surprise, on Saturday morning— Yankee Sullivan then lying dead in his cell— the streets were cleared for two blocks each way from the head-quarters, six brass pieces were mounted, swivels loaded with grape were placed on the roof, two cannon guarded by one hundred French musketeers, were pointed up Sacramento Street, and two, guarded by a hundred riflemen, pointed down Davis Street, and towards the steamboat landing. The whole committee was under arms, and the triangle was ready to summon other aid if necessary. There proved to be no need for this preparation, however, unless the very extent of it averted the danger. The Governor was unfortunate in his

solicitations with General Wool, and the *John* CHAP.
Adams, willing as that vessel's commander XXX.
probably was, did not interfere.

1856.

On the first Sunday in June the triangle June 1.
sounded the alarm. Charles P. Duane, a New
Yorker until 1849, but from 1852 for a couple of
years chief engineer of the San Francisco Fire
Department, was arrested. He made considerable resistance, but the clangor of the triangle
brought out the Vigilants, armed in such numbers that he surrendered and went to jail. Next
day, "Wooley Kearney" was arrested, in whose
house was found a ballot-box, innocent and
honest enough to look at, but curiously contrived, with sliding sides, from the grooves behind which, though locked and sealed, when
a concealed spring was pressed, hundreds of
ballots could be added to those deposited by the
voters.

The Vigilance Committee had been now,
for a fortnight, in vigorous action. It has been
shown that the newspapers almost unanimously
—the clergy with astonishing boldness—the
church almost as a church—the people, apparently for the time as one man—approved the
formation of the committee. But it was natural to look for a reaction after the committee
had begun to make arrests—after they had
hanged two men, and a third had gone a suicide from their prison into the hands of the

coroner, and his dead body had been exposed to the view of thousands of curious people.

But if a reaction was coming, it was time for it to show some tokens to that effect. Two daily newspapers had, after a little hesitation, come out in opposition to the Vigilance Committee. The lawyers, as a class, were opposed. Indeed, it was not so much the law as the lawyers that the people had rebelled against. The judges, from their very positions, must frown upon the movement which dared to act as if justice were more sacred even than law. One distinguished clergyman, Dr. Scott, was known to lack sympathy with the committee, although far the greater part of his congregation belonged to it. The politicians, bound hand and foot to party, soon perceived that opposition was their cue. There must be in a city of so many inhabitants no inconsiderable numbers of conservative men, who, after winking at the execution of Casey, would return to their old love of law and order.

So the politicians and the lawyers argued, and, supposing that the time had come, the *Herald* of June 2d called for a mass meeting of the friends of law and order, at two o'clock of that day, on the plaza.

When the hour arrived, there was a small gathering inside the plaza fence, and a great concourse outside it—placards having been posted in the neighborhood inviting sympathizers with the Vigilance Committee to stay outside. Alexander Campbell called the meeting to order, and, on his nomination, John H. Wade took the chair.

As Mr. Wade began to speak, there was a great rush into the plaza and towards the platform. The force of the placards was exhausted. The "Law and Order" men said that the Vigilants were trying to create a riot and break up the meeting. The Vigilants protested that they were simply seeking good places to hear.

All the speakers were lawyers—Wade, Campbell, C. H. Brosnan, Calhoun Benham, and Colonel E. D. Baker. While Benham glorified the law, and magnified the virtue of yielding it peaceful obedience, he unwittingly exposed the butt of a revolver stuck in his belt. The crowd cried out upon this evidence of distrust in his own doctrine. Benham coolly told them that he went prepared to enforce obedience to the law.

Colonel Baker had a hard task to secure a hearing. He had defended Cora, and the crowd hissed him, groaned at him, and uttered many expressions of disrespect, reminding him and each other of the ten-thousand-dollar fee he was reported to have taken for that defence, and of his eulogy of the woman whom Cora had made his wife on the morning of his execution. But the eloquent colonel battled bravely the storm, and conquered it at last. While he was speaking, an attempt was made to raise the United States flag to the top of the liberty pole. When it had neared the top, the halyards parted, and the bunting came to the ground. The Vigilants cheered the incident as an omen, saying that the flag declined to protect their opponents. Altogether, the meeting was admitted to have failed of its object.

CHAPTER XXXI.

COLLISION OF THE VIGILANCE COMMITTEE WITH THE STATE AUTHORITIES.

Next day—it was the third of June—Governor Johnson issued from the executive chamber at Sacramento a proclamation, which declared San Francisco in a state of insurrection. It commanded all volunteer companies, and all persons subject to military duty within the county, to report immediately to Major-General William T. Sherman (since, the hero of the Georgia march), and all within the third, fourth, and fifth districts—which included the whole territory from the northern line of Mendocino to the southern border of Tulare, and from the Sierras to the ocean—to be in readiness to respond to further orders. The Vigilance Committee it ordered to disband.

Perhaps, if the Governor had been more prompt, this proclamation might have stimulated the coveted reaction. It came too late to do the opposition much good, and the Vigilants heard it scornfully or with quiet unconcern. It did not commend itself to the masses. The city had been for weeks orderly to an unusual degree. The civil courts proceeded with their business unhindered, the criminal courts found little to do, and time hung heavy on the hands of the police. The coroner was seldom called, and inquests were few and far between. The morning papers omitted the item with the standing head—"A man found drowned." It was astonishing how few the man-traps on the wharves caught. The citizen went where he chose at night, and had no fear of robbery. The stranger saw silent men patrolling the streets after dark, and felt himself safe in any quarter. The good people of the interior agreed with those of the Bay City, that there was nothing to take up arms for; so, wherever the proclamation was read, it "was duly laughed at."

But the State military authorities opened recruiting offices in San Francisco, and invited enrolments. Nor was the appeal in vain. Some very shabby fellows, and not a few respectable men, who, in other times, would have avoided all military connections, as foreign to their taste, volunteered for the support of law and order.

Seeing these hostile preparations, the Vigilants opened their books for new enlistments. Meanwhile they kept on with their main work, notifying dangerous persons what day must be their last on the coast, and shipping some of their prisoners. They put their head-quarters in order and fortified them. To make sure against surprise, they constructed a bulwark six feet high, of a double row of gunny-bags filled with sand, from the front corners of their building to and along the centre of Sacramento Street. Chinks between the bags were left for port-holes, through which protruded occasionally the muzzles of sundry cannon—ships' guns mounted for land service. They called their secure retreat, thus fortified, "Fort Vigilance." The opposition named it "Fort Gunny-Bags." They forbade the use of spirituous liquors in their buildings. The triangle on the roof they replaced with a bell. They gathered in more small-arms, and the numbers on whom they could rely to use them grew daily. Their place was always well garrisoned, and they had twenty-five cannon at their command.

When the proclamation had been four days before the public, a committee of foremost citizens, among whom were Colonel Joseph B. Crockett, F. W. Macondray, Henry S. Foote, Balie Peyton, and John Sime, by previous arrangement, met Governor Johnson at Benicia, where he was in company with Volney E. Howard, Judge Terry, and other advisers, and respectfully petitioned His Excellency not to precipitate a collision. They represented that they were authorized to say that the Vigilance Committee would desist from the exhibition of armed forces in public, and would obey the writ of *habeas corpus,* if they could have assurances that the State authorities would proceed no farther in opposition. The Governor put his brief answer in writing. He would certainly do all that he could to avert unnecessary bloodshed, but he should execute the laws; and, if a collision occurred, the responsibility must rest on those who disregarded the authority of the State.

Before the parties separated after this fruitless meeting, General Sherman put into the hands of the Governor his resignation of the command of the second division of the State militia. In a card that he published, he reminded the public that he was no advocate of the Vigilance Committee. He had tried to enroll the militia of his district, and had promised to arm them, basing his promise upon the verbal assurance of General Wool (then commanding the Pacific Department of the United States Army) to Governor Johnson, that he would issue sufficient arms for the emergency, upon call. But when the requisition was made, General Wool had changed his mind, and refused the arms. He (General Sherman) had counselled moderation and forbearance; as this counsel did not seem to coincide with the Gov-

GENERAL SHERMAN RESIGNS. 459

ernor's views, he thought it best to resign his commission. The Governor accepted the resignation, and appointed Volney E. Howard Major-General in Sherman's stead.

CHAP. XXXI 1856.

General Wool took ample notice of this slur that Sherman cast on his firmness or veracity, afterward, when it was repeated from another quarter. For the present he simply ordered the observance, on the part of the army officers, of the strictest neutrality.

About this time news came from Washington that Philip Herbert, one of the California members of Congress, had killed a waiter at Willard's Hotel, because the waiter had answered impudently his imperious orders after a debauch. Then, on the same day that a fatal affray was telegraphed as occurring at Coloma, it was announced that a gambler, who had formerly drawn pay for work not done as a copying clerk at the San Francisco Hall of Records, had shot an officer of the law at Sacramento.

By the Herbert affair the people felt that they were disgraced throughout all Christendom. The other acts of violence would not have caused the slightest sensation at another time, but now they fell like sparks on tinder, kindling a determination all through the State to see the end at once of a condition in society wherein the average standard of morality was lower than that of the majority. They burned to let the world see, by the clearest proofs at home, that though their representative had proved a murderer, he did not fairly represent California society. They had meetings in many towns, in which they denounced the Governor's proclamation, and in some cases passed resolutions assuring the Vigilants that when they took up arms, it should be to defend reform and punish villains. Many military companies disbanded to prevent any awkward contingencies, in which they followed an example that had been set in San Francisco, where some on so doing surrendered their arms to the State, and others took theirs to the Vigilance Committee, as the real representatives of the people.

On the 9th of June the Vigilance Committee issued an address to the public, in which they rehearsed the circumstances that led to their organization, and put forth the philosophy on which they justified it:—

Self-government was the people's inalienable right. From the people emanated the right of their own representatives to enact laws, and of their honestly elected officers to execute them. When the enacted laws failed of execution, it was the people's right to resume the power that they had delegated, or which had been usurped. In this case, three-fourths of all the people of the State sympathized with and endorsed their efforts at reform. It did not follow, because they had not seen fit to resume *all* the powers confided to executive or legal officers, that they were not at liberty to withdraw the authority of unlawful servants who used authority to thwart justice. The committee had been intrusted by the people with the task of gathering evidence, and, after trial, of expelling ruffians and assassins who had outraged peace and good order, violated the ballot-box, and overruled law. They would spare no pains to avoid civil war, but their work they must do; the reform in hand they had pledged their lives, their fortunes, and their sacred honor to accomplish. When it was finished they would resign their power into the hands of the people.

In 1849 a Vigilance Committee had been organized to put down "The Hounds." In 1851, when the "Sydney Coves" became intolerable, a Vigilance Committee suddenly came to the rescue. A scrutiny of the names on its rolls showed that it was the still extant organization of 1849. In 1853 the dispersed Sydney thieves reappeared in town, and gave due notice of their arrival by a repetition of their old familiar acts of violence. One morning, a notice was published in a newspaper, requesting the Executive Committee of the Vigilants of 1851 to meet. That was enough. It does not appear whether the meeting called for was ever held, but the Sydneys took the hint and slipped out of sight. Upon the death of James King, the aroused people found the hull of the old organization, which had never been formally broken up, and built it up to the formidable Vigilance Committee of 1856.

Those who joined it signed a constitution, which explained its object in a general way, and agreed to be governed in matters of detail by a set of by-laws, which were never published. They denominated themselves "The Committee of Vigilance," an association for the protection of the ballot-box, the lives, liberty, and property of the citizens and residents of San Francisco. "We do bind ourselves," said they, "each unto the other by a solemn oath, to do and perform every just and lawful act for the maintenance of law and order, and to sustain the laws when faithfully and properly administered. But we are determined that no thief, burglar, incendiary, assassin, ballot-box stuffer, or other disturber of the peace, shall escape punishment, either by quibbles of the law, the carelessness or corruption of the police, or a laxity of those who pretend to administer justice." They agreed to keep open, night and day, rooms for their deliberations, with always one in attendance to receive from members reports of acts of violence, and, if an emergency demanded it, to summon the committee for

THE VIGILANCE ORGANIZATION. 463

such action as a majority when assembled should determine on. It was the duty of the Executive Committee chosen by the General Committee to decide upon the measures necessary to carry out the objects of the association, and to call into conference a Board of Delegates, consisting of three from each subdivision of the General Committee, when the subject of their determination was grave. The association was to be kept free from all considerations or discussions of sects, sections, or politics, and any orderly citizen, irrespective of nativity, party, or sect, could join it. No accused person could be punished until after fair and impartial trial and conviction. The General Committee were to be bound by the decision of the majority, on any question submitted by the Executive Committee; but, as to the punishment of criminals, the death penalty could only be enforced when two-thirds of those present approved it. Finally, they said, "believing ourselves to be executors of the will of a majority of our citizens, we do pledge our sacred honor to defend and sustain each other in carrying out the determined action of this committee, at the hazard of our lives and our fortunes."

The Executive Committee consisted at first of thirty-three members. A portion of the time they sat as a legislative body, and then again as a court. They had a prosecuting attorney, and counsel of their own number was always assigned to defend the party charged with crime. Their meetings were secret, and few of their proceedings were ever authoritatively published, or even announced to the body that appointed them.

Within the General Committee was a police organization, with a chief, and a sheriff with his deputies. The rest of the General Committee was divided into military companies—infantry, artillery, and dragoons—of about one hundred men to each company, which drilled, some at head-quarters, and some at apartments outside, provided for the purpose. A notice from the secretary to the captains was usually all that was necessary to obtain a general meeting; but for sudden emergencies, there was the triangle on the roof, or the bell that replaced it, a tap on which would summon such a swarm of men from their business as, in the older time, nothing but a general fire-alarm would have called together. The head-quarters was at once an armory, a drill-room, a court-room, a guard-house, a fort, and a secure prison.

They got most of their cannon from the shipping in the harbor; their muskets from their domiciles, from George Law's wandering stock, some with a lot of sabres from cases which the State took in charge as its contingent from the United States, and did not sufficiently guard, and some from the volunteer companies disbanded on the Governor's proclamation, who thought the people the safest guardians of their trust.

They never lacked funds. The wealthy men who went into the committee shed their money like water, while a great deal of the patrol, police, and other daily work of the organization, was rendered gratuitously. It was said, at the time, that five hundred dollars a day covered their expenses when most extended.

The committee often published brief proclamations, but they were only signed "No. 33, Secretary," and impressed with the committee's seal—an eye. It does not appear that this impersonal signature was ever forged, or that any person ever found it to his interest to utter an official paper with a bogus eye on it.

A great many citizens, who never signed the constitution of the Vigilance Committee, signified their readiness to assist, whenever it should need outside aid. On the 12th of June there was a meeting of such sympathizers, to the number of about three hundred, for conference. Judge D. O. Shattuck presided, and at a later session Balie Peyton. Ex-Recorder Baker said he had not joined the committee, because his oath as an attorney prohibited him. Ex-United States Senator Henry S. Foote announced his approval of the objects of the meet-

CHAP. XXXI.
1856.

ing, and his sympathy with the Vigilants. A committee, on which were H. M. Naglee, Lafayette Maynard, and Abel Guy, presented resolutions, which were adopted, expressing confidence in the Constitution of the United States, and of the State, respectfully requesting Governor Johnson to withdraw his proclamation, recommending the press to avoid exciting discussions and irritating appeals, protesting that the term "official corruption" should not be construed to embrace the acts of all the judicial officers of the county, a majority of whom were beyond reproach, and expressing a readiness, if disappointed in their hopes of an early peaceful termination of their difficulties, to organize and maintain the right.

This protest, limiting the scope of the term "official corruption," was timely and just. For, curiously enough, there were some excellent men on the bench even then in San Francisco. Edward Norton (who in 1861 received as high a compliment as the State often pays to a citizen, having been, while absent from the country, elected to a seat on the bench of the Supreme Court of California) was Judge of the Twelfth District Court; but partly because he was particularly averse to the trial of criminal cases, he had very seldom to deal with the notorious villains who cursed the community. On the bench of the Fourth District Court was

Judge Hager, whose integrity was not questioned. In the Superior Court, until the Consolidation Act legislated it out of existence, was Judge Shattuck, a Vigilance sympathizer. Freelon was County Judge, and Mayor Van Ness was Police Judge or Recorder.

As a fruit of these conference meetings was the great mass meeting before the Oriental Hotel, held on the 15th of June. Balie Peyton presided. Among the speakers was William Duer, who, in the course of his remarks, said that probably more than five hundred murders had been committed in California during the preceding year, yet not more than five of the perpetrators had been punished according to the forms of the law! He enumerated some cogent reasons why the ballot-box, under the guardianship of ruffians, could not be expected to cure the evils they endured. In a late election in St. Mateo County, from three precincts, where there were but three hundred voters, fifteen hundred votes had been returned. At Crystal Springs, where there were but about thirty voters, five hundred votes had been returned by the agency of the same ballot-box stuffers who controlled the San Francisco elections.

But the immense audience did not remember the meeting so much for the speeches as for their sight of the famous "patent ballot-box," which had been captured at Wooley Kearney's house, and which Colonel Peyton exhibited, as "the orator of the occasion."

Governor Johnson saw little at home to encourage him in the thankless job he had undertaken, so he appealed to the powers at Washington. By the steamer of the 20th of June, he wrote to President Pierce a statement of the awkward plight of himself and the State which he could not govern, and an appeal for aid in enforcing the local laws. To be sure that his letter should neither miscarry nor fail to be pressed upon the attention of the Administration, he also sent R. Augustus Thompson, and F. Forman, postmaster at Sacramento, to deliver it to Mr. Pierce, and furnish such details as could not be embodied in a written communication.

A month later, Secretary Marcy wrote to the Governor that the President had received it, and given it his most careful consideration, but being troubled with serious doubts of his lawful power to proceed in the manner desired, he had referred the subject to the Attorney-General, who found insuperable obstacles, which the President adopted as his own.

The Governor's communication briefly recited the events, which caused him to confess that he could not manage his own matters. Seeing things in a different light from that of San

Francisco, he reported them as they seemed to him. The Vigilance Committee, he said, was formed on the 16th of May, " secret in its character, and to the uninitiated its purposes unknown." A mob, before the committee's organization, had attempted to " rescue " Casey from the officers of the law, and summarily punish him, but the attempt was successfully resisted. Meanwhile the mayor had called out the military forces of the city, numbering some ten companies; but not more than fifty or sixty of all their numbers could be depended on. Several companies disbanded; a large number of their members joined the Vigilance Committee, carrying with them their arms and accoutrements, and the only two pieces of artillery belonging to the State. The sheriff did his utmost to obtain the aid of a *posse*, but not one in ten of those summoned would obey his call. On the 17th of May, three or four thousand men marched to the jail and demanded Casey and Cora. The sheriff, powerless, was fain to surrender them, and a few days later the committee hung their two captives from the windows of their place of meeting. They arrested other individuals, and established a system of espionage unknown to the laws or usages of a republic. The sheriff was, by armed resistance, prevented from serving a writ of *habeas corpus*, issued by a judge of the Supreme Court of the

CHAP. XXXI.
1856.

State, on one of their prisoners, and the person for whom the writ was issued was, with others, transported beyond the limits of the State, while one prisoner, rather than submit to be banished, committed suicide in his cell. The Governor said he had detailed to General Wool, in a personal interview, the condition of affairs, and shown him that he was almost destitute of arms, and entirely destitute of ammunition; and the general had "unhesitatingly promised" to furnish on his requisition what arms and ammunition he required. On the 3d of June he issued his proclamation, and a day or two after made a requisition, but then General Wool refused, alleging a lack of authority! In the mean time the Vigilance Committee continued to arm themselves with muskets, and their head-quarters with guns, varying in size from six to thirty-two pounders, numbering in all thirty pieces; they had erected fortifications; proceeded with the trial and conviction of prisoners; and held some still in custody, while others in fear had fled to remote parts of the State. In the streets, and throughout the city, they harangued the people "both against the General and State Governments," and at least one of their presses had defiantly come out against existing authority, and called upon the people to assemble and form a new government. He was powerless to arrest these unlawful proceedings, simply because he was destitute of arms and ammunition to equip a force capable of coping with them, who numbered now six or seven thousand, with sympathizers in large numbers outside. He had not muskets or rifles enough for six hundred men—of ordnance and ammunition he had none. He therefore asked that the United States officers commanding the Pacific Division be ordered to issue to the State arms and ammunition sufficient to suppress the insurrection now, and at any future time when required by the Governor.

Such, in substance, was the statement which President Pierce turned over to his Attorney-General, Caleb Cushing, for that distinguished lawyer to find good legal reasons for denying its petition. Mr. Cushing treated it precisely as if he thought it a story founded on facts. He perceived that Governor Johnson had forgotten to convene the Legislature, through whose call alone the President could be moved to action; and, moreover, that if the California Legislature had invited his interference, the statute only authorized him to call out the military of some other State, or to employ the United States forces—the law presuming that a Governor will always be competent to call out his own State militia. In the present case, there were no circumstances of superlative exigency, there was no actual shock of arms. The constitutional power of the State had not been exhausted—it had not even been exerted; and so Mr. Cushing, not presuming to say that the President had not moral authority in his discretion, concluded that he had not sufficient legal justification for acceding to Governor Johnson's request.

CHAPTER XXXII.

THE VIGILANCE COMMITTEE ASSUMES MORE DOUBTFUL POWERS.

IF the Governor had waited until the next steamer, he might have made even a stronger case to the Government, for the *Sierra Nevada* had not been twenty-four hours out of port when the Vigilance Committee assumed some new and still more startling responsibilities. They learned that the Governor, having obtained a portion of the State's quota of arms, was shipping them from up the river to the care of General Howard at San Francisco. They heard that some of these were on board the schooner *Julia*, which had already left Sacramento, and they deemed it essential to the public peace that they should never arrive at their appointed destination. So, on the evening of the 20th of June, J. L. Durkee, with a detachment of Vigilants in a craft obtained for the purpose, went up the bay as far as the islands called "The Sisters," and lay-to. In the course of the night the *Julia* came gliding down. Durkee's party boarded her, showed Vigilance

CHAP. XXXII.
1856.

authority for what they did, took out one hundred and fifty muskets and the ammunition, which were in charge of Reuben Maloney and John Phillips, let the men go, but conveyed the property to the city, and before the people were stirring, lodged it safely in the committee's arsenal.

Soon afterwards another party of Vigilants boarded a schooner in the bay which had neared the wharf, and was loaded with a cargo of bricks. The Vigilants, turning up a few courses of bricks, came down upon twelve cases of rifles and six cases of ammunition—another remittance from the Governor's treasured supply for General Howard's militia. Of course they were all transferred to the Vigilants' arsenal without delay.

June 21 When the Vigilants' Executive Committee met on Saturday (June 21st) to hear the reports from these expeditions, they concluded that they ought to have Reuben Maloney before them to testify as to the circumstances of the shipment of the arms, and ordered Sterling A. Hopkins, of their police, to produce him.

Hopkins, with two assistants, went at once to the office of Dr. H. P. Ashe, the United States Navy Agent, at the corner of Washington and Kearny streets, over Palmer, Cook & Company's banking-house. They found the man sought, and several others whom they did not seek—among them Dr. Ashe, who was a captain of one of the Governor's military companies, and David S. Terry, an Associate Justice of the Supreme Court. As these two gentlemen assured Hopkins that no arrest could be made in their presence, he returned to the committee-rooms, where, being furnished re-enforcements, he was ordered to make the arrest at all hazards.

So soon as the Vigilant police had left their presence, Judge Terry, armed with a rifle and bowie-knife, Dr. Ashe carrying a rifle, and others armed with pistols, descended to the street, as an escort for Maloney, whom they designed to take to the Dupont Street Armory, and leave him in care of the Law and Order troops. They had not gone far up Jackson Street, when Hopkins's party overtook them. Terry's company turned and faced them as they approached, bringing their arms into a threatening position and warning them to keep back. Hopkins sprang upon Terry, and Officer Bovee upon Dr. Ashe. The doctor surrendered, but Terry struggled manfully. A pistol was fired accidentally in the crowd that gathered, and the great confusion made the exact process of events a difficult thing to describe. Terry surrendered his rifle at last, but, as he did it, he caught out his bowie-knife and plunged its blade into Hopkins's neck, severing the carotid artery, and mak-

CHAP. XXXII.
1856.
June 21.

ing a wound which for many days thereafter threatened to prove fatal. In the excitement of the moment it was not generally known that Hopkins was wounded, nor until after Terry and his friends, including Maloney, had escaped to the armory.

Meanwhile the Vigilance bell sounded, and men from all corners of the city were gathering to head-quarters. Draymen stopped in the street, freed from their carts their horses, mounted, and went clattering to the rendezvous. Storekeepers locked up hastily and ran. Clerks leaped over their counters; carpenters left the shaving in the plane; blacksmiths dropped the hammer by the red-hot iron on the anvil; schoolmasters dismissed their pupils. It seemed as if the whole male population, on foot and on horseback, was hurrying to Sacramento Street. Occasionally one would be seen stemming the tide, running against the current to the armory. These were the Law and Order men, availing themselves of the Vigilant alarm to gather at their head-quarters. In three quarters of an hour after the alarm was sounded, every armory in the city, and every house where it was suspected that the Law and Order people had concealed any store of arms, was surrounded by armed Vigilants.

The iron doors and shutters of the Blues' armory on Dupont Street were closed as the main body of the Vigilant troops drew up about it, and for a time it was supposed that resistance would be made. But soon Dr. Ashe appeared at a window with a message from the beleaguered, asking a conference as to the terms of capitulation. The Vigilants demanded, first of all, the surrender of Judge Terry and Reuben Maloney. Very soon after, these worthies were produced, and, together with Dr. Ashe, were conveyed to Fort Vigilance. The armory, with its three hundred muskets, was soon turned over to the besiegers, who, with their prize, marched off to the next armory, planted a cannon before the door, drew up in line, and demanded a surrender. Colonel West commanded at the California Exchange Armory. When the order to surrender came, he ran his eye along his little force of seventy-five men, then glanced at the surging multitude outside and at the cannon, thought how useless it would be to sprinkle the streets with blood, and ordered his men to stack their arms. It was the same story at all the rest. By six o'clock the whole job was completed; there was not one of the two thousand muskets, and scarcely a pound of powder, which the Governor or his Law and Order men controlled in the morning, that was not now in Vigilant hands, and all the men found in the armories had been marched off, two and two, to

CHAP. XXXII.

1856.
June 21.

Fort Vigilance. Next morning all the State's soldiery were discharged.

It was a heavy day's work, that 21st of June. Three days before, the committee thought itself almost ready to lay down its power. Now it found itself possessed of arms enough, in an attitude of defiance of the State executive, in danger of a collision with the Federal authorities if it should turn out that the arms taken from the *Julia* and the *Mariposa* were not State but United States property, and with a Supreme Court judge on its hands as a prisoner whose victim was expected to die.

If Hopkins should die, it must go hard with Terry, for in those days murder by a judge was held to be as heinous a crime as murder committed by an untitled ruffian. It would be very awkward for the committee to hang a judge. If they should do it, it would be like suspending the whole Supreme Court. Judge Heydenfeldt was at the East on a visit. Chief-Justice Murray was still in the State, but he was under the ban. He had more than once had his personal encounter in the streets of Sacramento, and there was, on the part of the newspapers, a pretty vigorous demand for his removal.

While the ugly gash in Hopkins's neck refused to be healed, the shadow of the gallows must have darkened Terry's cell; something made him moody and tame. When it healed and the wounded man was clearly doing well, Terry recovered his defiant air, and bore himself like a high judicial officer, though in durance.

He had very busy friends at work planning his release. Major-General Volney E. Howard hurried up to Sacramento, and, to an assembly in front of the Orleans Hotel, told the story of his friend's capture; but his audience turned his speech into ridicule, and testified their sympathy with the committee.

The general then presented to the Governor an "official report" of all these late proceedings, in which the story was told with some variations from what was accepted popularly as the true version. He said Terry inflicted the wound on Hopkins while the later was trying to draw a pistol, and expressed his opinion that if Hopkins died it would be a clear case of justifiable homicide. Being authorized by Ashe, from the second-story window of the Blues' Armory, to negotiate for the judge, he promised the Vigilance Committee that Terry should deliver himself up to the civil authorities, if they would raise the siege. This they refused. He detailed the seizure of the State's arms in the city and on the bay. He said that George Law's roving muskets had arrived at the port, and had been seized or purchased by the Vigilants. He

CHAP. believed that the committee aimed at nothing
XXXII. less than the overthrow of the State Govern-
1856. ment and secession from the Federal Union! Though the French Consul had ordered all French citizens to withdraw from their treasonable connections, several hundred of them still remained in the Vigilance organization—and he blackened their character without scruple. He admitted that crime very often went unpunished in San Francisco; it was, however, not because judges were corrupt, but because the men who constituted the Vigilance Committee had so persistently shirked jury duty—in which statement the general told at least a portion of the truth.

Terry found another valuable friend in an unexpected quarter. Judge D. O. Shattuck, whose sympathies with the reformers had been clearly displayed, wrote a card to the public, in which he took the ground that, after the proclamation of the Governor, and the organization of the State forces in opposition to the people, they were in a state of war. When Terry stabbed Hopkins, he was in company with a legal armed force (that is, Dr. Ashe, captain of a militia company) resisting the officers of a belligerent. Hence he was entitled to be treated as a prisoner of war, and hanging him would be in contravention of the usages of civilized belligerents. The argument commanded no respect, but its author did, and still Judge Terry lay in the Sacramento Street prison, and was refused, after a few days, even the presence of his wife.

There was a deal of clamoring for Terry to resign his judgeship. While his prospects were most dubious, a letter from his wife to the people was published. In it that lady expressed her confidence that the judge would resign if the wish of the people to such effect could be clearly indicated.

After this, and while Hopkins was doing very well, three commissioners came down from Sacramento to negotiate for an adjustment of difficulties. They were Colonel Zabriskie, General James Allen, and Dr. C. B. Zabriskie. They met the Executive Committee of the Vigilants, stated their authority and errand, and received permission to pass a sealed letter to Judge Terry. In that letter they referred to Mrs. Terry's intimation, and asked what he would consider a satisfactory expression of the will of the people, and invited him to suggest some means of ascertaining it.

The judge replied that he would like to consult with his friends, but, he wrote, "If I leave this building alive, I leave it as Justice of the Supreme Court of this State, and no power on earth can make me change this resolution." Hopeless as this made the case, the commissioners obtained permission for A. P. Crittenden to visit the judge in his cell, and through him came a proposition for discovering the wish of the people. Let Terry be tried by an impartial jury, and, if found guilty of any offence, he would resign.

That ended negotiations. The committee would give him all the trial he would get.

The commission tried to keep its mission secret, but it leaked into the newspapers. Then it was whispered that the Governor never authorized the negotiation; then it was openly said that he repudiated it.

This brought a full statement, from Colonel Zabriskie, of the facts, though it was an ungracious task, as the Governor's wife was the colonel's daughter. The colonel said he had indeed no written authority, but none the less had attempted the negotiation at Governor Johnson's request, made before witnesses; just as, a while before, Judge Monson and Charles T. Botts had been intrusted with a similar undertaking. The terms of peace which he had been authorized to propose were these: The Vigilance Committee to deliver Terry over to the legal authorities, to restore the State arms to the Governor's possession, and to disband. The Governor to recommend to the Legislature the passage of a General Amnesty Act, to advise the authorities in San Francisco not to prosecute for acts done by or at the instance of the committee; to use his influence, if prosecutions were commenced, to have them quashed, and, if convictions were found, to grant unconditional pardon. This statement was indorsed by Colonel Zabriskie's colleague, and the names of witnesses to the executive's authorization were given. Still, when the negotiations fell through, the Governor repudiated the commissioners, and the father-in-law repudiated the Governor.

Terry found friends in still higher quarters. The news of his incarceration went to Texas, the State whence he emigrated to California. The Texas Legislature, being in session, promptly prepared a memorial to Congress, praying, if the Federal Government or Congress could consistently, that it would interfere in his behalf. This memorial Sam Houston presented to the Senate on the 29th of August, and the judge became the topic of the morning hour. Mr. Houston simply called attention to the evidence of the intense interest that the case excited in Texas, which was proven by the memorial. He remarked that while in Texas, Judge Terry had borne a high character as an honorable man, and was an ornament to the community. Mr. Brown stated that a more honorable man than Judge Terry did not breathe the air of heaven. He had known him from infancy, and his paents before him, and all his connections. There was not a blemish on his character.

But John Bell, of Tennessee, saw the matter in a different light. He had in his pocket a letter from a gentleman in whom he put great confidence, who bore testimony to Terry's high character, but who alleged that it was his rash impulsiveness that got him into this trouble; and that if it had not been for this unfortunate occurrence, the Vigilance Committee would have been dissolved before that time. The writer of the letter was not a member of the committee, but was deeply concerned for Terry's safety. He stated in his letter that there was no party interest involved in the formation of the committee, and no disloyal sentiment about it. An attempt was afterwards made to give it a party complexion, but it was without foundation or success.

Mr. Weller, of California, entirely disagreed with Mr. Bell. He believed that the committee, after executing two or three men, and causing the deportation of ten or fifteen more, would not stop there. If they had five thousand men under arms, he was satisfied they would preserve their organization until the next Presidential term. Judge Terry was an honorable, high-minded, prudent man, who felt bound to use the whole of his moral influence in favor of sustaining the laws. He would not undertake to say whether all the members of the Vigilance Committee were loyal to the Federal Government or not, but there were men in California who were not loyal, and who had openly advocated secession. From the first Wednesday in September of that year, until November, there was no Legislature that could be convened in California, and during that interregnum, he thought, the President, who had scruples about lending the Governor aid while the Legislature could be convened, had full legal authority to furnish arms and ammunition to help put down the revolution.

The memorial was referred to the Judiciary Committee, and never reported upon.

The 4th of July came and went, without any special celebration in the city. General Howard's charge of secession tendencies, which, as we have seen, Mr. Weller echoed a month or two later in the Senate, were not deemed of sufficient importance to require a formal exhibition of patriotism to disprove them.

Edward McGowan, who was under indictment as an accessory to the murder of James King, was, about this time, earning renown for his ubiquity. One day he was reported in Carson Valley, begrimed with the dust of the alkaline plains and the sweat of his rapid escape. The next he was said to be in Philadelphia. The next he was announced in Lower

California. Then he was seen near Hangtown Creek. Then he was at Santa Barbara. This last report came up fully verified. He arrived there on horseback, found that he was recognized, and took to the tule marsh. Somebody fired the tules, but they were green and would not burn. The Vigilance Committee, hearing this, dispatched a schooner with ten of its policemen to Santa Barbara to capture the fugitive. When they arrived McGowan had disappeared, and no one knew where he had gone.

The question was forced on the committee, what they would do if their banished should return to the city. Charles Duane, the exiled ex-chief of the Fire Department, left the *Golden Age* at Acapulco, on her downward trip. When the *John L. Stephens* touched at Acapulco on the upward trip, Duane got on board and stowed himself away until the *Stephens* was out of the harbor. Captain Pierson hailed the *Sonora*, bound to Panama, put his stow-away on board her, and so saved the San Franciscans an awkward job.

One of those who had been banished to the Sandwich Islands, soon after reappeared in San Francisco. The committee on investigation discovered, and published the fact, that owing to the exile's nervousness, the reading of his sentence in his hearing was omitted when he went abroad. This omission saved him from the death penalty.

It was the boast of the Vigilance Committee, that, since they had taken control, deeds of violence had become very uncommon. The streets at any hour of the night were safe. The man-traps in the wharves caught an astonishingly small number of victims. Whereas, before, it was rare to open a morning paper that did not have an item, "Found drowned"—and quite accidentally, of course; now the coroner seldom held an inquest.

But suddenly, on the 24th of July, a murder was committed in broad daylight. Joseph Hetherington, an Englishman by birth, who had lived at the South several years, and came to California from St. Louis—a gambler, an acquaintance (though not by his own volition) of the Vigilance Committee of 1851, and who, in 1853, fatally shot his man in a land dispute—this Hetherington had a business difficulty with Dr. Andrew Randall, a native of Ohio, who came first to California in 1859, bringing with him a commission as postmaster for Monterey. Randall was afterwards a member of Assembly; then a dealer in real estate; and he had acquired a good deal of wealth, especially in land. A judgment against him for a large amount had been bought by Hetherington, and Randall refused, or at least failed, promptly to pay it. So many hard words had passed between them, that they both went armed, expecting an encounter.

On the afternoon of the 24th, they met in the St Nicholas Hotel, on Sansome Street. Hetherington caught Randall by the beard, and uttered some insulting remarks. Randall felt for his pistol, and Hetherington fired. Several shots passed between them; Hetherington's third took effect, and Randall received a wound of which he died two days afterwards.

A city policeman arrested the murderer, but the Vigilance police relieved him of his charge, and Hetherington went to the Sacramento Street prison. His trial resulted in a conviction, and the Vigilance troops were ordered to be in their armories at two o'clock on the morning of the 29th. By three o'clock the troops, to the number of three thousand, took possession of the streets in the vicinity of the gallows, which was erected on Davis Street, between Sacramento and Commercial. An immense crowd flocked to see the execution.

At the signal from the bell, Hetherington was brought out, and with him Philander Brace, who had been tried and convicted of the murder of Captain Joseph B. West, near the Mission. Brace was a native of New York State, only twenty-one years of age, and not wanting in early education. He committed the murder for which he was now to suffer some two years before, and had passed unharmed through the farce of a trial by the court. After that, he spent a month in the county jail, in punishment for a petty larceny— was there arrested by the Vigilance Committee, tried for the murder, convicted, and condemned to death.

Preceding the two doomed and pinioned men, as they rode towards the gallows, walked twenty-nine members of the Executive Committee. On the scaffold, Hetherington bore himself decorously; but Brace, who in prison had evinced penitence, showed great impatience for the end. Hetherington addressed the crowd. He protested that he shot Randall in self-defence, denied that he had done a dishonorable act, and challenged them to observe that he would die, as he had lived, a gentleman. While he spoke, Brace frequently interrupted him with the most horrid blasphemies, and urged expedition. At ten minutes of six the Vigilance bell sounded, and the drop fell. The bodies of Brace and Hetherington were surrendered to the coroner, who held an inquest. The members of the Vigilance Committee, who were called in as witnesses, generally declined to answer any questions. The jury brought in a verdict of "death by hanging, at the hands of —— (they named the executioner) and a person unknown, aided and abetted by a party of men styling themselves the Committee of Vigilance of San Francisco."

This certainly was a reign of terror to evildoers, but not to others; for though the usually gay, volatile, driving town wore an air of "sad sincerity" during the three months of strict vigilance rule, men whose record was clean, and who intended right, felt a rare sense of freedom from danger. But dubious characters were in a very unhappy way. They felt unsafe in the cities, and they suffocated in the thin air of solitary places. They could not well escape out of the State except through San Francisco, and if they ventured into that port they were pretty sure to lodge the very first night in the Vigilance prison. A very bold, bad man might join the Committee of Vigilance to escape suspicion, but that required a genius for hypocrisy to prove a success.

Indeed, the Executive Committee arrested more than one of the members of the Vigilance Committee. The brothers Green were notable examples:—

Alfred A. Green had often heard old Californians, who when sober had never a word to say on the subject, babble in their cups about the stupid blunders of the Americans as to land titles; they said the Land Commission was always confirming the fraudulent titles, and rejecting genuine ones. Especially he had heard one Sanchez say, that there was no good title to land on the peninsula of San Francisco, north of the Buri Buri Ranche. General James McDougall filed a petition with the Land Commissioners in behalf of the city for the pueblo lands. Green was among those whom McDougall employed to assist him, and he had already reached the conclusion from what he had heard the tipsy babbler say, that there were in existence papers which would prove the clear title of the city, as the pueblo's successor, to all the common lands which claimants under a variety of fraudulent claims were appropriating. Green mentioned his surmises to McDougall, who encouraged him to proceed, then slipping a couple of bottles of liquor into his buggy, drove off to see Sanchez.

The old Californian was pleased to see his visitor, and especially his bottles. They drank together and grew confidential. They talked of the changes that had come over the times, of the old and the new, and of titles. At last, Green putting on an air of indignation, charged Sanchez with slandering his countrymen, and saying that they held possession of their land under forged papers. That aroused the Spanish pride of Sanchez, who proceeded to make good his charge, and to prove that it was no slander,

CHAP. XXXII.
1856.

but the honest truth. He said that when the Americans conquered the country, the old Californians believed the English would soon come and restore the Mexican Government. In this expectation, a few of them agreed to gather up the public titles, not to burn, but carefully to conceal them. They did so, and the precious papers were safe now under the floor of Tiburcio Vasquez's bedroom. Just as so much had been said, Sanchez's wife came in and begged Green not to pay the slightest attention to what he had heard, as if it were simply absurd. Green eased the lady's mind with a jest, and soon after returned home.

He reported proceedings to General McDougall, and was advised to get the papers by any stratagem. No court was at that hour in session; if he waited till morning, Sanchez would probably take measures to avert the mischief he had been beguiled into, and McDougall would be off in a few days to Washington, to take his seat in Congress. Time was precious.

Green went directly to a friend and said, "Nat., take your pen and write," and Nat. Hicks wrote at his dictation an order to Tiburcio Vasquez, to deliver to A. A. Green certain papers mentioned, signed it "By order of the Court," sealed it with a bit of red sealing-wax, and stamped the seal with the face of a coin. Then, with his accomplice and one of his own brothers, Green rode over to Vasquez's place, handed him the order, and in a stern voice demanded why the documents had been concealed so long. The old gentleman listened to the "order of the Court," looked at the seal, turned pale, produced at once the papers, and asked for a receipt. Green wrote a receipt, and signed it with his own name, though it looked more like a "Crane" than a "Green."

This is the version of the story that Green gave four years later in court. Vasquez, under oath, said he was administrator, and held the papers in charge as such; he kept them on a bench, not under the floor; they were not concealed. An American once before had them for two months, took copies of them, and returned them according to agreement. He could not read, but when Green showed and read to him a letter from the Government, he delivered the titles and took a receipt for them.

So Green had got the papers, but he very soon began to think he had won an elephant. He could not get rid of them again—at least not with any such profit as he had hoped. General McDougall's hasty departure for Washington forbade negotiations. He called on Mayor Brenham, and the mayor thought he might decently ask fifty thousand dollars for them. The mayor appointed a commission to see the papers. Green said that on the commission was one gentleman who, reading Spanish, saw their value, but, being interested in a fraudulent title, assured the rest of the commission that they were worthless. Distinguished counsel advised the mayor that there were valuable papers in the budget, but did not advise their purchase, and the city did not buy. When C. K. Garrison was elected mayor, Green called on him about this business. Over a bottle of wine, Garrison told him that he had an interest in the Potrero; after he got rid of that, and some other conflicting interests, he would join him to prosecute the city's title to the pueblo. He called on Colonel Crockett, but the colonel was retained for the Fund Commissioners to fix the Vallejo line. Green could not get the confidence of the press, and the lawyers were against him. He lectured at Musical Hall, and the people were stirred with his story; but when they asked the lawyers about it, they were told that it was all nonsense. So his suit nowhere prospered, and the papers lay in a box under Green's bed, more jealously watched than while Vasquez kept them.

Now among the multitude who rushed to sign the Vigilance roll, soon after James King's death, were this same Alfred A. Green, and John L. Green, his brother; indeed, some said that all the brothers were members of the committee, though probably none of them signed the constitution, which was not prepared for signatures until the committee had been about a month in operation. The question of their membership, however, was not debated when the Executive Committee determined, in view of the grave interests that might be involved, to possess these papers for the city's sake. As Green had obtained them by stratagem, it would not be surprising if he should attempt to drive a very hard bargain before surrendering them, if warned of their intentions. So, suddenly the two Greens, Alfred A. and John L., were arrested, confronted with Vasquez, and the papers demanded.

At first, Alfred asked fifty thousand dollars for his treasure. Afterwards, when he saw how matters were managed by his captors, he agreed to take twenty-five thousand. On that he was sent under escort to his house, but, when he arrived there, and learned how his family had suffered in his absence, he told his guards they should have his papers at no price. So he was taken back to his cell again, and there he lay a week longer. Then they gave him a memorandum "exculpating all his family," and tendered him twelve thousand five-hundred dollars for his papers, which he accepted, his brother being dispatched for the documents, and executing his errand faithfully. The committee paid the price, the Greens were free, and at a later date the papers, whatever they were worth, were turned over to the city.

All this while Judge Terry was a prisoner in Fort Vigilance. There was some talk of getting the United States Circuit Court judge to issue a writ of *habeas corpus* for him, which would have been a very good move if Judge McAllister could have been brought to issue it. Since Terry himself had vainly issued such a writ for Reuben Maloney's body, the committee had professed more respect for *habeas corpus*. State officers armed with it had been politely admitted to the building, and invited to rummage all cells and corners, though it happened that they could never find the men they sought. Maloney's testimony in court, years afterwards, threw a little light on this mystery. He said that once he was taken out of the main building, handcuffed, and secreted in another house near by; and he was told, at a later date, that it was because an officer was searching for him.

Then, by this time, the committee had come to be very chary of a collision with the Federal Government. They had not, indeed, scrupled to arrest Dr. Ashe, the United States Navy Agent, and they had possessed themselves of arms which had just gone out of Federal into State hands. But in that case, when the

United States Marshal wanted Durkee, he found him, and Durkee was a Federal prisoner until he was admitted to bail. If the Circuit judge had interposed, he would have made a very awkward complication of affairs. But he declined to interfere, and about that time news came from the East that President Pierce did not see his way clear to meddle with such local matters.

CHAP. XXXII.
1856.

Meanwhile Hopkins was pronounced out of danger, and that fact divested Terry's case of its most alarming features. Finally, his trial, which had occupied five weeks, and on which some hundred and fifty witnesses had been examined, came to an end. With the adoption of a resolution that he was unworthy the confidence of the people, and ought to resign his judgeship, his case was dismissed, and at two and a half o'clock on the morning of the 7th of August, he was set at liberty.

Aug. 7

The news was received almost angrily by the masses of the Vigilants. Seeing how strong the tide of sentiment ran against them, the Executive Committee called the Board of Delegates together, and talked over the reasons of the decision. There were but two ways of dealing with the committee's convicts—they were doomed either to banishment or death. Terry was not guilty of murder, for the man he had stabbed was alive yet, and quite recovered. He could not be banished without making a living martyr of him, and, with the influence he could rally, there could be no guarantee that he would not return though banished. After a three hours' session the delegates separated, and the Vigilants admitted the policy, if not the impartial justice, of the decision.

Free again, after nearly seven weeks of confinement, Terry took the advice of the Executive Committee, and sought refuge on board the United States vessel *John Adams*, which was still in the harbor. There he met sympathizing, admiring friends. When he was transferred to the steamer bound to Sacramento, a gun was fired from the *John Adams*, and cheers in his honor rang out from the men in the rigging. Arriving at Sacramento, a torchlight precession greeted and escorted him to the Orleans Hotel, where there were congratulatory speeches by Tod Robinson, Colonel E. D. Baker, Volney E. Howard, Vincent E. Geiger, Horace Smith, and others, and feasting until morning. A few weeks later he was with Judge Murray "running the Supreme Court," which, because Terry had been in seclusion, and Heydenfelt was in Europe, in lack of a quorum, had stood idle during these stirring times.

CHAPTER XXXIII.

THE VIGILANCE COMMITTEE DISBANDS.

AND now (August 12th) the cells of Fort Vigilance were empty. The Vigilants had evinced a moderation that was marvellous, joined with a promptness in execution that held the guilty in awe. They were disposed to restore the power they had used to the hands of those who gave it them. But dare they do it? Dare they let go the tiger that they held by the ears? Would not the banished swarm back and fill the courts with complaints against them? Of course their exiles who stayed away would lie in wait for the members as they arrived at the Atlantic ports, and annoy them in every conceivable way. Billy Mulligan had already in New York exercised his muscle, punishing some whom he came across. Would Judge Terry, on the Supreme Court bench, with Judge Murray ever ready to concur, let them live in peace? Would not the State employ its authority to punish them for past contempt? Would it be safe to disband before the Legislature should meet and pass a general Amnesty

CHAP. XXXIII.

1856.
Aug. 12

CHAP. XXXIII. 1856.

Act? What should they do with their arms? These were the sharp rocks long foreseen by the Vigilants, now earnestly desirous of bringing their ship to port and beaching her. In self-protection the committee must act shrewdly in this grave, final act of their career.

Their opponents had always prophesied that they would merge into a political concern. Perhaps it was the rapidly approaching Presidential election that hastened them to their conclusions.

The two National Conventions had met and nominated. The Democrats had put forward James Buchanan, of Pennsylvania; the Republicans had chosen as their standard-bearer John C. Fremont, of California. The news had reached the reputed State of the latter while Terry was in confinement, but had scarcely produced a ripple of sensation. The "honest miners" in the foot-hills were eager as ever to hear the news "from below," but it was vigilance news, not political, for which they were hungry. The Republicans had as yet no organization in the State, and leading Democrats were setting their faces against the Vigilants. The Young Men's Democratic Club refused to admit Vigilants to membership, and Superintendent Lott, of the Branch Mint, gave the employés in that establishment the alternative of going out of the Vigilance Committee, if they were in it, or, out of the mint. Clearly, it was time for the Vigilance Committee to disband, or be crowded into a false position; yet, before dissolving, it was natural to set in operation some method for preserving from waste the advantages that had been gained, and for insuring the continuance of the reforms they had begun.

There had been made several popular movements to induce the city officers, from mayor to constables, to resign. The Vigilance Committee had not openly given these movements any aid, the nearest approach to it being their arrest of some persons who were disturbing a public open-air meeting, called to forward the fruitless effort. The office-holders clung to their posts, and would not think of resigning. Happily, however, an act of the Legislature consolidating the city and county into one municipality had gone into effect, and there was to be an entirely new force of municipal officers elected in November. What the committee had to do with the party that sprang into existence in time to take good care of that election may hereafter be fairly inferred. So far as the open record goes, the Vigilance Committee, as such, had nothing to do with it, for now they proceeded to prove at once the fears of friends baseless, and the prophecies of foes false, that, whatever their original intentions, they would grow enamored of power. They gave notice of preparations to disband, and all concerned went into training for a demonstration that should carry conviction to the eye, that in their retirement they must not be trifled with, nor trampled on.

Monday, the 18th of August, was devoted to a grand final parade. Business was more generally suspended than was the custom on Sundays or ordinary holidays. From all the vicinity the people swarmed in, either to see or swell the pageantry. At noon there was a review of the Vigilance troops, when five thousand one hundred and thirty-seven men, all well armed and thoroughly equipped, answered at roll-call. After the review came the procession through the principal streets. It was like a floral procession or a triumphal march of veterans from the wars, so abounded the flowers which ladies showered on them as they passed, so gay was the display of flags, so cheerily rang out the music of the bands.

At the head of the column were three companies of artillery, with eighteen pieces of cannon. Next came the Executive Committee, on horseback, twenty-nine in number, with President Coleman and General Doane at their head; then the mounted dragoons, two hundred and ninety in number; then the medical staff of forty-nine physicians and surgeons, mounted; then one hundred and fifty members of the Executive Committee of 1851, carrying a flag, on one side of which was inscribed: "Presented to the Vigilance Committee of the City of San Francisco, by the ladies of Trinity Parish, as a testimony of their approval. Do right and fear not. August 9th, 1851;" and, on the other, "The Vigilance Committee of the City of San Francisco, instituted June 9th, 1851, for the protection of the citizens and residents of San Francisco.—*Art.* I., *Constitution.*" Next came thirty-three companies of infantry; then the vigilance police; and then citizens, mounted. On reaching the Sacramento Street head-quarters, which had already been partially dismantled, and its sand-bag barricades removed, the procession halted, the military broke up by regiments, the companies returning to their armories, which were still guarded by trusty men, and disposing of their arms.

The Executive Committee now published an address to the General Committee, which, after a brief rehearsal of the causes and motives of the organization, and a statement of its results, recommended the members to return to their avocations, and forget the animosities which may have estranged them from those good citizens who had honestly differed with them. They claimed that their errors had been on the side of clemency. Rogues there were still unpunished, but the archives of the committee contained a large amount of testimony which could hereafter be used to punish crime, and prevent political abuses, by the employment of those ordinary remedies which were not likely to remain, as they had been, inoperative. They advised the General Committee to retain its organization, but without active service. For themselves they promised to be ever vigilant, investigating and reforming abuses, urging and aiding the constituted authorities to the performance of their duties. They would reserve the discretion to reassemble the Board of Delegates or the general body, should either of the following occasions demand: The return of the banished; the necessity of protecting any member from violence or malicious prosecution, growing out of acts performed by authority of the committee; the assault of any citizen, should it be apparent that the laws were inefficient for his protection or for the pursuit of the offenders; or, in case of a violation of the purity of the ballot-box, or the sanctity of the elective franchise.

Two days later the rooms of the committee were thrown open to the inspection of the public, and many thousands of people embraced the opportunity to gratify their curiosity during the three days of the exhibition. On the first floor they found rooms devoted to the sutler's, quartermaster's, and commissary's departments, and a large hall, chiefly for the use of the artillery and cavalry companies. In the centre of the hall were several brass field-pieces. There were racks of arms along the walls, which were relieved by the bulletin-boards and framed muster-rolls of the various companies, paintings, portraits of notables, among which figured the head of General Wool, flags presented by ladies, floral wreaths, and emblematic devices wrought in evergreens. The air was fragrant with the bouquets and vases of flowers that loaded the tables.

On the second floor were the drill-rooms and head-quarters of a few of the infantry companies, most of them renting armories in different parts of the city. Here many relics were pointed out; the ropes with which men had been hanged; the burglars' tools found on Brace; "the pirate Durkee's sword"—a rusty blade used in the capture of the *Julia;* Terry's rifle; the original patent ballot-box, and the muster-roll of Balie Peyton's reserve corps, which was never regularly attached to the Vigilance Committee. Among the arms displayed was the lance which a whaleman bore, in the silent procession that captured the jail on Sunday morning.

The executive chamber on this floor was visited, not without a sense of awe, in remembrance of the grave deliberations it had witnessed. On a low platform was the president's

CHAP. XXXIII.
1856.

chair, behind a table furnished with bell and gavel. In front was the secretary's desk, and then the seats and tables of members. Ante-rooms for clerks, witnesses, and sub-committees opened into this room.

The cells in which Casey, Cora, Terry, and other notables were confined, were pointed out, on the second floor. They were not such apartments as men select, as especially roomy and commodious, at first-class hotels, but for cells they were tolerable, being about seven by twelve feet in dimensions, and ventilated by auger-holes and the cracks between the shrunken boards. The visitor was told that the former occupants had all the conveniences compatible with safe keeping, their meals being served at their order, from neighboring restaurants. If there were any subterranean paths or secret passages, through which prisoners were rushed to the adjoining buildings, to evade the *habeas corpus*, they escaped the eyes of the reporters, as well as of the multitude.

There was still some last work on the hands of the Executive Committee. General Kibbe, Aug. 23. on the 23d of August, demanded the State's arms and ammunition, which were needed to put down hostile Indians with, in Siskiyou County. Whether the committee doubted if the Indian hostilities were any thing more than a *ruse*, well calculated to enlist the sympathies of the interior with the State authorities, or thought it not yet safe to part with the arms, they refused to comply with the demand.

CHAP. XXXIII.
1856.

On the 27th, "33, Secretary," issued a public notice to certain parties, among whom was a former supervisor of the county, who, having been notified to leave the State, had fled to the interior, giving them opportunity to depart by either of the next two steamers, never to return, under penalty of death.

Aug.27.

Durkee and Rand were still to be tried in the Federal Court for piracy, in seizing the State arms on the high seas—that is, in San Pablo Bay. Both had been admitted to bail, soon after the offence was committed, in the sum of twenty-five thousand dollars each; E. W. Godard, James Dowes, J. W. Brittain, and Samuel Soulé being bondsmen for Durkee, and J. H. Fish, and T. J. L. Smiley, O. Arrington, and Jules David for Rand. On granting the application for admission to bail, Judge Hoffman had remarked upon the violation of law by the Vigilance Committee, whose order for the seizure was admitted. True, the people sustained them, he said, but, none the less for that, they had trampled on the law.

As the law and order people expressed loudly their confidence that "the pirates" would be convicted and punished, the committee opened its

CHAP. XXXIII.

1856.

books again for the enrolment of members, and many accessions to their roll were made.

A grand jury, consisting in part of Sacramentans, was impanelled, which found indictments. Durkee's trial came first. All members of the Vigilance Committee were rejected from the jury, as were all members of the Young Men's Democratic Club. The testimony was brief; the judge charged that unless it was found that the prisoner had taken the arms feloniously for his own benefit, he could not be convicted. The jury were out four minutes, and returned with a verdict of *not guilty*. The District Attorney declined to prosecute Rand, and that peril was passed.

And now the Executive Committee hauled down their flag, closed entirely their rooms, and sold their furniture at auction. They kept guard for a while longer, but never had occasion to summon the Board of Delegates, or to strike the bell for another rally.

Shall the Vigilants be judged by their fruits? They took the law into their own hands and executed it. Law had been used as a machinery for screening villains from punishment. They broke up the combinations of the lawless and set law in an honored seat again. They purified the city. At first it seemed as if this had been done at the expense of the rest of the State. The dispersal of the city rogues led to an unusual number of highway robberies in the interior; but the villains soon learned how truly the whole State sympathized with the Vigilants, and that they were ready on the spur of an aggravated case to imitate the Vigilant method of quickening the steps of Justice. They made the ballot-box sacred once more. It was very certain that there would be no more farces on election-day, and that men would be elected by honest votes or left in private life. Guilds of crime and organized gangs of thieves, burglars, and murderers were thoroughly broken up. It was loosely estimated that eight hundred persons, the scum of society, had been forced to leave the country. To secure that happy result, they had arrested not a few who were set free again on their parole. They had inflicted the death-penalty upon four: Casey, Cora, Brace, and Hetherington. The list of those whom they banished from the State was officially published by the secretary "No. 33," on the 4th of October, as follows:—

June 5th, Charles P. Duane, William Mulligan, and William *alias* Wooley Kearney, shipped by the *Golden Age* to New York; William Carr and Martin Gallagher, shipped by the bark *Yankee* to the Sandwich Islands. June 20th, John Crowe, shipped by the *Sonora* to New Orleans; William Lewis, John Lawler, William Hamilton, and Terence Kelly, shipped by the *Sierra Nevada* to New York. July 5th, James Reuben Maloney, Alexander Purffle, *alias* Purple, Thomas Mulloy, Daniel Aldrich, and F. B. Cunningham, shipped by the *John L. Stephens* to New York. July 21st, James White, James Burke *alias* Activity, William McLean, and Abraham Kraft, shipped by the *Golden Age* to New York. August 5th, Edward Bulger, Michael Brannegan, and John Cooney, shipped by the *Sonora* to New York. September 5th, John Thompson, *alias* Liverpool Jack, and John Stephens, shipped by the *Golden Age* to New York.

The following were ordered to leave by the steamers of August 20th and September 5th:—

W. Bagley, James Henessy, James Cusick, and J. D. Musgrove.

Two of the banished and one of the executed were members of the Board of Supervisors.

The Vigilance Committee had not accomplished their reforms by sprinkling with rosewater; they had performed a most ungracious task. They drew a long breath and felt a grateful sense of relief when it was clearly safe to retire again to their private pursuits, and they had laid again upon all the people alike the burden of preserving the peace and maintaining order.

We have said that most of the clergy either went into the Vigilance movement heartily, or at least stood aloof from its opponents. There was one notable exception. The Rev. Dr. Scott (Presbyterian), of Calvary Church, was away when Casey was executed, and, when he returned to town, he refused to recognize the new measures as just or right. It was evident from his public prayers that he did not believe in them; still he did not say any thing to offend his congregation, nine-tenths of whom sympathized with, or were themselves active Vigilants. Not until the organization had disbanded and a letter got back to San Francisco, which he had addressed to the editor of the *Pacific*, through a Philadelphia Presbyterian paper, was it seen that the Doctor had ranged himself with the opposition, and put himself on record as against it, while the excitement was the greatest. Of course the papers pounced upon him; he was drawn into a discussion; the whole matter was argued over again, and much hard feeling was produced.

To the scandal of everybody, one Sabbath morning, an effigy, labelled with the Doctor's name, was found hanging by Calvary Church door. The law and order men said the Vigilants did it. The Vigilants denied it, asking what they could gain by hanging a bundle of rags; and intimated that their enemies did it, knowing it would be charged on them. The Doctor took the matter to heart and resigned his place. His people refused to accept the resignation, the matter blew over, and Dr. Scott was spared to enjoy the popularity that one earns who buffets a strong tide and emerges without damage.

The great political reform had not been achieved without some other social disturbances. All the passions that are aroused by a civil war had been stirred. Bosom friends, and brothers in business together, divided and avoided each other. A Vigilant met one whom he had not seen for several weeks, and extended his hand with a friendly salutation. "There's blood on it," said the old acquaintance, drawing back; "I don't know you, sir." The papers were not remarkably violent, but they were very rough in their treatment of men in public life. They did not much abuse each other, perhaps not more than in an ordinary election campaign, when party spirit runs high; but they published official records, and raked up forgotten facts, and blurted out stories which they thought they had reason to believe concerning men in public positions, without the slightest regard to the law of libel.

Allusion was made to the general sympathy of the people of the interior of the State with the Vigilants. It was manifested by the tone of the press; by the loss of subscribers that some papers suffered because they spoke sneeringly of King, and would not take back their words; by the closing of stores and the tolling of bells at Sacramento, Marysville, Stockton, and elsewhere, on the day of King's funeral; and by public meetings at San Jose, Columbia, and many other places, which adopted resolutions approving the committee's decisive action. In the mining districts the public sentiment was not at all shocked to learn that men in the Bay City were taking a short cut to justice—they were rather fond of short cuts themselves. Down the coast, too, the people were quite resigned, as a random example shall prove:— Within one week four persons were taken out of the Monterey jail and hanged. However, between an infuriated populace met to lynch a heinous transgressor, and a coolly deliberating, thoroughly organized Vigilance Committee, there was as wide a difference as between a mob and a court. Nothing similar to the San Francisco Vigilance Committee was ever organized in the interior.

Happy for all that the Presidential election was approaching. Its excitement would help distract attention from the painful events of the past three months, and give the wounds of society opportunity to heal.

On the 3d of November, the committee, having surrendered the State arms to the authorities, the Governor withdrew his proclamation of insurrection, and so the local election which followed in San Francisco had no cloud of illegality about it. Then, by swift degrees, the subject dropped out of the list of topics that men much debated. The Democratic State Convention, that met in the fall of 1856, was expected to glance by resolution at the subject, but wiser counsels prevailed, and no mention of it was made. In the American State Convention a resolution condemnatory of the Vigilants was introduced, but instantly tabled with hisses. Governor Johnson unbosomed himself to the Legislature in 1857, but most that came of it was a controversy between His Excellency and General Wool. Governor Weller indulged in a fling at the committee, when in 1855 he wrote his inaugural, but in the same connection admitted that the necessities of the times demanded something of the sort. The Legislature has generally kept their hands off, only through its relief bills for McGowan, Duane, and others, showing that its animus was hostile, though policy dictated forgiving and forgetting. Occasionally some speaker, young to the platform on the Pacific coast, has branched off upon the subject, but he seldom has found his audience demonstrative about that time. The suits for damages that have been brought by the returned exiles fill the court-rooms with thoughtful, earnest-looking men, who say little, and hear all.

SUITS BROUGHT AGAINST THE VIGILANTS. 515

The members of the committee were subjected to some annoyances at the East. Several of them were assaulted in the streets of New York by the friends of the banished. Maloney, Duane, and Mulligan brought suits for damages against William T. Coleman, and others of the committee, whom they found in New York, but the courts denied their jurisdiction, and the complainants obtained no satisfaction. In 1859, Martin Gallagher got a decree from Judge Hoffman, of the United States District Court in California, awarding to him three thousand dollars damages and costs against the master of the bark *Yankee*. The brothers Green brought suit separately for damages in the Twelfth District Court of California. The first case that came to trial was that of John L. Green, before Judge Norton, in 1860. The complainant alleged fifty thousand dollars damages by the injury to his own health from imprisonment in the committee's jail, and by the death of his wife, which, he said, was hastened by the shock it gave her. The trial occupied several days, and, while it lasted, was the sensation of the town. The jury gave a verdict for the plaintiff, awarding the damages at one hundred and fifty dollars, which left the plaintiff to pay his own costs, and made it necessary for him to pay the jurors' fees. The result was not so flattering as to encourage the brothers to urge

CHAP. XXXIII.

1857–1860.

1859.

1860.

CHAP. XXXIII.

1860.

1864.

their cases, and they have not yet been determined.

Duane, returning to the State in 1860, filed libels in the United States District Court against Captain Goodall, the master of the steam-tug *Hercules*, which conveyed him, when banished, manacled to the *Golden Age*, off the mouth of San Francisco harbor; against Captain Watkins, of the steamer *Age*, which took him to Acapulco; and against Captain Pearson, of the steamer *John L. Stephens*, who, finding him on board, a stow-away, trying to return to San Francisco from Acapulco, transferred him to the steamer *Sonora*, bound to Panama. The aggregate damages claimed were one hundred and twenty-five thousand dollars. In the case of Pearson, Judge Hoffman decreed four thousand dollars damages in 1864, and Circuit Judge Field affirmed the decision. The other cases were understood to be compromised, at rates sufficient to give the returned exile a comfortable living.

Several of the banished manifested an overweening desire to return to San Frsucisco, as if mischief done in any other place lacked its relish, and reform nowhere else were half as meritorious. Some of them were helped back by Vigilants themselves years later, and, while some became tolerably fair citizens, practising their old tricks only at *primary* elections, which

the law does not recognize, and where conse- CHAP. XXXIII.
quently stuffing and colonizing are not misdemeanors, except in the moral sense, no one of   1864.
them has so distinguished himself for either private or public virtues, as to start a suspicion of
any gross injustice in his sentence.

By common consent, old San Franciscans
still avoid discussing the revolution of 1856 in
miscellaneous company, as one on which neither
party has tempered its acerbity, unprofitable,
and a quarrel-breeder. Occasionally, some one
in his wrath calls a Vigilant "a strangler," and
the other retorts upon him as one of the "law
and murder party." It would have seemed
scarcely time yet to write the history of these
doings, but that, in the great events that have
lately convulsed our country, these local matters,
that used to hold the peaceful, law-abiding
world breathless, will be forgotten, if the record
is much longer delayed; and then, again, a large
portion of the people now in the State were not
here in 1856, and they, a sort of premature posterity, have a right to know what was going
on in the home that was preparing for them,
before their arrival.

CHAPTER XXXIV.

PRESERVING THE FRUITS OF THE REFORM.

CHAP. XXXIV.

1856.
Aug.

About a week before the Vigilance Committee disbanded, there was a mass meeting of citizens in front of the American Exchange in San Francisco, to organize a party, irrespective of all political leanings, which should rescue the city offices from the clutch of irresponsible men, and keep unsullied its rights—in short, a People's Reform Party. The names of the men who figured in it were not those of prominent Vigilants, though its opponents charge that it was the heir of the Vigilance Committee's opinions, and was inaugurated, in degree, at least, for their protection.

Ira P. Rankin was called to the chair, a previous nominee having been voted down. Mr. Rankin admitted that he was not sure whether he was in favor of the objects of the meeting, but as it was a people's gathering, he would obey their orders. A preamble and resolutions were introduced. These charged that the political parties, as organized, had bred many of their troubles. They had tried the American party, but discovered in it no higher grade of political integrity than in the old parties. Now the politicians must stand back; the people would attend to their own affairs. With the Presidential nominations they had nothing to do, with their local affairs every thing. The practical proposition of the resolutions was to appoint a committee of twenty-one, among whom were named J. B. Thomas, E. H. Washburn, Louis McLean, Frederick Billings, A. B. Forbes, and T. O. Larkin, to encourage and recommend the election of members of the Legislature, pledged to reform, and to nominate city and county officers.

If, as was averred, the meeting was packed by the Vigilants, it is very curious that it was not better managed, for at an early hour it was captured by the Republicans, and its object almost frustrated. Trenor W. Park opposed nominating until the other parties had completed their tickets. After his speech, the resolutions were put and lost. William Duer essayed to save them, but he had already committed himself so openly to the Know Nothings that his appeal lost its force. Others spoke, but it was wasting words, until E. H. Washburn took the stand, and, with an address which turned the tide of feeling, induced a reconsideration, and finally the adoption of the

CHAP. XXXIV.

1856.

policy of the resolutions. The committee of twenty-one was appointed.

In good time it submitted a reform ticket to the people for their votes, and on election-day it was carried by a large majority.

The Consolidation Act was now in force in San Francisco. It greatly reduced the powers of the city legislature, limited the tax that might be levied for each specific object, required the scrupulous separation of the funds, prohibited the use of money in one fund for objects legitimately covered by another fund, and tied the officers down to a very strict accountability. This act, devised by Horace Hawes, was adopted by a Legislature which got little credit for good intentions towards the city, but it was an admirable measure for the thriftless times. It has been said, in later days, that to this act rather than to the election of the people's tickets is due the good order and improved financial condition of the city. That this was not so is clear enough from a solitary consideration: Sacramento obtained a similar charter for its use, but failed to put good men in office, and to watch them with all diligence. So, while San Francisco from that time prospered in her finances, Sacramento dashed on in her old career until she stood on the verge of bankruptcy.

Nov. The newly-elected city and county officers

were for the most part good men; and those in whom the people afterwards concluded that they were mistaken, they watched so narrowly that abuses were infrequent, corruption went out of practice, and economy became the rule in office. When the gas-bills were complained of as unreasonably large, and the gas company denied that it could make them less, the reformers brought tallow dips into the supervisors' chamber, and transacted business by their flickering light. When the district judges asked for stoves to warm their court-rooms, the supervisors reminded them that, in the favored climate of California, stoves were a costly luxury, and fuel an unnecessary bill of expense. City improvements—the reduction of the streets over the irregular surface of the city to the official grade—had been the ruin of many who unfortunately owned real estate. The new authorities were, by the new charter and their own pledges, required to stop improving, except as property-owners petitioned for it. The city did not spread itself quite so rapidly as before, but bankruptcy was avoided by the delay. It was estimated that not less than eight hundred persons—the scum of the earth's villany—had left the city, and most of them the State, during the Vigilance Committee's rule. Relieved of this great burden, the criminal courts travelled easily in the road of justice, and rogues found that crime was the swift forerunner of punishment. It remains so to this day. The police are few in number, but active and vigilant. There have, indeed, been some mysterious murders, of which the perpetrators were never discovered; still, in no other city of its size in the Union is there a more cheerful assurance that life is safe from violence, and property from thieves and robbers. The period was not by any means supposed to be within millennial limits, yet the city rapidly became famous for its economy, its good order, and its financial responsibility.

The extent of the financial reform will be obvious from a few comparisons. The revolution occurred in 1856. The year before that, things were at the worst. The second year after it, the reform was fairly fruit-bearing. The city's bills for advertising and stationery, in 1855, were $65,231; in 1858, $2,727. Assessment expenses, in 1855, were $45,011; in 1858, $9,100. Election expenses, in 1855, were $22,920; in 1858, nothing. The fire department, in 1855, cost $263,120; in 1858 it was in better condition for $29,972. The hospital department, in 1855, cost $278,328; in 1858, the sick were better cared for at $43,880. For extra legal services, in 1855, the city was taxed $31,821; in 1858 the amount was a little over one-fourth that sum. The police and prisoners cost the city, in 1855, $236,690; in 1858, $59,943. The salaries of officers amounted, in 1858, to little more than one-fourth as much as in 1855. The annual expenditures of the city and county were as follows: In 1854, $1,831,-825; in 1855, $2,646,190; in 1856, $856,120; in 1857, $353,292; in 1858, $366,427; in 1859, 480,895; in 1860, $706,719; in 1861, $512,896.

The largest item of expenditure every year, with a solitary exception, since 1856, has been paid in satisfaction of old debts contracted during the old *régime;* and in 1863 nearly one-third of all the city taxes went to meet the interest of these debts. The city has no floating debt. Every demand against it is paid upon presentation.

Each successive year, as the municipal election draws nigh, several thousands of the people petition the nominating committees of the two preceding years to nominate a committee as its successor. This new committee pledges its members, as its predecessors did, to receive no nomination in a given number of years following. This system avoids the primary elections of the political parties, where trickery and money shape tickets for honest men to indorse at the legalized election, and experience seems to show it the best that has been devised. The nominating committee thus selected, canvasses quietly and secretly the merits of candidates, and gives the result in a full municipal ticket. Except in the case of here and there an individual, these tickets have always been elected. The people rule San Francisco, and in consequence it has abroad, as at home, the reputation of being the best-governed city in the Union.

CHAPTER XXXV.

FINANCIAL BREAKERS.

But just as the people were beginning to manage their own affairs creditably in San Francisco, the financial credit of the State received a most damaging blow. When the interest on the State bonds came due at New York, July, 1856, no funds were there to meet it. The Treasurer had punctually deposited enough with Palmer, Cook & Co. for the purpose, and that firm alleged that its agent, ex-Congressman Wright, one of the partners, had instructions to attend to the punctual payment, but he had no money when the fatal day arrived, and the State was disgraced. The same thing had happened in 1854, when Duncan, Sherman & Co. came to the rescue, and saved California's honor; but the Legislature allowed Palmer, Cook & Co. to reimburse that house months afterwards without interest. Of course no one acquainted with that story would be in haste to sacrifice himself now.

The Treasurer scraped together what he could, and as soon as he could, and, forwarding it to

New York, paid the interest, and the affair redounded more to the discredit of the bankers than of the State. But Californians were much stirred up about it, and demanded that there should be no more of bankers going between them and their creditors—taking their money on deposit, with a pledge of expressing it seasonably, and instead turning it to electioneering account. For by this time it was known that Palmer, Cook & Co. were Fremont's bankers, as well as California's, and it was suspected that they were furnishing money for the Presidential campaign, with the Mariposa mine as security.

But the bankers were not alone to blame. The Constitution prohibited the creation of a debt exceeding three hundred thousand dollars; yet the excess of State expenditures above the receipts into the treasury for the year ending with June, 1856, was more than double that amount. By New Year's Day, 1857, the State debt was over four million dollars. It had been contracted to carry on the legislative, judicial, and executive functions of the Government on an extravagant scale, for hospital, prison, and school purposes, for taking the census of 1852, for printing, and for Indian war expenses. But whatever its object, it was contracted in clear violation of the organic law. The Supreme Court decided that so much of it as was in excess of three hundred thousand dollars was unconstitutional and void, and that, though the Legislature should tax the people to pay it, that tax would be illegal, and its collection could not be enforced.

Here was a frightful vision of repudiation presented to the good people, who gloried in an exclusive metallic currency, and that they had no bill-emitting banks. Now they began to doubt if they had not been too fast in rushing into the responsibilities of a State. Except Texas, all the other Western States had been kept a while in Territorial leading-strings, and during their patient waiting had their expenses paid out of the national treasury. California had set up housekeeping without a dollar to buy furniture, pay rent, or hire service with. To run the State at the start, she issued bonds, bearing interest at three per cent. a month. When she redeemed them in 1856, the interest had far outgrown the principal. Had not the Constitution provided too much government machinery for the little governing that was wanted?—too grand an engine for a craft that had but a handful of a crew to man it? Too many officers, too high salaries, exorbitant fees, extravagant jobs; too frequent and too long legislative sessions; swarms about the treasury, clamoring that party services gave them a right to live off the State—these were sucking the life out of the commonwealth. The people suspected that they had been too ambitious; that they would better have waited a while in Territorial pupilage.

But regrets were in vain. Besides, it had never been a question of admission as a State or remaining a Territory. Congress refused California any kind of government; it was a choice between a State organization or nothing. Indeed, if they had another commonwealth to found under similar circumstances, they would do the job in the same way. They would prefer a State's dignity to a Territory's economy and thrift—genteel sovereignty rather than full-fed dependence—officers of their choice, bad as they might be, rather than those of other men's appointment. Certainly the love of the Union was strengthened by early admission into it; and whatever California may have lost in money by her haste, she gained in patriotism. As to the Union, none could doubt that it lost nothing and made much by California's early welcome to all its honors.

The Supreme Court had indicated a solitary way for the State's escape from the disgrace of repudiation. That was for the question of assuming the unconstitutional debt to be submitted to the people. The Legislature quickly passed an act of submission, and the people, by overwhelming numbers, voted to pay every dollar of the debt. But it was one thing cheerfully to assume the debt illegally contracted by careless servants, and another to pay it.

Governor Johnson zealously urged retrenchment, and the Legislature vigorously essayed reform. Year by year, hoping to abolish the scrip system, the debt had been funded at seven per cent. annual interest. Still, there was a great deal of scrip afloat, some of which, being unsupported by any satisfactory vouchers, was refused payment. A board of examiners was created, to pass upon all claims and comptroller's warrants required, where the cash could not be paid for authorized expenditures. The Governor made one more effort to induce Congress to restore the "civil fund" to the State, but it was vain. The Supreme Court of the United States had decided the action of the Federal authorities in collecting customs after the cession of California as a conquered province of Mexico, and while it was under the sway of military officers, though in a time of peace, warrantable and right; so that long-cherished resource for extinguishing the debt was abandoned. The appropriation by Congress towards meeting the Indian war debt was ample to have covered the whole claim; but Jefferson Davis, Secretary of War, refused to transfer the money called for by the appropriation, and required the production of original accounts and vouchers, many of which were lost. Under this delay the debt grew by the accumulation of interest, and the State was at some expense to obtain an additional appropriation. The effort was fruitless, and there was nothing better than to divide what had been appropriated, so far as it would go among the claimants.

Free, fearless taxation was resorted to as the only means left to reduce the debt, but expenditures, after all the legislative pruning, were enormous. It was hard to conquer the extravagant habits of early days. Governor Downey estimated the local indebtedness of the cities and counties, on the first of January, 1861, at near ten million dollars; and Governor Stanford quoted the State debt in the beginning of 1863 at over five and a half millions.

For neither the local nor the State debts was there much to show; a few court-houses and jails, a few public halls, a State-prison at San Quentin inadequate to its purpose, an insane asylum at Stockton, not half large enough for the number of its inmates, the foundations of a capitol at Sacramento, a small State library, richest in law books, a reform-school building at Marysville, with a handful of boys in its echoing halls—one wonders where the millions of borrowed money went. Salaries, fees, interest consumed a large share of it; some charitable institutions, mainly maintained by the

contributions of churches and individuals, enjoyed a meagre portion; peace with Indians
cost something almost every year, and the pets
of party and the sharpers of the lobby took
toll of all they could reach.

The resources of the State are so abundant,
the prosperity of the inhabitants so general,
that the debt does not much trouble the people
now. Its interest is met with punctuality.
The bonds of the State and of most of the cities
stand well in the market, and our general credit
is excellent at home and abroad.

But the debt rather waxes than wanes, and
there is no such wholesome impatience to be
rid of it as a proper regard to economy would
require. During the war of the rebellion, a
new source of indebtedness was necessarily
created. Bounties to soldiers, arming and
drilling the militia, all means of defence against
foreign foes or traitors at home, were welcomed
by those who most cherished thrift. Yet each
new outlay demanded sharper watch that none
be wasted, closer scrutiny that disbursing
agents make no illegal commissions.

CHAP.
XXXV.

1863.

1865.

CHAPTER XXXVI.

LAND TITLES.

It is scarcely possible to overstate the annoyances that Californians have suffered in the past from the uncertainty of land titles. Before the country came into the possession of the United States a very considerable portion of the best lands for agricultural purposes, and of the region about the bays, including the natural sites for many future cities, had been granted to individuals by the Mexican authorities. They valued their gifts very cheaply, because there were few competitors, and bounded them most loosely. The grant might convey a definite number of square leagues within a certain valley, or inside the exterior limits of a named rancho, leaving the grantee to locate his tract anywhere within those limits. As little accurate surveying was done and little attention paid to topography, grants often overlapped and encroached upon each other, and sometimes a person was given all the gores, corners, and odd pieces of some favorite tract, not appropriated by grants of earlier date. Though there had been never a fraudulent claim for a rood of ground, the lax method of Mexican conveyancing would have insured a rich harvest of litigation, for, by the treaty of Guadalupe Hidalgo, the American Government agreed not to disturb existing titles, and to respect all grants derived through the Mexican or Spanish authorities.

The gold discovery opened the gates to a flood of population which must have homes of some sort, and land to build their homes on. When the new-comers asked who owned the soil, they were distracted with the variety of answers. One authority named a distant ranchman as the proprietor. Another pointed out the man whose cattle ranged over it. Another quoted a clamorous claimant, but admitted that his title was generally supposed to be fraudulent—for, as lands came into demand, there sprang up a populous tribe of claimants, with manufactured papers sufficiently resembling the genuine in the breadth of boundaries and uncertainty of extent and location called for, and, perhaps, more careful than they to bear abundance of seals and signatures.

Most of the American settlers bought the lots they coveted of the claimant presumed to have the best title; others were satisfied to buy the cheapest, and still others put up their fences and cabins as if settling on Government land, asking no one's permission, confident that possession and a rifle would give them as good a chance as was to be bought. They were not at liberty to wait for conflicting claims to be adjudicated, for the homeless must have shelter, the markets must be supplied with vegetables and grain, and there was no movement to determine by law who owned the land, until busy cities replaced the drowsy solitude of the coast, and a vigorous American State was improving the premises that so long lay waste as a sleepy province of Mexico.

In 1851, three years after the treaty of peace was signed, Congress enacted a law for the settlement of land claims in California—it might with propriety have been entitled an act to retard their settlement. Colonel Benton insisted that patents ought to issue to all lands whose titles should be found perfect and fairly recorded at Mexico; but he was overruled, and a commission was created to sit in San Francisco, and decide the validity of claims according to the usages, laws, and customs of the Government from which the titles were derived.

Before this Board of Land Commissioners all claimants under Spanish or Mexican grants must present their evidences of title within two years of the date of the passage of the act, or the land would be deemed part of the domain of the United States. The board must decide upon the validity of the claim within thirty days after its presentation. The claimant, or the district attorney, could appeal from the board's decision to the United States District Court, and from that to the Federal Supreme Court. When a claim was finally confirmed, unless other claimants intervened, a patent for the land was to issue, and the surveyor-general was to "locate" it. From his survey the appeal was to the Department of the Interior, at Washington.

For commissioners, President Fillmore appointed Harry L. Thornton, Augustus Thompson, and Alpheus L. Felch. His Democratic successor thrust them out, and appointed others in their places.

As neither commissioners nor counsel were familiar with Mexican law and practice, tedious delays and grave blunders were unavoidable. The board, before its final adjournment, March, 1856, to which time the amended law extended its existence, had some eight hundred claims presented. More than half of them it confirmed; some, for obvious fraud, it rejected, and some for gross informalities; while some, because they called for land, afterwards granted in a large tract to the same parties, were withdrawn.

The area of land called for by the claims presented was nineteen thousand one hundred and forty-eight square miles. Many of the rejected claims were allowed, and confirmed in the district courts, which also finally rejected some very important ones that the board confirmed. The labor is by no means ended yet. Some stubborn cases are still pending in the district courts; the Supreme Court of the United States has its docket still burdened with appeals, and Congress at every session is invoked for special enactments to relieve some party who suffers by virtue of a decision that the testimony made inevitable.

Indeed, it is scarcely possible that every final decision should not work a hardship to somebody. Every genuine claim that is confirmed requires a large body of squatters and holders under adverse titles to be ousted. Seldom can a survey be approved for a claim whose genuineness is no surprise, without forfeiting some honest settler's improvements. It was a grievance loudly complained of, that an appeal from the survey made necessary a journey to Washington to watch proceedings under a subordinate of the Land Office, and many a disappointed claimant has come home, alleging that the party which accommodated the clerk with the largest loan won the decision.

Few of the original grantees have found their fortune in the grants that seemed princely to the landless. Though their claims were confirmed, they were generally fought with ruinous obstinacy. Enormous counsel fees, huge bills of cost, money hired at frightful interest, and its payment secured by mortgage upon mortgage, have compelled many an original grantee to lament the day that he asked for a grant, and when his patent has come, it was not for him, but for his lawyers. Some relief was afforded when the Supreme Court, in 1858, decided that the district courts had power to supervise the surveys, and so spare the trip to Washington. Congress has tried to relieve sufferers by opening cases once closed, but every such opening has involved another set of claimants in litigation.

President Buchanan, in 1860, sent a message to the House of Representatives, accompanied by some correspondence concerning this subject, that caused a sensation. Appropriations, amounting to $114,000, had been made by the Thirty-fourth and Thirty-fifth Congresses for legal assistance, and other expenditures, in the disposal of private land claims in California. The House of the Thirty-sixth Congress asked for a detailed statement of these expenditures, and Mr. Buchanan furnished it.

Judge Black, of Pennsylvania, was Attorney-General. His letters said it was incredible that so many grants could have been made in good faith by any Government as were claimed in California, under titles, real or fabricated, from Governors Alvarado, Micheltorena, or Pio Pico. They covered a very large portion of the best mineral and agricultural regions. There seemed to be not an island or place for a fort, a custom-house, hospital, or post-office but must be purchased on his own terms from some private claimant. But they were supported by an array of testimony that had already secured their confirmation by the Land Commissioners and the district courts, and rendered defence hopeless unless extraordinary means for investigation were resorted to. The examination of records in the city of Mexico, "led to the conclusion that even the archives of that Government had, in some way, become an instrument of sanctioning frauds against the United States." In February, 1858, Edwin M. Stanton (since United States Secretary of War) was sent to San Francisco as special counsel for the Government in pending cases, and especially charged to resist the Limantour claim. The scattered archives of the Mexican Government were hunted out of their careless concealment, whether in public offices or in the keeping of ex-officials, and deposited with the Surveyor-General. Official correspondence, seals, and suspicious grants were copied photographically, and important documents translated for the use of the court at Washington. Irresistible proof was obtained "that there had been an organized system of fabricating land titles carried on for a long time in California by Mexican officials; that forgery and perjury had been reduced to a regular occupation; that the making of false grants, with the subornation of false witnesses to prove them, had become a trade and a business." "The richest part of San Francisco was found to be covered by no less than five different grants, every one of them forged after the conquest: Sacramento, Marysville, Stockton, and Petaluma were claimed on titles no better." The value of the lands claimed under fraudulent titles was estimated at not less than one hundred and fifty million dollars! More than two-thirds of them (in value) had already been exposed and defeated.

He enumerated some of the cases disposed of in favor of the Government. Prominent in the list was Limantour's claim for two square leagues of San Francisco land, and for Alcatras, the Farallones, and Fort Point. Mr. Stanton, before the District Court, produced overwhelming proofs of its fraud. Its rejection by Judge Hoffman has already been noticed. Limantour was prosecuted for forgery and setting up a claim known to be false. He gave bail in the sum of thirty-five thousand dollars for his appearance, and left the country. To this day his sureties have not paid the forfeited bonds. Captain Sutter, under two grants, claimed thirty-five square leagues in the Sacramento Valley. One of them, made by Alvarado, in 1841, for eleven leagues, was genuine. The other, professing to be from Micheltorena, for twenty-two leagues, covering the sites of Sacramento and Marysville, and embracing portions of five counties, was shown to have been made, if by Micheltorena at all, after a successful revolution had expelled him from his capital. The Supreme Court rejected it. In this case, as in many others, not the slightest suspicion was cast on the claimant who held in good faith, and in perfect honesty conveyed large tracts covered by his title to third parties. Nye's claim to four leagues on the Sacramento was a sample of claims under the general permission granted by Micheltorena, after his expulsion from office, to Sutter to issue certificates of title to persons who had previously petitioned for land. The Supreme Court treated the general title as a nullity. The claim of Fuentes, a young nephew of Micheltorena, for eleven leagues near the Mission of San José, was rejected when the Supreme Court was shown that, though it was dated at Monterey, 1843, the Governor whose signature was attached had never at that time been to Monterey. The claim of the two brothers of General Vallejo, better known as the Teschemacher claim, for sixteen leagues, was rejected as spurious. The claim of Santillan, a priest at the Mission Dolores, to the site of San Francisco, purported to be derived from a grant by Pio Pico in 1846. It was prosecuted in the name of James R. Bolton, and held by Palmer, Cook & Co. and a Philadelphia company, when the Supreme Court, to the great joy of San Franciscans, reversed the judgment of the commissioners and the District Court, and rejected it. Other claims of less note and value it rejected, some for lack of proof of their genuineness, some for clearly discovered though adroitly perpetrated fraud.

The Attorney-General's figures, as quoted above, especially his estimate of the value of the land saved from the operation of spurious titles, were recklessly extravagant; but though he wrote as an attorney, and not as a judge, even he does not picture too vividly the audacity and gigantic proportions of the frauds attempted.

The chaotic confusion concerning land titles in California that prevailed a few years ago can never again return. Most of the important claims have been determined by the highest judicial authorities, and Congress grows less and less disposed to reopen cases adjudicated, or by enactment to disturb what is apparently firm. Most that now remains is to settle and appoint the boundaries of grants confirmed. A man may at last buy a homestead lot in the city, or a farm in the country, with some comfortable assurance that, if he has the proper searches for title made, he is not simply purchasing a lawsuit.

CHAPTER XXXVII.

BITTER PARTY STRIFES.

WITHIN the eight years after the Vigilance revolution, California enjoyed or suffered the control of four different political parties: the Know Nothing, Democratic, Republican, and Union. The Know Nothing, or American, as it called itself, rode into power on the wave of reform. Governor Johnson kept faith with the reformers, and under his spur the Legislature did really apply the pruning-knife to governmental expenses with effect. But his administration committed an egregious blunder in the matter of the State Prison.

In 1851, by an unfortunate contract for a term of ten years, that institution was turned over to the control of James M. Estill. There were so many abuses, so many escapes of prisoners, sometimes encouraged if not even planned by the keepers, so much and such well-grounded complaint, that the Legislature declared the lease forfeited, and the State officers resumed its management. They erected a wall twenty feet high about the premises at San Quentin,

CHAP. XXXVII.

1856–1864.

enclosing a square of five hundred feet on each side, and initiated many reforms.

1856. Still the concern did not prosper, and the Legislature of 1856, doubtless thinking it wise economy, made a new lease of the prison buildings and labor to the same Estill, he engaging to maintain and keep safely the convicts, and the State to pay him ten thousand dollars a year for five years. Very soon he assigned the lease to one McCauley at half the agreed rate of compensation. The abuses now were worse than ever. Prisoners were maltreated and continually escaping.

The Legislature again declared the lease forfeited, and Governer Weller, in the spring of 1858, took forcible possession of the property, and gave the keys to a new warden. The assignee prosecuted for his rights and for damages, and the Supreme Court sustained him. A compromise was effected, but its terms were not punctually met on the part of the State. Finally, a bonus was paid the assignee in Governor Downey's day, and, though there have been several wholesale escapes, the management has improved ever since, and, but for the lack of room to classify prisoners and keep the adepts in crime separate from mere novices, it is in tolerable condition.

1857. The Administration suffered also from the scandal of a defalcation by one of its principal officers. There was suddenly missing from the treasury some one hundred and forty thousand dollars. Dr. Bates, the Treasurer, pretended that it was set aside to pay the interest on the debt, but all he could show for it was a penal bond of the Pacific Express Company, engaging to pay one hundred and twenty-four thousand dollars into the treasury in default of the payment of the interest due in New York in July. Bates was impeached, convicted, and declared by the Senate disqualified to hold office. He was indicted, too, for embezzlement, stood two or three trials, but by virtue of a change of venue, was finally acquitted. His sureties were prosecuted, and judgment recovered against them, but they proved insolvent, and the State abandoned the claim.

CHAP XXXVII.

1857.

Know Nothingism was a temporary expedient, and short-lived. Here, as elsewhere, it died before the term of its first victors expired. Johnson sent his second annual message (1857) to a Legislature which on joint ballot had forty-six Democratic majority.

As Gwin's seat in the United States Senate had been vacant nearly two years, and Weller's was just about to be, there should be no difficulty, if the two factions would be satisfied each with an abundant prize. Broderick was king of caucus that year. On the 10th of January (1857), in joint convention, he had seventy-

Jan. 10.

35

nine votes, E. C. Stanley fourteen, and J. W. Coffroth seventeen, on the first ballot, and Broderick was declared elected United States Senator, to fill the place that Weller would vacate in March.

But who should be his colleague? who occupy for four years Gwin's long-vacant seat? Broderick wanted Judge McCorkle, but caucus, rebelling, refused him. Gwin, Broderick's bitter enemy, bade high for it. Milton S. Latham wanted it, who, as member of Congress, and especially as Collector of the Port of San Francisco, had earned a fair reputation. Both paid court to Broderick, for the decision lay with him. Gwin professed great disgust of Federal patronage; meddling with it had caused all his woes; men whom he helped to office were working for Latham; he would be glad to give up all pretensions to any claim in the appointments. But Broderick distrusted him. Latham, with reservations about two or three trivial places, had assured Broderick's friends that they should have his aid to obtain whatever they wanted, and it was understood that Latham was to be the lucky man.

Suddenly Frank Tilford, candidate for the San Francisco collectorship, told Broderick that he missed a letter from his desk in which Latham had pledged his support of him for the position; he suspected that Latham had surreptitiously regained possession of it. On this, Broderick professed that all faith in Latham deserted him, and he ordered caucus to give its vote for Gwin.

When Broderick told this story on the stump two years afterwards, Latham indignantly denied the petty larceny, and Tilford in writing indorsed the denial, saying that he found the letter next morning, on closer search, where he left it.

Latham's version of his defeat was this: Broderick sent for him to visit him at the "Magnolia," in Sacramento. He declined to go to his room, but consented to meet him at David Mahoney's room, in the same house. So at night, between eleven and a half and two o'clock, the Senator elect, and the young aspirant for senatorial honors, met. Broderick told Latham he would make him Senator if he would write a full relinquishment of all his claims upon the Federal patronage. Latham answered that he should lose his self-respect if he did it, and declined. Upon that they separated, but Estill, of infragrant State Prison memory, essayed to compromise their differences. Finally, Latham consented that if Estill would write, he would sign the required relinquishment, except as to three persons and places. Broderick's ultimatum was an unconditional surrender, which Latham refused.

Caucus obeyed orders promptly. At its next session, on the fourteenth ballot, Gwin received forty-seven votes (seven more than was necessary to a choice), Latham but twenty-six. On the 13th of January, the Legislative Joint Convention met again, when the first ballot stood: Gwin, eighty-one; H. A. Crabb, seventeen; A. M. Sargent, eleven; E. C. Stanley, one; O. L. Shafter, one; so Gwin was at last elected his own successor, to serve four years.

As if to convince even the simplest that it was not Broderick's magnanimity, but a most corrupt and disgraceful bargain that restored Gwin to the Senate, there appeared in print, a day or two later, an astounding "Letter to the People," bearing even date with his election, and signed with Gwin's name. In it occurred the following remarkable sentences: "A representative whose evil destiny it is to be the indirect dispenser of Federal patronage, will strangely miscalculate if he expects to evade the malice of disappointed men. To the Federal patronage in the State do I attribute, in a great degree, the malice and hostile energy which, after years of faithful service, have nearly cost me the indorsement of a re-election to the United States Senate. From patronage, then, and the curse it entails, I shall gladly in future turn, and my sole labor and ambition shall be to deserve well of the State, and to justify the choice of the Legislature in honoring me a second time as a representative of its interests. * * * * I have hinted at aid other than that received from those whom I regarded as friends. I refer to the timely assistance accorded to me by Mr. Broderick and his friends. Although at one time a rival, and recognizing in him a fierce but manly opponent, I do not hesitate to acknowledge, in this public manner, his forgetfulness of all grounds of dissension and hostility, in what he conceives to be a step necessary to allay the strifes and discords which had distracted the party and the State. To him I conceive, in a great degree, my election is due; and I feel bound to him and them in common efforts to unite and heal, where the result heretofore has been to break down and destroy."

That spring, there was a grand hegira of the politicians to Washington, to secure the spoils that Buchanan had to distribute. But at the national capital Broderick's rod had no magic power, while Gwin's open house and profuse hospitality, and Mrs. Gwin's fancy balls and gay receptions, had all the effect that such things aim to produce on impressible senators and cabinet officers. Though Gwin may have kept the promise of his letter, the choicest of the Federal patronage for California came out with the senior Senator's brand upon it. Washington, whom Broderick did not love, was given the collectorship at San Francisco. Bigler was exiled with a mission to Chili.

At home, in the fall, Broderick tried to get McCorkle nominated for Governor on an Anti-Lecompton platform, but failed. Weller received the nomination, and was elected by the undivided Democracy over Edward Stanley, the candidate of the Whigs.

The Legislature chosen that fall was largely Democratic. Meeting in 1858, it adopted a resolution indorsing the President's Kansas policy, and instructing the State's senators to vote accordingly.

There was occasion this year to try the virtue of the Fugitive Slave Law, one of the series of Compromise Acts of 1850. A Mr. Stovall, from Mississippi, came into the State with his slave, Archy, in the summer of 1857. Though he professed that he did not intend to stay long, he so far settled as to engage for a while as teacher of a private school in Sacramento. In January, he prepared to send the slave South again, when suddenly Archy assumed his liberty, and declined to go. Stovall had the boy arrested; but the friends of the alleged slave sued out a writ of *habeas corpus*, under which he was discharged, on the ground that Stovall was not a traveller, and Archy not a fugitive, under the act of 1850. Instantly that he was discharged, he was rearrested, and his case hastened up to CHAP. XXXVII. the Supreme Court, where Chief-Justice Burnett gave the law to the negro, and, Terry concurring, the negro to his claimant. Stovall now brought his chattel to San Francisco, and took the steamer for home; but when off the Heads, both were arrested and brought back—the former on a charge of kidnapping; the latter by writ of *habeas corpus*. The U. S. Commissioner, George Pen Johnston, though a man of strong Southern sympathies, heard the case, when it came up before him, with impartiality. Colonel Baker befriended Archy; J. A. Hardy (who was impeached, in 1862, for using treasonable language) pleaded the cause of Stovall. After an exciting trial, in course of which counsel came once to the verge of a physical collision, and the blacks in town were very much stirred up, the negro was set free.

1858.

The second Legislature during Weller's gubernatorial term was more than simply Democratic; it was chivalric and very "high-toned" on the Lecompton question. By resolution it denounced a speech made by Broderick in the Senate—in which he had spoken with great freedom of the Executive—as insulting to the nation and humiliating to the people.

1859.

So soon as Congress adjourned the two senators came home to have the fight over again, on the soil native to it. Gwin brought with him the good wishes of the Administration; Broderick the sympathies of the Douglas Democrats and the Republicans, who had fraternized on many matters, though maintaining distinctly party lines. In Administrative circles, Weller was the candidate of the ultra Southern men, Latham of the Conservatives, and in Convention Latham won the nomination for Governor. For Congressmen, Burch and Scott were nominated by the same convention. The anti-Lecompton Convention nominated John Curry for Governor, and Joseph C. McKibben and S. A. Booker for Congress. The Republicans nominated Leland Stanford for Governor, and Colonel E. H. Baker and P. H. Sibley for Congress.

Here there was ample occasion for the hostile senators to get a verdict, principle enough involved in the contest to dignify it, personal animosity enough to make sure that each would struggle to the extent of his power for victory. Gwin had on his side the patronage of the Government, the custom-house, the post-office, the mint, each of which had a long list of employés, and a list ten times longer of expectants of places there. Besides, he had the odor of regularity, so dear to Democrats. Broderick had the sympathies of the Republicans, but their votes were thought to be mortgaged to candidates of their own. As was the Democratic custom, the candidates went into the outskirts, avoiding San Francisco, and even Sacramento, as long as possible, evidently dreading the phonographers and the press of the chief cities.

But at the very opening of the campaign, an affair occurred which was augury of a bitter strife coming. Judge Terry was a defeated candidate before the Lecompton Convention for a renomination to the supreme bench. In a speech professing resignation to the will of the majority, he said some harsh things of Broderick, intimating that while it was true enough that he rallied to the call of a Douglas, it was not of Stephen A., but of Frederick Douglass, the eloquent mulatto. Broderick read the report of this speech at the breakfast-table of the International Hotel in San Francisco, and as he laid aside the paper uttered some remark not complimentary to Terry. D. W. Perley heard the remark, and replied to it. Broderick retorted. Perley, seeing there were ladies at the table, withdrew, and soon after sent a hostile message to Broderick by the hands of S. H. Brooks, Lecompton candidate for State Comptroller. E. J. C. Kewen, arriving the same night, relieved Brooks, and himself took on the part of Perley's friend. Broderick, because there was some informality about it, chose to send his reply—it was dated June 29th, 1859—to Perley direct. He said the publicity given to the affair put it out of his power to afford the satisfaction demanded. He had told him in the presence of gentlemen, at the time of the alleged insult, that he would not accept a challenge from him, who, within a few days, had made oath that he was a subject of Great Britain, and, consequently, had no political rights to be affected by giving or receiving a challenge. "For many years," wrote Broderick, "and up to the time of my elevation to the position I now occupy, it was well known that I would not have avoided any issue of the character proposed. If compelled to accept a challenge, it could only be with a gentleman holding a position equally elevated and responsible, and there are no circumstances which could induce me even to do thus during the pendency of the present canvass. When I authorized the announcement that I would address the people of California during the campaign, it was suggested that efforts would be made to force me into difficulties, and I determined to take no notice of attacks from any source during the canvass. If I were to accept your challenge, there are probably many other gentlemen who would seek similar opportunities for hostile meetings, for the purpose of accomplishing a political object, or to obtain public notoriety. I cannot afford, at the present time, to descend to a violation of the Constitution and the State laws to subserve either their or your purposes."

Perley then issued a card to the public, pronouncing Broderick's letter a tissue of falsehoods, a mean, quibbling, dastardly evasion, and expressing the opinion that Broderick was as devoid of courage as of principle, and had no longer any right to call himself a gentleman.

Broderick made his first stump speech at Placerville, July 9th. He recited the points of his career in California. He was elected to the first Senate of the State, and in 1851 re-elected for two years, and chosen by that body to preside over it, when the Lieutenant-Governor, McDougall, was called to fill the chair of Governor, made vacant by Burnett's resignation. In 1852 and 1853 he was chairman of the State Central Committee. In 1852 he was a candidate for the United States Senate, but caucus preferred the claims of Weller. In 1854 he was again a candidate, and caucus gave him the nomination, but a combination of Americans, Old Line Whigs, and Federal officeholders defeated him. He protested that "no thieving bill, or corrupt measure, designed to rob the treasury, ever received support or countenance" from him.

Said he, "I have lived among you for more than ten years. From the commencement, and during the period when the gross vices of public men were winked at or forgotten, on account of the general laxity of morals that prevailed in society unleavened by the presence of virtuous woman, no man, living or dead, ever saw me at a gaming-table, or in a brothel, or under the influence of liquors, or ever knew me to refuse to pay an honest debt. No one ever dared to charge me with being influenced by pecuniary considerations in any vote which I gave." He had been told that the San Francisco Vigilance Committee undertook to investigate his history. The principles of that organization he did not approve; he had no sympathy with them; but many men in it had since become friendly. He had sought to reduce the salaries of Federal officers in California. He claimed credit for defeating the Lime Point swindle; read letters from Governor Weller, urging the purchase of the Point at three hundred thousand dollars; produced the evidence of a clerk in the Treasury Department, describing that precipitous rock at the door of the ocean, as a property valuable for warehouses, and eligible for villas and suburban residences, and stating that six hundred acres of it was good for agricultural purposes!

At Nevada, Broderick told the story of Gwin's last election to the Senate, giving that version which made Latham party to the larceny of the Tilford letter. Latham, at Shasta, pronounced the story untrue in every respect. Gwin, at Yreka, called it a "lie," and vile and slanderous. In another place he ridiculed Broderick's pretensions to ability to address intelligent audiences; his first speech in the Senate was a failure, his second he read from a manuscript. Broderick, at Quincy, July 21st, spoke of "Gwin's low scurrility," accused him of being the paid agent of the Pacific Mail Steamship Company, and repeated a confident belief that both Gwin and Weller were interested in the Line Point swindle. Latham, at Nevada, told his version of the Senatorial bargain, which is incorporated in our account of that abominable transaction. At Sacramento he said, in a strain quite foreign to the campaign, that the future historian would put this down among the remarkable features of the year 1859, that while Barnum was lecturing in England upon honesty, and Lola Montez was lecturing in Scotland upon feminine virtue, David C. Broderick was lecturing in California upon political honesty. Broderick, at Red Bluff, spoke of Gwin's "utter worthlessness of character, his unreliability of word, his sneaking manner of acting." Gwin, at Alleghany Town, said of Broderick, "He is at my feet; I have my foot upon his neck.... I intend... to lash him with a scourge of scorpions, and shingle him over with the falsehoods and libels he has uttered against me and others." He pronounced the charge of his being the paid agent of the

CHAP. XXXVII.
1859.

Pacific Mail Steamship Company false, and the author of it a slanderer and calumniator. "Such a man will soon be banished from every gentleman's house, if he is now tolerated in any." In a card, dated August 11th, Gwin claimed it proven that Broderick intended to use the position he held to pay his electioneering debts.

The Republicans, all this time, were much divided as to whether they should fuse with the anti-Lecompton party, with a fair prospect of electing a portion of their ticket, or maintain their isolation, plead their distinctive doctrines from the stump, avoid all entangling alliances, and boldly accept immediate defeat as part of the drill necessary to "organize victory" in the future.

A distinguished stranger had arrived—Horace Greeley, of the New York *Tribune*, covered with boils, and very much fatigued with the overland journey, yet lecturing on literary subjects, addressing great crowds concerning the Pacific Railroad, giving audience to admirers, and not loath to tender advice to his Republican friends. Being urged to do so, he wrote a letter to the public (August 20th), giving the reasons why it is better to take half a loaf than no bread, why McKibben, Democrat as he was, should be re-elected to Congress, and why Republicans and anti-Lecompton men should unite to defeat the Lecompton ticket.

The advice was not well relished in all Republican quarters. Frank M. Pixley published in pamphlet form a bold denunciation of the fusing scheme. He believed that all the rough things Broderick had said of Gwin, Weller, and Denver were true, but he charged that Broderick was no better. He regarded Broderick responsible for the acts of the Executive of the State " while Bigler cumbered the gubernatorial chair," for he ruled the Governor with a rod of iron, dispensed his patronage, and disposed of his bounty. He could see nothing to choose between Gwin and Broderick; both were " equally bad, equally corrupt, both unscrupulous, and both surrounded by equally bad and contemptible men." Broderick had voted with Republicans in the Senate simply because the President had tabooed him, and there was no place for him on the Administration benches. In his political career he saw nothing but the shrewd, imperious, self-willed, unscrupulous politician. While admitting his freedom from the stain of personal immorality, if he " should give a list of all the blackguards that ever infested San Francisco, that ever stuffed a ballot-box, or raised a plug-muss on election-day, he would name the political friends of the Hon. David C. Broderick."

One of the Republican candidates for Congress withdrew on the eve of election, and the

Republicans cast their votes for Baker and McKibben. It was in vain, however; Latham was elected Governor, and Burch and Scott to Congress.

CHAPTER XXXVIII.

BRODERICK'S DEATH.—NOTABLE DUELS.

ELECTION being over, Judge Terry descended from the Supreme bench, to demand of Broderick an apology for the uncomplimentary remark which Perley heard at the breakfast-table of the International more than two months previous, and excepted to. By note he asked a retraction of the language used. Broderick asked what he understood the language to be. Terry replied: "You said, 'I have heretofore considered and spoken of him (Terry) as the only honest man on the Supreme Court bench; but I now take it all back.'" But if that was not the exact language, it made no difference; he asked a retraction of any words which were calculated to reflect on his character as an officer or a gentleman. Broderick responded, repeating his exact language, which was about as the other had heard it, with this addition, "During Judge Terry's incarceration by the Vigilance Committee, I paid two hundred dollars a week to support a newspaper in his defence." "You are the best judge," added the writer of this note, evidently surprised that at a time when such violence of speech was tolerated, language so very temperate and mild should be selected to shoot him for, "as to whether the language affords good grounds of offence."

As mortal combat was predetermined, they wasted little more time on preliminaries. Broderick's friends held, that if his remarks at the International table were to be withdrawn, Terry's, at Mr. Benton's church, which provoked them, should also be withdrawn. But Terry had nothing to retract, nor had Broderick. So, on the morning of the 11th, they met for a duel just over the San Francisco line, in San Mateo County; but Chief Burke, armed with a warrant from each county, came suddenly up, arrested them, and put a stop to proceedings. The police court dismissed the charge, because no violation of the law had been committed.

At seven o'clock on the morning of September 13th, the combatants met again at another point in San Mateo County, some twelve miles from the city, and no police interfered. About fifty spectators were present. Terry's seconds were Thomas Hayes and Calhoun Benham; Broderick's were McKibben and D. D. Colton. Broderick won the choice of positions and the word of fire. Terry won the choice of weapons, which were duelling pistols; distance, ten paces.

At the word, the principals raised their pistols, but Broderick's discharged itself before being brought to a level—the ball striking the ground some distance in front of his opponent. Terry's fire followed but a second later—he exclaiming, "The shot is not mortal; I have struck two inches to the right;" then, as he saw Broderick slowly falling, he and his friends retired. The ball had entered Broderick's breast near the right nipple, and lodged in the left side. He was taken on a litter to the road, and then conveyed to Leonidas Haskell's residence at Black Point. He was in great pain, and oppressed with a heavy load on the chest, except when relieved of sensibility by anæsthetics. One who was by his bedside says that he exclaimed, "They have killed me because I was opposed to the extension of slavery and a corrupt Administration." Occasionally he appeared to rally, but he soon fell into delirium again, and, at twenty minutes after nine on the morning of the 17th of September, he died.

On the coroner's inquest, the gunsmith who loaded the pistol Broderick used said it was more delicate on the trigger than Terry's; though the seconds declared that they were ignorant of the fact. S. H. Brooks, the newly elected State Comptroller, loaded Terry's weapon.

The remains of the deceased Senator were

removed to the Union Hotel, there to lie in state for a time. On Sunday, the 18th, the funeral was celebrated. Colonel Baker delivered one of his matchless orations over the body, to a great crowd assembled on the plaza. It was a glowing tribute to the memory of his friend, which told the more emphatically because it was not unrelieved eulogy. He said, that in his judgment, when Broderick sought to anticipate the senatorial election, he committed an error which he lived to regret. He urged that no man suppose his friend's death " was caused by any other reason than that to which his own words assigned it. It had been long foreshadowed; it was predicted by his friends; it was threatened by his enemies; it was the consequence of intense political hatred. His death was a political necessity, poorly veiled beneath the guise of private quarrel." Concerning the code to which this costly sacrifice was brought, the orator said: "Fellow-citizens, one year ago I performed a duty such as I perform to-day, over the remains of Senator Ferguson, who died as Mr. Broderick died, tangled in the meshes of the code of honor. To-day there is another and a more eminent sacrifice. To-day I renew my protest; to-day I utter yours. The code of honor is a delusion and a snare; it palters with the hope of a true courage, and binds it at the feet of crafty and cruel skill. It surrounds its victim with the pomp and grace of the procession, but leaves him bleeding on the altar. It substitutes cold and deliberate preparation for courageous and manly impulse, and arms the one to disarm the other. It may prevent fraud between practised duellists, who should be forever without its pale, but it makes the mere 'trick of the weapon' superior to the noblest cause and truest courage. Its pretence of equality is a lie: it is equal in all the form; it is unjust in all the substance—the habitude of arms—the early training—the frontier life—the border war—the sectional custom—the life of leisure;—all these are advantages which no negotiation can neutralize, and which no courage can overcome."

From the Plaza, the body was borne to Lone Mountain Cemetery, accompanied by the Pioneers, a benevolent society, some two thousand citizens on foot, and a long procession of carriages. At the grave, two Catholic clergymen officiated. Father Gallagher, to the mourners, said their friend died repenting his misguided act: "He addressed me as a father; I regarded him as a son in Christ." A monument of granite has since been erected on the highest ground in the cemetery, whence the ocean and the city, and the mountains of the coast range across the bay, are together visible, marking the spot where Broderick's remains repose. At a short distance from it is the grave of his friend who pronounced the oration over his bier. Colonel Baker, soon after these funeral ceremonies, went to Oregon, assisted in the political campaign that carried that State in opposition to the Buchanan Democracy, and was elected (1860) United States Senator. On his way to Washington, he was received at San Francisco with triumphal honors by the Republicans, who claimed him to be theirs quite as much as Oregon's Senator. In the Senate chamber, his eloquence shone no less illustriously than in the halls and from "the stump" of the Pacific coast.

Baker was born in England, but reared, since six years of age, in America. Deprived in youth of all near relatives, except a younger brother, whom he supported by his work as a weaver, in Philadelphia, he went to Illinois, studied law, was elected to Congress, raised a regiment of Illinoisans, whom he led into the Mexican war, where he won distinction, and in 1851 removed to San Francisco.

The Slaveholders' Rebellion bursting out into open war soon after he had taken his seat as Senator from Oregon, he raised a regiment of volunteers at the East, during the Congressional recess, which gloried in the name of the "California Regiment," and took it into service.

At Ball's Bluff, while gallantly leading his brigade against the enemy, he fell pierced by six bullets. His body was taken to San Francisco, where it was received with memorable ceremonies, including a funeral oration by Edward Stanly, and another at the grave by the Rev. T. Starr King, and buried at Lone Mountain.

A will was found in Washington bearing Broderick's signature. As the property it disposed of was valued at some four hundred thousand dollars, the will was vigorously contested, but it was finally admitted to probate.

Terry, when he saw that he had seriously wounded his opponent, hastened to Sacramento, and thence to his farm near Stockton. He had left with a friend his resignation of the judgeship before the duel came off, to be sent in to the Governor only on condition of such a result as did follow. And now he signified his readiness for trial. The case was postponed from time to time, moved from court to court, and at last, on a change of venue, taken into Marin County, where the Seventh District Court was in session, temporarily presided over by Judge Hardy, who came all the way from Mokelumne Hill for the purpose. On the day set for trial, the witnesses from San Francisco were becalmed on the bay. The court waited a little while, then the prosecuting attorney moved a *nolle prosequi*, and the farce was ended. After the war of the rebellion broke out, Terry went overland to Texas, joined the rebels, and troubled California no more.

There had been some notable duels in the State before this one which proved fatal to Broderick. The bloodless ones brought a storm of ridicule upon all concerned; some very bloody ones, where the principals hacked each other with swords till both were shockingly mutilated, and one party or the other butchered, were quite as much calculated to disgust sensible people with "the code."

Edward Gilbert, senior editor of the *Alta California* newspaper, and one of the first Congressmen chosen by the State after its organization, challenged J. W. Denver, State Senator from Trinity, for reflections on him in a political letter. Denver accepted, and on the 2d of August, 1852, at Oak Grove, near Sacramento, the duel came off, the weapons being rifles, the distance forty paces. At the first fire both missed—Denver purposely, it was said. At the second Gilbert fell, and in a few minutes died.

On the 21st of August, 1858, at Angel Island, George Pen Johnston, and Mr. Ferguson, of Sacramento, a State Senator, fought a duel, the cause being the offensive way in which the Senator, in a drinking saloon, told a story in which a young lady of Johnston's acquaintance figured. They fought with pistols, at ten paces distance, which, in the unsatisfactory progress of the engagement, was shortened to six paces. Four shots were exchanged. On the fourth, Ferguson fell with a fractured thigh-bone. Twenty-four days afterwards he died, while the surgeons were amputating his leg. Johnston surrendered himself to the Marin County authorities, was tried, and acquitted, on the ground that Ferguson died not from the effects of the wound, but because he had refused to allow an earlier amputation.

Since the Broderick duel, there has been but one "affair of honor" that has caused much sensation in the State. It was between Daniel Showalter, of Mariposa, aged thirty-two, of Breckinridge Democratic politics, and Speaker *pro tempore* of the Assembly of 1861, and Charles W. Piercy, aged twenty-four, Douglas Democratic member from San Bernardino. The Union resolutions came to a vote in Assembly under operation of the previous question. Showalter asked leave to explain his vote. Piercy objected. Showalter said he had "nothing but contempt for any gentleman who objects." The quarrel was nursed till the Legislature adjourned. Then Piercy sent a challenge, which was accepted. They met eight miles from San Rafael, at four o'clock of the 25th of May (1861), with rifles, at forty paces, and in presence, as was customary, of a considerable number of witnesses. At the second shot Piercy fell dead.

The law is stringent enough in letter, but it has never punished the duellist, and still it is felt that duelling is not likely again to be resorted to by gentlemen in the State. A drunken vagabond may, and not unfrequently does, challenge some one to mortal combat, with the effect of bringing himself into the station-house and into contempt. The change of politics, the decay of bogus Chivalry, and the constantly increasing influence of the New England sentiment, have effected the reform.

Governor Weller surprised the people by appointing Henry P. Haun, of Marysville, to occupy the Senatorial seat made vacant by Broderick's death, until the Legislature should choose a permanent occupant. Haun served for one term, and then died. On the 13th of February he announced to the Senate his predecessor's death. He said that he fell "in an unfortunate conflict, which was engendered by the use of unguarded expressions by the deceased, personal in their character towards another distinguished gentleman, who occupied a high and honorable position in the State of California." He moved resolutions of respect, and an adjournment for the day.

Mr. Crittenden reminded Senators that Broderick always made his mark wherever he stood. Mr. Seward said impartiality would require the historian to raise Houston, and Rusk, and Broderick to the rank among the organizers of our States, which the world has assigned to Winthrop and Villiers, Raleigh and Penn, Baltimore and Oglethorpe. Foster said he must vote against the resolutions, on the ground that the subject of their eulogy died by a duel They were adopted.

CHAPTER XXXIX.

A POLITICAL REVOLUTION.

CHAP.
XXXIX.
1860.

So soon as the Legislature of 1860 assembled, the struggle for Broderick's place began. The Democrats were in power as usual. Ninety-seven of them went into caucus together, and on the first ballot Ex-Governor Weller had thirty-eight votes; Ex-Congressman Denver, thirty-one; Judge Baldwin, eleven; Collector Washington, nine; and General McDougall, eight. They tried it again on an early ensuing evening; Baldwin was withdrawn, Denver stepped aside, and the first ballot showed Latham, fifty-one; Weller, forty-three; Washington, two. The result startled the people, who had just elected Latham Governor, but caucus asked no permission from the people. The two houses met in Joint Convention on the 11th of January. A Sacramento member nominated Latham, a San Franciscan nominated Oscar L. Shafter, and John Conness for the Anti-Lecomptonites nominated Edmund Randolph. The first ballot gave Latham (who the day before was inaugurated Governor) ninety-seven, Randolph fourteen, Shafter three.

Latham, having achieved the object of his ambition, resigned the reins of State Government to John G. Downey, Lieutenant-Governor, a man without political history or experience, but not destined to be without a popularity, especially in San Francisco, quite new to Chief Executives in California. The Legislature shaped its labors mainly with the view of securing all the patronage possible for the Democratic party, that it might go with reasonable expectations into the Presidential election of the coming fall. It passed bills for the inspection of beef and pork, and multiplied licenses, not so much for revenue purposes, or because those staples needed inspection, as because favorites and men skilled in the tactics of primary conventions wanted paying places. It crowned its unwelcome labors with an act authorizing substantially the joint wharf companies of San Francisco to build a sea-wall, or bulkhead, along the city front, and to take toll of all that passed it into the city for fifty years to come; meanwhile mocking the State with the tender of the reserved right to buy the work on completion at cost and ten per cent. yearly interest. It was a barefaced imposition of a heavy tax on commerce for the benefit of speculators, which

San Francisco resented with profound indignation.

Now it had been claimed that Latham was pledged against the scheme, and that, knowing he could not be moved to favor it, he was sent to the Senate by the Bulkheaders' influence, to get him out of the way. If so, they calculated without their true host. Governor Downey lacked experience, but not resolution, and when the enrolled bill went to him for the executive sanction he vetoed it.

The Bulkheaders were boiling with wrath; San Francisco went into ecstasies. The citizens demanded a visit from the little Governor of Irish birth and iron backbone, and, when he reluctantly consented, they met him at the Sacramento boat, with a torchlight procession that shamed every precedent in that line. They escorted him to his temporary residence with music, and banners, and cheers, through streets illuminated with bonfires, costly pyrotechnics, and transparencies, exhibiting mottoes of welcome, and with rockets and Roman candles, often defined triumphal arches, over the route.

This veto killed the bulkhead, which, in one form or another, had been the great topic of strife ever since Bigler advised the water-front extension. After that it was heard of no more as a living lobby scheme. The Union Legislature of 1863 passed an act creating a commission composed of three citizens, to be elected in a way satisfactory to the whole people, to manage the wharves and apply their revenues, hitherto stopping mostly in private hands, to needful repairs and the construction of such a sea-wall as the wants of commerce and the protection of the harbor demand. The work, though just beginning, is in satisfactory shape, and promises the happiest results.

Downey won the gratitude of the friends of a free press, too, by pocketing a bill concerning libel, intended to punish for their outspoken, honest editorials, certain papers at the Bay that lashed the Treasury thieves into continuous fury. The gratitude of the Bay City people towards the Los Angeles apothecary, who played the part of Governor so much better than any of his predecessors had done, was unbounded. There was nothing they would not have given him, but that his Southern proclivities drew him, towards the close of his term, upon a rock which, in the stormy times, no craft could graze without serious damage.

That year, for the third time, the people, by direct vote, repudiated the proposition for a convention to revise the Constitution. Desirous as they were to secure and enjoy certain changes in the organic law, especially to place the Supreme Court on a more satisfactory footing, and reduce the ordinary expenses of government,

CHAP.
XXXIX.
1860.

they refused the risks incident to a general revisal. As early as 1852 the Chivalry had unsuccessfully attempted a convention, with the secret purpose of dividing the State and erecting the southern half into a Slave Territory. From that time the friends of Union and of freedom were very chary of creating any opportunities that secessionists or slavery extensionists might possibly use mischievously.

The result of the fall election (1860) proved that the anti-slavery doctrines, urged with so much persistency in regions that seemed to give no token of respect for them, by Republican stump speakers and a portion of the press, not always without peril of insult, and for the orators showers of stale eggs, had taken unexpected hold of the interior; that the Northern sentiment was strengthening in the larger cities; that the quarrels of the Democracy and the corruption of a party that ran the State for its spoils, had worked out their legitimate result in the disgust of its more intelligent adherents. The popular vote gave Lincoln, for President, a plurality of seven hundred over Douglas, and three thousand more for Douglas than for Breckinridge—the total vote cast being one hundred and nineteen thousand eight hundred and twelve. Mr. Lincoln received the four votes of the State in the Electoral College. The influence of Broderick dead was even greater than he had exerted living. To the party of which he had been the leader belonged half the credit of the change. The Chivalry were utterly crushed.

CHAP. XXXIX.
1860.

The Legislature then elected, and which met in January, 1861, had few Republicans in it, but the color of the new Democracy differed materially from that of the old. Both houses adopted a concurrent resolution pronouncing untrue and expunging the resolutions of censure on Broderick, passed two years before. They rather distinguished themselves by their more generous than just gifts and franchises to individuals and companies, of which the privilege of laying horse railroads in the streets of San Francisco was chief. The first three of these popular institutions were granted that year, and, whether the scandal about the corrupt appliances used to obtain their charters was true or not, it is certain that on the railroad question, as on a pivot, turned almost all the other local legislation.

1861.

That Legislature accomplished also the always difficult job of electing a United States Senator, taking nearly three months for it. Gwin's seat was to become vacant on the 3d of March. The split in the Democracy was too wide to be bridged by any caucus, and it was not attempted. The Assembly, willing to try the paces of candidates, invited all aspirants to

CHAP. address it publicly. General McDougall alone
XXXIX. ventured to the platform, for it was a time, just
1861. on the eve of war, when trimming politicians
shrank from committing themselves. Edmund
Randolph was sick in bed, and lost that opportunity to pledge himself to loyalty. But
McDougall made an excellent Union speech.

About the middle of February the Douglas
men began to assemble in caucus. One evening, twenty-six members being present, McDougall received thirteen votes, Randolph six (notwithstanding that his name was withdrawn
during the progress of the voting), Edgerton
three, Griffith two. So McDougall was the
nominee of the Douglas caucus.

The other kind of Democrats tried in vain to
obtain a caucus. The Republicans were more
harmonious, and on the twelfth ballot nominated Timothy G. Phelps.

The Legislature went into joint convention
on the 9th of March, with the following result:
Weller twenty-seven, Phelps twenty-three, McDougall twenty-seven, Nugent nine, Denver
sixteen, Whitesides sixteen, Hoge five, and
others three. On the 19th, the Breckinridge
and anti-McDougall Democrats met to the number of forty-six in caucus, and nominated John
Nugent, formerly proprietor and editor of the
San Francisco *Herald*. In joint convention
next day, on the twenty-second and last ballot,

McDougall had fifty-six, Nugent forty-seven, Weller six, Phelps one, Creanor one. To obtain this result, which gave just the necessary number to elect McDougall, Phelps changed his vote when he saw that the Republicans, by uniting with the Douglas men, could elect a man firmly pledged to the Union, and save the State from being represented in the United States Senate by John Nugent.

The news that Secessionists had fired on Fort Sumter reached the Pacific coast late in April, and it fired the Union-loving heart of California. A great meeting was held in San Francisco on the 11th of May, business being suspended, and the day devoted to it. Several prominent citizens, of dubious tendencies before, took then their stand openly for the Federal Government and against the seceders. In September, Captains Halleck, Naglee, and others of military education went East, tendering their services to the Administration. The election that fall was a positive triumph for the Republicans, an overwhelming one for the two Union parties. Three candidates for Governor were in the field: Leland Stanford, Republican; John Conness, Douglas Democrat; J. R. McConnell, Breckinridge Democrat. Their votes were, for Stanford, fifty-six thousand and thirty-six; for Conness, thirty thousand nine hundred and forty-four; for McConnell, thirty-two thousand seven hundred and fifty-one.

1862. Still, the Legislature that met January, 1862, was not Republican; the party never had a nominal control in the Legislature, though that year the Federal and State offices were filled by Republicans. The majority of the members were of Democratic antecedents, elected by a union of the Republican and Free-Soil Democratic votes. For the local reputation of the party that elected Mr. Lincoln it was just as well so. A flood that submerged Sacramento, and made its streets only passable for boats, compelled an early adjournment of the Legislature to San Francisco, where the session was completed. It did a wholesale business in the way of franchises for ferries, bridges, and toll-roads. It abounded in local and special legislation. But it submitted some wholesome amendments of the Constitution, which the people adopted cheerfully, and on the great national question it was sound. It impeached Judge Hardy (of the Terry farce), and the Senate, sitting as a court, found him guilty of using treasonable language, and deposed him from the bench of the Sixteenth District.

1863. The Legislature of 1863 was almost entirely Union. The distinction between Republican and Douglas Democrat had vanished. It is strange that, without opposition enough to act as a brake upon it, the party did nothing to damage the commonwealth; for it cannot be denied that party needs party to check it, and that nothing is so wholesome for a majority as a compact, stubborn minority to watch it. Phelps and Sargent, who were both in the House of Representatives, Trenor W. Park, and John Conness, were candidates before caucus for United States Senator. After a long and heated struggle, Conness won the caucus nomination, and the joint convention ratified it.

The Legislature of 1864 was, like its predecessor, loyal in all its utterances, and reflecting by its acts no discredit upon the party to which an overwhelming majority of its members belonged. But the importance of the subject justifies a more extended reference to the temper with which California has regarded her relations to the Federal Government.

CHAPTER XL.

RELATIONS TO THE FEDERAL GOVERNMENT.

CHAP. XL.

1861.

When the Southern States began to secede, California was ruled by a Democratic Governor, a Democratic Legislature occupied its capital, and four Democrats were its representatives in Congress. Her forts were garrisoned by men whose loyalty in so trying an hour could only be surmised. It was not without fears for the result that the position of the State was observed from Washington.

The Republicans and Douglas Democrats in the Legislature united to elect General James A. McDougall to the United States Senate, who, though a Democrat, placed himself squarely on a coercion and war platform. They also secured the passage of a resolution declaring that the people would not fail in fidelity and fealty to the Constitution and the Union, and the State would at all times respond to any requisition that might be made upon it to defend the republic against foreign and domestic foes.

Brigadier-General Albert Sydney Johnston,

a native of Kentucky, commanded the Pacific Department. While it was not supposed that a soldier of his honorable antecedents could betray a trust as Twiggs had done in Texas, his sympathies were known to be with the South, and if Kentucky should secede it was feared that he might "go with his State," as was the political fashion of the time.

It is said that Edmund Randolph (for till Virginia seceded he was for the Union) communicated information, which, through Colonel Baker, was transmitted to President Lincoln, to the effect that a scheme was meditated for turning California over to the Confederacy. It was known, too, at Washington, that Jefferson Davis had offered Johnston the major-generalship of the rebel armies, a fact which Johnston did not communicate to his superiors in authority. General Edwin V. Sumner received orders to proceed to the Pacific coast at once. He boarded the Aspinwall steamer after she left her wharf at New York, and came unannounced. Arriving at San Francisco, he immediately called upon General Johnston, and conveyed to him the proofs that he was relieved. Johnston was not surprised. A friend in Washington, who was afterwards dismissed the service, had surreptitiously notified him by pony express that Sumner was coming, and, availing himself of that information, Johnston had already dispatched his resignation to the Department. He turned over the forts, arsenals, &c., to his successor, and soon proceeded South by the overland route through Texas. He was intrusted with an important command in the Confederate service, and was killed in battle on the field of Shiloh. Sumner arrived here in April (1861), but not a day too early.

The great May meeting in San Francisco cheered the friends of the Administration as to the stand of that city, but whether the State would back up the city was still somewhat in doubt. The leading independent papers which, while there was any hope of a compromise, pleaded for peace, and deprecated coercion, with the news of the attack on Fort Sumter earnestly pronounced for the war, and brought their support to the Administration, in its most vigorous efforts to crush out the rebellion. The pulpit was eloquent for Union, and for the war necessary to preserve it. In San Francisco the national flag was hoisted over most of the churches, not including those of the Episcopalians and Catholics, who, though professing equal respect for the flag and all it symbolizes, thought that even it should not be placed on a consecrated building.

But to the rule of loyal utterance from the pulpit there was one marked exception. The Rev. Dr. Scott, of Calvary, preached peace with offensive zeal. In his public prayers he would not omit the petition for blessings on "all presidents and vice-presidents," which the public interpreted into a prayer for Jefferson Davis as fervent as for Lincoln. One morning, in September (1861), an effigy of the doctor was found hanging in front of his church. He trimmed his words, and read carefully written prayers, but he could not conceal his sympathy with the seceders. Great crowds gathered about his church on Sunday, and there was much danger of some disgraceful outbreak. But the bold stand of the independent press against mob law, and the prudent management of the police, averted the dreaded riot. Happily, Dr. Scott resigned and left the country. His warmest friends (and his personal traits and popular preaching made him many friends) were glad to see him safely out of the way of the mischief that his inability to keep silence on stirring pertinent themes was always brewing.

Among the clergy who did great service to the Union was the Rev. T. Starr King, who came from Boston to San Francisco to take pastoral charge of the First Unitarian Church. Besides his reputation as a pulpit orator, he brought with him an enviable name as a lecturer. He delivered a course of lectures, soon after his arrival in 1860, on miscellaneous literary subjects, which were very much relished by critical audiences. Being pretty fully reported by the press, every corner of the State was soon demanding him to repeat the course, and invitations were showered in upon him to speak on extraordinary occasions and special topics. Though his first lectures were purely literary, he soon began to mix in the wholesome doctrines of free speech, human rights, abhorrence of slavery, and the imperative necessity of Union. There was a charm in his delivery that few could resist. He was received with applause where Republican orators, saying things no more radical, could not be heard without hisses. Delicately feeling his way, and never arousing the prejudices of his hearers, he adroitly educated his audiences to a lofty style of patriotism. The effect was obvious in San Francisco, where audiences were accustomed to every style of address; it was far more noticeable in the interior.

Afterwards, as politics became simply a question of Union or Dissolution, he construed sermons, lectures, addresses, orations, all to the one end of deepening the Union sentiment, and even occasionally took the stump for candidates who promised best to keep the State headed right for Union.

When, in 1863, a United States Senator was to be elected, there was much desire to secure his services for the honorable position, but he modestly dissuaded his friends, and discouraged all thought of it. He had a higher ambition. The senatorship was for six years; of the sacred office he already held, his tenure was for life. Though holding a faith rejected by most of the clergy with whom he cordially co-operated for his country, they allowed no question of sectarianism to divide their patriotic labors. His valuable life was cut short by *diphtheria*, in the Spring of 1864. The people of the State mourned his departure as if news of the loss of a battle had been telegraphed to them. He was buried in the enclosure of the beautiful church which his enterprise had just pushed to completion, and which constitutes his appropriate monument.

The political parties had soon found their places and taken them. The Republicans dropped all but their name, and came out unconditionally for the Union. The Central Committee of the Breckinridge Democrats coquetted with the Committee of the Douglas Democrats for a fusion, but the latter declined all offers, and the factions parted company. The convention of the Douglas Democrats met on the 4th of July (1861), under the name of the Union Democratic party—Douglas was dead—and nominated John Conness for Governor; Downey having ruined his chances for a nomination, by a letter to the great May meeting at San Francisco, in which he said: "I did not believe, nor do I now, that an aggressive war should be waged upon any section of the Confederacy, nor do I believe that this Union can be preserved by a coercive policy."

The Breckinridge Democracy met July 23d. Their convention was less remarkable for its milk-and-water resolutions, and its list of unsuccessful candidates nominated for office, than for a crazy speech, made by the eccentric Edmund Randolph. That able lawyer, who had a passion for siding with hopeless minorities, was almost dying with the disease that shortly afterwards proved fatal to him. Appearing in this convention, where his presence was a surprise, and being tempted into a speech, he said, among other things: "Gentlemen, my thoughts and my heart are not here to-night in this house. Far to the East, in the homes from which we came, tyranny and usurpation, with arms in its hands, is this night, perhaps, slaughtering our fathers, our brothers, and our sisters, and outraging our homes in every conceivable way shocking to the heart of humanity and freedom. To me, it seems a waste of time to talk. For God's sake, gentlemen, tell me of battles fought and won. Tell me of usurpers overthrown; that Missouri is again a free State, no longer crushed under the armed heel of a reckless and odious despot. Tell me that the

State of Maryland lives again; and oh! gentlemen, let us read, let us hear at the first moment that not one hostile foot now treads the soil of Virginia. [Applause and cheers.] If this be rebellion, then I am a rebel. Do you want a traitor, then I am a traitor. For God's sake speed the ball; may the lead go quick to his heart, and may our country be free from this despot usurper that now claims the name of President of the United States. [Cheers.]"

The result of the election settled the status of California abroad. The Republicans and Union Democrats together polled eighty-six thousand nine hundred and eighty votes; the Breckinridge Democrats, thirty-two thousand seven hundred and fifty-one. In his retiring message, Governor Downey claimed that he had faithfully represented the people on the Union and War questions. "Although," said he, "with one single exception, the only Executive of all the Free States entertaining political proclivities at variance with the party administering the National Government, not one of them can have displayed a greater promptitude in obeying every constitutional requisition of the President." However, when, a few days later, Leland Stanford was inaugurated, the people breathed more freely, for now their Executive was unequivocally, and without any reservations, for the Union.

CHAP.
XL.

1861-
1864.

In Congress, California was unfortunately represented at first. The course that Senator Gwin has since taken was expected of him. Still, in his last session, he denied that he had said in case of a disruption California would go with the South, and protested that she was for the Union. His exit from the Senate was occasion of great joy to the State that so long honored him.

Senator Latham, before the election of Lincoln, had predicted that California, if the division came, would either go with the South or set up for herself. At the session of 1860-61, he took back the prediction, saying he was satisfied he had mistaken the sentiments of the people. Returning to California in the spring of 1861, he made Union speeches on the stump. In the Senate, he voted generally to sustain the war policy of the Administration; but, returning in the summer of 1862 to California, he went about denouncing the Administration, parading its alleged corruption, charging that it had perverted the war into a war of abolition. So he was quietly shelved.

Senator McDougall, who succeeded Gwin, grievously disappointed those to whom he owed his election. He voted most war measures, but he seemed at heart with the opposition. The Legislature of 1864, by concurrent resolution, charged him with violating the letter and spirit of his pledges, and repudiated him as a wilful misrepresentative of the wishes, the opinions, and habits of the people.

Senator Conness, who succeeded Latham on the great questions involving the life of the nation, has, so far, truly represented his constituents.

In the early summer of 1862, impressed with the necessity of uniting more firmly all friends of the Union to prevent accidents that would damage the reputation of the State, or cause in the General Government any possible suspicion of the loyalty of California, the Republicans and Union Democrats united in one strong Union party. The Republicans laid down their old organization at once; the Union Democratic leaders, lagging behind the rank and file, still adhered to theirs. The only State officer to be elected that year was the Superintendent of Common Schools. The Union candidate received some thirteen thousand majority over both the other candidates, though one of them was the nominee of the still surviving Union Democratic organization. In the fall of 1863 a better opportunity was afforded for a test of the strength of parties. The Union party nominated F. F. Low for Governor; the Democrats chose their strongest man, ex-Governor Downey, who still professed Unionism; and there was no third candidate. Low had nineteen thousand six hundred and sixty-one majority, and was elected. Three members of Congress were elected—all thoroughly for the Union, and disposed to stand by the Administration in its most earnest measures for the vigorous prosecution of the war. The Legislatures for the years 1862, 1863, and 1864 vied with each other in the expression of the immovable determination of the people to sustain the Union at every hazard. Nothing more could be asked in the way of pledges.

And now, as in every department the State was right loyally represented, it was fortunate that the amendments to the Constitution had gone into effect, under which the State officers were to serve four years, the Legislature to meet but once in two years, and the Supreme Court to be reorganized by the election of five judges, and the one of them who drew the longest term to hold office for ten years. The Judicial election (1863) resulted in the election of five first-class lawyers to the bench—S. W. Sanderson, O. L. Shafter, John Curry, Lorenzo Sawyer, and A. L. Rhodes; men whose ability, purity, and patriotism were alike unquestioned.

In whatever other way California could prove her loyalty, she did it heartily. In accordance with the requisition of the General Government, two regiments of cavalry and five of infantry were organized in the fall of 1861. A part of these troops were set to garrison the forts on the Pacific, a part were sent East by steamer, and a column of seventeen companies, five of them cavalry, crossed the plains for New Mexico. There was no draft in California, her quota never having been announced to the provost-marshal.

She expressed her eagerness through the press and her representatives to furnish her full quota of men for the army, but her great distance from the seat of war led the Government to decline her tendered aid to any large extent. However, many citizens left business, went East, and entered the service, being accredited to other States.

There was not the zeal for volunteering here that sometimes swept over that portion of the North nearer to the field of action; for the prospect of being shut up in Pacific coast forts, or sent to hunt Indians, was not as well calculated to kindle enthusiasm, as when, by enlisting, one might reasonably expect to meet rebel foes, and expend on them the indignation he felt at the sight of traitors struggling to overthrow the best of human governments.

At a time when relief for wounded soldiers was most needed, citizens of the State contributed seven hundred thousand dollars in gold to the Sanitary Commission; and to other organized devices for aiding those on whom the war bore heavily, they were proportionately generous.

Congress, at the special session of 1861, imposed a direct tax upon all the States. California was the first to collect and pay her proportion, which amounted to nearly two hundred and fifty-five thousand dollars. Though mostly collected in gold, the State Treasurer paid it over in greenbacks, to the great disgust and indignation of the people, who felt that such economy was at the expense of their reputation. The Legislature turned the difference in the exchange over to the benefit of the United States volunteers from the State.

There was only one point on which the patriotism of California could be misunderstood. Gold and silver constituted the exclusive currency of the State, yet United States paper, which early depreciated from the gold value expressed by its face, had been made a legal tender by act of Congress. To avoid collisions between debtors and creditors, and to maintain credit upon a sound basis, the Legislature of 1863 enacted a law which required the payment of debts in any specified currency agreed upon by a written contract. The whole mercantile community had urged the law. Without it, they said, credit must vanish; no man would lend gold, or sell goods at gold prices, when there was danger that on the day

of settlement he would be tendered depreciated
paper in payment. The opponents of the law
protested that it was a virtual nullification of
an act of Congress; every State should encourage the Government by accepting its money.
Then, would capital flow into a country where
the national dollar lost half its value making
the transit?

The act went into instant operation, and the
same Supreme Court that pronounced the legal-tender act in accordance with the Constitution
of the United States, decided the specific contract act in harmony with the State Constitution. The result was gratifying. Public sentiment settled down upon the use of two distinct currencies. Even without a written contract it was understood that an honorable man
paid his debts in gold, unless he had originally
stipulated to pay in paper. The difference in
exchange upon Eastern capitals greatly favored
purchasers in those markets under the high
prices ruling there. Californians, on striking
the balance, could scarcely discover that they
suffered at all from the war or war prices. One
obtains a fresh impression of the extent of our
country when he sees so vast a war raging over
such wide fields, yet sees a State within the
Union, sympathizing heartily with the Government, busy in all the arts of peace, experiencing

no financial inconvenience, and feeling no appreciable share of the burden.

No political party had dared for years to suggest the propriety of a tax upon the mines. The General Government owned them, yet it was obviously to the general benefit that they be diligently worked, and that nothing hinder their production. Without the gold of California the expenses of the war could not be met; nothing must discourage its constant and steady flow. But every thing else was being roundly taxed. Was it right to exempt one business so profitable—one class of laborers so able to pay? In 1864, Congress levied a tax of one-half of one per cent. upon gold and silver bullion, to be paid by the assayer; and the patriotism of the people restrained them from even a murmur of objection.

When, in November, the fairest of opportunities was afforded, by a Presidential election, to test the sentiment of the State, the ticket pledged to Lincoln and Johnson was elected by thirty thousand majority.

Californians could not be indifferent spectators of the great events passing in the Mississippi Valley and the Atlantic and Gulf States. Even if they had had no stake in the struggle between barbarism and civilization, no share in the glory of establishing the Union in perpetuity, or the shame of permitting its dissolution, they knew too many of the actors on both sides to stand by as cool observers without emotion.

The regular army and navy being small before the war, most of the officers of rank had in their turn spent some time upon the Pacific coast. Grant was long stationed in Oregon. The leading men of California were on terms of intimacy with Sherman, who was resident partner of the banking house of Lucas, Turner & Co., having narrowly escaped with his life on his arrival, in 1853, by swimming ashore from the wreck of the steamer *S. S. Lewis*, just north of the Golden Gate; with Farragut, the hero of New Orleans and Mobile, who was at Mare Island during the Vigilance Committee rule; with Hooker, who owned a ranch in Sonoma County; with Fremont, whose Mariposa estate embraced a notable gold mine; with Halleck and Baker and Shields, who had practised law in San Francisco; with Stoneman, who tried with Hooker, but failed, to make a saw-mill profitable at Bodega; with McPherson, who went from Alcatraz to the war, and was killed in front of Atlanta; with Lander, Buell, Ord, Keyes, Heintzelman, and Sumner, who chafed at his long detention on the Pacific side while younger men were reaping such harvests of fame; with the veteran Wool, with Harney, Denver, Naglee, and Geary, the first

CHAP. XL.

1864.

mayor of San Francisco; with Hancock and Stone, Porter, Boggs, and many others whose achievements, in different degrees, contributed to the lustre of American arms, and helped to crush the great rebellion.

Nor in the enemy's ranks were there lacking men who had cut some figure in the State's history. Gwin maintained a show of neutrality at first; then escaped through the lines to Mississippi. When Grant's army came into those parts, the house where his daughter lived was burned; the family retired to Richmond, and afterwards, running the blockade at Wilmington, escaped into France. Albert Sydney Johnston went from commanding the Pacific Department to commanding Confederate soldiers. Major Garnett, who was sent out with T. Butler King by President Taylor, to urge the organization of a State Government, and who devised the State seal, which, with amendments, was adopted, went East when Virginia seceded, and fell in battle, rallying his men to resist McClellan's force in West Virginia. B. F. Cheatham, of Stockton, was made a major-general in the Confederate service, and was at Belmont and Shiloh, Perryville, Murfreesboro', and Chickamauga. Comptroller Brooks was a volunteer aide in Cheatham's staff at Chickamauga. Calhoun Benham was on Johnston's staff at Shiloh, and afterwards with Breckinridge.

Judge Terry was on Bragg's staff at Chickamauga. Magruder, famous, when a captain in the United States army on this coast, for being so generally intoxicated, had charge of the defences of Yorktown when McClellan attempted the peninsular route to Richmond. Herbert, the member of Congress who killed the Irish waiter, was killed on occasion of Banks's Red River expedition. Many another resident, whom California was happy to spare, joined the Confederates, and kept their sympathizers at home well posted with rebel news.

The patriotism of California, in its popular form, was excessively radical. It believed in the extirpation of slavery as the root and cause of the war. The loyal press maintained jealous watch over suspicious quarters. Loyal Leagues were extensively organized, and did good service quietly in keeping the peace.

One little schooner, the *Chapman*, was fitted out from San Francisco secretly, for a piratical excursion, but she was overhauled before sailing, and confiscated. The two principals to this nefarious scheme were tried, convicted, and imprisoned. But one of them (Rubery, the Englishman) was pardoned by the President, at the solicitation of John Bright; the other (Ridgley Greathouse) was released, after a brief confinement, by Judge Hoffman's strict con-

CHAP. XL.
1864.

struction of the President's Amnesty Proclamation.

Until the Presidential campaign of 1864, it was rare to hear a public disloyal utterance in California. A few violent haranguers, such as "General" Chipman, E. J. C. Kewen, and C. L. Weller, ex-postmaster of San Francisco, were arrested and lodged in Alcatraz, for using treasonable language publicly and defiantly, but their own political friends refused them any capital or special consideration in the conventions on the strength of their martyrdom. Brigadier-General Wright, who, after Sumner's return East, and until General McDowell in 1864 relieved him, had command of the Pacific Department, was as prudent as prompt, and as delicate as firm, in the exercise of military authority. The general unanimity of the people made his task easy; yet a less judicious commander might have precipitated trouble any month.

CHAPTER XLI.

RESOURCES OF THE STATE.

Notwithstanding that every year more and more of the treasure of the mines is detained in the country for permanent investment in its enterprises, and for improvement of its homes, the export keeps steadily on at nearly the old figures. The steamers, for years leaving three times a month, with a regularity quite surprising, took each more than a million to cast into the circulation of the world. This is a marvel, considering the alleged hazards of every mine, and the lottery that gold-hunting is said to be, even when the enlarged area of the gold-field is taken into account. It forces the conclusion that the business, after all, is much more steady and regular than is generally admitted.

The export of treasure from San Francisco, as manifested at the Custom-House, was, in 1857, $48,976,697; in 1858, $47,548,025; in 1859, $47,640,462; in 1860, $42,303,345; in 1861, $40,639,089; in 1862, $42,561,761; and in 1863, $46,071,920. Since 1858, the amounts named embrace several millions a year, from

CHAP. XLI.
1864.

mines outside of California; more than enough to balance the increasing amounts retained in the State, for it is not to be doubted that the gold yield of California, after increasing till 1853, when over fifty-seven millions were exported, has since gradually fallen off, for reasons to be named hereafter.

The shallow placers or "dry diggings" of 1849 and 1850 appeared, before 1862, to be, for profitable American work, about exhausted. They were wrought almost exclusively by Chinese, whose earnings are a clear gain to the country, for they glean with profit where whites could not make wages. John hoards some of it, but he is a good liver after his fashion, and is by no means a bad customer of the mountain storekeepers. The heavy rains of the winter of 1861 and 1862, by supplying the mines with plenty of water at just the right time for their operations, and still more by washing away the accumulated tailings of several years' work, laid bare many a rich deposit, and made the placer-mining profitable again.

The hydraulic method still pays well, though not as well as a year or two ago; for the richest hills have been sifted, and hydraulicing involves such large expenditures for water, for sluice-boxes, for quicksilver, and for gunpowder to loosen the compact gravel, that, unless the ground is very rich, they cannot be afforded.

Very costly, rather risky, yet, on the whole, very remunerative is the system of tunnelling, which, by 1862, had outgrown in favor most other methods. It bores deep into mountains to the supposed beds of ancient rivers. The peril of missing the deposit is great, but when it is hit the reward is munificent.

Attempts to separate gold from the quartz rock were early made on a large scale, and with results that discouraged capitalists. In 1856 quartz-mining took a new start, and now there is not a mining county in the State but has several large, expensive, well-appointed mills, stamping and crushing the rock to a powder, and yielding lucrative returns to owners.

The yield of gold has been further affected by drought, by excessive rains, and lately by a series of rushes to other mining fields, that threatened to leave the interior of the State a desert: to Fraser River, in 1858, draining the State, it was estimated, of twenty thousand of its population, most of which, however, found its way back again not long afterwards; to Washoe, in 1860 and 1861, when about the same number crossed from California to the eastern slope of the Sierra Nevadas, and most of them stayed there; to the Salmon River, and other Washington Territory placers, in 1861 and 1862; to Idaho, as the Salmon River district is now

CHAP. XLI.

1864.

called, and Arizona, in 1863; and to Idaho, the Colorado region, and Mexico, in 1864.

These annual rushes have left many a locality, that was all alive with busy, boisterous men in the fall, desolate and silent in the spring; and many a village that was full of excitement in 1858, is now drowsy and still, having parted with half its population since then. The largest interior cities suffered much by the depletion. Sacramento has not the population to-day that it had four years ago; Marysville's growth was checked, Stockton's progress arrested, though not so violently.

Since the spring of 1861, mines of silver, copper, and coal have been opened within the State. The silver veins of finest promise were chiefly found in the tier of counties lying along the western base of the Sierra Nevada, and in the Owen's River region.

Of copper, the richest and most explored deposits are in Calaveras County, where the new business has started a new city into existence—Copperopolis. The copper ore is convertible into cash at the mouth of the mine. It is all smelted abroad, and no outlay for mills or furnaces is required. The ore goes East or to Europe as freight, and already appreciably helps returning ships to eke out a return cargo.

The coal is not of the secondary, but of the tertiary formation, good enough for creating

NEW MINERAL DISCOVERIES. 605

steam or for purposes of fuel, but not the best to work iron with. It is bituminous, breaks readily, kindles easily, and burns with a flame. It is already produced in large quantity, and at a price that makes it unprofitable to import coal for ordinary uses.

CHAP. XLI.
1864.

Inexhaustible quantities of iron have been developed, but none is yet rendered available for use. Asphaltum in immense beds, and petroleum springs, if geologists and experts are to be trusted, are found in the southern part of the State. The former article, taken from the sea-shore, near Santa Barbara, is already extensively used for pavements and roofs.

Besides these staples, other useful minerals, in wonderful variety and astonishing abundance, are found. Borax—a lake of it—salt, soda, sulphur, flavoring a thousand springs, chalk, gypsum, nitre, marble, and building-stone—the catalogue of those not found here would be briefer than of those which are—are plenty. Yet some that make up the bulk of mountains, and are quite accessible, must wait for capital to abound, and wages to fall, before coming into market.

A curious mania possessed the people through 1863. "Prospecting" was the fever in the blood of the masses. There was a general scouring of the State; a ransacking in all gulches; a testing of the character of the rocks

1863.

in all localities. In the most isolated regions, and up to the fire limits of the cities, there were little parties of men with pick and hammer breaking off the outcroppings of ledges, and with acids testing them for copper, silver, quicksilver, and other metals. Astonishing results followed. The coveted minerals were found in thousands of places. In the "cow counties" as well as in the mining counties, in the Coast Range as well as in the foot-hills of the Sierras, north and south, and up to the bluffs of the ocean, amazing discoveries were reported.

These prospecters generally had their expenses paid by a company, the members at home furnishing capital, and the travellers the work. Other enterprising men went out alone, and on their own account, searched diligently, and when they found what they sought, broke off a bagful of specimens, entered their claims at the nearest Recorder's office, and hastened to San Francisco to organize a company to hold and develop them.

There was, no doubt, a great deal of false information paraded, and many companies located on ledges that had no existence, to open "leads" entirely imaginary. Yet the greater number acted upon honest if mistaken reports; if the members had visited the locality where their hopes lay locked, they would not have been undeceived; though now to see the spot would excite only merriment at the thought that such a commonplace rock could be accepted as the corner-stone of the grand fortune fancy once reared on it. More than a thousand companies were organized in the State. Brokers' offices, with their windows full of choice specimens, threatened to monopolize the best business stands in the cities. Long-established firms sacrificed the advertisement of their plate-glass windows, brokers offering such tempting rent for a desk and a few feet of glazed frontage. Several boards of brokers were started, where shares in all sorts of companies were sold and reported daily.

The assessments upon stockholders in the mining companies were very light at first, just enough to pay for office rent, a set of books, the engraving of a handsome certificate of stock, and possibly to keep a man or two developing the claim.

Almost everybody bought mining stock. Nothing but war news could check the perpetual talk of "feet," "outcroppings," "indications," "sulphurets," and "ores." No profession or class, age or sex, was exempt from the epidemic. Shrewd merchants and careful bankers invested the profits of their legitimate business, sometimes infringed upon their invested capital. Sharp lawyers sold their homesteads for shares. Clerks anticipated their salaries, laborers "salt-

CHAP. XLI.

1864.

ed away" their wages, and washerwomen their earnings in "promising mines."

Some, getting their "feet" rapidly off their hands at an advance, made large gains, and their good luck stimulated all the rest. Oftener, as the assessments increased, the shareholders agreed to consider the company that hired them a "bilk," forfeit the stock, and plunge the deeper into some other stock, to make amends. The lists of delinquent stockholders had to be published for a given time, before the shares could be sold at auction. These lists occupied a full page in more than one of the largest newspapers daily. It excited no surprise to see the soundest merchants' names figuring in these lists for large delinquencies, nor did it damage their credit. Perhaps they were there to "bear the stock"—then the small holders would cling the tighter, determined not to be "frozen out." Commercial speculations were almost entirely neglected, and Front Street took its heaviest risks in feet. The companies always had a nominal capital of immense amount. Any thing under hundreds of thousands of dollars was deemed a small affair.

The engraved mining-field was not limited to California. The prospecters and claim-takers traversed the desert far east of Virginia City and Aurora, and made populous the barren mountains of Reese River and Humboldt. They crossed the Colorado to the San Francisco Mountains of Arizona. They "took up" the islands of the coast. They overran the Mexican border, and to the eastward of the Gulf of California, and among the sterile mountains of Lower California made their camps.

A stranger coming into the State and inoculated against the strange infection, in view of the immense nominal capital of the companies, observing how every knot of men discussed little lumps of commonplace rock, and talked geologically, hearing the wild talk of Presidents, Secretaries, and Directors as to the value of their claims, yet noting that many a President of a company incorporated for a million dollars could not pay for his lunch in lack of either cash or credit, would have pronounced it a sweeping madness, in which high and low, educated and ignorant, men, women, and children, timid capitalists and penniless paupers, were alike involved.

Some said they had seen fortune beckon before, and, in their scepticism refusing to follow, lost what proved to be a splendid chance; they trusted they were wiser now. Some bought as speculators, seldom paying cash, but exchanging scrip—"wild-cat" for "promising," and that for dividend-paying, of which, curiously enough, there were but four or five companies in the market, for few of the old, faithfully-wrought

610   THE HISTORY OF CALIFORNIA.

CHAP.
XLI.

1863.

mines were called on Exchange. Their hope was that, by turning over their purchases every few days, and selling enough to pay assessments, they would escape every peril of loss; and they did, until the crash came, and they still had a hatful on hand worth only its weight at the paper-maker's. Others said the man was a fool who neglected such an opportunity, and sent for all their brothers to come out with what they could scrape together and be rich.

If one said the whole thing was a delusion, he was pointed to the fact that the founderies were busy day and night filling orders for machinery to go to these mines in Mexico, Nevada, and unnamed because unknown regions both near and afar off. The few sober ones, who were not carried away by the excitement, held that, while many must suffer as the result of their stock speculations, the general effect of the prospecting out of which they grew would not be bad; that the soil of the State, for all this ransacking, would develop a noble harvest of minerals at some early future day.

1864.

The bubble burst without any noise of explosion. In the summer of 1864 there was a sudden fall in the shares of the few dividend-paying mines. Ophir dropped fifty per cent.; Gould and Curry, which had been taken as the standard of successful mines, sank still more. Then the wild-cat quietly stole out of sight.

THE BUBBLE BURSTS.

CHAP. XLI.
1864.

The brokers vacated their offices; a few men went into insolvency. The masses pocketed their losses, and said little about them. They filed away their certificates of stock, lately so carefully treasured, as curious, useless pictures, tokens of experience gained, and pushed on with their legitimate business. It is astonishing, considering the amount of money that changed hands during the popular possession by this mania, how few were seriously injured by it. Wages were good, salaries high, business brisk. They paid high for their experience, and could afford it. The map of the country was written over with the localities of mineral deposits rich and abiding, though it might not pay to work them for some time to come. The prospecters had made a geological reconnoissance in force. As of all such preliminary surveys, the advantages were not immediately developed.

Agriculture grows rapidly in importance. Though little more than a third of the area of the State is tillable land, not over a fortieth part of that tillable portion is cultivated. With the disadvantage of a summer so dry that much of the grain land will not, or rather has not produced vegetables and fruit without irrigation, the farmer is amply compensated in the warmth of the winter, the length of the growing season, the prolific character of all vegetable life in California, and the needlessness of barns and granaries. No vegetables are raised between Boston and Charleston that do not thrive in its soil. Fruit in every variety, common in semi-tropical or temperate climates, comes into early bearing, and for abundance, size, or flavor, has no competitor.

It is held by some who have been in the business abroad, that there is no better grape land. All foreign varieties flourish, as well as the old mission stock. The crop never fails. No disease affects the vines thus far, and they are productive beyond precedent. Our wine is in the Eastern markets, and, though susceptible of great improvement, stands well, and is likely to be in greater demand every year.

It is settled that California can feed herself, and compete on favorable terms in supplying Europe when its grain crop fails. The California wheat exceeds in strength and dryness, qualities that especially adapt it for transportation through the tropics. The same qualities added to its whiteness, thin skin, plumpness and weight, make it a favorite in all markets. In 1861 the wheat and flour exported from San Francisco was valued half a million of dollars higher than the provisions imported, including tea, coffee, and spices.

Hitherto little has been manufactured in California which could be as well imported.

Wages, though still higher than in any other equally civilized country, are gradually falling, and with their fall manufactures will multiply.

Nothing else prevents the making of our finest woollen cloths, for the finest qualities of wool are liberally produced. The experiments that have been made in manufacturing the coarser woollen goods, glass, powder, paper, and wooden ware, are flattering. Raising no cotton, smelting no iron as yet, here are large classes of goods long hence to be imported. We make our own lumber, and export much, but since there is a lack of tough woods in the State, our carriages, or at least our carriage materials, must be imported.

San Francisco is inevitably destined to be the principal port of the Pacific. Her imports and her exports are about equal. Of the latter, gold is the chief. It is easy to handle, and the market is always clamorous for it. Unlike wheat, which becomes a drug whenever all wheat-fields yield abundantly, our principal export always commands a fixed, unvarying price.

Of our other exports, hides are at present an important item, but that resource will fail as better notions of ranching come into fashion, and cattle are esteemed for something else than their hides and tallow. Besides the vast amounts of quicksilver used in the State, more than a million dollars' worth was exported in

1861. The silver and copper ore sent abroad are rapidly increasing. The exports other than gold in 1861 equalled more than one-sixth of the gold export—a fact of great significance and promise.

Of the arrivals, during the year named, nearly half the tonnage was from domestic Pacific ports. Since then, the trade with Mexico has grown beyond calculation, and that with the northern coast enjoys a wholesome increase. The tonnage arriving from China was almost equal to that from Europe. Every year more and more whalers turn in for supplies.

Business constantly assumes more stability, and less the character of speculation. In 1859, the applications for the benefit of the insolvent act were less than one-third the applications in 1855, and the number still decreases. Yet, the ruling rate of interest, from one per cent. a month on the best securities, to two and a half per cent., shows that capital still regards all business as perilous, or, at least, acts on the suspicion.

Gold and silver coins of the United States are the almost exclusive currency, but no coin less than a dime is in general use, though half-dimes are occasionally given and taken at retail stores in the cities. Coppers and nickels are curious rarities. Legal-tender notes of the United States are accepted for Federal taxes, for judgments rendered (in default of a specific contract) or fines inflicted by the courts. Otherwise they pass only at the ruling discount from gold.

CHAPTER XLII.

QUARRELS WITH NATURE.—COMPENSATIONS FOR APPARENT MISFORTUNES.

CHAP. XLII.
1864.

It has been supposed that Nature, so lavish of gifts to California, like a jealous lover, had many quarrels with her. If it was so in the beginning, time, society, and the presence of strangers are effecting a cure.

The earthquakes which tradition and the early Mission records make really serious affairs, though frequent, have seldom of late done even the slightest harm. They inspire no more terror than a thunderstorm at the East, and are less to be dreaded.

Ignorance, or neglect of the warnings of natives and old residents, exposed the sites of several inland cities to overflow from the streams on whose banks they were built. Thus Sacramento was flooded January, 1850, in March, 1852, and from Christmas of that year to New Years of 1853, while the place was still black with the ruins of the great November fire, that destroyed the entire business portion of the city; and Marysville was flooded in 1852. Experience taught the necessity of building strong levees above the level of the river at flood, and of raising the street grades.

This done, the cities enjoyed immunity from floods until the winter of 1861–2, when double the amount of rain fell that California had seen any year since the American conquest. The snows on the mountains melted under the warm rain, and the rivers, whose beds were filled with the tailings from the mines, soon overflowed their banks.

The Sacramento levees would have held up against it, but that a railroad company had carelessly filled in with an embankment a space intended to be left as a bridge. The waters of the American, overflowing above the city, and being prevented by the dam of the railroad embankment from passing off behind it, flowed over the eastern levee and filled the city. This was the 9th of December. In a few hours the southern levee burst, and the waters in the city began to subside—small houses, furniture, cattle, and horses being carried away in the torrent through the crevasse. A million dollars' worth of property was destroyed in this brief submergence, and more than five thousand sufferers required aid from the Howard Association of Sacramento, which disbursed some sixty thousand dollars for their relief, two-thirds of it being contributed by San Francisco.

CHAP. XLII.
1862.

On the 10th of January, 1862, the flood came again, stronger and more devastating than before. The effort to repair the levees had proved a failure. As the waters rose in their dwellings, the occupants of the larger buildings took to the upper stories. Those in smaller houses either fled to the pavilion prepared for them, or, if too late for that, climbed up on beds, tables, chairs, keeping their flag or light of distress out to guide the relief-boats to their rescue. The streets for weeks were traversed only by boats. From the capitol roof no land was visible in or near the city, except a small portion of the levee. Perhaps half the population of fifteen thousand sought refuge temporarily in other cities, chiefly in San Francisco, which sent up relief steamers with cooked provisions, money, and men, and put Platt's Hall at the service of the rescued.

But not Sacramento alone; Stockton, Marysville, Napa, Knight's Ferry, Ione, Jacksonville, and numerous other places were drowned. Houses, furniture, goods, fences were washed away. The cattle crowded in herds to the knolls, and in herds perished, as, after days of shivering and starvation, they tumbled into the sea. Their carcasses dotted the plains a year later. From the foot-hills of the Sierra to those of the Coast Range, from the foot of Shasta to the hills that lead up to the Tehon Pass, all the plain was converted into a lake, not unlike in shape and size Lake Michigan. This immense body of water discharged itself through Suisun Bay, the Straits of Carquines, San Francisco Bay, and the Golden Gate to the ocean. The height of the waters in the bay was not much increased, but there ceased to flow in any flood-tide through the Golden Gate. For weeks the turbid yellow stream rolled continuously out, bearing tules, brush, and trees with it far out to sea.

Is a flood to be anticipated periodically? Is it to be provided against and still dreaded? The straits at the head of Suisun Bay were too narrow an outlet for the waters accumulated in the Sacramento and San Joaquin valleys; that cause of a wide-spread overflow is not likely to be remedied until some other similar disaster indicates the necessity. But the flood itself washed out the tailings from thousands of flumes that had filled the river-beds. As there will be less hereafter than heretofore of the kind of mining which disturbs the courses of the rivers, that prominent cause of floods is to a large extent removed. The exposed cities have lifted their main streets and levees above the highest water-mark. The farmers on the plains recognize the advantage of erecting their houses on a shallow mound, or at least of having one spot of higher ground on their premises

CHAP. XLII.
1862.

as a place of refuge for the cattle. As there had been no precedent for such a flood within the memory of living men in the State, so no other such is anticipated, especially as the change from sluice and placer and hydraulic to quartz mining, will diminish the main cause of overflows that is subject to human control.

California has occasionally suffered in several leading interests from drought. The stranger travelling through the southern part of the State in the late summer or early fall, would fancy himself on a desert. The rivers that were swollen in December, are mere rills in their broad, dry beds. The earth that in May was carpeted with verdure, and gay with an endless variety of flowers, is brown, and no sign of grass appears. Yet, to his astonishment, thousands of cattle browse on the apparent desert and grow fat. Closer examination shows the earth covered with the burs and stalks of a clover which the cattle enjoy and thrive on finely. With the first rains of November the grasses start, and as the winter deepens and spring approaches, flowers of all hues glorify the abundant pasture-grounds.

But occasionally the fall rains come early and spoil the dry feed, and the spring rains late, which is hard for the cattle; or the rains fail altogether.

The season of 1809 and 1810 was an almost rainless one. The old missionaries took the hint, and after that saw that a stock of corn, dried beef, and beans sufficient for two years were laid in. They set their Indians to fishing, too, that the sea might on emergency eke out the food-supplies of the land.

Again in 1820 and 1821 there was little rain. The great flocks and herds were straitened for pasture, and, by order of Governor Sola, hundreds of mares were killed, to save the pasture they would eat. The Indians were sent out by the Fathers to gather pine-nuts and acorns, and thus economize their store.

Between 1828 and 1830, a drought of nearly two years' duration afflicted the land, so that, as was estimated, forty thousand cattle died. The crops (of the Southern Missions) were scarcely more than sufficed for seed, and the wells and springs of Monterey gave out.

In 1840 and 1841, there was no rain at the south for fourteen months, but the range of the cattle was greater, and they suffered less than before. It is said that in 1855 and 1856, there were seventy thousand cattle lost below Monterey—dying of starvation and cold, after the fall rains destroyed the old feed, and before the new was fit to be eaten.

The winters of 1862-3 and 1863-4 were unusually dry, and the cattle of the South suffered severely. Thousands were driven to the Matanzas to be slaughtered for their hides, and other thousands, too much wasted to endure the drive to the coast, perished on the plains. The grain crop of the central part of the State was scarcely half what was expected. But the Russian River region, and certain other localities near the coast and in the foot-hills, were singularly favored with rain, so that there was no scarcity of grain, and in the short supply the farmers got for their small crops about as much as for their larger ones before.

The apparent misfortunes of California have not generally proved as serious hinderances to her growth as was anticipated. Some of them have soon discovered themselves blessings in disguise, while some, though very costly and at first glance altogether ruinous, have developed afterwards undreamed-of compensations. Fires in the early days ravaged the towns, and the value of the destroyed improvements seemed utterly lost. The Mission Fathers used to require the Indians to build their huts of combustible material, so that when they became intolerably filthy they could be burned down and out of the way. Some of our early fires did the same kindly office for the pioneers. Often badly chosen sites for cities were deserted because a fire swept off all that tempted the settlers—already aware of their mistake—to stay, and then a better site was chosen. The floods, that seemed to fetch nothing but ruin, had their compensations. Interior towns, built below a safe grade, were graded up while it cost comparatively little to do it, and levees were seasonably constructed; sterile hill-sides were made fruitful; the breadth of the grain crop largely extended from the valleys up the slopes; the tailings of old mines were washed off, and new placers revealed.

The drought of 1863 and 1864 was not altogether evil. The markets of meats, vegetables, and grains were still abundantly supplied, and the enhanced prices made the round year a better one than its flushed predecessor, for many farmers and ranchmen. If the event shows that the negligent system prevalent in the southern counties is to any large degree abandoned by the owners of herds, the drought will prove to have benefited them immeasurably. A man owns a hundred wild cattle, and cannot produce a pound of butter or cheese from them: to get a glass of milk, perhaps will require an hour's labor with a vaquero to lasso the "tame cow," and an assistant or two to milk her. If drought or flood or famine will conspire to break up the lazy style of herding and farming at the south, the plains that are at times deserts may become fruitful prairies, and homesteads dot the long, dreary, solitary leagues that lie waste between San Juan and Los Angeles. A dozen well-conditioned tame cattle might make richer than he is the owner of hundreds of wild cattle, worth only the tallow and hides of their carcasses.

Every enforced change in the method of mining has seemed to threaten ruin, yet generally has resulted in permanent benefit to the region accepting the change. The exhausted placers went into the hands of Chinamen, whose aggregate washings and pickings are all clear gain to the gold in circulation. The old placer diggers, provided with the capital that the pan and rocker helped them to, turned to tunnels and hydraulics, which paid better dividends. When the richest hills are worked and sifted, and water charges are too high to leave hydraulicing profitable any longer, the rivers scoop out their beds again, and the danger of floods is reduced. In some of the rivers, where three years ago only a thin, yellow, muddy stream was moving, the bars already begin to be removed, and the channel to deepen, along which pours a clear tide again, reminding the early settlers of the look it bore when they first saw it. Again, every failure of a paying bar disperses a camp of miners to prospecting, and new resources are brought to light. The returning wave from Washoe, in 1861, developed the copper of Calaveras, and many a deposit of silver; for the miners, when not too fiercely bitten with the fury for the last discovery, pick both ways as they travel, and, especially as they return, question all the promising croppings, and are geological surveyors of the most practical sort.

From 1860 to 1862, inclusive, the State's interior population apparently decreased. As it was owing principally to the rush to Washington Territory, Idaho, and Washoe, it did not seem like so utter a loss as when, in 1858 and 1859, British Columbia was absorbing its enterprise and industry. This drifting into other Territories belonging to the Union could be borne the better, since it was only sowing, beyond the border, harvests that California and the Union would jointly reap. But it was rough at first on California. The middle tier of counties suffered most. Some of their mining towns lost half their population. But the compensation was surprisingly quick in coming. Splendid roads over the mountains were constructed, to meet the demands of the new settlements beyond the eastern border. A new and profitable market was opened for all that the orchardists and gardeners and farmers in the foot-hills could raise, and agriculture competed with mining as a profitable employment in what had been deemed exclusively mining counties. Factors appeared at the door of every man who had any thing in the shape of produce or grain to sell, with tempting prices

CHAP. XLII.
1862.

in hand. It stimulated the permanent settlement of the rich little valleys, and men, who had drifted ever since their arrival, sent for their families and improved homesteads. Washoe did for Californians what Congress should have done long ago; it gave the miner an interest in the land. Then founderies started up in all the cities to supply a clamorous demand for machinery; and when Washoe abated her demand, the stock of machinery that could be so easily turned out of these founderies stimulated prospecting for other fields within our borders to employ it.

The social compensations for those rushes, that looked so frightful as they approached, were still more remarkable. With each rush went the worst class first. The gambling and drinking saloons and houses of ill-fame were the first to close up. They who remained gave more attention to their homes, to the education of their growing families, to their moral training. Cottages took on paint, flowers crept more boldly up to the windows, vines trailed their glories to the sun; and the cottage owners were not ashamed of these evidences of a taste that was deemed effeminate by the departed roysterers. School-houses were open longer in the year; churches lost their musty, unventilated air.

It is growing all the while clearer that these

rushes cause far more apparent than real loss to the community. The class that runs, quick as the mercury in the tilted level, at the first report of great diggings in the distance, is not the most desirable class, though it is the noisiest. Streets that were ringing with the songs of a score or two of riotous fellows, perambulating them through the early night, and brilliant with the light of open gambling and drinking saloons, are still and dark now, and the hasty observer might conclude that the life of the town had gone. It is only its wild, unprofitable life that has vanished. A thousand well-to-do, steady people, in their homes, are not as noisy as the score of spendthrifts; a new mining camp of five hundred makes more noise at night than a New England village of five thousand people. But send a popular lecturer, or a good stump speaker, into these dull towns, and he will see the population swarm out to meet and cheer him. Unquestionably there are more elements of permanent prosperity in the State to-day than ever before; and though it is not true of particular localities, of the State as a whole, it is true that the growth has been steady and healthful.

CHAPTER XLIII.

THE PEOPLE AND THE PROSPECTS.

CHAP.
XLIII.
1864.

The sixteen years of its occupation have not changed the early impression of the salubrity of the climate of California. In the low districts, subject to overflow from the rivers, and in the parts where the miners constantly turn new soil to the sun, miasmatic diseases prevail. Rheumatism naturally waits upon the miner who exposes himself in ditches, or lies drilling and picking all day or night in a damp tunnel; for, deep in a tunnel, night and day are indistinguishable.

The strong winds of the coast are severe for persons with sensitive throat or lungs. In San Francisco, throughout the year, the air is bracing, and tempting to work. Probably most of the ailments of the males in that city are due to the inspiriting air—in winter sufficiently cool to make gentle exercise agreeable, yet scarcely cold enough to require a fire, except as a cheerful addition to the picture of an evening at home; in summer serene and delicious in the morning, a little chilly and invigorating with the westerly afternoon winds, which would be always grateful but for the dust and sand with which they are laden—a nuisance that will disappear as the streets come to be more generally planked down or paved, and new blocks of buildings furnish a lee. This very bracing, always stimulating condition of the air, tempts to overwork, and induces the diseases that grow out of constant, unremitting excitement.

It will be remedied in part by fashion, which will establish certain times of the year as the proper ones to visit the coast or retire to the interior, to fly to watering-places, to loiter about the medicinal springs, to see the natural curiosities of the country, Yosemite Valley, the Big Tree groves of Mariposa and Calaveras, the Geysers, or to make excursions to the grape counties in the time of the vintage. At present, fashion only dictates, when one is overworked, a trip to the Sandwich Islands, or overland or by steamer to the East, or to Europe.

Society has wondrously improved since the Vigilance era. Most Californians were enterprising, or they would not have migrated so long a distance; intelligent, or they would have lacked the enterprise their very presence proves. They are great readers, because the majority received at least a common-school education at home, and their love of home, and their isolation, make reading a necessity to obtain the news and pass their leisure pleasantly. The newspaper is in every man's house, and it is doubtful if anywhere the newspaper is more admirably conducted to meet the wants of a people that believe in it. No American papers pay more for the earliest news than the leading journals of San Francisco and Sacramento; none pay more attention to local news and interests; few, if any, are more carefully conducted to prevent misleading those who leave their paper to do their thinking for them. Almost every sect and party has a representative and advocate, if not an organ; and the religious press, though not at all profitable as a business speculation, is influential.

The common schools are at last upon such a basis that in the settled parts of the State any child may obtain as fair a primary education as in an Eastern public school; of course there are regions sparsely populated, where the school-houses are long distances apart, and the schools kept but a small portion of the year. Private and select schools of superior excellence abound in the cities and their vicinity, and are extensively patronized, because parents are suspicious that their children learn too fast and too much in the public schools. Several colleges and professional schools have been planted. Such institutions are of slow growth, but they are rooting firmly and springing with fine promise. As the people of the American colonies long preferred to send their children to Europe to be educated, so hitherto the custom has prevailed in California of sending the boys to the colleges and the girls to the seminaries of the East. The custom will cease as the parents are weaned from their old homes, for motives of economy and the natural desire to keep one's family together conspire to give home schools the preference over even better ones abroad.

The census of 1860 was so shabbily taken, that it almost demands an apology to quote it; yet, in its rude approximation to truth, it exhibits some curious facts. According to its returns, only a little more than one-fourth of the white inhabitants were females. This disproportion of the sexes, greatest in the mining districts and least in the chief cities, accounts for the large though decreasing number of divorces, perhaps for some of the insanity and suicides that startle the community. Add to this that the mildness of the climate makes the people, to a large extent, an out-door people, permits them to hold exchange on the side-walk, tempts them to pleasure excursions into the country the year round, and requires no firesides in their homes, and there are suggested some of the chief social dangers of the State.

CHAP. XLIII.

1864.

In San Francisco the Sabbath is scarcely less generally observed than in the Eastern cities. The most notable difference is, that the theatres are open on the Sabbath as on other evenings, though principally attended by French, German, and Spanish residents. In the country, though church spires and towers give the Christian aspect to all thriving interior towns, the proportion of attendants is exceedingly small, and it is easy to find men brought up under church influences who have not heard a sermon in a year, or only as among the curiosities of the metropolis on visiting it.

Away from the conserving influence of woman and home, living lives of hazard and excitement, there was danger that the masses would acquire habits of intemperance in drinking. The fear was not unfounded, nor the result other than was feared. The bracing climate sustained the hard drinker, and deluded him with the hope of longevity in spite of his excesses, until sudden death terminated his career. The influence of exemplary business partnerships, of Sabbath-school, of church, of home, were potent within their circle, but the mass was outside their circle. A reform which proved widely influential was inaugurated January 1st, 1859. A company of firemen ("Howard, No. 3"), sitting in their engine-house late at night, celebrating New Year after the custom of the country, fell to musing over their prospects, and were vouchsafed a vision of their probable fate. At last they agreed solemnly to discontinue the use of intoxicating liquor—to "dash away the cup." They organized a society of Dashaways, with Frank E. R. Whitney, chief engineer of the fire department of San Francisco, as their president, pledging themselves to drink nothing intoxicating for five and a half months. They kept their promise, and, before reaching the limit of their self-imposed pledge, renewed it for all time. They rented a hall, started a library, opened an intelligence office, had meetings every Sabbath, at which clergymen and others were invited to address them, experience meetings in the afternoon, business and debating meetings in the evenings, went out seeking among their acquaintance for new men to be pledged, played the Good Samaritan to all drunkards, established branch Dashaway associations in other cities, and were felt for good wherever they went. Out of their efforts grew up the Asylum for Inebriates, which has a fine permanent building. They erected a hall of their own, where all strangers are welcome. Many who have been pledged have fallen away and been lost; but scores and hundreds it has saved. Many have doubted if the experiment could finally and lastingly succeed, querying whether the reformation it achieves is radical enough to affect the fruit of a lifetime. Thus far it has succeeded beyond all expectation; it has done immense good at a time when it was most needed, and to a class not accessible to other means of reform.

One question connected with this subject still perplexes the people. The State is to become a great wine-making country. But in wine-growing States the thin wines supplant tea and coffee as table drinks. How will this affect California society? The grapes of the land are rich in sugar and excessive in the production of alcohol. Will the common use of wine made from them lead to abstinence from the poisonous adulterations of imported liquors? or will it but stimulate the appetite to a demand for still fiercer drinks? Opinion is divided on the question, and there is too little experience yet to guide to a correct conclusion.

There is no poor-house in California, and one reason is because there are not many poor. The generation that settled the country is still young and able-bodied. The high cost of removal to the State prohibits poverty from invading it in force, so that its poor are its own. The people directly relieve utter destitution when they hear of it, and, because at San Francisco there are hospitals, asylums, and many societies organized to relieve suffering, ease poverty "over the centre," and assist the ailing, a prevalent method of relief in the country is to help the afflicted down to the city; if there they have no friends, and if to their other griefs they add home-sickness, San Franciscans cheerfully help them back to their Eastern homes.

The Indians are estimated to number, instead of the hundred thousand of the time of admission, from ten thousand to fifteen thousand; and diseases acquired by their contact with the whites, whiskey, to which they are devotedly attached, and frequent skirmishes with the whites, are rapidly reducing that number. The opportunity to benefit them, the question what to do with them, will soon pass. They only haunt the outskirts, and are little real trouble even now.

Governor Weller estimated the expenditures of the State and General Government, in taking care of and fighting Indians, from the admission of the State to 1859, at three million dollars. The Government, observing how the old missionaries made the Indians support themselves and lay up fat stores for the Fathers, devised, in 1853, the Reservation system, but committed the radical blunder of sending out professional politicians as Indian Agents rather than men with some tolerable idea of controlling Indians by moral means, of winning their respect and benefiting them. The result was a digraceful failure. An appropriation of two hundred and fifty thousand dollars annually, for six or seven years, built ample granaries for the prospective crops, furnished pleasant head-quarters for the superintendents and employés, and helped to carry local elections as the Administration at Washington wished them carried, but gave the Indians very little employment or clothing or provisions.

The money was wasted. The fertile nooks composing the Reservations were coveted by the encroaching whites, and pretexts for "clearing out" the Indians were easy. In 1858–9, at Nova Cult, one hundred and fifty Indians, including women and children, were slaughtered—the settlers said they killed their cattle, but neither settlers nor their cattle had any business in the valley. The settlers said the Government did nothing for its wards at King's River, so they drove them over to Fresno. At a station near Mendocino several Indians were murdered. About Humboldt Bay and Pitt River there was a series of massacres; the blood curdles at the recital of the story by those who apologize for the murderers. The massacres were generally called "wars;" sometimes the State took a hand, oftener the Government troops came to the rescue, and, more by over-awing whites than by shooting Indians, re-established peace.

Since 1860 the annual appropriation has been

about fifty thousand dollars. The Indians perhaps get as much as when the sum was five times greater. Probably all that can be done for the miserable remnant, is to give them agents who will treat them with kindness and deal with the Government honestly. Men fit for the post can secure their confidence and rule them by kindness, can save their squaws from being stolen, and their children from being kidnapped. Do that, and they are as harmless as cattle, as inoffensive as sheep. If the General Government will only furnish them supplies enough to pass them over seasons of drought, so that the alternative shall not be famine or cattle-stealing, and compel the whites to let them alone, the Indian question would be settled. They are the wards of the Government at Washington. It, more than the State, is to blame for their maltreatment and abuse. If their fate reflects shame upon the settlers, so does the fate of all their race upon the settlers of the continent—a suggestion that is not made in a spirit of apology, but that any may consider well who meditate throwing the first stone.

The Chinese puzzle is not solved yet. The number of Chinese in the State is estimated at from fifty to sixty thousand, and all belong to one or other of the fur companies that have their head-quarters at San Francisco.

In 1859 the miners in one of the northern counties attempted to eject the Chinese from the mines. The local authorities interfered to prevent the outrage, and Governor Weller, to his credit, aided them against the mob. The Legislature, impelled by a clamor about the competition of coolie with white labor, indulged in a series of spiteful legislation to the annoyance of the Chinese. In 1857 it levied a tax on Chinese immigrants, but the Supreme Court annulled it. In 1859 it taxed Chinese fishermen four dollars a month, and the chief effect was to cause the whites to pay John a little more than they would have done for every pound of fish they bought. In 1862 it passed an act with the direct purpose of discouraging immigration, but the Supreme Court declared it unconstitutional and void. The cigar-makers raised a howl against the Chinese in 1862, and an attempt was made to drive them out of the gardens about San Francisco. But because they were neat and nimble-fingered and worked cheaply, they outlived the persecution; and now they make the cigars, pick the berries for market, do light mechanical work in the woollen and other factories, and are appreciated as quiet, profitable help. The State over, they are creating values out of nothing, of which Americans receive the lion's share. As society grows stable they are sure to get better treatment than hitherto.

If the heathen moralist could say "whatever is human pertains to me," Christians certainly will not oppress these pioneers, though of a heathen race, whose presence is a perpetual challenge to the expansive missionary spirit to do what it can for their Christianization. If, when they meet us half-way, our Christianity cannot impress them, what prospect that their teeming land can be affected by any thing that our missionaries can do?

Kindness tells upon them as upon other folks. A few gather every Sabbath in San Francisco to the Mission Church, which, under the Rev. Mr. Speer, of the Presbyterian Board, or the Rev. Mr. Loomis, his successor, has been maintained since 1852. A few stray into the Sabbath schools and are welcome, while a considerable number attend the evening school established by the City Board of Education for their benefit, and where competent teachers instruct them in English.

There are a few other elements composing the population that do not easily mix with Europeans, but they are feeble in numbers and threaten no trouble. Cosmopolitan beyond all other lands, there is every reason to believe that after the first generation the people will seem homogeneous.

CHAP. XLIII.
1864.

California has conquered ocean and desert, distance and isolation. Regular lines of steamers were early established to convey mails and passengers from New York to San Francisco. At first these steamers ran monthly; then every fortnight, and then, for several years, three times a month. The favorite line is by Panama, especially since the railroad over that narrow isthmus is finished from ocean to ocean. The fare is always high, seldom, except when sharp competition reduces it, falling below two hundred and thirty dollars for the best, and eighty dollars for the meanest accommodations. Other routes occasionally compete for a share of the travel.

In the early days there was much suffering on the journey, whatever the route. The detention and hardships of the isthmus-crossing predisposed to cholera, and the steerage passengers especially were swept off with frightful mortality. Now, however, the trip is generally made in little over twenty-one days, and if the passenger affords himself the comforts that money and experience can command, he may with ordinary weather make his first voyage a pleasure excursion, though, after that, at the best it will prove tedious and tiresome.

The terrors of the overland route, too, have been greatly diminished. In October, 1858, by act of Congress, a daily overland mail was started, and the contractors put upon the line stages which whisk the passenger, paying about the same as first-class steamer fare, from Atchison to Placerville, in nineteen days.

In the spring of 1860 the pony mail was started. Light, well-armed riders, carrying nothing but letters, dashed from station to station, on small, tough, fleet-footed horses, making the trip across the continent in nine days. It was a stirring thing to meet the pony in the mountains. By the winding of his horn the rider announced his coming, when teamster, emigrant, and even aristocratic stage-driver pulled his team closer to the bank and let the pony pass. With a yell, perhaps, but no stop to parley, the rider flashed by on his galloping mustang, and the next winding of his horn showed him far off, already clambering the hill or plunging into the distant cañon.

But the pony was stabled forever on the completion of the telegraph across the continent. This constant marvel was finished early in 1861, and one of the first messages that travelled the mysterious wire announced the death of Colonel Baker at Ball's Bluff. With occasional interruptions, chiefly from atmospheric causes east of Omaha, the telegraph has kept the people of California posted during the war with the news of the day almost as promptly as were they of the Eastern cities. The same dispatches that went from Washington over night to New York and Boston were read next morning in San Francisco. The difference in longitude operated to the advantage of the West, and atoned for the loss of time in repeating the message at Chicago, Salt Lake, or elsewhere.

There still remains to be built that great bond of union, the Pacific Railroad. It is, begun, however, and the least sanguine expect it to be completed so that one may ride by rail from the ports of the Atlantic to the great metropolis of the Pacific within the next dozen years. Give us this, and the glory of the situation of California will be as apparent at the East as at the West. There will be a continuous line of settlements from the Missouri to the Sacramento, and both East and West must speedily reap benefits tenfold the cost of the gigantic undertaking.

Events in California have occurred so rapidly, the country so lately an unknown land has so quickly overtaken the civilization of the Eastern States, that the incidents of sixteen years ago seem as truly antique as if a century intervened between them and the present. The actors in the most stirring scenes of the coast still live. It is a delicate task to write of them with the same impartiality as if they were dead. It is awkward to have the men who have figured in history usurping the place of posterity and criticising the historian's labors.

But though the State has passed through so much, produced so largely, achieved so nobly, it is clearly, as yet, on the threshold of its great career. With all its drawbacks, which are but temporary, so charming is its climate, so rich its resources, and so accessible are they to all the industrious and energetic, that the intelligent immigrant now, as he did in the past, and doubtless will in the future for many a year, feels the force of the State's motto, and for himself exclaims, *Eureka*.

Steadily the State grows in material wealth; rapidly it improves in its social aspect as a home for a free, intelligent people. Even if the next census should not show as great a growth in population during the current decennial period as was anticipated a few years ago, it must be remembered how that may happen without permanent injury to the State.

California is, like the older Eastern States, a busy hive, whence new swarms go off annually, yet are not lost to her. From her borders have gone out the men who are developing the resources of a region four times as great as the original thirteen States. The Union is a perpetual gainer, though California may appear to be checked by this wonderfully elastic expansion. Nevada, Idaho, Western Utah, Arizona, and the four northern States of Mexico owe their population chiefly to California. They are fast repaying her for the outlay on them in the trade and commerce that they have created for her principal port, in the market they make for her agricultural products, in their demand for the work of her factories and founderies, and the gold, silver, copper, and other mineral products that go through San Francisco into the markets of the world. Looking at California in connection with the colonies that have gone from her, and will ever be tributary to her, there is not a more marvellous State growth recorded in all the pages of history.

INDEX.

INDEX.

A.

ALARCON finds mouth of the Colorado, 11.
ABARONI's grand scheme for California, 57.
ALVARADO's insurrection successful, 142.
ALCALDES of San Francisco, 216.
ALTA CALIFORNIA, 292.
ADAMS & Co., 405.
AMERICAN FLAG hoisted at Monterey, 180.
       San Francisco, 181.
AREA of the State, 275.
AGRICULTURE, 353, 611.
ANIAN, Straits of, 16, 22.
ABORIGINES of California, 88.

B.

BRANNAN, Samuel, 214.
BARTLETT, Washington A., 216.
BRACE's crime and punishment, 488.
BAKER's eulogy on Broderick, 564.
BRANCIFORTE established, 105.
BANISHED persons, list of, 509.
BALBOA's discovery of the South Sea, 4.
BEAR FLAG, 173.
BENNETT elected Governor, 282.
BENTON, Colonel, writes to California, 254.
BIGLER, Governor, and the Chinese, 370.
BRITISH plots to get California, 179.
BROWN, Captain John, 118.
BOSCANA's account of the Aborigines, 90.
BRODERICK, D. C., 305, 417.
      elected Senator, 546.

BRODERICK and Gwin, 549.
  on the stump, 555.
  death of, 563.
BOUNDARY question vetoed, 275.
BULKHEAD bill vetoed, 574.
BULLETIN, Evening, 408.

C.

CATTLE RODEOS, 157.
CASEY, James P., 432.
  and Cora hung, 446.
CABRILLO goes up the North American coast, 12
CALIFORNIA, meaning of the word, 13.
  under Mexican rule, 121.
  independence of, 152.
  in 1849-50, 331.
  bill for admission passes Senate, 319.
  admitted to the Union, 321.
  a mother of Territories, 343.
  Star, 215.
CALM half century, 111.
CAPITOL on wheels, 391.
CHARITIES and benevolence, 635.
CALHOUN's efforts for Slavery, 250, 313.
CLAY's Compromise Measures, 309, 317, 321.
CLIMATE of California, 629.
CHINESE, 369.
  puzzle, 637.
CITIES, incorporation of, 289.
CORTEZ's exploration on Mexican coast, 7.
COMMERCE while under Mexico, 158.
CONGRESS on California, 249.
CONVENTION, expenses of, 277.
CONSERVATIVE influences, 343.
COMMERCE, 355.
COMPENSATION for misfortunes, 625.
CONSTITUTIONAL Convention, 262.
CONSTITUTION adopted, 282.
  provisions of, 277.

INDEX. 649

Cook, Captain, beware, 116.
Colonial Spanish scheme, 126.
Common law adopted, 287.
Columbus's theory of the South Sea, 3.
Columbia, warning against ship, 117.
County names, 299.
Currency in 1849, 328.
        questions, 595.
Church, first Protestant, 294.

D.

Dashaways, 633.
Drake on coast of California, 22.
        probably in San Francisco Bay, 23.
Drake's report of climate and gold of California, 21, 26.
Dragons that defended the coast, 2.
Deseret's delegates to California, 287.
Dress of natives, 158.
Democrat, first meeting, 295.
Dwinelle's Colonial History, 107.
Difficulty between Kearny, Fremont, and Stockton, 207.
Domestic habits of natives, 156.
Downey, Governor, 573.
Douglas's efforts for the admission of California, 254.
Droughts, 621.
Duelling in California, 569.

E.

Earthquakes, 116.
Echeandria, Governor, 130.
Emigrants, suffering of, 217.
        rush of, 237.
Exiles attempt to return to San Francisco, 486.
Exports of treasure, 601.
Exports and imports, 613.
Educational condition, 631.

F.

Franciscans take Jesuit Missions of Lower California, 68.
        occupy Upper California, 72.

FRAUDULENT land claims, 539.
FREMONT and Castro confront each other, 162.
    threatened by Castro, 163.
    overtaken by Lieutenant Gillespie, 166.
    turns back to revolutionize the Government, 167.
    battalion, 173, 201.
    pursues Castro, 174.
    and Sloat, 182.
    pardons Jesus Pico, 203.
    as Governor of California, 208.
    disobeys orders, 211.
    is disgraced, 212.
    indignation at, 223.
FINANCIAL storm, 402.
FINANCES of the State, 410.
FINANCIAL breakers, 525.
FIRES in San Francisco, 333.
FIELD, Californians on the, 597.
FILLIBUSTERISM, 393.
FLOODS, 617.
FIGUEROA, 134.
    his labors and death, 139.
FLORES's revolt, 191.
FUGITIVE Slave Act, 550.

G.

GRAHAM, Isaac, 142.
    arrested, 146.
GRASS VALLEY, 389.
GALVEZ's expeditions to Upper California, 72.
GAMBLING, 337.
GREEN, A. A., obtains Pueblo papers, 490.
GREELEY, Horace, at San Francisco, 558.
GWIN, Dr., 417.
    on the stump, 557.
GOVERNORS of California under Spain, 123.
        Mexico, 151.
GOLD, discovery of, 226.
    how found, 231.
    Dana's report, 232.

GOLD, Sutter and Marshall on, 232.
    Isaac Humphrey on, 233.
    Baptiste on, 234.
GULF of California explored by Ugarte, 61.

H.

HABEAS CORPUS, how respected by Vigilance Committee, 496.
HANGING, 287.
HARBORS, why difficult to find on the Pacific, 40.
HETHERINGTON's crime and punishment, 487.
HIJAR's colony, 136.
HOUNDS, the, 293.
HOUSES in 1849–50, 331.

I.

INTEREST, rate of, 286.
IDE's Proclamation of Independence, 171.
INDIAN customs, 91.
    wars, 359.
    reservations, 367.
INDIANS, 636.

J.

JEALOUSY of foreigners, 116.
JESUIT missions in Lower California, 51.
    life at, 64.
JESUITS' account of Lower California, 68.
JIGGERS, remedy for, 110.
JONES, Commodore, mistake in hoisting the flag, 148.
JUNIPERO SERRA, 81.
    characteristics of, 82.
    his life, by Palou, 83.

K.

KEARNY, General, in trouble, 195.
KING, James, 407.
KING, James, shot, 435.
    Rev. T. STARR, 585.
        death of, 587.

KINO, his antecedents, 42.
    his attempts to colonize Lower California, 38.

L.

LAND claims, 533.
LAND Commissioners, 535.
LATHAM elected Senator, 573.
LAW in California, 246.
LANGUAGE: Missionaries' devices to convey ideas, 38.
LEGISLATURE, first, 284.
LIBELS, 275.
LIMANTOUR's claim, 382, 539.
LOYALTY of California, 577.
LORETTO, mission of, 44.
LOWER CALIFORNIA proved to be a peninsula, 52.
LOTTERIES, 276.
LYNCH LAW, 339, 428.

M.

MAGELLAN on the Pacific, 5.
MASON, Governor, report of, 227.
MARYSVILLE, 387.
McKEE, Redick, 364.
MERVINE, repulse of, 193.
MENDOZA's fruitless expeditions, 10.
MENDOCINO visited by Viscaino, 33.
                     Cabrillo, 12.
MICHELTORENA's arrival, 147.
MINES, yield of, in 1848-56, 347.
MINERAL discoveries, 605
MIRACLE at Loretto, 46.
MISSIONS in Upper California, order of foundation, 86, 87.
        theory of, 98, 108.
        population of, 113.
        meridian of prosperity, 129.
        secularized, 130.
        jurisdiction of, divided, 135.
        government of, 100.
MINING processes, 349.

INDEX.   653

MINING, various methods of, 603.
    stock mania, 607.
McGOWAN, Edwards, ubiquity, 485.
MORAL aspects, 633.
MONTEREY discovered, 30.
MORMONS arrive, 214.
McDOUGALL, elected Senator, 579.

N.

NATIVES of California, as found by Drake, 25.
NATIVES of California, 153.
    great horsemen, 154.
NEWSPAPERS on the Vigilance Committee, 437.
NEGROES, question of free, 271.
NEGROES in California, 376.

O.

OTONDO, Admiral, attempts to colonize, 37.

P.

PADREZ, 136.
PLACERVILLE, 389.
PAGE, BACON & Co., 403.
PACIFIC Railroad, 642.
PALOU's life of Junipero Serra, 83.
PERLEY challenges Broderick, 553.
PRESIDIOS, 101.
PEOPLE's party organization, 519.
PRIESTS' and soldiers' quarrels, 102.
PIO PICO, Governor, 150.
PIONEER miners, 245.
PIOUS fund, 67.
    diverted, 127.
    sold, 128.
POLK and the Pacific Coast, 253.
POLITICAL blunders, 341.
POLITICS of California, 413.
PORTILLA's treachery, 133.
POPULATION of the State, 357.

PONY mail, 641.
PUEBLO papers, 491.
    Vigilance Committee buy them, 495.
PUEBLOS, 105, 106.
    various kinds, 109.
    was San Francisco one? 107.
PULPIT on the Vigilance Committee, 439.

Q.

QUARTZ crushing, 350.

R.

RANDOLPH, Edmund, 589.
REVENUE laws extend to California, 261.
REFORM city government, 521.
RILEY, General Bennett, 247, 262.
RUSSIANS in California, 118, 120.
RUSH to California, 237.

S.

SAN FRANCISCO, mysterious allusions to, 31
    found by Portalá, 77.
    its growth, 289, 291.
    in 1856, 381.
SACRAMENTO, 297, 386.
STATE resources, 601.
SLAVERY, 248, 269, 315.
SAN DIEGO discovered, 29.
    settled, 76.
SEAL of the State, 278.
SEWARD on admission of California, 313.
SENATORSHIP, United States, 421.
SMITH, Jedediah S., first overlander, 124.
SMITH, Persifer F., 247.
SMITH, Peter, judgments, 384.
SLOAT, Commodore, at Monterey, 176.
    alarmed, 182, 184.
    returns home, 186.

SOLIZ's insurrection, 130.
SONORA captured by American insurgents, 170.
SCHOOL, first public, 291.
STOCKTON, arrives at San Francisco, 184.
         proclamation of, 186.
         his march to Los Angeles, 189.
         recovers his lost fruits, 193.
         marches from San Diego to Los Angeles, 199.
SCOTT, Dr., and the Vigilance Committee, 511.
SQUATTER riots, 337.
SUTTER and Micheltorena, 149.
SUTTER, John A., 302.
SUITS against the Vigilance Committee, 515.

T.

TAYLOR's first message, 307.
TENT age of California, 325.
TREATY of Couengo, 205.
         ignored, 209.
    between United States and Mexico, 235.
TERRY, Judge, in prison, 477.
         friends at work, 480.
         friends in United States Senate, 483.
         freed, 497.
         fêted, 498.
         and Broderick, 561.
         escapes unpunished, 567.
TIERRA, Salva, 43.
         his death, 58.

U.

UGARTE in Lower California, 48.
         death of, 61.
UNITED STATES Senators on Union, 590.
UNION meeting, May, 1861, 579.
ULLOA's explorations on Lower California coast, 9.
UNCONSTITUTIONAL debt, 527.
         assumed by the people, 531.

V.

VESSEL, first one built in California, 60.
VENEGA's History of California, 70.
VISCAINO's explorations of the coast, 28.
                results of, 35.
                did he visit San Francisco? 32.
                visits Mendocino, 33.
VIGILANCE Committee of 1856, 432, 461.
                and Governor Johnson, 458.
                and General Sherman, 458.
                and General Wool, 458.
                organization, 461.
                and President of United States, 468.
                board the Julia, 473.
                collision with authorities, 475.
                Governor Johnson repudiates commission to, 482.
                disbands, 499.
                final parade, 502.
                address of Executive Committee, 503.
                rooms inspected, 505.
                winding up, 507.
                summary of their work, 509.
VICTORIA, Governor, 131.
                resigns, 133.

W.

WHALERS' visits, 160.
WAGES in 1849, 329.
WALKER, William, 393.
                schemes of, 397.
                death of, 398.
WEBSTER on admission of California, 313.
WELLER on Terry and the Vigilance Committee, 484.

X.

XIMENES discovers Lower California, 8.

Y.

YANKEE Sullivan, 449.
YERBA, Buena, 215.

Z.

ZABRISKIE, Colonel, on Vigilance Committee, 481, 482.

www.ingramcontent.com/pod-product-compliance
Lightning Source LLC
Chambersburg PA
CBHW021220300426
44111CB00007B/366